The Way of the Prophet

A Selection of Hadith

ʻABD AL-GHAFFĀR ḤASAN

TRANSLATED AND EDITED BY
USAMA HASAN

WITH A PREFACE BY
KHURSHID AHMAD

THE ISLAMIC FOUNDATION

Published by
THE ISLAMIC FOUNDATION
Markfield Conference Centre, Ratby Lane, Markfield,
Leicestershire LE67 9SY, United Kingdom
E-mail: publications@islamic-foundation.com
Website: www.islamic-foundation.com

Quran House, PO Box 30611, Nairobi, Kenya

PMB 3193, Kano Nigeria

Distributed by: Kube Publishing Ltd.
Tel: +44 (0) 1530 249230, Fax: +44 (0) 1530 249656
Email: info@kubepublishing.com

2nd Impression 2012/1433 H.

British Library Cataloguing in Publication Data

Hasan, Abd al-Ghaffar
The way of the Prophet: a selection of Hadith
1. Hadith - Commentaries 2. Hadith - Texts
I. Title II. Hasan, Usama
297.1'2407

ISBNs
978-0-860374-33-6 *casebound*
978-0-860374-57-2 *paperback*

Typeset by: N.A. Qaddoura
Cover Design by: Nasir Cadir

Printed by Imak Offset, TURKEY

بسم الله الرحمن الرحيم

Contents

Transliteration Table x

Preface (by Khurshid Ahmad) xi

Foreword (by Usama Hasan) xxxii

1. Objective of Compiling this Work 1

2. Introduction to the Sciences of *Ḥadīth* 5
   - 2.1 Three Methods of Preserving *Ḥadīth* 5
   - 2.2 Four Phases of *Ḥadīth* Preservation 6
   - 2.3 *Ḥadīth* Terminology 24
   - 2.4 A Tree of *Ḥadīth* Transmission 27

3. Fundamentals of Islam 31
   - 3.1 Beliefs and Pillars of Islam 31
   - 3.2 *Tawḥīd* (Affirming the Unity of God) 33
   - 3.3 Faith in Prophethood 34
   - 3.4 Following the Messenger of Allah ﷺ 35
   - 3.5 Loving the Messenger of Allah ﷺ 36
   - 3.6 Avoiding Extremism and Having a Balanced Belief Regarding the Messenger of Allah ﷺ 36
   - 3.7 Faith in Predestination 38
   - 3.8 Accountability in the Hereafter 39
   - 3.9 The Transitory Nature of the World 40
   - 3.10 The Spirit of Islam (Sincerity) 42
   - 3.11 Moderation and Balance 43
   - 3.12 A Comprehensive Concept of Virtue 47
   - 3.13 The Believer's View of the Worldly Life 48

4. Teachings of the Religion 52
4.1 Virtues of Knowledge, Wisdom and Teaching the Religion 52
4.2 Wisdom in Preaching and Reform 53
4.3 Religious Education and Upbringing of One's Children and Family 56
4.4 Forbiddance of Irresponsible Talk Regarding the Religion 57
4.5 Evil People of Knowledge 60

5. Establishing the Religion (*Dīn*) 63
5.1 The Effort to Renew and Revive the Religion (*Dīn*) 63
5.2 A Religious Sense of Honour 66
5.3 *Jihād* in the Path of Allah ﷻ 69

6. Ritual Worship 70
6.1 The Importance of Prayer (*Ṣalāt*) 70
6.2 *Zakāt* (Giving Alms) 72
6.3 Fasting 73
6.4 *Ḥajj* (Pilgrimage) 73
6.5 The Importance of Voluntary Worship 73
6.6 Remembrance and Recitation 75
6.7 Abundant Remembrance of Allah ﷻ 76
6.8 Supplication and its Etiquette 77

7. Morality and Character 82
7.1 The Importance of Morality in Islam 82
7.2 The Relationship between Faith and Morality 83

8. The Foundations of the Noblest Ethics 85
8.1 Piety 85
8.2 Purity of Methods and Means of Livelihood 86
8.3 The Seat of Piety 87
8.4 Signs of Piety 88
8.5 Extremism in Piety 89
8.6 Trust in God 90
8.7 A Model of Trust in God 91
8.8 Gratitude 92

	8.9	*Ṣabr* (Patience, Perseverance, Steadfastness)	92
	8.10	Patience in Difficulty	93
	8.11	Patience in Obeying Allah ﷻ	93
	8.12	Patience in One's Principles: a Principled Life	94
	8.13	Steadfastness in Facing the Enemy	95
	8.14	Patience in Poverty and Destitution	95
	8.15	Discipline Against the Desire for Revenge	96
9.	Personal Character		98
	9.1	Self-Control	98
	9.2	Forgiveness and Forbearance	99
	9.3	Magnanimity	99
	9.4	*Ḥayā'* (Modesty, Shame, Shyness)	100
	9.5	Dignity and Solemnity	101
	9.6	Keeping Secrets	101
	9.7	Humility	102
	9.8	Humility and Self-Effacement	103
	9.9	Avoiding Fame	103
	9.10	Contentment	104
	9.11	Simplicity in Lifestyle	106
	9.12	Moderation	109
	9.13	Constancy	110
	9.14	Generosity	112
	9.15	Honesty and Trustworthiness	113
10.	Despicable Qualities		114
	10.1	Narcissism (Self-Admiration)	114
	10.2	Preventing Self-Admiration	115
	10.3	Avoiding Self-Admiration	115
	10.4	Love of Fame	116
	10.5	Arrogance	116
	10.6	Self-Abasement	117
	10.7	Tight-Fistedness	118
	10.8	Selfishness	118
	10.9	Miserliness and Narrow-Mindedness	118
	10.10	Dishonourable and Mean Behaviour	119
	10.11	Greed	119
	10.12	Artificiality and Unnatural Behaviour	120
	10.13	Artificiality and Affectation in Conversation	121
	10.14	False Formality	121

	10.15	Extravagance and Exaggerated Formality	122
	10.16	Extravagance and Luxury	123
	10.17	Despair and Loss of Aspiration	124
	10.18	Self-Delusion	125
11.	Virtuous Living		126
	11.1	Understanding and Intelligence	126
	11.2	Intelligence and Experience	127
	11.3	Purification and Cleanliness	128
	11.4	Etiquette of Eating	132
	11.5	Dignity	134
	11.6	Beauty of Voice	134
	11.7	Clarity of Discourse	135
	11.8	Purity of Tongue	135
	11.9	Correcting Undignified Appearances	135
	11.10	Good-Naturedness	136
	11.11	Avoiding Excessive Laughter	136
	11.12	Etiquette of Travelling	137
	11.13	Taking Precautions	138
	11.14	Etiquette of Sleeping	138
	11.15	Protecting Health	139
	11.16	Etiquette of Walking	139
12.	A Virtuous Society		140
	12.1	Rights of Parents	140
	12.2	Maintaining Family Ties	141
	12.3	Obeying the Husband	142
	12.4	The Virtuous Wife	142
	12.5	The Importance of Accepting Proposals from the Virtuous	143
	12.6	A Happy Married Life	143
	12.7	The Importance of a Happy Married Life	144
	12.8	An Easy-Going Relationship	144
	12.9	Winning the Wife's Heart	145
	12.10	Treating One's Wives Equally	145
	12.11	The Rights of Family	146
	12.12	Equal Treatment of Children	149
	12.13	Maintaining Family Ties	150
	12.14	Serving Humanity	150
	12.15	Good Neighbourliness	151
	12.16	Rights of the Guest	152

12.17 Rights of Slaves and Servants 153
12.18 Kind Treatment of Prisoners 154
12.19 Caring for the Poor 156
12.20 The Rights of the Poor over the Wealth of the Rich 156
12.21 Helping Those Afflicted by Tribulations 157
12.22 Respect for Elders 157
12.23 Social Etiquette 158
12.24 Rights of Friendship and Companionship 158
12.25 Informality with Close Friends 159
12.26 Moderation in Cheerfulness 160
12.27 Concern for the Weak and Disadvantaged 160
12.28 Concern for Workers 161
12.29 Concern for Poor or Uninfluential Persons 162
12.30 Helping the Needy 163
12.31 Kind Treatment of Orphans 163
12.32 Kind Treatment of Servants 164
12.33 Compassion Towards Animals 164
12.34 Showing Mercy to People in General 165

13. Social Virtues 166
13.1 Sincere Advice 166
13.2 Preventing Oppression 167
13.3 Love and Compassion 168
13.4 Generosity in Dealings 169
13.5 Defending a Muslim Brother 170
13.6 Thinking Well of Others 170
13.7 Etiquette of Social Interaction 171
13.8 Etiquette of Entering and Leaving Houses 172
13.9 Etiquette of Friendship 172
13.10 Effects of Friendship 173
13.11 Moderation in Friendship and Enmity 173
13.12 Being Good-Natured 174

14. Social Ills 176
14.1 Having a Careless Tongue 176
14.2 Irresponsible Talk 176
14.3 Vulgarity 178
14.4 Frequent Swearing of Oaths 178
14.5 Ridiculing Others 179
14.6 Being Suspicious of Others 179

14.7 Spying and Fault-Finding 180
14.8 Carrying Tales 180
14.9 The Limits of Backbiting 182
14.10 Speaking Ill of the Dead 183
14.11 Being Two-Faced 183
14.12 Enmity and Hatred 184
14.13 Mutual Severing of Relations 184
14.14 Haughtiness 185
14.15 Being Unscrupulous 186
14.16 Harmful and Frivolous Poetry 186
14.17 Breaking Promises 187
14.18 The Corruption of Hypocrisy 187
14.19 Inconsistency of Speech and Action 188
14.20 Supporting the Oppressor 188
14.21 Usurping the Rights of Others 189
14.22 Usurping Property 189
14.23 Treachery 190
14.24 Bribery 191
14.25 Blocking the Hidden Avenues to Bribery 192
14.26 Blocking the Hidden Avenues to Usury 193
14.27 Preventing the Causes of Disputes and Fights 193
14.28 Dissension and Dispute 194
14.29 Killing a Muslim 194
14.30 Deception and Dishonesty 195
14.31 Hoarding 196
14.32 Exploiting Legal Tricks 196
14.33 Irresponsible Actions 197
14.34 Selfishness 198
14.35 Miserliness 198
14.36 Ingratitude 199
14.37 Contrived and False Appearances 200
14.38 Having an Inferiority Complex and Imitating Others 200
14.39 Idolatry and Personality-Worship 201
14.40 Royal Pomp 201
14.41 *Jāhilī* Royal Special Treatment 202
14.42 Elitism 202
14.43 Partisanship for One's Group, Tribe or Nation 203

14.44 Class Distinction 204
14.45 Blocking the Hidden Avenues to Obscenity 204
14.46 Spreading Indecency 208
14.47 A Corrupting Environment 208
14.48 Greed for Power 209
14.49 Interceding on Behalf of a Criminal 210
14.50 Breaking Covenants 210
14.51 Dangerous Social Ills 211
14.52 Greed for the World 211

15. A Sound Social System 213
15.1 Social Order 213
15.2 Holding to the Congregation 213
15.3 The Importance of a Social Order 214
15.4 Abiding by Rules 215
15.5 The Limits of Obedience to Authority 216
15.6 No Agreement or Declaration is Allowed that Contravenes Divine Limits 216
15.7 Responsibilities of the *Amīr* (Leader) 217
15.8 The Obligations of Islamic Governance 218
15.9 The Qualities of Imamate and Leadership 219
15.10 Seeking Position 221
15.11 The Limits of Seeking Positions 222
15.12 Reform of the Government Depends on Reform of the Public 222
15.13 The Importance of a System of Consultation 223
15.14 Responsibilities of the Judiciary 224
15.15 Equality in Enforcing Laws 225
15.16 Legal Equality 225
15.17 The Limits of Legal Pardon 226
15.18 Principles and Etiquette of Judgment 227
15.19 Etiquette of War 228
15.20 International Relations 229
15.21 Religion and Politics 230

16. Translator's Bibliography 236

Transliteration Table

Arabic Consonants

Initial, unexpressed medial and final:

ء	ʾ	د	d	ض	ḍ	ك	k
ب	b	ذ	dh	ط	ṭ	ل	l
ت	t	ر	r	ظ	ẓ	م	m
ث	th	ز	z	ع	ʿ	ن	n
ج	j	س	s	غ	gh	هـ	h
ح	ḥ	ش	sh	ف	f	و	w
خ	kh	ص	ṣ	ق	q	ي	y

Vowels, diphthongs, etc.

Short:	ـَ	a	ـِ	i	ـُ	u
Long:	ـَا	ā	ـِي	ī	ـُو	ū
Diphthongs:			ـَوْ	aw		
			ـَيْ	ay		

Preface

The Greatness of the Prophet's Way

Allah's bounties and favours upon humankind are countless and unending; but, His greatest blessing has been His Guidance to enable humanity to understand His Reality, to recognize their Creator and the scheme of things He has designed for them, including the role and place of the humans within it. This Guidance, among other things, spells out the ideals and objectives of human life and the values, norms and rules of conduct that can establish justice (*'adl*) in human affairs and lead to the good life here and success and salvation in the Hereafter (Qur'ān 6: 73; 29: 44).

The creation of the heavens, the earth and all that lies in between is a basic premise on which the entire Islamic vision of life rests. This is how a leading Muslim thinker expounds this foundational principle:

> It has been asserted again and again in the Qur'ān that God created the heavens and the earth "in Truth". This covers a wide range of meanings:
>
> First, that the heavens and the earth have not been created just for the fun of it. This state of existence is not a theatrical farce. This world is not a child's toy with which to amuse oneself as long as one wishes before crushing it to bits and throwing it away. Creation is rather an act of great seriousness. A great objective motivates it, and a wise and benevolent purpose underlies it. Hence, after the lapse

> of a certain stage it is necessary for the Creator to take full account of the work that has been done and to use those results as the basis for the next stage.
>
> Second, it means that God has created this entire system of the universe on solid foundations of Truth. The whole of the universe is based on Justice, Wisdom and Truth. Hence, there is no scope in the system for falsehood to take root and prosper. The phenomenon of the prosperity of falsehood which we observe is to be ascribed to the will of God Who grants the followers of falsehood the opportunity, if they so wish, to expend their efforts in promoting unrighteousness, injustice and untruth. In the end, however, the earth will throw up all the seeds of untruth that have been sown, and, in the final reckoning, every follower of falsehood will see that the efforts he devoted to cultivating and watering this pernicious tree have all gone to waste.
>
> Third, it means that God has founded the universe on the basis of right, and it is on account of being its Creator that He governs it. His Command in the Universe is supreme since He alone has the right to govern it, the Universe being nothing but His creation. No one else has any right to enforce his will.[1]

The need and provision of *hidāyah* is a logical requirement of the creation of the universe in Truth and the endowment of humans with free will and the opportunity to choose between right and wrong, truth and falsehood, and justice and oppression. The Qur'ānic paradigm is very clear.

Men and women, as Allah's vicegerents, were endowed with intellect and with knowledge, both the 'names of all things', along with the capacity to differentiate and choose between good and evil. Inculcated within every human being is the potential for both virtue and God-consciousness (*taqwā*) and evil and disobedience (*fujūr*). The test lies in whether we voluntarily and

1. Sayyid Abul A'lā Mawdūdī, *Towards Understanding the Qur'ān* (Leicester: Islamic Foundation, 1989), Vol. II, pp. 243-44, with slight revisions.

consciously opt for the guidance (*hidāyah*) that leads to success in life. Many verses of the Qur'ān illuminate different aspects of this paradigm (2: 31; 64: 3; 87: 1-3; 91: 7-10; 95: 4). The challenging assignment of stewardship and vicegerency (*istikhlāf*) on the earth was combined with the light of Divine guidance (*hidāyah*), clearly marking out the road to success and salvation (*Sūrah al-Baqarah* 2: 38-39).

The Islamic paradigm of guidance is founded on three pillars:

a. First, creation of the universe and all that is in it, is done by the Creator on the basis of Truth, and, as an integral part of that, the creation of human beings in the best of moulds, endowing them with the intellect and capacity to acquire knowledge using reason and resorting to imagination, innovation, experimentation, discretion and wisdom (*ḥikmah*).
b. Divine revelation (*waḥy*) in the form of the Book (*al-Kitāb*) revealed through Allah's prophets, and final revelation in its complete form through the last Prophet Muḥammad ﷺ in the form of the Noble Qur'ān, preserved in its original form as the Word of God, to serve as the source of guidance for all times and places.
c. The life-example (*uswah*) of the Prophet ﷺ, a human being selected (*istifā*) and guided by Allah ﷻ, so as to provide the Model for all human beings in all aspects of their lives.

The human intellect is the starting point for benefiting from Divine guidance – through use of the faculties to learn, think, reflect, discuss, discern, judge and resolve and then to act righteously. All those endowed with intellect have the responsibility to make this effort and to pursue the right path (Qur'ān 3: 190-191; 10: 5-6; 51: 20-21). Only the mentally-impaired are deemed to be exempted from this and are thus excused.

The role of intellect in discovering, understanding and responding to Allah's guidance has been described by the Qur'ān as an integral part of this process. In *Sūrah al-Jāthiyah*, the discourse begins with:

حمٓ ۝ تَنزِيلُ ٱلْكِتَٰبِ مِنَ ٱللَّهِ ٱلْعَزِيزِ ٱلْحَكِيمِ ۝

Hā'. Mīm. This Book is a revelation from the Most Mighty, the Most Wise. (*Sūrah al-Jāthiyah* 45: 1-2)

Then the people are invited to reflect on the signs of Allah around them:

إِنَّ فِى ٱلسَّمَٰوَٰتِ وَٱلْأَرْضِ لَءَايَٰتٍ لِّلْمُؤْمِنِينَ ۝ وَفِى خَلْقِكُمْ وَمَا يَبُثُّ مِن دَآبَّةٍ ءَايَٰتٌ لِّقَوْمٍ يُوقِنُونَ ۝ وَٱخْتِلَٰفِ ٱلَّيْلِ وَٱلنَّهَارِ وَمَآ أَنزَلَ ٱللَّهُ مِنَ ٱلسَّمَآءِ مِن رِّزْقٍ فَأَحْيَا بِهِ ٱلْأَرْضَ بَعْدَ مَوْتِهَا وَتَصْرِيفِ ٱلرِّيَٰحِ ءَايَٰتٌ لِّقَوْمٍ يَعْقِلُونَ ۝

Behold, for those who believe there are [myriad] signs in the heavens and the earth and in your own creation; and in the animals which He spreads out over the earth and in the succession of night and day, and in the provision that Allah sends down from the sky wherewith He gives life to the earth after it had been lifeless, and in the change of the winds: [in all these] there are signs for people who use reason. (*Sūrah al-Jāthiyah* 45: 3-5)

Finally they are treated to a kind of shock therapy by asking them why they do not use their intellect to see the Reality:

تِلْكَ ءَايَٰتُ ٱللَّهِ نَتْلُوهَا عَلَيْكَ بِٱلْحَقِّ ۖ فَبِأَىِّ حَدِيثٍۭ بَعْدَ ٱللَّهِ وَءَايَٰتِهِۦ يُؤْمِنُونَ ۝

These are Allah's Signs that We rehearse to you in Truth. In what kind of discourse after Allah and His Signs will they, then, believe? (*Sūrah al-Jāthiyah* 45: 6)

It is through intellect and understanding that the Qur'ān brings humankind to the Divine revelation (10: 24; 21: 10). The centrepiece of this guidance is the Qur'ān, the unadulterated Word of God, preserved in its fullness. This is the principal source of Divine guidance (Qur'ān 2: 1-2; 3: 138; 10: 57; 17: 9-10).

The Qur'ān has not been revealed as an abstraction. It has been revealed through Archangel Jibrīl عليه السلام to the Prophet

Muḥammad ﷺ to be communicated to the whole of mankind. It is on the Prophet's testimony that we believe in it as the Revealed Word of God. It is he who was assigned to convey it to mankind as it was revealed to him and also to explain it, live by it, purify the believers through it, translate it into the lives of people and society, organize and lead a movement in history to transform individuals and communities to become the living symbols of this guidance and the upholders of this Divine message for mankind for all eternity.

The role of the Prophet ﷺ is pivotal in this process of guidance. The Qur'ān is the ultimate guide and the source of light; the Prophet Muḥammad ﷺ is the model, the authentic interpreter and teacher of the Book and a living embodiment of the Qur'ānic vision of life and society. It is the life-example of the Prophet Muḥammad ﷺ, a human being like all humans, except that he received Divine revelation and was guided by Allah ﷻ to be the perfect and noble model (*uswah ḥasanah*) for all humanity. The Mother of the Believers 'Ā'ishah رضي الله عنها is reported to have said that he was the embodiment of the Qur'ān. This is what the *Sunnah* is.

The Qur'ān clearly spells out the status, authority and role of the Prophet ﷺ so as to illumine the entire process of Divine guidance:

يَٰٓأَيُّهَا ٱلنَّاسُ قَدْ جَآءَكُمُ ٱلرَّسُولُ بِٱلْحَقِّ مِن رَّبِّكُمْ فَـَٔامِنُوا۟ خَيْرًا لَّكُمْ ۚ وَإِن تَكْفُرُوا۟ فَإِنَّ لِلَّهِ مَا فِى
ٱلسَّمَٰوَٰتِ وَٱلْأَرْضِ ۚ وَكَانَ ٱللَّهُ عَلِيمًا حَكِيمًا ۝

O People! Now that the Messenger has come to you bearing the Truth from your Lord, believe in him, it will be good for you. If you reject, know well that to Allah belongs all that is in the heavens and the earth. Allah is All-Knowing, All-Wise. (*Sūrah al-Nisā'* 4: 170)

هُوَ ٱلَّذِى بَعَثَ فِى ٱلْأُمِّيِّـۧنَ رَسُولًا مِّنْهُمْ يَتْلُوا۟ عَلَيْهِمْ ءَايَٰتِهِۦ وَيُزَكِّيهِمْ وَيُعَلِّمُهُمُ ٱلْكِتَٰبَ وَٱلْحِكْمَةَ
وَإِن كَانُوا۟ مِن قَبْلُ لَفِى ضَلَٰلٍ مُّبِينٍ ۝ وَءَاخَرِينَ مِنْهُمْ لَمَّا يَلْحَقُوا۟ بِهِمْ ۚ وَهُوَ ٱلْعَزِيزُ ٱلْحَكِيمُ ۝

He it is Who has sent to the gentiles a Messenger from among themselves, one who rehearses to them His verses, purifies their lives, and imparts to them the [*meanings of the*] *Book and the Wisdom although before that they were in utter error; and [He has also] sent him to those others who have not yet joined them. He is the Most Mighty, the Most Wise.* (*Sūrah al-Jumu'ah* 62: 2-3)

لَقَدْ أَرْسَلْنَا رُسُلَنَا بِٱلْبَيِّنَٰتِ وَأَنزَلْنَا مَعَهُمُ ٱلْكِتَٰبَ وَٱلْمِيزَانَ لِيَقُومَ ٱلنَّاسُ بِٱلْقِسْطِ ... ۝

Indeed We sent Our Messengers with Clear Signs, and send down with them the Books and the Balance that people may uphold justice. (*Sūrah al-Ḥadīd* 57: 25)

يَٰٓأَيُّهَا ٱلنَّبِيُّ إِنَّآ أَرْسَلْنَٰكَ شَٰهِدًا وَمُبَشِّرًا وَنَذِيرًا ۝ وَدَاعِيًا إِلَى ٱللَّهِ بِإِذْنِهِۦ وَسِرَاجًا مُّنِيرًا ۝

O Prophet! We have sent you forth as a Witness, a Bearer of good tidings, and a Warner, as one who calls people to Allah by His leave, and as an Upright Shining Lamp. (*Sūrah al-Aḥzāb* 33: 45-46)

The life of the Prophet ﷺ is a noble example, a perfect model, a beautiful and balanced life story, a framework for human conduct and a standard for emulation:

وَإِنَّكَ لَعَلَىٰ خُلُقٍ عَظِيمٍ ۝

And [O Prophet] you are certainly on the most exalted standard of moral excellence. (*Sūrah al-Qalam* 68: 4)

وَمَآ أَرْسَلْنَٰكَ إِلَّا رَحْمَةً لِّلْعَٰلَمِينَ ۝

We have sent you [Muḥammad] forth as nothing but a mercy to people of the whole world. (*Sūrah al-Anbiyā'* 21: 107)

And that is why he is the model and guide for all and for all times to come:

لَّقَدْ كَانَ لَكُمْ فِى رَسُولِ ٱللَّهِ أُسْوَةٌ حَسَنَةٌ لِّمَن كَانَ يَرْجُوا۟ ٱللَّهَ وَٱلْيَوْمَ ٱلْءَاخِرَ وَذَكَرَ ٱللَّهَ كَثِيرًا ۝

Surely there was a good example for you in the Messenger of Allah, for all those who look forward to Allah and the Last Day and remember Allah much. (*Sūrah al-Aḥzāb* 33: 21)

The prescription and the criterion for success here and hereafter consists in (a) *belief* in Allah ﷻ and His Prophet ﷺ, and (b) a *life-long effort* to *follow* and *obey* them and to *strive* hard to *fulfill* the mission and the assignment given to human beings as Allah's vicegerents on the earth (*Sūrah al-Nisā'* 4: 13-14).

Those who follow Allah ﷻ and His Messenger ﷺ will be in the best of company in the life to come.

وَمَن يُطِعِ ٱللَّهَ وَٱلرَّسُولَ فَأُو۟لَـٰٓئِكَ مَعَ ٱلَّذِينَ أَنْعَمَ ٱللَّهُ عَلَيْهِم مِّنَ ٱلنَّبِيِّـۧنَ وَٱلصِّدِّيقِينَ وَٱلشُّهَدَآءِ
وَٱلصَّـٰلِحِينَ ۚ وَحَسُنَ أُو۟لَـٰٓئِكَ رَفِيقًا ۝ ذَٰلِكَ ٱلْفَضْلُ مِنَ ٱللَّهِ ۚ وَكَفَىٰ بِٱللَّهِ عَلِيمًا ۝

He who obeys Allah and the Messenger – such shall be with those whom Allah has favoured – the Prophets, those steadfast in truthfulness, the martyrs, and the righteous. How excellent will they be for companionship. That is a bounty from Allah, and Allah suffices to know the truth. (*Sūrah al-Nisā'* 4: 69-70)

The Prophet Muḥammad ﷺ is the only authentic and authorized representative of Allah ﷻ for all ages. In the Islamic scheme of authority no one else other than the Prophet Muḥammad ﷺ enjoys the power to speak in the name of Allah stating what Allah ﷻ wants from the believers. Everyone, howsoever high or low, is subject to the guidance and value framework laid down by Allah ﷻ and His Prophet Muḥammad ﷺ. This establishes the principle of equality of all before the law. This discredits the concept of theocracy wherein a certain class of men of religion is given the power to speak in the name of God. The principle of the finality of Prophethood in the person of Muḥammad ﷺ is the greatest guarantor of human dignity and equality.

As Muḥammad ﷺ is the only intermediary by dint of his being Allah's Messenger ﷺ, it is important to clearly understand the foundations of the relationship believers have with him. The five most important of these are as follows:

1. *Faith in the Prophet* ﷺ

Faith (*īmān*) in the Prophet Muḥammad ﷺ as Allah's Prophet and Messenger. To accept all that he received from Allah ﷻ as

Allah's revelation i.e. the Book, and to believe in all the articles of faith as spelled out by Allah ﷻ and His Prophet ﷺ: belief in Allah, His angels, His Books, His prophets, the Day of Judgment, and life after death.

Faith in Muḥammad ﷺ is much more than a formal acknowledgement of his Prophethood as Allah's Messenger. It involves an unwavering belief in its truthfulness, an unshakable trust in his integrity and an uninflinching commitment to follow in his footsteps in order to seek Allah's pleasure, success in this life and salvation in the life-to-come. It is to have a faith of conviction, confidence and understanding, both in one's person and in the path he ﷺ has shown. This requirement to hold fast to him was not meant solely for his Companions ﷺ who had the honour of seeing him, but is also for those who came later. Holding fast to him is the everlasting path of success. His pleasure with us, his teachings and his example are the gateway to Allah's good pleasure. This faith is characterized by a sense of complete satisfaction of mind, heart and soul with Allah ﷻ, His Prophet ﷺ and the path spelled out by them. This has been summed up by the Prophet ﷺ in these words:

ذَاقَ طُعْمَ الإِيْمَانِ مَنْ رَضِيَ بِاللهِ رَبًّا وَبِالْإِسْلاَمِ دِيْنًا وَبِمُحَمَّدٍ رَسُولاً. صحيح مسلم، كتاب الإيمان، ٤٩

He has tasted the real flavour of faith who is content with Allah as the Lord, with Islam as the Way of Life and with Muḥammad ﷺ as Prophet and Guide. Muslim, Book of Faith, *Ḥadīth* no. 49.

2. *The Prophet ﷺ as Guide*

The second foundation is to accept the Prophet Muḥammad ﷺ as the guide, the model, the lawgiver under Allah's authority, the ultimate arbiter in all matters amongst the Muslims for all times to come. He alone can speak on behalf of Allah ﷻ and for that purpose his word and conduct are protected under Allah's grace.

قُلْ إِنَّمَآ أَنَا۠ بَشَرٌ مِّثْلُكُمْ يُوحَىٰٓ إِلَىَّ أَنَّمَآ إِلَٰهُكُمْ إِلَٰهٌ وَٰحِدٌ فَمَن كَانَ يَرْجُوا۟ لِقَآءَ رَبِّهِۦ فَلْيَعْمَلْ عَمَلًا
صَٰلِحًا وَلَا يُشْرِكْ بِعِبَادَةِ رَبِّهِۦٓ أَحَدًا ۝

Say [*O Muḥammad*]*: I am no more than a human being like you; one to whom Revelation is made: Your Lord is the One and Only God! Hence whoever looks forward to meet his Lord, let him do righteous works, and let him associate none with the worship of his Lord.* (*Sūrah al-Kahf* 18: 110)

The authority and the functions of the Prophet ﷺ are clearly stated in the Qur'ān as under:

ٱلَّذِينَ يَتَّبِعُونَ ٱلرَّسُولَ ٱلنَّبِىَّ ٱلْأُمِّىَّ ٱلَّذِى يَجِدُونَهُۥ مَكْتُوبًا عِندَهُمْ فِى ٱلتَّوْرَىٰةِ وَٱلْإِنجِيلِ يَأْمُرُهُم
بِٱلْمَعْرُوفِ وَيَنْهَىٰهُمْ عَنِ ٱلْمُنكَرِ وَيُحِلُّ لَهُمُ ٱلطَّيِّبَٰتِ وَيُحَرِّمُ عَلَيْهِمُ ٱلْخَبَٰٓئِثَ وَيَضَعُ عَنْهُمْ إِصْرَهُمْ
وَٱلْأَغْلَٰلَ ٱلَّتِى كَانَتْ عَلَيْهِمْ ۚ فَٱلَّذِينَ ءَامَنُوا۟ بِهِۦ وَعَزَّرُوهُ وَنَصَرُوهُ وَٱتَّبَعُوا۟ ٱلنُّورَ ٱلَّذِىٓ أُنزِلَ مَعَهُۥٓ ۙ
أُو۟لَٰٓئِكَ هُمُ ٱلْمُفْلِحُونَ ۝

[*Today this Mercy is for*] *those who follow the* ummī *Prophet, whom they find mentioned in the Torah, and the Gospel that they have. He enjoins upon them what is good and forbids them what is evil. He makes the clean things lawful to them and prohibits all corrupt things and removes from them their burdens and the shackles that were upon them. So those who believe in him and assist him, and succour him and follow the Light which has been sent down with him, it is they who shall prosper.* (*Sūrah al-A'rāf* 7: 157)

Numerous verses of the Qur'ān establish the Prophet ﷺ as the final authority in all matters of the Muslims (4: 64-65; 53: 1-4; 59: 8).

3. *Love of the Prophet* ﷺ

Accepting the authority of the Prophet ﷺ is not merely a legalistic or formal relationship. It is an intensely personal, spiritual and reverential relationship rooted in faith, love and reverence. This brings us to the *third* foundation of this relationship – that of love, trust, reverence and devotion. This is a unique dimension of the relationship between the Muslims and the Prophet ﷺ who is their greatest benefactor and a mercy unto mankind. His own feelings towards the believers set the tone for this profoundly personal relationship.

لَقَدْ جَآءَكُمْ رَسُولٌ مِّنْ أَنفُسِكُمْ عَزِيزٌ عَلَيْهِ مَا عَنِتُّمْ حَرِيصٌ عَلَيْكُم بِٱلْمُؤْمِنِينَ رَءُوفٌ رَّحِيمٌ

There has come to you a Messenger from Allah from among yourselves, who is distressed by the losses you sustain, who is ardently desirous of your welfare and is tender and merciful to those that believe. (*Sūrah al-Tawbah* 9: 128)

Love for him and preferring him to everyone else is a cardinal virtue and a natural dimension of this relationship (Qur'ān 9: 24; 33: 6). As the Prophet ﷺ has said:

لَايُؤْمِنُ أَحَدُكُمْ حَتَّىٰ أَكُونَ أَحَبَّ اِلَيْهِ مِنْ وَلَدِهِ وَوَالِدِهِ وَالنَّاسِ اَجْمَعِينَ. صحيح مسلم، كتاب الإيمان، ٦٣

No one can be a true believer unless I am closer and dearer to him than his children, parents and all other persons. Muslim, Book of Faith, *Ḥadīth* no. 63.

In Makkah and Madīnah, during the life of the Prophet ﷺ, one could see, feel and breathe this bond of love and affection between the Prophet ﷺ and his Companions ؓ – each loving the other. But this bond was not specific to the lifetime of the Prophet ﷺ, but integral to the sum and substance of *īmān* and represents an eternal feature of the Islamic ethos. The Companions ؓ valued his pleasure much more than their own, would be hurt by what hurt him and preferred what he preferred. They would gladly sacrifice their wealth, even their lives, to protect him and fulfil his commands and wishes. This relationship was much more intense than simple kinship as it was spiritual, emotional and ideological. It also indicated their commitment to him: to his teachings, to his message and to his mission. His personality remains pivotal to the lives of Muslims, and the fruits of this relationship can be seen in the entire lifestyles of the faithful and their efforts to dedicate themselves scrupulously to the fulfilment of his mission by following in his footsteps.

So following the Prophet ﷺ is a logical consequence of love for Allah ﷻ. The counterpart of this equation and the greatest prize that can be thought of and yearned for is that the believers who follow the Prophet ﷺ are loved by Allah ﷻ.

قُلْ إِن كُنتُمْ تُحِبُّونَ ٱللَّهَ فَٱتَّبِعُونِى يُحْبِبْكُمُ ٱللَّهُ وَيَغْفِرْ لَكُمْ ذُنُوبَكُمْ ۗ وَٱللَّهُ غَفُورٌ رَّحِيمٌ ۝

[*O Messenger*], *tell people: "If you indeed love Allah, follow me, and Allah will love you and will forgive you your sins, Allah is All-Forgiving, All-Compassionate.* (*Sūrah Āl 'Imrān* 3: 31)

It is this intense personal relationship of love and reverence for Allah ﷻ and His Prophet ﷺ that characterizes the Muslim psyche. That is why the Prophet Muḥammad ﷺ is central to the life of Muslims – men and women, young and old, individuals and communities.

4. *Obedience of the Prophet* ﷺ

This brings us to the *fourth* foundation of the Muslims' relationship with the Prophet ﷺ and that is obedience (*ṭā'ah*). It is a logical demand of all the above three foundations of faith, authority and love. That is why the test of a Muslim's acceptance of the Prophetic authority with trust and love, lies in following the letter and spirit of his instructions (Qur'ān 3: 132; 24: 52; 33: 71), and obedience to the Prophet ﷺ has been proclaimed to be synonymous with the obedience of Allah ﷻ (*Sūrah al-Nisā'* 4: 80). The test of *īmān*, loyalty and authority and love of the Prophet ﷺ lies in obeying his directives and commands.

5. *Emulation of the Prophet* ﷺ

This obedience to Allah ﷻ and His Prophet ﷺ has been the hallmark of Muslim life and identity. However, obedience relates primarily to following Divine laws and commands and the Prophet's instructions and directives. But the Islamic paradigm of relationship with Allah ﷻ and His Prophet ﷺ has another unique dimension, or something that goes beyond obedience. It is *iṭṭibāʿ* or imitation and emulation of the life-example of the Prophet ﷺ, or seeking to come into conformity with the Prophetic ideal. This makes the role of the Prophet cardinal to this process of Divine Guidance – transforming the lives of men, women and communities through the Way set by the Prophet ﷺ. That brings us to the *fifth* foundation, which completes the process that imparts to the life of Muslims its distinct hue and colour.

It is important to understand this subtle difference between *ṭāʿah* (obedience) and *iṭṭibāʿ* (emulation). Obedience (*ṭāʿah*) is in respect of laws, instructions and rules of conduct. But the relationship with the Prophet ﷺ goes beyond obedience: it is emulation of his model, casting one's life in the mould or life-pattern set by the Prophet ﷺ. This calls for something more than *ṭāʿah*. It is *iṭṭibāʿ* or the enthusiastic following of his personal example, emulating his conduct and behaviour. Allah's commands are to be obeyed; the Qur'ānic edicts are to be followed, but it is only the life-example of the Prophet ﷺ that can be emulated. This is the process through which one strives to pattern one's life and conduct to the life-example (*uswah*) of the Prophet ﷺ.[2]

The Companions ﷺ of the Prophet ﷺ not only obeyed his commands and instructions, they also emulated his life and behaviour, his mode and manner and even the very style of everything he did from worship to governance in its full measure. They did not stop at following what he commanded and avoiding what he forbade. They lovingly and keenly observed each and every one of his acts, assimilating every fine detail of his behaviour and manners into their own lives. They strived hard to refashion their own lives in complete harmony with his. Allah's love for the believers is the result not merely of their love of Allah and obedience (*ṭāʿah*) to Allah ﷻ and His Prophet ﷺ but also emulation (*iṭṭibāʿ*) of the Prophet ﷺ, casting themselves in the life-pattern of the Prophet (*Sūrah Āl ʿImrān* 3: 31).

---

2. For a very candid discussion on *ṭāʿah* and *iṭṭibāʿ*, see Mawlānā Amīn Aḥsan Iṣlāḥī, *Tazkiyyah Nafs* (Urdu), Pakistan, 5th edition, 2008, pp. 113-123.

These are the five foundations upon which the relationship of the Muslim with the Prophet of Allah ﷺ rests. That is why his Way (*Sunnah*) is central to the lives of Muslims, for each individual as well as to the *Ummah* as community and nation. The *Sunnah* fashions their identity, providing the common elements in the lives and behaviour of the Muslims regardless of whenever or wherever they may be.

Thus the Qur'ān and the *Sunnah*, the Message and the Messenger are inseparable. That is why the *Sunnah* gives the life of a Muslim its real identity and direction. It is a *spiritual phenomenon* based on faith and love, but it is also a *sociological process* that imparts unity, homogeneity and commonality to the lives of Muslims individually and collectively, in every place and in every period from the days of the Prophet ﷺ to the end of days. It is adherence to the *Sunnah* that is the most powerful and solidifying force in the Muslim's life, character and identity. That makes the *Sunnah* not just a norm, but a living reality that has ensured a remarkable degree of continuity and solidarity in Muslim life, something that is unparalleled in the history of human societies and civilizations. With rites and rituals from birth to death, personal conduct to social behaviour, how to greet and meet, principles and norms of family life, social conduct, economic dealings and dynamics of governance, every sphere of life is illumined with the light of the *Sunnah*.

The *Sunnah* constitutes the everlasting framework for Muslim life and behaviour; it is the sheet-anchor and mainstay of Islam and Muslim life. This was guaranteed by the command of Islam: عَلَيْكُمْ بِسُنَّتِي (You must follow my *Sunnah* (Way)) and مَنْ رَغِبَ عَنْ سُنَّتِي فَلَيْسَ مِنِّيْ (Whoever detests my *Sunnah* does not belong to me (i.e. among my followers or my community)). He is also reported to have said:

تَرَكْتُ فِيْكُمْ اَمْرَيْنِ لَنْ تَضِلُّوا مَا تَمَسَّكْتُمْ بِهِمَا: كِتَابَ اللهِ وَسُنَّتَ رَسُوْلِهِ. موطأ مالك، كتاب الجامع، ١٣٩٥

I am leaving behind with you two things. You will never go astray if you firmly adhere to them: the Book of Allah and the *Sunnah* of His Messenger. *Muwaṭṭa'* Imām Mālik, Book of the Congregation, *Ḥadīth* no. 1395.

The Qur'ān is the paramount source of guidance; the *Sunnah* is the application of that guidance to all aspects of individual and collective life. It is the key to understanding the Qur'ānic guidance and the process through which it is translated into reality in our lives.

The *Sunnah* is the most authentic explanation and elaboration of the Word of God. As the Prophet ﷺ was the living example of Divine guidance, his *Sunnah* shows us how to live in accordance with the Divine command. The *Sunnah* makes the *hidāyah* revealed in the Book easy to understand, follow, and put into practice. The Qur'ān and the *Sunnah* represent two sides of the same coin; they are inseparable. That is the reason why the Qur'ān says:

مَّن يُطِعِ ٱلرَّسُولَ فَقَدْ أَطَاعَ ٱللَّهَ ...

He who obeys the Messenger thereby obeys Allah (*Sūrah al-Nisā'* 4: 80).

And the Prophet ﷺ reiterates the same when he says:

مَـنْ اَطَاعَنِي فَقَـدْ اَطَاعَ اللهَ وَمَـنْ عَصَـانِي فَقَـدْ عَصَىٰ اللهَ. البـخاري، كتاب الأحكام، ٦٦٠٤

Whoever obeys me obeys Allah and whoever disobeys me disobeys Allah. Bukhārī, Book of Laws, *Ḥadīth* no. 6604.

The *Sunnah* is not only the unifying force of the Muslims, but it also defines, highlights and operationalizes the nature of spirituality in Islam which permeates every aspect of the worldly life and relations over and above the formal acts of worship. Seyyed Hossein Nasr brings this into sharp focus:

> The sunnah is central to all aspects of Islamic spirituality, for it is through the emulation of the sunnah of the Prophet

> that the Muslim is able to gain certain of the virtues which are possessed in their fullness by the Prophet. The Muslims see the Prophet through his sunnah – how he acted, spoke, walked, ate, judged, loved and worshipped. The sunnah is, therefore, in a sense the continuation of the life of the Prophet for later generations.[3]

A modern scholar of Islam steeped in the mystical tradition describes the importance of the *Sunnah* in the following words:

> It is inconceivable that these virtues (of the sunnah) could have been practiced through the centuries down to our time if the founder of Islam had not personified them in the highest degree; it is also inconceivable that they should have been borrowed from elsewhere – and one cannot imagine from where since their conditioning and their style are specifically Islamic. For Muslims the moral and spiritual worth of the Prophet is not an abstraction or a supposition; it is a lived reality and it is precisely this which proves its authenticity retrospectively.[4]

Annemarie Schimmel, a keen observer of the Islamic ethos, regards *imitatio Muhammadi*, an imitation of the Prophet's actions and activity, as the principal force that has shaped Muslim identity:

> But it was through this imitation of Muhammad's actions as transmitted through the *ḥadīth,* that Islamic life assumed a unique uniformity in social behavior, a fact that has always impressed visitors of all parts of the Muslim world. [...] It is this ideal of the *imitatio Muhammadi* that has provided Muslims from Morocco to Indonesia with such a

---

3. Seyyed Hossein Nasr, '*Sunnah* and *Ḥadīth*' in Seyyed Hossein Nasr (ed.), *Islamic Spirituality* (New York: Crossroad Publishing, 1997), 2 vols., Vol. I, pp. 97-110, quotation at p. 98.
4. Frithjof Schuon, *Islam and the Perennial Philosophy*, trans. by J.P. Hobson (London: Al-Tajir World of Islam Trust, 1976), p. 29.

> uniformity of action: wherever one may be, one knows how to behave when entering a house, which formulas of greeting to employ, what to avoid in good company, how to eat, and how to travel. For centuries Muslim children have been brought up in these ways.[5]

Two more aspects of the *Sunnah* deserve to be mentioned. The first is that it covers *all* aspects of human life, from faith and worship to individual and collective life, from personal hygiene to social manners and mores, from individual piety to public morality, from family relations to economic and political dealings, from the depths of spiritual experience to the length and breadth of socio-economic life and the problems of good governance. The *Sunnah* provides guidance for all these dimensions of life and imparts to them a unity of purpose and vision. It is through the instrumentality of the *Sunnah* that all aspects of life are welded together into a comprehensive, holistic, integrated and harmonious *Weltanschauung*.

The other historic contribution of the *Sunnah* relates to its role in bringing about a complete reconciliation between the moral and the material, the spiritual and the mundane sides of life. Prayer and progress no longer represent different worlds: they are integrated into an organic whole. Devotional and spiritual matters are fully taken care of and the questions of daily life and social conduct have been permeated with a moral and spiritual ideal.

The Prophet ﷺ has bequeathed a model that treats life as a compound entity, a sum total of moral, spiritual, practical, individual, social, political and cultural manifestations. Life is not divided into the sacred and the secular, that-worldly and this-worldly, the spiritual and the mundane. The *Sunnah* shows how this integrated model of life can be actualized in both individual and collective behaviour. This is not to assert that

5. Annemarie Schimmel, *And Muhammad is His Messenger: The Veneration of the Prophet in Islamic Piety* (Chapel Hill: The University of North Carolina Press, 1985), pp. 32, 55.

life is free from tensions, lapses and disappointments; these are indeed part of the human existence. The *Sunnah* shows how these human situations are to be faced with faith, fortitude and fraternal support and cooperation. The *Sunnah* helps us to engage in a process of interaction between our ideals and reality to discern the ways and means that can represent a plausible blend of the two. The *Sunnah* is, therefore, a norm, a process, and a methodology, all rolled into one, and herein lies the historical dynamic that the *Sunnah* has played in Muslim life and history. That is why the *Sunnah*, in the words of Muhammad Asad, constitutes 'the iron-framework of the House of Islam' and that 'to follow him all he commanded is to follow Islam; to discard his Sunnah is to discard the reality of Islam.'[6]

It is this effort to follow the Prophet ﷺ and to bring one's life and behaviour into consonance with his life and behaviour that makes a Muslim's whole life a conscious, disciplined and meaningful exercise to pursue what is right and just and to avoid what is wrong and unjust.

Every saying (*qawl*), action (*'amal*) or actions that had his tacit approval (*taqrīr*) is a *Sunnah* and every *Sunnah* is a gem of virtue and piety. It radiates light that can illuminate our whole lives. But there is yet another very important dimension that must not be ignored. It is the totality of the life-model of the Prophet ﷺ in which all the *Sunan* (plural of *Sunnah*) taken together go to make up what may be described as the grand *Sunnah* – i.e. his role as *dāʿiyah ilā Allāh*, one who calls people to the path of their Creator, or namely, the totality of his mission to imbibe the Divine message, convey it to others, live by it and strive to establish it in its entirety (*iqāmat al-Dīn* or establishing the Islamic order). This grand *Sunnah* begins from the moment he received the Divine Call in Ḥirāʾ and shared it with his wife, the Mother of the Believers, Sayyidah Khadījah ﵂ and his nearest relatives and friends. His efforts, throughout the Makkan and the Madīnan periods until he breathed his last, centred round

---

6. Muhammad Asad, *Islam at the Crossroads* (Gibraltar: Dar al-Andalus, 1993 [1934]), pp. 82, 97.

this message (*da'wah*). He lived, he strived, and suffered for only one purpose: witness (*shahādah*) of Truth and establishment of the *Dīn* in all areas of human existence.

If all of his *Sunan* are taken together, they go to make a beautiful mosaic, with a clear pattern and design. It is this struggle for sharing and establishing *Dīn* that constitutes his grand *Sunnah*. It is this prophetic mission for which he was raised by Allah and for which he strived all his life. It was a historic mission that he fulfilled; it is this mission that he has bequeathed to the *Ummah*, and to humanity at large, as our mission and destiny. Iqbal beautifully identifies this defining role of the Prophet ﷺ in his *Reconstruction of Religious Thought in Islam*. Reflecting on the experience of the historic event of the *Mi'rāj* (Ascension) in the Prophet's life, Iqbal writes:

> 'Muhammad of Arabia ascended the highest heaven and returned. I swear by God that if I had reached that point, I should have never returned.' These are the words of a great Muslim saint, 'Abdul Quddus of Gangoh. In the whole range of Sufi literature it will probably be difficult to find words which, in a single sentence, disclose such an acute perception of the psychological difference between the prophetic and the mystic types of consciousness. The mystic does not wish to return from the repose of 'unitarian experience', and even when he does return, as he must, his return does not mean much for mankind at large. The prophet's return is creative. He returns to insert himself into the sweep of time with a view to control the forces of history, and thereby to create a fresh world of ideals. For the mystic the repose of 'unitary experience' is something final; for the prophet it is the awakening, within him, of world-shaking psychological forces, calculated to completely transform the human world. The desire to see his religious experience transformed into a living world-force is supreme in the prophet.[7]

---

7. Muhammad Iqbal, *The Reconstruction of Religious Thought in Islam*, Lahore: Shaikh Muhammad Ashraf, 1977, p. 124.

This missionary effort, spread over the twenty-three years of his prophetic ministry, directed towards sharing the truth, bearing witness to it and engaging in a ceaseless effort to transform the world constitutes the grand *Sunnah* of the Prophet Muḥammad ﷺ, the final Messenger and the Seal of the Prophets. All of his sayings and actions taken in their entirety were directed towards sharing the Divine message with humanity. He spared no individual and collective effort to transform the human condition so as to bring it into harmony with the Divine Will. He strived night and day to infuse the lives of the people with the light that has been bestowed upon him. He spent every effort to produce a new people, a new society and a new history so as to fulfil the task assigned to him as the Prophet of Allah ﷺ. While we must make every effort to learn, understand and live in accord with each and every *Sunnah* of the Prophet ﷺ, we must be equally mindful of pursuing the grand *Sunnah* of the Prophet ﷺ, in order to continue the Prophetic mission that was the be-all and end-all of his life and effort. The Qur'ān obligates Muslims, individually and collectively, to bear witness to the Truth before humanity, just as the Prophet ﷺ was a witness unto them:

وَكَذَٰلِكَ جَعَلْنَٰكُمْ أُمَّةً وَسَطًا لِّتَكُونُوا۟ شُهَدَآءَ عَلَى ٱلنَّاسِ وَيَكُونَ ٱلرَّسُولُ عَلَيْكُمْ شَهِيدًا ...

And it is thus that We appointed you to be the community of the middle way so that you might be witnesses to all mankind as the Messenger was made to be a witness to you. (*Sūrah al-Baqarah* 2: 143)

وَجَٰهِدُوا۟ فِى ٱللَّهِ حَقَّ جِهَادِهِۦ ۚ هُوَ ٱجْتَبَىٰكُمْ وَمَا جَعَلَ عَلَيْكُمْ فِى ٱلدِّينِ مِنْ حَرَجٍ ۚ مِّلَّةَ أَبِيكُمْ
إِبْرَٰهِيمَ ۚ هُوَ سَمَّىٰكُمُ ٱلْمُسْلِمِينَ مِن قَبْلُ وَفِى هَٰذَا لِيَكُونَ ٱلرَّسُولُ شَهِيدًا عَلَيْكُمْ وَتَكُونُوا۟ شُهَدَآءَ عَلَى
ٱلنَّاسِ ۚ فَأَقِيمُوا۟ ٱلصَّلَوٰةَ وَءَاتُوا۟ ٱلزَّكَوٰةَ وَٱعْتَصِمُوا۟ بِٱللَّهِ هُوَ مَوْلَىٰكُمْ ۖ فَنِعْمَ ٱلْمَوْلَىٰ وَنِعْمَ ٱلنَّصِيرُ

You strive in the cause of Allah in a manner worthy of that striving. He has chosen you [for His task], and He has not laid upon you any hardship in religion. Keep to the faith of your father Abraham. Allah named you Muslims earlier and even in this [Book] that the Messenger may be a witness over you, and that you may be witnesses over all mankind.

So establish Prayer, and pay Zakāt, *and hold fast to Allah. He is your Protector. What an excellent Protector; what an excellent Helper!* (*Sūrah al-Ḥajj* 22: 78)

The Way of the Prophet is the translation of *Intikhāb-e-Ḥadīth,* a collection of the sayings of the Prophet ﷺ compiled in 1956 by the late Mawlānā ʿAbd al-Ghaffār Ḥasan, who was then head of the training department of the Jamāʿat-i-Islāmī Pakistan. The respected Mawlānā was a key resource person in the training programmes of the Islamic Movement in the 1950s. This collection grew out of the teaching sessions in *Ḥadīth* that Mawlānā ʿAbd al-Ghaffār Ḥasan used to conduct on a regular basis. In my student days from 1950 to 1956, I had the good fortune of learning at his feet most of the *Aḥādīth* contained in this collection. He used to live with us during these training programmes, spending all his time not only in formal lectures but in long-lasting sessions explaining the meaning and implications of these gems of wisdom. His effort was not confined to teaching us these *Aḥādīth*. He was always eager to ensure that we imbibed these *Aḥādīth* in our souls and articulated them in our conduct. His style of teaching and training was remarkable – clear, direct, affectionate, and friendly. He would generously welcome our questions and was never offended even if some of them were stupid. He always tried to explain difficult points in a very simple and pleasant manner with words that would sink directly into our hearts. For those of us who experienced this, it was the best and most enjoyable period of our lives.

This collection was originally made with a purpose. Within a span of some four hundred *Aḥādīth*, an effort was undertaken to give the course participant a feel for the immeasurable richness of the Prophetic guidance. This course was meant primarily for the students and workers of the Islamic Movement who were undertaking modern education and who had had no opportunity to learn the traditional Islamic sciences. After introducing them to the basic terms and concepts of *Uṣūl al-Ḥadīth*, including a brief account of *Ḥadīth* compilation and criticism, the sayings of the Prophet ﷺ, dealing with different aspects of life were taught, together with short explanations. The participants were asked to memorize some of the shorter *Aḥādīth*. This present collection, with explanatory notes, reproduces what was taught to us.

I have given this background to highlight the major distinctions of this collection: its comprehensiveness and its educative role as a training manual for the workers of the Islamic Movement. However, its usefulness goes far beyond its immediate audience. In its present form, it can best be described as a beautiful handbook of *Ḥadīth*, making the radiant gems of Prophetic wisdom available to a wider public. With admirable brevity, it helpfully gives the sum and substance of the Prophet's Way, of the *Sunnah*. It is important too in the sense that the collection as a whole brings into sharp focus the grand *Sunnah* of the Prophet ﷺ that I have tried to highlight in this preface. This has been a very popular compendium of *Ḥadīth*: in Pakistan, some thirty editions of this collection have been published.

It is my hope that the publication of the English translation will be a blessing for young Muslims in the English-speaking world. For non-Muslims it also provides a window into the life and mission of the Prophet of Islam. At a time when Islam is constantly misrepresented, particularly in the West, this short collection of the sayings of the Prophet ﷺ can enable all and sundry to get a clearer picture of Islam from the words of none other than the Last Prophet of Allah. May Allah ﷻ give the best of rewards to the late Mawlānā ʿAbd al-Ghaffār Ḥasan for whom this constitutes a perpetual benefit (*ṣadaqah jāriyah*). May Allah ﷻ also reward his grandson Dr. Usama Hasan, who has ably translated this book into modern English, and all our colleagues at the Islamic Foundation and Kube Publications who have helped to bring out this noble collection in the best of forms.

Islamabad Khurshid Ahmad
1st Safar 1430 H
27th January 2009

Foreword

It gives me great pleasure to present, by the grace of Allah Almighty, this translation of a concise yet profound work on *Ḥadīth* by my esteemed teacher and paternal grandfather, Shaykh ʿAbd al-Ghaffār Ḥasan, may Allah shower His Mercy upon him, for he departed from this world in March 2007.

This translation was begun in 2002 at the request of Professor Khurshid Ahmad, Chairman of the Islamic Foundation, and a student of the author from nearly half a century ago. I am extremely grateful to Professor Khurshid for his constant support and encouragement during the course of this work. The bulk of the translation work was carried out between 2002 and 2004 in London and Islamabad, where I lived and worked for most of 2003 and was able to benefit from the presence of my grandfather and many of his students.

Upon my return to London, I was able to complete the translation with the invaluable aid of my beloved father and teacher, Dr. Suhaib Hasan, who helped me with the work's difficult passages, both Urdu and Arabic, and clarified their meaning.

I would like to thank Dr. Manazir Ahsan, Mr. Abdul Rashid Siddiqui, Yahya Birt and Haris Ahmad for their tireless efforts to bring this book to publication. Thanks are due to Nasir Cadir for designing the cover. I am also indebted to Naeem Qaddoura and Medhat Singhab for their invaluable help with the layout of the manuscript.

Finally, citations from the Qur'ān have been taken from Zafar Ishaq Ansari's translation of Mawdūdī's *Tafhīm al-Qur'ān*, published by the Islamic Foundation (Markfield, 2006).

In conclusion, I pray to Allah to accept and bless the contributions of all those who have participated in this work, and to enable this book to be an ongoing charitable act initiated by our dear departed teacher.

London — Usama Hasan
Jumādā al-Ākhir 1429
June 2008

1

Objective of Compiling this Work

The objective of establishing the Jamāʿat-i-Islāmī as explained in its constitution is:

> The objective of the Jamāʿat-i-Islāmī Pakistan and the goal of all its efforts is to establish the *dīn* [i.e. the establishment of the supremacy of Divine law, or the Islamic system of life in its entirety] and ultimately to earn the Divine pleasure and success in the Hereafter.

Clearly, it is necessary for those who adopt this vision to present to the world a resolve rooted in faith, spiritual zeal and sincere determination. Their word and deed must correspond, and they must be the embodiment of good deeds and true pictures of sincerity. For the sake of this lofty aim, they must be ready to sacrifice their most beloved possessions, and they must have in their sights neither worldly profit nor material benefit, but only the Divine pleasure.

In order to keep these important requirements of the vision fresh in the minds, the Central *Majlis-i-Shūrā* of Jamāʿat-i-Islāmī decided quite some time ago to establish such training centres in whose curricula the study of the Qur'ān and the study of *Ḥadīth* would occupy prominent and distinct positions.

For Qur'ānic study, one can benefit from *Tafhīm al-Qur'ān*[1] and other reliable *tafsīrs* and commentaries. However, for the study of *Ḥadīth*, as far as my knowledge goes, there was no comprehensive and concise collection in Urdu that would be totally suitable and beneficial for the nurturing of character and the building of personality. Therefore, keeping this objective in mind, this work has been compiled.

Features of this Compilation

1. In selecting the *Aḥādīth*, the idea has been that all aspects of human life related to individual and collective personality and morality should be illuminated in the light of the *Sunnah* of the Messenger, ﷺ, and that in this respect no important example should be neglected. It can be gauged by glancing at the index of topics that, from individual dealings to international relations, there is no significant aspect of life that the Messenger of Allah, may Allah bless him and his family and grant them peace, has not been illuminated with guidance by his words and deeds.
2. In this compilation in general, those teachings of morality and matters of *Fiqh* (Islamic Law) have been included upon which the entire Islamic nation is agreed. As far as possible, I have avoided going into matters of detail about which there is disagreement: such a need can be fulfilled by a separate work.
3. (a) Righteous personality and pure character spring from sound beliefs and ideas, and are polished and refreshed precisely by the rituals of worship established in the *Sharī'ah*.[2]

---

1. *Tafhīm al-Qur'ān*, by Sayyid Abul A'lā Mawdūdī, Lahore, (six volumes). The English translation is being published under the auspices of the Islamic Foundation, Leicester, U.K., under the title: *Towards Understanding the Qur'ān*, with vols. I to VIII published as of 2007.

2. Generally, the *Sharī'ah* refers to the way of Divine guidance received through Allah's Messenger ﷺ by which salvation and success may be attained in this worldly life and in the Hereafter. More specifically, it refers to the revealed

On this basis, *Aḥādīth* dealing with these two topics have been placed first in this collection.

(b) A Muslim's fundamental vision is to establish Islam in this world. However, this duty of establishing Islam cannot be fulfilled in a real sense unless the person is aware of the profound principles of *da'wah* and *tablīgh* (calling to Allah and sharing the message of Islam). Therefore, narrations regarding these two topics have also been placed before the chapter on morality.

4. By studying the *Aḥādīth*, filled with jewels of wisdom, that constitute this collection, it can be seen how worthless is the position of those people who pick and choose some narrations out of context and then pronounce them to be repugnant to reason and morality.[3] They have been spreading false propaganda against the entire treasure of *Ḥadīth*. This is irrational as it is ignoble.

   It is an accepted principle of *Uṣūl al-Ḥadīth* that if any narration, in the wealth of *Ḥadīth* literature that has reached us through reliable means, apparently contradicts the intellect, then one can ponder and reflect and, as a last resort, abstain from commenting. However, this does not mean that on the basis of a few such narrations, this entire treasure of righteous guidance should be thrown away! This collection is like a mirror in which the entire spectrum of the teachings of the Prophet ﷺ can be seen.

---

or sacred law of Islam which establishes the commandments and prohibitions of religion. Its main sources are the Qur'ān and the *Sunnah* and therafter other juristic principles such as consensus (*ijmā'*) and argument by analogy (*qiyās*). Its scope includes not just law but worship, ethics and personal conduct. – Trans. Note

3. Swami Diyanand, a nineteenth-century Hindu revivalist, separated some *āyāt* from their contexts and attributed false meanings to them in his *Sathyartha Parkash* in order to spread hatred against the Noble Qur'ān. Similar vicious efforts have been made by others in the name of "reform" of *Ḥadīth*. Detractors have always behaved in the same manner, their hearts throbbing in unison. This collection gives a comprehensive and integrated picture of the *Sunnah* of the Prophet ﷺ.

5. In translation and commentary, an effort has been made to use plain language and explanation for the ordinary mind, and to mention only concepts that are free from the confusion and complexity of philosophy and *kalām*. In this way, not only will the students at the training centres benefit, but this collection will also be beneficial for the ordinary Muslim who has only received a basic education.

   It cannot be claimed that this collection is comprehensive, covering every field of human activity and behaviour. However, every care has been taken not to leave out any major area of human endeavour and education.

   The respected readers, especially the honoured people of knowledge, are requested, upon finding any shortcoming or mistake, to alert the author accordingly and to keep him informed of their sincere suggestions and constructive advice.

I pray to Allah that He makes this humble attempt a means of happiness and success in the Hereafter for me, and that He grants travellers on the path of Truth the capability to derive as much benefit as possible from it. *Āmīn*!

10th Rabīʿ al-Thānī, 1376 — ʿAbd al-Ghaffār Ḥasan
14th November, 1956

2

Introduction to the Sciences of *Ḥadīth*

Not all the necessary and important issues in *Ḥadīth* can be covered by this brief introduction: that would require a separate and independent work. The following brief sketch of the gathering and compilation of *Ḥadīth* is presented, giving an idea of the stages through which the priceless treasure of the Prophetic *Ḥadīth* has passed during thirteen centuries in reaching us. It also indicates who those pure souls were who dedicated their entire lives to transmitting these treasures of wisdom and guidance to future generations, and who would even risk their lives in this path if required.

2.1 THREE METHODS OF PRESERVING *ḤADĪTH*

The *Aḥādīth* of the Messenger of Allah ﷺ have reached us through three reliable methods:

1. The practice of the Ummah.
2. Written memory-aids and compilations.
3. Memory-aided narration and transmission, i.e. the continuous sequence of study and teaching.

2.2 FOUR PHASES OF *ḤADĪTH* PRESERVATION

In this sense, the total period of collection and arrangement, and of composition and compilation of *Ḥadīth*, can be divided into four phases.

2.2.1 *The First Phase: From the Prophetic era to the end of the first century* hijri

In this phase, the details of the preservers of *Ḥadīth* and of written memory-aids and compilations are as follows:

2.2.1.1 Famous Preservers of *Ḥadīth*

The Companions (*Ṣaḥābah*, ﷺ)

1. Abū Hurayrah ʿAbd al-Raḥmān b. Ṣakhr, ﷺ, d. 59 H, aged 78, 5374 narrations. His students reach 800 in number.
2. ʿAbdullāh b. ʿAbbās, ﷺ, d. 68 H, aged 71, 2660 narrations.
3. ʿĀ'ishah Ṣiddīqah, ﷺ, d. 58 H, aged 67, 2210 narrations.
4. ʿAbdullāh b. ʿUmar, ﷺ, d. 73 H, aged 84, 1630 narrations.
5. Jābir b. ʿAbdullāh, ﷺ, d. 78 H, aged 94, 1560 narrations.
6. Anas b. Mālik, ﷺ, d. 93 H, aged 103, 1286 narrations.
7. Abū Saʿīd al-Khudrī, ﷺ, d. 74 H, aged 84, 1170 narrations.

These are the majestic Companions who preserved more than a thousand *Aḥādīth* each. Apart from them, ʿAbdullāh b. ʿAmr b. al-ʿĀṣ ﷺ, (d. 63 H), ʿAlī ﷺ, (d. 40 H) and ʿUmar ﷺ, (d. 23 H) fall into the category of those Companions whose narrations number between five hundred and a thousand each.

Similarly, Abū Bakr ﷺ, (d. 13 H), ʿUthmān ﷺ, (d. 36 H), Umm Salamah ﷺ, (d. 59 H), Abū Mūsā al-Ashʿarī ﷺ, (d. 52 H), Abū Dharr al-Ghifārī ﷺ, (d. 32 H), Abū Ayyūb al-Anṣārī ﷺ, (d. 51 H), Ubayy b. Kaʿb ﷺ, (d. 19 H) and Muʿādh b. Jabal ﷺ, (d. 18 H) have narrated between one hundred and five hundred *Aḥādīth* each.

The Followers (*Tābi'īn*)

Besides the Companions, the period of those senior Followers cannot be forgotten: those by whose wealth of selfless and sincere efforts, the Ummah of Muḥammad will be enriched with the treasures of the *Sunnah* until the Day of Judgment. Some of these seniors are introduced as follows:

1. Sa'īd b. al-Musayyib, ﵁. He was born in Madīnah in the second year of the reign of al-Fārūq [i.e. 'Umar], d. 105 H. He took the knowledge of *Ḥadīth* from 'Uthmān, 'Ā'ishah, Abū Hurayrah and Zayd b. Thābit, ﵃ all.
2. 'Urwah b. al-Zubayr, ﵁. He is regarded as one of the outstanding people of knowledge in Madīnah. He was the nephew of 'Ā'ishah, and narrated *Aḥādīth* mostly from his honourable maternal aunt. He also had the honour of being the student of Abū Hurayrah and Zayd b. Thābit. Many people of knowledge, including the likes of Ṣāliḥ b. Kaysān and Imām al-Zuhrī, were amongst his students. He died in 94 H.
3. Sālim b. 'Abdullāh b. 'Umar, ﵁, is counted amongst the Seven *Fuqahā'*[4] of Madīnah. He took the knowledge of *Ḥadīth* from his illustrious father and other Companions. His students included Nāfi', al-Zuhrī and other famous Followers. He passed away in 106 H.
4. Nāfi', freed slave of 'Abdullāh b. 'Umar ﵁. He is the special student of 'Abdullāh b. 'Umar ﵁, and the teacher of Imām Mālik, may Allah have mercy on him. The traditionists regard this chain of narration (Mālik from Nāfi' from 'Abdullāh b. 'Umar ﵁ from the Messenger of Allah ﷺ as the "Golden Chain". He passed away in 117 H.

2.2.1.2 Written Legacy of the First Phase

1. *Ṣaḥīfah Ṣādiqah*. This was compiled by 'Abdullāh b. 'Amr b. al-'Āṣ ﵁, d. 63 H, aged 77. He had a special inclination

4. Or jurists, literally "men of understanding".

towards writing and compilation. Whatever he heard from the Prophet ﷺ, he would write down, and had permission from the Prophet ﷺ to do so.[5] This compilation consisted of about a thousand *Aḥādīth*, and remained preserved amongst his family for a period; it can now be found in full within the *Musnad* of Imām Aḥmad, may Allah have mercy upon him.

2. *Ṣaḥīfah Ṣaḥīḥah*, compiled by Hammām b. Munabbih (d. 101 H), one of Abū Hurayrah's famous students who used to write down the narrations from his illustrious teacher. Manuscripts of this work are found in the libraries of Berlin and Damascus. Imām Aḥmad b. Ḥanbal has included this entire *ṣaḥīfah* in his famous *Musnad* under Abū Hurayrah's section.[6] A few years ago, the document was published in Hyderabad through the efforts of Dr. Hamidullah; it consists of 138 narrations. This *ṣaḥīfah* is a subset of the totality of Abū Hurayrah's narrations, and most of its narrations are also found in Bukhārī and Muslim, with similar wording and no significant differences.
3. Another of Abū Hurayrah's students, Bashīr b. Nuhayk, also compiled a collection of *Ḥadīth*. Upon parting from Abū Hurayrah, Bashīr recited it to his teacher and received the latter's approval.[7]
4. *Musnad* of Abū Hurayrah ؓ. Copies of this were written during the time of the Companions. One of these copies was in the possession of the father of 'Umar b. 'Abd al-'Azīz, 'Abd al-'Azīz b. Marwān (d. 86 H), the governor of Egypt. He wrote to Kathīr b. Murrah, "Write down those *Aḥādīth* that you have from the Noble Companions, but there is no need to send the narrations of Abū Hurayrah, since we have those with us in written form."[8] A copy of the

5. *Mukhtaṣar Jāmi' Bayān al-'Ilm*, pp. 36-37.
6. See *Musnad Aḥmad*, Vol. 2, pp. 312-8. For details, see the preface to *Ṣaḥīfah Hammām b. Munabbih*, ed. Dr. Hamidullah.
7. *Jāmi' Bayān al-'Ilm*, Vol. 1, p. 72; *Tahdhīb al-Tahdhīb*, Vol. 1, p. 470.
8. Preface to *Ṣaḥīfah Hammām*, p. 50, quoting from *Ṭabaqāt Ibn Sa'd*, Vol. 7, p. 157.

Musnad of Abū Hurayrah, written by the hand of Imām Ibn Taymiyyah, exists in a library in Germany.[9]

5. *Ṣaḥīfah* of ʿAlī ﵁. Through Imām Bukhārī's description, we know that this collection was quite bulky.[10] Points related to *zakāt*, the sanctity of Madīnah, the Sermon at the Farewell *Ḥajj* and the constitution of the Islamic amirate were recorded therein.
6. The written form of the Prophet's Sermon, ﷺ. On the occasion of the conquest of Makkah, the Prophet, ﷺ, ordered Abū Shāh of Yemen to record in writing his detailed sermon, upon the latter's request.[11] This sermon consisted of important explanations regarding human rights.
7. *Ṣaḥīfah* of Jābir ﵁. The narrations of Jābir b. ʿAbdullāh ﵄ were compiled in written form by his students Wahb b. Munabbih (d. 110 H) and Sulaymān b. Qays al-Shukrī.[12] This collection covered the rites of *Ḥajj* and the Sermon of the Farewell *Ḥajj*.
8. Narrations of ʿĀ'ishah Ṣiddīqah ﵂. The *Aḥādīth* of ʿĀ'ishah ﵂ were recorded in writing by her nephew and student, ʿUrwah b. al-Zubayr ﵁.[13]
9. *Aḥādīth* of Ibn ʿAbbās ﵁. There were a number of collections of the narrations of ʿAbdullāh b. ʿAbbās ﵁. Saʿīd b. Jubayr (may Allah have mercy on him), the Follower, was one of those who used to compile his narrations in written form.[14]
10. The *Ṣaḥīfahs* of Anas b. Mālik ﵁. Saʿīd b. Hilāl (may Allah have mercy on him) says that Anas b. Mālik ﵁ used to bring out his written notes and show them to us, saying, "I heard these statements personally from the Messenger of Allah, ﷺ.

---

9. Introduction to *Tuḥfat al-Aḥwadhī Sharḥ Tirmidhī*, p. 165.
10. *Ṣaḥīḥ al-Bukhārī, Kitāb al-Iʿtiṣām bi'l-Kitāb wa'l-Sunnah*, Vol. 1, p. 451.
11. *Ibid.*, Vol. 1, p. 20; *Mukhtaṣar Jāmiʿ Bayān al-ʿIlm*, p. 36; *Ṣaḥīḥ Muslim*, vol. 1, p. 439.
12. *Tahdhīb al-Tahdhīb*, Vol. 4, p. 215.
13. *Ibid.*, Vol. 7, p. 183.
14. *Sunan al-Dārimī*, p. 68.

After recording them in writing, I confirmed them by reading them back to him."[15]

11. ʿAmr b. Ḥazm ﷺ. When the Prophet ﷺ was sending him to Yemen as governor, he gave him a written code of instructions. He not only preserved this letter, but included other Prophetic statements alongside it, thus compiling a significantly-sized book.[16]
12. The treatise of Samurah b. Jundub ﷺ. This was inherited by his son, and was a very large treasure of narrations.[17]
13. *Ṣaḥīfah* of Saʿd b. ʿUbādah ﷺ, the Companion who knew how to read and write from the *Jāhiliyyah* period.
14. The writings of Nāfiʿ ﷺ. Sulaymān b. Mūsā narrated that ʿAbdullāh b. ʿUmar ﷺ would dictate and Nāfiʿ ﷺ would record what he said in writing.[18]
15. Maʿn narrated that ʿAbd al-Raḥmān b. ʿAbdullāh b. Masʿūd brought out a book before him and took an oath, saying that it was written by the hand of his father, ʿAbdullāh b. Masʿūd ﷺ.[19]

Were the process of investigation and verification to be continued, many more such examples and instances would be found.

In this phase, the Noble Companions (*Ṣaḥābah*) and Senior Followers (*Tābiʿūn*) concentrated on writing down the contents of their own memories. In the second phase, the work of collection and compilation increased and widened. As well as their own information, the collectors of *Ḥadīth* met with the people of knowledge in their city or area and also consolidated their narrations.

---

15. Preface to *Ṣaḥīfah Hammām*, p. 34, quoting from Khaṭīb Baghdādī. Cf. *Mustadrak Ḥākim*, Vol. 3, p. 574.

16. *Al-Wathāʾiq al-Siyāsiyyah*, p. 105. Also Dr. Hamidullah, quoting from Ṭabarī, p. 104.

17. *Tahdhīb al-Tahdhīb* of Ibn Ḥajar, Vol. 4, p. 236.

18. Dārimī, p. 69. Cf. Preface to *Ṣaḥīfah Hammām*, p. 45, quoting from *Ṭabaqāt Ibn Saʿd*.

19. *Mukhtaṣar Jāmiʿ Bayān al-ʿIlm*, p. 37.

2.2.2 *The Second Phase*

This second phase ends around the middle of the second century *hijrī*. In this phase was produced a large group of Followers who absorbed the literature of the first phase into wider compilations.

2.2.2.1 Compilers of *Ḥadīth*

1. Muḥammad b. Shihāb al-Zuhrī (d. 124 H). He is one of the outstanding *muḥaddithūn* of his time, and gained knowledge of *Ḥadīth* from the following illustrious personalities: from the Companions, ʿAbdullāh b. ʿUmar, Anas b. Mālik and Sahl b. Saʿd ﷺ; from the Followers, Saʿīd b. al-Musayyib, Maḥmūd b. Rabīʿ and others. His students included Imāms of *Ḥadīth* such as Imām Awzāʿī, Imām Mālik and Sufyān b. ʿUyaynah. In 101 H, ʿUmar b. ʿAbd al-ʿAzīz ordered him to gather and collect *Aḥādīth*. Apart from him, ʿUmar b. ʿAbd al-ʿAzīz also instructed the governor of Madīnah, Abū Bakr Muḥammad b. ʿAmr b. Ḥazm, to record in writing the treasure of *Ḥadīth* possessed by ʿAmrah bint ʿAbd al-Raḥmān and Qāsim b. Muḥammad. (ʿAmrah was one of the distinguished students of ʿĀ'ishah ﷺ, and Qāsim b. Muḥammad was the latter's fraternal nephew – ʿĀ'ishah ﷺ had personally supervised their upbringing and education.)[20] This was not all, for ʿUmar b. ʿAbd al-ʿAziz further issued a special directive to all people of authority in the Islamic lands to gather and compile all sources of *Ḥadīth*. As a result of this, volumes upon volumes of *Aḥādīth* were sent to the seat of the Caliphate in Damascus. The Caliph of the time distributed copies of these to every corner of the empire.[21] After Imām Zuhrī's compilation of a collection of *Ḥadīth*, other people of knowledge of this era also began to work on recording and compiling *Ḥadīth*. The following personalities achieved the honour of being amongst the forerunners in this regard.

---

20. *Tahdhīb al-Tahdhīb* of Ibn Ḥajar, Vol. 7, p. 172.
21. *Tadhkirat al-Ḥuffāẓ*, Vol. 1, p. 106. *Mukhtaṣar Jāmiʿ Bayān al-ʿIlm*, p. 38.

2. ʿAbd al-Malik b. Jurayj (d. 150 H), in Makkah;
3. Imām Awzāʿī (d. 157 H), in Syria;
4. Maʿmar b. Rāshid (d. 153 H), in Yemen;
5. Imām Sufyān Thawrī (d. 161), in Kufa;
6. Imām Ḥammād b. Salamah (d. 167 H), in Basra; and
7. Imām ʿAbdullāh b. al-Mubārak (d. 181 H), in Khurasan.
8. Imām Mālik b. Anas (b. 93 H, died 179 H). After Imām Zuhrī, the distinction of compiling *Ḥadīth* in Madīnah was achieved by him. He learnt from Nāfiʿ, Zuhrī and other outstanding people of knowledge; his teachers reached 900 in number. By way of his overflowing spring, thousands of thirsty seekers of the *Sunnah* were quenched in the Hijaz, Syria, Iraq, Palestine, Egypt and Africa. His students included such famous personalities as Layth b. Saʿd (d. 175 H), Ibn al-Mubārak (d. 181 H), Imām Shāfiʿī (d. 204 H) and Imām Muḥammad b. Ḥasan al-Shaybānī (d. 189 H).

2.2.2.2 Written Legacy of the Second Phase

1. *Muwaṭṭaʾ* of Imām Mālik. In this phase, many collections of *Ḥadīth* were compiled, amongst which Imām Mālik's *Muwaṭṭaʾ* occupies the highest rank. Compiled during the period 130-141 H, it has a total of over 1700 narrations, of which 600 are *marfūʿ* (narrations from the Prophet ﷺ), 228 are *mursal* (where a Follower quotes the Prophet directly without naming the Companion), 613 are *mawqūf* (statements of the Companions), and 285 are *maqṭūʿ* (statements of the Followers).

   The following are the names of some of the other compilations from this phase.
2. The *Jāmiʿ* of Sufyān Thawrī (d. 161 H).
3. The *Jāmiʿ* of Ibn al-Mubārak (d. 181 H).
4. The *Jāmiʿ* of Imām Awzāʿī (d. 157 H).
5. The *Jāmiʿ* of Ibn Jurayj (d. 150 H).
6. *Kitāb al-Kharāj* of Qāḍī Abū Yūsuf (d. 182 H).
7. *Kitāb al-Āthār* of Imām Muḥammad (d. 189 H).

In this phase, the *Aḥādīth* of the Messenger of Allah ﷺ, the *āthār* of the Companions and *fatāwā* of the Followers used to be arranged in the same collection. However, it was always made clear whether a statement was that of a Companion or Follower, or the *Ḥadīth* of the Messenger of Allah ﷺ.

2.2.3 *The Third Phase*

This phase starts around the second half of the second century *hijrī* and extends until the end of the fourth century.

2.2.3.1 Distinguishing Features of the Third Phase

The distinguishing features of this phase are as follows:

1. *Aḥādīth* of the Prophet, ﷺ, were compiled separately to the *āthār* of the Companions and statements of the Followers.
2. Separate compilations of reliable transmissions were prepared. In this way, after investigation and verification, the works of the second phase were absorbed into the bulky books of the third phase.
3. Not only were narrations gathered in this phase, but in order to preserve the knowledge of *Ḥadīth*, the noble *muḥaddithūn* laid the foundations of over a hundred sciences related to *Ḥadīth*. Until today, thousands of books have been written on these sciences. May Allah accept their effort and grant them the best reward on our behalf!

2.2.3.2 The Sciences of *Ḥadīth*

In concise terms, some of these sciences are introduced here:

1. *Asmā' al-Rijāl* (Names of the Narrators). In this science, the situations of narrators, their dates of birth and death, details of their teachers and students and journeys seeking knowledge, and the verdicts of *Ḥadīth* experts regarding their reliability (whether reliable or unreliable) are recorded.

This science is extremely vast, very beneficial and highly interesting. Even some bigoted Orientalists were not able to avoid admitting that, as a result of this science, the biographies of 500,000 narrators have been preserved. This distinguishing feature is one in which the Muslim nation is unrivalled.[22]

Numerous books have been written in this science, of which some are:

a. *Tahdhīb al-Kamāl* by Imām Yūsuf al-Mizzī (d. 742 H), the most important and authoritative work in its field.
b. *Tahdhīb al-Tahdhīb* by Ḥāfiẓ Ibn Ḥajar, commentator on Bukhārī. This work is in twelve volumes, and has been published from Hyderabad-Deccan.
c. *Tadhkirat al-Ḥuffāẓ* by 'Allāmah Dhahabī (d. 748).

2. *Muṣṭalaḥ* or *Uṣūl al-Ḥadīth* ("Terminology or Foundations of *Ḥadīth*"). In the light of this science the principles and conditions relating to the authenticity or weakness of *Aḥādīth* come to be known.[23] The most famous book in this field is *'Ulūm al-Ḥadīth*, also known as *Muqaddimah Ibn al-Ṣalāḥ*, written by Abū 'Amr 'Uthmān b. al-Ṣalāḥ (d. 577 H). In the recent past, two books on *Uṣūl al-Ḥadīth* have been produced:

a. *Tawjīh al-Naẓar* by 'Allāmah Ṭāhir b. Ṣāliḥ al-Jazā'irī (d. 1338 H);
b. *Qawā'id al-Taḥdīth* by 'Allāmah Sayyid Jamāl al-Dīn al-Qāsimī (d. 1332 H). The former is distinguished by its breadth of coverage, the latter by its excellent arrangement.

3. *Gharīb al-Ḥadīth* ("Rare words in *Ḥadīth*"). In this science, linguistic analysis of difficult words occurring in *Aḥādīth*

22. Introduction to *al-Iṣābah*, English ed., Springer, Calcutta, 1864.
23. See a brief discussion on the classification and terminology of *Ḥadīth* in the later pages of this Introduction.

has been carried out. Famous works in this field are *al-Fā'iq* by 'Allāmah Zamakhsharī (d. 538 H) and *al-Nihāyah* by Ibn al-Athīr (d. 606 H).

4. *Takhrīj al-Ḥadīth* – Through this science, the original sources of narrations found in famous books of *tafsīr*, *fiqh*, *taṣawwuf* and *'aqā'id* are traced. For example, the *Hidāyah* by Burhān al-Dīn 'Alī b. Abī Bakr al-Marghīnānī (d. 592 H) and *Iḥyā' 'Ulūm al-Dīn* by Imām Ghazālī (d. 505 H) contain many narrations without a chain of narration or reference. Now, if someone would like to find out the grade of authenticity of these narrations and which major works of *Ḥadīth* they are found in, they should refer to *Naṣb al-Rāyah* by Ḥāfiẓ Zayla'ī (d. 792 H) and *al-Dirāyah* by Ḥāfiẓ Ibn Ḥajar 'Asqalānī (d. 852 H) for the former, and to *al-Mughnī 'an Ḥaml al-Asfār* by Ḥāfiẓ Zayn al-Dīn al-'Irāqī (d. 806 H) for the latter.
5. *Al-Aḥādīth al-Mawḍū'ah* ("Fabricated *Aḥādīth*"). In this field, the people of knowledge have compiled independent books into which *mawḍū'* (fabricated) narrations have been sifted out. In this regard, *al-Fawā'id al-Majmū'ah* by Qāḍī Shawkānī (d. 1255 H) and *al-La'āli' al-Maṣnū'ah* ("Artificial Pearls") by Ḥāfiẓ Jalāl al-Dīn Suyūṭī (d. 911 H) are most prominent.
6. *Al-Nāsikh wa'l-Mansūkh* ("Abrogating and Abrogated *Ḥadīth*"). In this field, *Kitāb al-I'tibār* by Imām Muḥammad b. Mūsā Ḥāzimī (d. 784 H aged 35) is the most famous and authoritative.
7. *Al-Tawfīq bayn al-Aḥādīth* ("Reconciling *Aḥādīth*"). In this science, the correct explanation is given of those narrations which are apparently mutually contradictory or conflicting. The first to discuss this field was Imām Shāfi'ī (d. 204 H), and his treatise is famously known as *Mukhtalif al-Ḥadīth*. Another beneficial book in this field is *Mushkil al-Āthār* by Imām Ṭaḥāwī (d. 321 H).
8. *Al-Mukhtalif wa'l-Mu'talif* ("Narrators with similar names"). In this science, special attention is given to those narrators whose names, bynames, nicknames and names of fathers, grandfathers or teachers are similar, leading to the possibility of a person unfamiliar with these matters to become

embroiled in error. In this field, the most comprehensive book is Ḥāfiẓ Ibn Ḥajar's *Ta'bīr al-Munabbih*.

9. *Aṭrāf al-Ḥadīth* ("Phrases from *Ḥadīth*"). Through this science, it is possible to find out the narrator and reference of phrases from *Ḥadīth*. For example, if someone remembers a sentence from *Ḥadīth* such as "Actions are only by intention," and wishes to know the complete narration and its sources and narrators, then recourse must be had to this science. In this field, the book *Tuḥfat al-Ashrāf* by Ḥāfiẓ Mizzī (d. 742 H) is very detailed, comprising an index of all narrations in the *Ṣiḥāḥ Sittah* ("Six Authentic Books"). Ḥāfiẓ Yūsuf Mizzī spent 26 years compiling this book, and completed it after extremely difficult toil. Today's Orientalists have taken a leaf out of books such as these and compiled indexes of *Ḥadīth* in a rather new fashion. For example, *Miftāḥ Kunūz al-Sunnah* ("Key to the Treasures of the *Sunnah*") was published in English and its Arabic translation was published in Cairo in 1934. Now, there is another comprehensive index compiled under the name *al-Mu'jam al-Mufahras*, of which twenty parts have been published so far.[24]

10. *Fiqh al-Ḥadīth* ("Jurisprudence of *Ḥadīth*"). In this science, the secrets and wisdoms in *Aḥādīth* related to legal rulings are unveiled. On this subject, one can benefit from the book *I'lām al-Muwaqqi'īn* of Ḥāfiẓ Ibn Qayyim (d. 751 H) and *Ḥujjat Allāh al-Bālighah* of Shāh Walīullāh of Delhi. Apart from these, the people of knowledge have also devoted separate compilations to different aspects of life. For example, in the area of transactions, *Kitāb al-Amwāl* ("Book of Wealth") by Abū 'Ubayd Qāsim b. Sallām (d. 224 H) is well-known, and in the issues related to land, *'ushr*, *kharāj* (land-tax) etc., the best work is *Kitāb al-Kharāj* by Qāḍī Abū Yūsuf. Therefore, study of the following works can establish the authority of the *Sunnah* as a source of Law and expose the misconceptions spread by the rejecters of *Ḥadīth*:

24. The latest encyclopaedias of *Ḥadīth*, in both printed and electronic form, now have vast indexes of *Ḥadīth* narrations. – Trans. Note

a. *Kitāb al-Umm* by Imām Shāfiʿī
b. *Al-Risālah* of Imām Shāfiʿī
c. *Al-Muwāfaqāt* by Abū Isḥāq Shāṭibī (d. 790 H)
d. *Ṣawāʿiq Mursalah* by Ibn Qayyim
e. *Al-Iḥkām* by Ibn Ḥazm al-Andalusī (d. 456 H)
f. The introduction to *Tarjumān al-Sunnah* (Urdu) by Mawlānā Badr-i-ʿAlam Mirthī
g. *Ithbāt al-Khabar* by my respected father, Mawlānā Ḥāfiẓ ʿAbd al-Sattār Ḥasan ʿUmarpūrī (d. 1916/1334 H aged 34)[25]
h. *Sunnat kī Āʾīnī Ḥaithīyat* ("The Constitutional Status of the *Sunnah*") by Mawlānā Sayyid Abul Aʿlā Mawdūdī.
i. *Inkār-e-Ḥadīth kā Manẓar awr Pas Manẓar* ("The Background and Context of Ḥadīth-Rejection") by Iftikhar Ahmad Balkhi is also interesting and informative. So far, two parts of it have been published.
j. A while ago, ʿAllāmah Muṣṭafā Sibāʿī began an extremely beneficial series of articles on the authority of *Ḥadīth* in *Risālah al-Muslimūn*, Damascus. This has been translated into Urdu by my colleague Malik Ghulam ʿAli, and published as a booklet named *Sunnat-e-Rasūl ṣallaʾLlāhu ʿalayhi wa sallam*.

The following works on the history of the science of *Ḥadīth* and related topics are models of comprehensiveness and benefit: the introduction to *Fatḥ al-Bārī* by Ḥāfiẓ Ibn Ḥajar; *Jāmiʿ Bayān al-ʿIlm wa Ahlih* by Ḥāfiẓ Ibn ʿAbd al-Barr al-Andalusī (d. 463 H); *Maʿrifah ʿUlūm al-Ḥadīth* by Imām Ḥākim (d. 405 H); and the introduction to *Tuḥfat al-Aḥwadhī* by the *muḥaddith* Mawlānā ʿAbd al-Raḥmān Mubārakpūrī (d. 1353 H/1935). In the works of the recent past, this book is a masterpiece in terms of its comprehensiveness and benefit. Similarly, the introduction

25. It was during the lifetime of my esteemed grandfather, Mawlānā Ḥāfiẓ ʿAbd al-Jabbār Muḥaddith ʿUmarpūrī (d. 1334/1916) that the *Ḥadīth*-rejection *fitnah* of Maulvī ʿAbdullāh Chakrālwī reared its head. My respected grandfather began a series of beneficial refutations and researched articles in his monthly *Ḍiyāʾ al-Sunnah* at the time.

to *Fatḥ al-Mulhim* by Mawlānā Shabbīr Aḥmad ʿUthmānī and *Tadwīn-i-Ḥadith* (in Urdu) by the late Mawlānā Manāẓir Aḥsan Gīlānī are jewels in their breadth of information.

2.2.3.3 The Compilers of *Ḥadīth* in the Third Phase

The following is an introduction to the outstanding and well-known compilers of *Ḥadīth* and reliable works of this phase:

1. Imām Aḥmad b. Ḥanbal (b. 164 H, d. 241 H). His most important compilation is known as *Musnad Aḥmad*, and [it] comprises 30,000 narrations. In its twenty volumes, every *Ḥadīth* worth mentioning has been included. Instead of arrangement by subject, all narrations by a particular Companion are arranged in one place. The work of arranging this book by chapter and subject was begun by the learned father of Ḥasan al-Bannā, Aḥmad ʿAbd al-Raḥmān Sāʿātī. So far, 14 volumes have been published. The famous scholar of Egypt, Aḥmad Shākir, is also working on this. Until now, almost 15 parts have been compiled.
2. Imām Muḥammad b. Ismāʿīl al-Bukhārī (b. 194 H, d. 256 H). His year of birth equates to *ṣidq*[26] ("truthfulness"), and his year of death to *nūr* ("light"). Of all his works, Imām Bukhārī's most important and authoritative book is *Ṣaḥīḥ al-Bukhārī*. Its full name is *al-Jāmiʿ al-Ṣaḥīḥ al-Musnad al-Mukhtaṣar min Umūr Rasūl Allāh ṣalla'Llāhu ʿalayhi wa ālihi wa sallam wa ayyāmih* (The Comprehensive, Authentic, Fully-Traced Abridgement from the Matters of the Messenger of Allah, may Allah bless him and his family and grant them peace, and his Days), and took sixteen years to compile. The number of students that studied the *Ṣaḥīḥ* directly with Imām Bukhārī reached 90,000. Sometimes, the audience in one sitting would reach 30,000 in number. In such a

26. This equivalence is worked out according to the *Abjad* numerical system, where the 28 letters of the Arabic alphabet take numerical values ranging from 1 (*alif*) to 1,000 (*ghayn*). – Trans. Note

gathering, the number of people conveying words to the audience would exceed 300. The total number of *Aḥādīth* in the *Ṣaḥīḥ* is 9,684. If repeated narrations, *ta'līqāt* (narrations without *isnād*), reports from the Companions and *mursal Aḥādīth* are omitted, the number of *marfū'* narrations is 2,623. Compared to other *muḥaddithūn*, Imām Bukhārī kept his criteria for accepting narrators very high.

3. Imām Muslim b. Ḥajjāj Qushayrī (b. 202 H, d. 261 H). Imām Bukhārī and Imām Aḥmad b. Ḥanbal are amongst his teachers, and Imām Tirmidhī, Abū Ḥātim Rāzī, and Abū Bakr b. Khuzaymah are counted amongst his students. His book *Ṣaḥīḥ Muslim* is regarded as most outstanding in terms of its excellent arrangement.
4. Imām Abū Dāwūd, Ash'ath b. Sulaymān Sijistānī (b. 202, d. 275 H). His most important work is famous by the name of *Sunan Abū Dāwūd*, and comprehensively gathers narrations mostly regarding legal rulings. It is a brilliant source for juristic and legal issues, and consists of 4,800 *Aḥādīth*.
5. Imām Abū 'Īsā Tirmidhī (b. 209 H, d. 279 H). In his *Jāmi' Tirmidhī*, different *fiqhī* positions are explained in detail.
6. Imām Aḥmad b. Shu'ayb Nasā'ī (d. 303 H). His work is called *al-Sunan al-Mujtaba*.
7. Imām Muḥammad b. Yazīd ibn Mājah Qazwīnī (d. 273 H). His book is famous by the name of *Sunan Ibn Mājah*.

Apart from *Musnad Aḥmad*, the other six books in the terminology of the *muḥaddithūn* are known as the *Ṣiḥāḥ Sittah* ("Six Authentic Collections"). Some of the people of knowledge include the *Muwaṭṭa'* of Imām Mālik amongst the *Ṣiḥaḥ Sittah* instead of *Sunan Ibn Mājah*. Apart from these, many other beneficial and comprehensive compilations were produced in this phase, but there is no scope here for going into details of those.

The collections of Bukhārī, Muslim and Tirmidhī are known as *Jāmi'* ("Comprehensive Works"), i.e. they include *Aḥādīth* about beliefs, worship, manners, transactions and many other topics.

The works of Abū Dāwūd, Nasā'ī and Ibn Mājah are known as *Sunan* ("Traditions"), i.e. they mostly have narrations related to practical matters of life.

2.2.3.4 Grades of *Ḥadīth* Books

With regards to authenticity and strength, the *muḥaddithūn* have graded all books of *Ḥadīth* into four levels:

1. *Muwaṭṭa' Imām Mālik*, *Ṣaḥīḥ al-Bukhārī* and *Ṣaḥīḥ Muslim*. With regards to the authenticity of their chains of narration and reliability of transmitters, these three books occupy the highest station.
2. The *Sunan* collections of Abū Dāwūd, Tirmidhī and Nasā'ī. Some of the narrators in these books are below those of the highest grade in terms of reliability. However, they are nevertheless regarded as reliable. *Musnad Aḥmad* is also included in this category.
3. The *Sunan* works of Dārimī (d. 225 H), Ibn Mājah, Bayhaqī and Darāquṭnī (d. 385 H), the books of Ṭabarānī (d. 360 H), the works of Ṭaḥāwī (d. 321 H), the *Musnad* of Imām Shāfi'ī, and the *Mustadrak* of Ḥākim (d. 405 H). In these books, every type of narration is found, including weak as well as authentic ones. However, the majority of narrations are reliable.
4. The works of Ibn Jarīr Ṭabarī (d. 310 H), Khaṭīb Baghdādī (d. 463 H), Abū Nu'aym (d. 403 H), Ibn 'Asākir (d. 571 H), Daylamī (author of *Musnad al-Firdaws*, d. 509 H), *Kāmil* of Ibn 'Adī (d. 365 H), the compilations of Ibn Mardawayh (d. 410 H), Wāqidī (d. 207 H) and the works of other authors such as these are included in this category. These compilations are a collection of "ripe" as well as "rotten" material, and even include many fabricated narrations. Public preachers, historians and Sufis mostly depend upon these books. However, with careful sifting, precious gems can be extracted from them, acceptable for presentation.

2.2.4 *The Fourth Phase*

This begins around the fifth century *hijrī*, and continues even today.

2.2.4.1 Types of Work in this Phase

At the beginning of this phase, the style of compilation of the third phase had reached its conclusion. Since then, the details of the work that has been done during this long period is as follows:

1. Important books of *Ḥadīth* had commentaries and marginal notes written upon them, and were translated into other languages.
2. In the sciences of *Ḥadīth* mentioned earlier, many works were produced and commentaries and abridgements were made based upon them.
3. The people of knowledge have compiled beneficial books by selecting *Aḥādīth* from the works of the third phase, according to taste or necessity. Some of these are:

    a. *Mishkāt al-Maṣābīḥ* ("The Niche of Lamps") by Walī al-Dīn Khaṭīb Tabrīzī. This gathers narrations related to beliefs, worship, transactions, character, manners and the Resurrection and Judgment.
    b. *Riyāḍ al-Ṣāliḥīn* ("Gardens of the Righteous") by Imām Abū Zakariyyā Yaḥya b. Sharaf al-Nawawī, commentator on *Ṣaḥīḥ* Muslim (d. 676 H). This is a selection of *Ḥadīth* mostly related to character and manners. At the beginning of each chapter, Qur'ānic verses related to the subject have also been mentioned, and this is the important distinguishing feature of this book. It has the same style of compilation and arrangement as that of *Ṣaḥīḥ al-Bukhārī*.
    c. *Muntaqā al-Akhbār* ("Selection of Reports") by Majd al-Dīn Abū'l-Barakāt 'Abd al-Salām b. Taymiyyah

(d. 652 H), the grandfather of the famous Shaykh al-Islām Taqī al-Dīn Aḥmad ibn Taymiyyah (d. 728 H). A commentary on this work in eight volumes has been written by Qāḍī Shawkānī, with the name *Nayl al-Awṭār* ("Achieving the Aims").

d. *Bulūgh al-Marām* ("Attaining the Objective") by Ḥāfiẓ Ibn Ḥajar (d. 852 H), commentator on *Ṣaḥīḥ Bukhārī*. This contains *Aḥādīth* mostly related to worship and transactions. The commentary in Arabic, *Subul al-Salām* ("Paths of Peace"), flowed from the pen of Muḥammad b. Ismā'īl al-San'ānī (d. 1182 H). Another commentary, *Misk al-Khitām* ("Musk of the Seal"), was compiled in Persian by Nawāb Ṣiddīq Ḥasan Khān (d. 1307 H).

Most of these works were translated and published in Urdu, quite some time ago.

2.2.4.2 The Science of *Ḥadīth* in Undivided India

The first person to shine the candle of the science of *Ḥadīth* in undivided India was Shaykh 'Abd al-Ḥaqq Muḥaddith Dehlawī b. Sayf al-Dīn Turk (d. 1052 H). After him, the lifelong sacrifices and strenuous efforts of Shāh Walīullāh (d. 1176 H) and his children, grandchildren and inspired students led to the Light of the *Sunnah* shining brightly in this land. *And the earth shall shine by the light of its Lord.*[27]

Since Shāh Walīullāh, may the Mercy of Allah be upon him, the sacred work of preparing and publishing translations, commentaries, and selections of *Ḥadīth* has continued to this day. It is hoped that this work, *Intikhāb-e-Ḥadīth* ("Selection of *Ḥadīth*"), will also be a link in this chain.

It is a favour from Allah that the author of this collection achieves the good fortune of imitating the servants of *Ḥadīth*, otherwise, where is this humble servant compared to those great

27. *Sūrah al-Zumar*, 39: 69.

souls who devoted their entire lives to collecting and spreading the *Ḥadīth* of the Messenger of Allah ﷺ?

> *I love the righteous, without being of them:*
> *Perhaps Allah will grant me righteousness.*[28]

By consulting the above survey of the science of *Ḥadīth*, it can be gauged that from the Prophetic era until today, there has never been a period when the chain of writing and transmitting *Ḥadīth* has been interrupted. This is that chain of knowledge whose day is bright and its night is also full of shining lights and illuminating lamps. [As is related in an authentic *Ḥadīth*:] its night is like its day.

Between the beloved Prophet Muḥammad ﷺ and present-day students of *Ḥadīth*, there is a chain of 23 or 24 teachers. On the following pages, following the way of the *muḥaddithūn*, the *sanad* (chain of transmission) of the author of this book is presented diagrammatically, bringing some 1,400 years of the chain of narrators of *Ḥadīth* right before the eyes. *And their cry will always end with: "All praise be to Allah, the Lord of the entire Universe".*[29] *Our Lord! Accept this from us; You are All-Hearing, All-Knowing!*[30] *My Lord, dispose me that I may give thanks for the bounty that You have bestowed upon me and my parents, and dispose me that I may do righteous deeds that would please You, and also make my descendants righteous. I repent to You, and I am one of those who surrender themselves to You.*[31]

16th Rabīʿ al-Thānī 1376 H — ʿAbd al-Ghaffār Ḥasan
20th November 1956

---

28. This is a couplet attributed to Imām al-Shāfiʿī, as it occurs in his *Dīwān*. In one version, the lines continue thus:
I hate the one whose trade is in vice,
Although we're involved in the same business! [Trans. Note]

29. *Sūrah Yūnus*, 10: 10.

30. *Sūrah al-Baqarah*, 2: 127.

31. *Sūrah al-Aḥqāf*, 46: 15.

2.3 *ḤADĪTH* TERMINOLOGY

Ḥadīth: The sayings, actions and approvals[32] of the Messenger of Allah ﷺ are known as *Ḥadīth*.

Athar: The saying or action of a Companion is known as *athar* (pl. *Āthār*)

Sanad: The chain of narrators of a *Ḥadīth*.

Matn: The text of a *Ḥadīth*.

Mutāwatir report: The narrators are so many in each stage that it is ordinarily impossible for them all to agree upon a lie. There are several types of *tawātur*:

i. in every era, transmission and narration continue for generation after generation, widely and generally, e.g. the Majestic Qur'ān;
ii. practical *tawātur*, e.g. the prayer times, and the basic forms of *adhān* and *ṣalāt*;
iii. *tawātur* in *isnād*, e.g. the *Ḥadīth*, "He who invents a lie upon my authority, let him prepare his seat in the Fire", has over a hundred narrators in just the generation of the Companions, and, similarly, the narration about the Finality of Prophethood;
iv. *tawātur* in meaning: i.e. the common content of numerous narrations reaches the level of *tawātur*, e.g. the miracles of the Prophet, raising hands in supplication, etc. (from the introduction to *Fatḥ al-Mulhim*).

*Aḥad (*pl. *āḥād*) or *wāḥid* report: The number of narrators does not reach the level of being *mutāwatir*. *Ḥadīth* scholars divide this into three categories:

a. *mashhūr*: where the number of narrators is never less than three, after the stage of the Companions;

32. Approval (*taqrīr*) means that something was done in the presence of the Prophet, and he did not forbid it.

b. *'azīz*: where the number of narrators is at least two in every stage;
c. *gharīb*: where there is only one narrator in any stage.

Marfū': A *Ḥadīth* attributed to the Messenger of Allah ﷺ.

Mawqūf: A narration attributed to a Companion, i.e. his/her saying or action.

Muttaṣil (continuous): There is no reporter missing from the chain of narration.

Munqaṭi' (discontinuous): Opposite of *muttaṣil*.

Mu'allaq: One or more narrators are omitted from the beginning of the *sanad*, or the entire *sanad* is omitted. The act of omission is called *ta'līq*.

Mu'ḍal: Two or more consecutive reporters are missing from a *sanad*.

Mursal: No Companion is mentioned between a Follower (*Tābi'ī*) and the Prophet ﷺ.

Shādhdh (peculiar): A narration where a reliable narrator contradicts a stronger narrator. The narration of the stronger narrator is known as *maḥfūẓ* (preserved).

Munkar (rejected): If a weak reporter contradicts a reliable reporter, the former's narration is called *munkar* (rejected); the latter's is called *ma'rūf* (approved).

Mu'allal (subtly flawed): A narration that has a hidden defect, such that only experts in the science of *Ḥadīth* can detect it, e.g. erroneously making a *mawqūf* narration *marfū'* or vice-versa.

Ṣaḥīḥ (genuine, authentic): a narration that satisfies the following conditions:

a. the chain is *muttaṣil* (continuous);
b. the reporters are trustworthy, i.e. reliable based on their biographies and character;
c. their memory is sound;

d. the narration is not *shādhdh*;
e. the narration is not *mu'allal.*

Ḥasan: A narration that satisfies the conditions of *ṣaḥīḥ*, except that the narrators are of a slightly lesser grade with regard to memory. If such a *ḥasan* narration is supported by another *ḥasan* narration, it is known as *ṣaḥīḥ li ghayrihī* (*ṣaḥīḥ* due to external support).

Ḍa'īf (weak): A narration that does not meet the conditions of *ṣaḥīḥ* or *ḥasan*. Several *ḍa'īf* narrations can collectively rise to the level of *ḥasan li ghayrihī* (*ḥasan* due to external support), with the condition that the weakness is not due to corruption in the character and morality of the reporters (*Qawā'id al-Taḥdīth*, p. 90). The most unreliable level of weakness is that where the reporters' own *taqwā* is suspect; such a narration is called *mawḍū'* (fabricated).

2.4 A TREE OF *ḤADĪTH* TRANSMISSION

THE MOST NOBLE MESSENGER
MUḤAMMAD, ﷺ

↓

Anas b. Mālik ؓ
(d. 93 H)

↓

Ḥumayd al-Ṭawil b. Abī Ḥumayd
(68-143 H)

↓

Muḥammad b. ʿAbdullāh al-Anṣārī
(118-215 H)

↓

Muḥammad b. Ismāʿīl al-Bukhārī
(194-256 H)

↓

Muḥammad b. Yūsuf al-Firabrī
(231-320 H)

↓

ʿAbdullāh b. Aḥmad al-Sarkhasī
(d. 381 H)

↓

ʿAbd al-Raḥmān b. Muẓaffar al-Dawūdī
(374-467 H)

↓

ʿAbd al-Awwal b. ʿĪsā al-Sijizzī
(458-553 H)

↓

Ḥusayn b. Mubārak al-Zubaydī
(546-631 H)

↓

Aḥmad b. Abī Ṭālib al-Ḥajjār
(d. 730 H)

↓ (to both)

Ibrāhīm b. Aḥmad al-Tanūkhī
(d. 800 H)

ʿAbd al-Raḥīm b. Ḥusayn al-ʿIrāqī
(725-806 H)

↓ (from both)

Aḥmad b. ʿAlī b. Ḥajr al-ʿAsqalānī
(774-852 H)

↓

Aḥmad Zakariyyā al-Anṣārī,
commentator on *Ṣaḥīḥ al-Bukhārī* (d. 925 H)

↓

Muḥammad b. Aḥmad al-Ramlī
(d. 1004 H)

↓

Aḥmad b. ʿAbd al-Quddūs al-Shinawī
(d. 1028 H)

⋮
↓

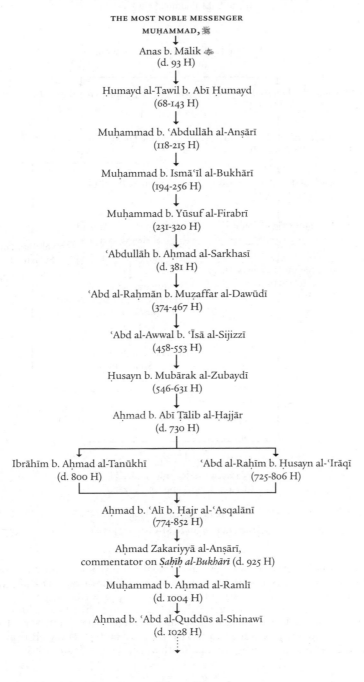

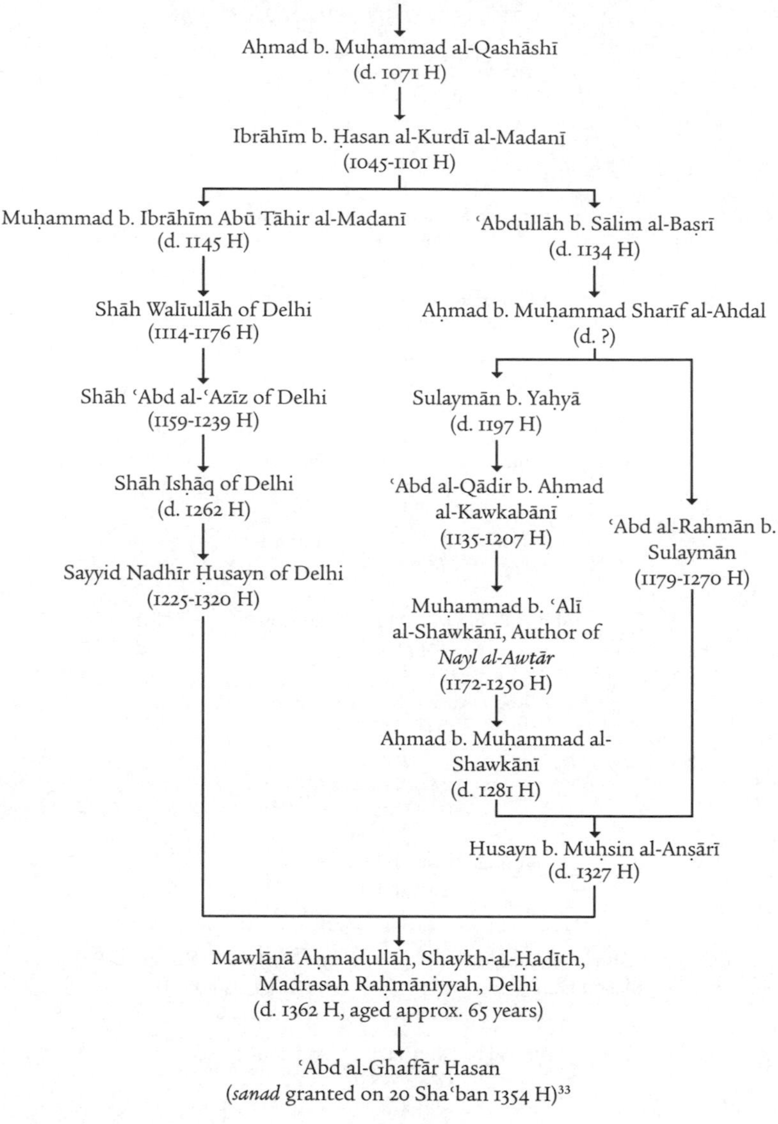

33. Shaykh ʿAbd al-Ghaffār Ḥasan taught thousands of students from over eighty countries around the world and granted the *isnād* and *ijāzah* (chain of transmission with permission to teach) to many of them. They include his own sons and scholars of *Ḥadīth*, Suhaib Hasan and Suhail Hasan, and Prof. Khurshid Ahmad of the Pakistan Senate, amongst other luminaries. I was therefore extremely honoured to receive the *isnād* and *ijāzah* myself from my grandfather on 14th Muharram, 1421 (20th April, 2000). – Trans. Note

2.4.1 *Clarifications*

1. The respected teacher Mawlānā Aḥmadullāh (may Allah have mercy upon him) took knowledge of *Ḥadīth* from two famous *Ḥadīth* teachers of his time: a) Mawlānā Sayyid Nadhīr Ḥusayn, and b) 'Allāmah Ḥusayn b. Muḥsin al-Anṣārī. The former is a pupil of the respected Shaykh Ibrāhīm b. Ḥasan Kurdī via four intermediaries; the latter via six. The son of Qāḍī Muḥammad b. 'Alī al-Shawkānī , Aḥmad b. Muḥammad , took knowledge of *Ḥadīth* from both his respected father and from 'Allāmah 'Abd al-Raḥmān b. Sulaymān, who benefited fully and directly from his father Sulaymān b. Yaḥyā. Thus, the number of intermediaries between the respected Shaykh Ḥusayn b. Muḥsin Anṣārī and Ibrāhīm b. Ḥasan Kurdī is five instead of six. The *isnād* chains of Mawlānā Sayyid Nadhīr Ḥusayn and 'Allāmah Ḥusayn b. Muḥsin Anṣārī meet above at Ibrāhīm b. Ḥasan Kurdī.
2. Only the *sanad* of *Ṣaḥīḥ al-Bukhārī* is presented here as a "Tree of *Ḥadīth* Transmission". Besides this there are other chains for other important sources of *Ḥadīth*, for details of which there is insufficient space here. There are numerous chains of narration from Imām Bukhārī to the Prophet ﷺ. Here, just one of the minimum-length chains is given.
3. Apart from Mawlānā Aḥmadullāh , the writer of these lines has also studied some of the books of *Ḥadīth* with Mawlānā 'Abd al-Raḥmān Nigranhsāwī , Mawlānā Muḥammad Surtī and Mawlānā 'Ubaydullāh Raḥmānī Mubārakpūrī. He has also had the opportunity to benefit briefly from Mawlānā 'Abd al-Raḥmān Muḥaddith Mubārakpūrī, commentator on *Sunan al-Tirmidhī*.

All praise is due to Allah, by Whose Favour righteous actions are completed.

17th Jumādā al-Ūlā 1376 H — 'Abd al-Ghaffār Ḥasan
30th December 1956.

Fundamentals of Islam

3.1 BELIEFS AND PILLARS OF ISLAM

عَنْ عُمَرَ بْنِ الْخَطَّابِ ﷺ قَالَ: بَيْنَمَا نَحْنُ جُلُوسٌ عِنْدَ رَسُولِ اللهِ ﷺ ذَاتَ يَوْمٍ، إِذْ طَلَعَ عَلَيْنَا رَجُلٌ شَدِيدُ بَيَاضِ الثِّيَابِ، شَدِيدُ سَوَادِ الشَّعَرِ، لَا يُرَى عَلَيْهِ أَثَرُ السَّفَرِ، وَلَا يَعْرِفُهُ مِنَّا أَحَدٌ، حَتَّى جَلَسَ إِلَى النَّبِيِّ ﷺ، فَأَسْنَدَ رُكْبَتَيْهِ إِلَى رُكْبَتَيْهِ وَوَضَعَ كَفَّيْهِ عَلَى فَخِذَيْهِ، وَقَالَ: يَا مُحَمَّدُ أَخْبِرْنِي عَنِ الْإِسْلَامِ. فَقَالَ رَسُولُ اللهِ ﷺ: الْإِسْلَامُ أَنْ تَشْهَدَ أَنْ لَا إِلَهَ إِلَّا اللهُ، وَأَنَّ مُحَمَّدًا رَسُولُ اللهِ، وَتُقِيمَ الصَّلَاةَ، وَتُؤْتِيَ الزَّكَاةَ، وَتَصُومَ رَمَضَانَ، وَتَحُجَّ الْبَيْتَ إِنِ اسْتَطَعْتَ إِلَيْهِ سَبِيلًا. قَالَ: صَدَقْتَ. قَالَ: فَعَجِبْنَا لَهُ يَسْأَلُهُ وَيُصَدِّقُهُ. قَالَ: فَأَخْبِرْنِي عَنِ الْإِيمَانِ. قَالَ: أَنْ تُؤْمِنَ بِاللهِ وَمَلَائِكَتِهِ وَكُتُبِهِ وَرُسُلِهِ وَالْيَوْمِ الْآخِرِ وَتُؤْمِنَ بِالْقَدَرِ خَيْرِهِ وَشَرِّهِ. قَالَ: صَدَقْتَ. قَالَ: فَأَخْبِرْنِي عَنِ الْإِحْسَانِ. قَالَ: أَنْ تَعْبُدَ اللهَ كَأَنَّكَ تَرَاهُ فَإِنْ لَمْ تَكُنْ تَرَاهُ فَإِنَّهُ يَرَاكَ. قَالَ: فَأَخْبِرْنِي عَنِ السَّاعَةِ. قَالَ: مَا الْمَسْؤُولُ عَنْهَا بِأَعْلَمَ مِنَ السَّائِلِ. قَالَ: فَأَخْبِرْنِي عَنْ أَمَارَتِهَا. قَالَ: أَنْ تَلِدَ الْأَمَةُ رَبَّتَهَا، وَأَنْ تَرَى الْحُفَاةَ الْعُرَاةَ الْعَالَةَ رِعَاءَ الشَّاءِ يَتَطَاوَلُونَ فِي الْبُنْيَانِ. قَالَ: ثُمَّ انْطَلَقَ، فَلَبِثْتُ مَلِيًّا، ثُمَّ قَالَ لِي: يَا عُمَرُ أَتَدْرِي مَنِ السَّائِلُ؟ قُلْتُ: اللهُ وَرَسُولُهُ أَعْلَمُ. قَالَ: فَإِنَّهُ جِبْرِيلُ أَتَاكُمْ يُعَلِّمُكُمْ دِينَكُمْ. رواه مسلم.

[1] On the authority of 'Umar b. al-Khaṭṭāb, ﷺ, who said: Whilst we were sitting with the Messenger of Allah, ﷺ, that day, a man appeared before us. His clothes were extremely white, his hair intensely black. No trace of travelling was visible upon him,

and none of us knew him. (He proceeded) until he sat before the Prophet, ﷺ, placing his knees against his knees and his palms upon his thighs. He then said, "O Muḥammad! Tell me about *Islam* [Submission]." He replied, "*Islam* is that you bear witness that there is no god except Allah and that Muḥammad is the Messenger of Allah, and you establish the *Ṣalāt* [Prayer] and pay the *zakāt* [Alms-tax], fast Ramaḍān and make the pilgrimage to the House if you are able to find a way to do that." He said, "You have spoken the truth." We were amazed at him: asking him and then confirming what he said. He said, "Then tell me about *Īmān* [Faith]." He replied, "[*Īmān* is] that you have faith in Allah, His Angels, His Books, His Messengers and the Last Day, and you have faith in Predestination: its Good and its Evil." He said, "You have spoken the truth." He further said, "Then tell me about *Iḥsān* [Excellence]." He replied, "[*Iḥsān* is] that you worship Allah as though you are seeing Him. But if you are not able to see Him, then He sees you." He said, "Then tell me about the Hour." He replied, "The one questioned does not know any more about it than the questioner." He said, "Then tell me about its signs." He replied, "[Its signs are] that the slave-woman gives birth to her mistress, and you see the barefoot, naked, destitute shepherds competing in the construction of lofty buildings." He then departed. I stayed for a long while, after which he said to me, "O ʿUmar, do you know who the questioner was?" I said, "Allah and His Messenger know best." He said, "It was Jibrīl [Gabriel]: he came to teach you your religion." Muslim (*Mishkāt*, Book of Faith, *Ḥadīth* no. 2).

Commentary

1. The meanings of *Islām*, *Īmān* and *Iḥsān* have been explained in this *Ḥadīth*. In the Qur'ān and *Ḥadīth*, wherever *Īmān* and *Islām* are mentioned together, *Īmān* denotes certainty and affirmation by the heart, whilst *Islām* means verbal affirmation of *Tawḥīd* and Prophethood as well as regular performance of the physical rites of worship.

The word *Iḥsān* is derived from *Ḥusn*, which means beauty. Beauty can only appear in worship when the awareness is deeply-rooted in the mind that we are present before Allah Exalted, as though we are seeing Him. Even if this awareness is not able to settle in the mind, then no-one can dispute the reality that Allah Exalted is nevertheless watching us. No action of the servants is hidden from His Gaze.

2. "The slave-woman gives birth to her mistress" means that near the Day of Resurrection, mutual co-operation, compassion and maintenance of family ties amongst people will instead be generally replaced by greed, selfishness and the breaking of family ties. The culture of respecting and obeying elders will end, to such an extent that even the daughter, who naturally has a strong affection for her mother, will treat her mother the way a mistress treats her slave-girl. Thus, the mother will not have given birth to her daughter, but to her mistress.
3. Barefoot and bare-bodied paupers and shepherds taking pride in rivalry regarding huge buildings means that uncivilised and uneducated people, bereft of nobility and character, will possess untold money and wealth. The urges of competition and ostentation in material matters will increase.

3.2 *TAWḤĪD* (AFFIRMING THE UNITY OF GOD)

وعَنْ أَبِي ذَرّ ﷺ قَالَ: أَتَيْتُ النَّبِيّ ﷺ، وَعَلَيْهِ ثَوْبٌ أَبْيَضُ، وَهُوَ نَائِمٌ، ثُمَّ أَتَيْتُهُ وَقَدْ اسْتَيْقَظَ، فَقَالَ: مَا مِنْ عَبْدٍ قَالَ لا إِلَهَ إِلَّا اللهُ، ثُمَّ مَاتَ عَلى ذَلِكَ إلا دَخَلَ الْجَنَّةَ .متفق عليه.

[2] On the authority of Abū Dharr ﷺ, who said: I came to the Prophet ﷺ but he was asleep, dressed in a white garment. I came to him again when he had woken up. He said, "Any servant [of Allah] who says, 'There is no god except Allah,' and then dies upon that, will [definitely] enter [nothing but] the Garden." Bukhārī and Muslim (*Mishkāt*, Book of Faith, *Ḥadīth* no. 26).

Commentary

In this *Ḥadīth*, "He who says, '*Lā ilāha illa'Llāh*'," does not mean simply a ritual declaration of the tongue. Rather, what is meant is such a declaration that is accompanied by certainty and affirmation of the heart, as occurs in other narrations, "with certainty in his heart", or "with affirmation by his heart", i.e. this declaration and confession must come with certainty and truthfulness of the heart. Clearly, when the declaration is made in this way, there will be a distinct change in a person's life and behaviour, and there will be positive effects upon all aspects of life.

وعَنْ سُفْيَانَ بْنِ عَبْدِ اللهِ الثَّقَفِيِّ ﵁ قَالَ: قُلْتُ يَا رَسُولَ اللهِ، قُلْ لِي فِي الْإِسْـــلَامِ قَوْلًا لَا أَسْأَلُ عَنْهُ أَحَدًا بَعْدَكَ. قَالَ: قُلْ آمَنْتُ بِاللهِ، ثُمَّ اسْتَقِمْ. رواه مسلم.

[3] On the authority of Sufyān b. ʿAbdullāh al-Thaqafī ﵁, who said: I asked, "O Messenger of Allah! Tell me a word in Islam that I need not ask of anyone after you." He replied, "Say: 'I have believed in Allah', and then remain steadfast [upon that]." Muslim (*Mishkāt*, Book of Faith, *Ḥadīth* no. 15).

وعَنْ الْعَبَّاسِ بْنِ عَبْدِ الْمُطَّلِبِ ﵁، أَنَّهُ سَمِعَ رَسُولَ اللهِ ﷺ يَقُولُ: ذَاقَ طَعْمَ الْإِيمَانِ مَنْ رَضِيَ بِاللهِ رَبًّا وَبِالْإِسْلَامِ دِينًا وَبِمُحَمَّدٍ رَسُولًا. رواه مسلم.

[4] On the authority of al-ʿAbbās b. ʿAbd al-Muṭṭalib ﵁, who said: the Messenger of Allah ﷺ said, "He has tasted the delight of faith: he who is pleased with Allah as Lord, with Islam as religion, and with Muḥammad as Messenger." Muslim (*Mishkāt*, Book of Faith, *Ḥadīth* no. 9).

3.3 FAITH IN PROPHETHOOD

عَنْ جَابِرٍ ﵁ أَنَّ عُمَرَ بْنَ الْخَطَّابِ ﵁ أَتَى رَسُولَ اللهِ ﷺ بِنُسْخَةٍ مِنْ التَّوْرَاةِ، فَقَـــالَ: يَا رَسُولَ اللهِ هَذِهِ نُسْخَةٌ مِنْ التَّوْرَاةِ. فَسَكَتَ، فَجَعَلَ يَقْرَأُ وَوَجْهُ رَسُولِ اللهِ يَتَغَيَّرُ. فَقَالَ

أَبُو بَكْرٍ: ثَكِلَتْكَ الثَّوَاكِلُ مَا تَرَى مَا بِوَجْهِ رَسُولِ اللهِ ﷺ. فَنَظَرَ عُمَرُ إِلَى وَجْهِ رَسُولِ اللهِ ﷺ، فَقَالَ: أَعُوذُ بِاللهِ مِنْ غَضَبِ اللهِ وَغَضَبِ رَسُولِهِ ﷺ، رَضِينَا بِاللهِ رَبًّا وَبِالْإِسْلَامِ دِينًا وَبِمُحَمَّدٍ نَبِيًّا. فَقَالَ رَسُولُ اللهِ ﷺ: وَالَّذِي نَفْسُ مُحَمَّدٍ بِيَدِهِ، لَوْ بَدَا لَكُمْ مُوسَى فَاتَّبَعْتُمُوهُ وَتَرَكْتُمُونِي لَضَلَلْتُمْ عَنْ سَوَاءِ السَّبِيلِ، وَلَوْ كَانَ حَيًّا وَأَدْرَكَ نُبُوَّتِي لَاتَّبَعَنِي.

وفي رِوَايَةٍ: مَا وَسِعَهُ إِلَّا اتِّبَاعِيْ. رواه الدارمي.

[5] On the authority of Jābir ﷺ that ʿUmar b. al-Khaṭṭāb ﷺ brought a copy of the Torah to the Messenger of Allah ﷺ and said, "O Messenger of Allah! This is a copy of the Torah." The Prophet remained silent. ʿUmar began to read from the Torah upon which the Prophet's face changed colour [with anger]. Abū Bakr said, "May bereaved ones be bereaved of you! Do you not see the expression in the face of the Messenger of Allah ﷺ?" ʿUmar looked at the face of the Messenger of Allah and said, "I seek refuge with Allah from the anger of Allah and the anger of His Messenger ﷺ. We are pleased with Allah as our Lord, with Islam as our religion and with Muḥammad as our Prophet." The Messenger of Allah ﷺ said, "By the One in Whose Hand is the life of Muḥammad! Were Moses to appear to you, and were you to follow him and leave me, you would stray from the Straight Path. Were he to be alive and to witness my Prophethood, he would follow me." In one narration, "He would have no option but to follow me." Aḥmad and Dārimī (*Mishkāt*, Book of Faith, *Ḥadīth* nos. 177 and 194).

3.4 FOLLOWING THE MESSENGER OF ALLAH ﷺ

وَعَنْ عَبْدِ اللهِ بْنِ عَمْرٍو ﷺ قَالَ: قَالَ رَسُولُ اللهِ ﷺ: لا يُؤْمِن أَحَدكُمْ حَتَّى يَكُوْنَ هَوَاهُ تَبَعًا لِمَا جِئْتُ بِهِ .رواه البغوي في شرح السنّة، وقال النووي في أربعينه: هذا حديث صحيح رويناه في كتاب الحجة بإسناد صحيح.

[6] On the authority of ʿAbdullāh b. ʿAmr ﷺ, who said: The Messenger of Allah ﷺ said, "None of you will be a believer until his desires follow that [Law] which I have brought."

Transmitted by Baghawī in his *Sharḥ al-Sunnah* and Nawawī, who authenticated it in his *Forty Ḥadīth* by saying, "This is an authentic tradition that we have transmitted in *The Book of Proof* with a genuine chain of narration." (*Mishkāt*, Book of Faith, *Ḥadīth* no. 167).

3.5 LOVING THE MESSENGER OF ALLAH ﷺ

وعَنْ أَنَس بْنِ مَالِكٍ رضي الله عنه قَالَ: قَالَ رَسُولُ الله ﷺ: لا يُؤْمِنُ أَحَدُكُمْ حَتَّى أَكُونَ أَحَبَّ إِلَيْهِ مِنْ وَالِدِهِ وَوَلَدِهِ وَالنَّاسِ أَجْمَعِينَ .متفق عليه.

[7] On the authority of Anas رضي الله عنه, who said: The Messenger of Allah ﷺ said, "None of you will be a believer until I become more beloved to him than his father, his son and all mankind." Bukhārī and Muslim (*Mishkāt*, Book of Faith, *Ḥadīth* no. 7).

وعَنْ أَنَس رضي الله عنه قَالَ: قَالَ لِي رَسُولُ الله ﷺ: يَا بُنَيَّ إِنْ قَدَرْتَ أَنْ تُصْبِحَ وَتُمْسِيَ لَيْسَ فِي قَلْبِكَ غِشٌّ لِأَحَدٍ فَافْعَلْ، ثُمَّ قَالَ لِي: يَا بُنَيَّ وَذَلِكَ مِنْ سُنَّتِي، وَمَنْ أَحَبَّ سُنَّتِي فَقَدْ أَحَبَّنِي، وَمَنْ أَحَبَّنِي كَانَ مَعِي فِي الْجَنَّةِ. رواه الترمذي.

[8] On the authority of Anas رضي الله عنه, who said: The Messenger of Allah ﷺ said to me, "O my son! If you are able to begin the morning and begin the evening with no malice towards anyone, then do so." He then said, "O my son! For that is my Way: he who loves my Way has loved me; and he who loves me will be with me in the Garden." Tirmidhī (*Mishkāt*, Book of Faith, *Ḥadīth* no. 175).

3.6 AVOIDING EXTREMISM AND HAVING A BALANCED BELIEF REGARDING THE MESSENGER OF ALLAH ﷺ

وعَنْ رَافِعِ بْنِ خَدِيجٍ رضي الله عنه قَالَ: قَدِمَ نَبِيُّ الله ﷺ، الْمَدِينَةَ وَهُمْ يَأْبُرُونَ النَّخْلَ، يَقُولُونَ يُلَقِّحُونَ النَّخْلَ، فَقَالَ: مَا تَصْنَعُونَ . قَالُوا: كُنَّا نَصْنَعُهُ. قَالَ: لَعَلَّكُمْ لَوْ لَمْ تَفْعَلُوا كَانَ خَيْرًا. فَتَرَكُوهُ فَنَفَضَتْ. قَالَ: فَذَكَرُوا ذَلِكَ لَهُ. فَقَالَ: إِنَّمَا أَنَا بَشَرٌ، إِذَا أَمَرْتُكُمْ بِشَيْءٍ مِنْ

دِينِكُمْ فَخُذُوا بِهِ، وَإِذَا أَمَرْتُكُمْ بِشَيْءٍ مِنْ رَأْيٍ، فَإِنَّمَا أَنَا بَشَرٌ. رواه مسلم ــ وفي رواية قَالَ
رَسُولُ اللهِ ﷺ: أَنْتُمْ أَعْلَمُ بِأُمُورِ دُنْيَاكُمْ.

[9]   On the authority of Rāfiʿ b. Khadīj ⬥, who said: The
Messenger of Allah ﷺ came to Madinah, and the people were
cross-pollinating the date-palms. He said, "What are you doing?"
They replied, "We are used to doing this." He said, "Perhaps, if
you did not do so, it would be better." So they ceased doing it, and
the yield decreased. They mentioned that to him, upon which
he said, "I am only a man. If I command you with something
from the matter of your religion, take it. If I command you
with something from my opinion, then I am only a man." In
another narration, the Messenger of Allah ﷺ said, "You are more
knowledgeable about the matters of your world." Muslim (*Mishkāt*,
Book of Faith, *Ḥadīth* no. 147).

Commentary

This *Ḥadīth* sheds light on several important matters:

1.   The Messenger of Allah ﷺ was a human being, and not
     superhuman. Thus it was not necessary that his personal
     view on worldly crafts and transactions should turn out
     to be correct. However, no doubt should be created about
     anything that he stated based on revelation.

2.   This *Ḥadīth* apparently distinguishes between *dīn* and *dunyā*
     ("religion" and "the world", respectively); however, the
     reality is that this is not the case. By "matters of the world"
     is meant issues related to crafts, e.g. crafts, agriculture,
     carpentry, etc. Clearly, the noble Prophets do not come
     to this world in order to teach such sciences and crafts.
     The context and text of this *Ḥadīth* also support this
     meaning. There remain the different branches of life, such
     as economics, social matters, politics and ethics. Just as
     the noble Prophets explain the details of ritual worship,
     their duties also include conveying the Divine instructions
     regarding these other branches of life.

3.7 FAITH IN PREDESTINATION

وعَنْ أَبي هُرَيْرَةَ ﷺ قَالَ: قَالَ رَسُولُ اللهِ ﷺ: الْمُؤْمِنُ الْقَوِيُّ خَيْرٌ وَأَحَبُّ إِلى اللهِ مِنْ الْمُؤْمِنِ الضَّعِيفِ وَفِي كُلٍّ خَيْرٌ، احْرِصْ عَلى مَا يَنْفَعُكَ وَاسْتَعِنْ بِاللهِ وَلا تَعْجَزْ وَإِنْ أَصَابَكَ شَيْءٌ فَلا تَقُلْ لَوْ أَني فَعَلْتُ كَانَ كَذَا وَكَذَا، وَلَكِنْ قُلْ: قَدَرُ اللهِ وَمَا شَاءَ فَعَلَ، فَإِنَّ لَوْ تَفْتَحُ عَمَلَ الشَّيْطَانِ. رواه مسلم.

[10] On the authority of Abū Hurayrah ﷺ, who said: The Messenger of Allah ﷺ said, "The strong believer is better and more beloved to Allah than the weak believer; nevertheless, there is goodness in both of them. Covet that which benefits you. Seek Allah's help, and do not lose resolve. If any difficulty befalls you, do not say, 'If only I had done such-and-such, such-and-such would have happened,' but say, 'Allah predetermined: whatever He wished, He did'; for saying, 'If only' opens the door to Satan's work." Muslim (*Mishkāt*, Book of Heart-Softening Matters, *Ḥadīth* no. 5298).

Commentary

In this *Ḥadīth*, the "strong believer" means one who is firm in his resolve and determination. Conversely, the "weak believer" is a Muslim who loses all resolve at the slightest failure.

وعَنْ ابْنِ عَبَّاس ﷺ قَالَ: كُنْتُ خَلْفَ رَسُولِ اللَّهِ ﷺ يَوْمًا، فَقَالَ: يَا غُلَامُ إِني أُعَلِّمُكَ كَلِمَاتٍ، احْفَظْ اللَّهَ يَحْفَظْكَ، احْفَظْ اللَّهَ تَجِدْهُ تُجَاهَكَ، إِذَا سَأَلْتَ فَاسْأَلْ اللَّهَ، وَإِذَا اسْتَعَنْتَ فَاسْتَعِنْ بِاللَّهِ، وَاعْلَمْ أَنَّ الأُمَّةَ لَوْ اجْتَمَعَتْ عَلى أَنْ يَنْفَعُوكَ بِشَيْءٍ لَمْ يَنْفَعُوكَ إِلا بِشَيْءٍ قَدْ كَتَبَهُ اللَّهُ لَكَ وَلَوْ اجْتَمَعُوا عَلى أَنْ يَضُرُّوكَ بِشَيْءٍ لَمْ يَضُرُّوكَ إِلا بِشَيْءٍ قَدْ كَتَبَهُ اللَّهُ عَلَيْكَ، رُفِعَتْ الأَقْلَامُ وَجَفَّتْ الصُّحُفُ . رواه أحمد والترمذي.

[11] On the authority of Ibn 'Abbās ﷺ, who said: I was [seated on a mount] behind the Prophet ﷺ one day, when he said, "Young man! I will teach you some important matters. (1) Guard [the limits of] Allah, and He will guard you. (2) Guard [the limits of] Allah, and you will find Him before you [with His Mercy].

(3) When you ask, ask from Allah. (4) When you need help, ask for Allah's help. (5) Know that if the people were to come together to benefit you with something, they could only benefit you as much as Allah had pre-ordained for you; if they were to come together to harm you in some way, they could only harm you as much as Allah had decreed for you. The pens have been lifted and the pages have dried." Aḥmad and Tirmidhī (*Mishkāt*, Book of Heart-Softening Matters, *Ḥadīth* no. 5302).

عن أَبِي خِزَامَةَ، عن أَبِيه ﷺ قال :سَأَلْتُ رَسُولَ الله، قُلْتُ: يا رسولَ الله، أَرَأَيْتَ رُقًى نَسْتَرْقِيهَا وَدَوَاءً نَتَدَاوَى بِهِ وَتُقَاةً نَتَّقِيهَا، هل تَرُدُّ مِنْ قَدَرِ الله شَيْئاً؟ قالَ :هِيَ مِنْ قَدَرِ الله. رواه الترمذي.

[12] On the authority of Abū Khizāmah's father ﷺ, who said: I asked, "O Messenger of Allah! Do you see the spiritual cures we use, the medicines by which we treat each other, the defences that we set up [against enemy attack] – do they repulse any of Allah's Predetermination?" He replied, "They are part of Allah's Predetermination." Aḥmad, Tirmidhī and Ibn Mājah (*Mishkāt*, Book of Faith, *Ḥadīth* no. 97).

3.8 ACCOUNTABILITY IN THE HEREAFTER

عن ابْنِ مَسْعُودٍ ﷺ، عن النبيِّ ﷺ قالَ :لاَ تَزُولُ قَدَمَا ابنِ آدَمَ يَوْمَ القِيَامَةِ مِنْ عِنْدِ رَبِّه حَتَّى يُسْأَلَ عن خَمْسٍ :عن عُمْرِهِ فِيما أَفْنَاهُ، وعن شَبَابِهِ فِيما أَبْلاَهُ، وَعن مَالِهِ مِنْ أَيْنَ اكْتَسَبَهُ وَفِيما أَنْفَقَهُ، وَمَاذَا عَمِلَ فِيما عَلِمَ. رواه الترمذي.

[13] On the authority of Ibn Mas'ūd ﷺ, that the Prophet ﷺ said, "The feet of the son of Ādam will not move from their place [on the Day of Judgment] until he is asked about five things: (1) About his life, in which deeds he spent it? (2) About his youth, how he utilised it? (3) About his wealth, from where did he earn it and (4) on what did he spend it? (5) What did he do, based on what he knew?" Tirmidhī (*Mishkāt*, Book of Heart-Softening Matters, *Ḥadīth* no. 5197).

3.9 THE TRANSITORY NATURE OF THE WORLD

وعَنْ ابْنِ مَسْعُودٍ ﵁، أَنَّ رَسُولَ الله ﷺ قَالَ: كُنْتُ نَهَيْتُكُمْ عَنْ زِيَارَةِ الْقُبُورِ، فَزُورُوهَا، فَإِنَّهَا تُزَهِّدُ فِي الدُّنْيَا وَتُذَكِّرُ الْآخِرَةَ. رواه ابن ماجه.

[14] On the authority of Ibn Masʿūd ﵁, that the Messenger of Allah ﷺ said, "I used to forbid you from visiting the graves. Now visit them, for they teach non-attachment to the world, and remind you of the Hereafter." Ibn Mājah (*Mishkāt*, Book of Funerals, *Ḥadīth* no. 1769).

وعَنْ عَبْدِ اللَّهِ بْنِ عُمَرَ ﵄ قَالَ: أَخَذَ رَسُولُ الله ﷺ بِمَنْكِبِي، فَقَالَ: كُنْ فِي الدُّنْيَا كَأَنَّكَ غَرِيبٌ أَوْ عَابِرُ سَبِيلٍ. وَكَانَ ابْنُ عُمَرَ يَقُولُ: إِذَا أَمْسَيْتَ فَلَا تَنْتَظِرْ الصَّبَاحَ وَإِذَا أَصْبَحْتَ فَلَا تَنْتَظِرْ الْمَسَاءَ، وَخُذْ مِنْ صِحَّتِكَ لِمَرَضِكَ، وَمِنْ حَيَاتِكَ لِمَوْتِكَ. رواه البخاري.

[15] On the authority of ʿAbdullāh b. ʿUmar ﵄, who said: The Messenger of Allah ﷺ took my shoulder and said, "Be in the world as though you are a stranger or a traveller." Ibn ʿUmar used to say, "When you reach the evening, do not wait for the morning. When you reach the morning, do not wait for the evening. Take [a provision of righteous deeds] from your health for your illness, and [a wealth of good action] from your life for your death." Bukhārī (*Mishkāt*, Book of Funerals, *Ḥadīth* no. 1604).

وعَنْ عَمْرِو بْنِ مَيْمُونٍ الأَوْدِي ﵁ قَالَ: قَالَ رَسُولُ الله ﷺ لِرَجُلٍ، وَهُوَ يَعِظُهُ: اِغْتَنِمْ خَمْسًا قَبْلَ خَمْسٍ: شَبَابَكَ قَبْلَ هَرَمِكَ، وَصِحَّتَكَ قَبْلَ سَقَمِكَ، وَغِنَاكَ قَبْلَ فَقْرِكَ، وَفَرَاغَكَ قَبْلَ شُغْلِكَ، وَحَيَاتَكَ قَبْلَ مَوْتِكَ. رَوَاهُ التِرْمِذِي مُرْسَلًا.

[16] On the authority of ʿAmr b. Maymūn al-Awdī ﵁, who said: The Messenger of Allah ﷺ said to a man, advising him, "Take advantage of five matters before five matters: (1) your youth before your old age; (2) your good health before your ill-health;

(3) your wealth before your poverty; (4) your spare time before your preoccupations; (5) your life before your death." Tirmidhī, in *mursal* form (*Mishkāt*, Book of Heart-Softening Matters, *Ḥadīth* no. 5174). The Ḥadīth is also transmitted by Ḥākim, Ibn Abī'l-Dunyā and Bayhaqī (*Ṣaḥīḥ al-Jāmi' al-Ṣaghīr*, no. 1077).

عَنْ أَبِي أَيُّوبَ الأَنْصَارِي ﷺ قَالَ: جَاءَ رَجُلٌ إِلَى النَّبِيِّ ﷺ، فَقَالَ: عِظْنِي وَأَوْجِزْ. فَقَالَ: إِذَا قُمْتَ فِي صَلَاتِكَ، فَصَلِّ صَلَاةَ مُوَدِّعٍ، وَلَا تَكَلَّمْ بِكَلَامٍ تَعْتَذِرُ مِنْهُ غَدًا، وَاجْمَعِ الإِيَاسَ مِمَّا فِي أَيْدِي النَّاسِ. رواه أحمد.

[17] On the authority of Abū Ayyūb al-Anṣārī ﷺ, who said: A man came to the Prophet ﷺ and said, "Give me some brief advice." He replied, "When you stand for prayer, pray the prayer of one who is bidding farewell. Do not say words for which you will apologise the following day. Finally, despair totally of that which is in the hands of people." Aḥmad (*Mishkāt*, Book of Heart-Softening Matters, *Ḥadīth* no. 5226) and Ibn Mājah (*Ṣaḥīḥ al-Jāmi' al-Ṣaghīr*, no. 742).

وَعَنْ عُقْبَةَ بْنِ عَامِرٍ ﷺ، عَنِ النَّبِيِّ ﷺ قَالَ: إِذَا رَأَيْتَ اللهَ، عَزَّ وَجَلَّ، يُعْطِي الْعَبْدَ مِنَ الدُّنْيَا عَلَى مَعَاصِيهِ مَا يُحِبُّ، فَإِنَّمَا هُوَ اسْتِدْرَاجٌ، ثُمَّ تَلَا رَسُولُ اللهِ ﷺ:« فَلَمَّا نَسُوا مَا ذُكِّرُوا بِهِ فَتَحْنَا عَلَيْهِمْ أَبْوَابَ كُلِّ شَيْءٍ حَتَّى إِذَا فَرِحُوا بِمَا أُوتُوا أَخَذْنَاهُمْ بَغْتَةً فَإِذَا هُمْ مُبْلِسُونَ». رواه أحمد.

[18] On the authority of 'Uqbah b. 'Āmir ﷺ, from the Prophet ﷺ, who said, "When you see Allah, Mighty and Magnificent, granting a servant things that he loves from the world despite his disobedience, then [know that] this is nothing but a gradual respite [before punishment]." The Messenger of Allah ﷺ then recited, *So when they forgot what they had been reminded of, We opened the gates of all things so that while they rejoiced in what they had been granted We suddenly seized them and they were plunged into despair.* [al-An'ām, 6: 44] Aḥmad (*Mishkāt*, Book of Heart-Softening Matters, *Ḥadīth* no. 5201).

Commentary

It is incorrect for a person or nation to think that Allah is happy with them based purely on worldly affluence or power. Rather, it is the form of a severe affliction that after such affluence, the Divine Punishment suddenly envelops wrongdoers. A similitude of the Divine Law of gradual respite is that of a fisherman who does not extract the fish from the water immediately after catching the hook in its throat. Rather, he keeps the tackle loose. When the fish becomes tired after swimming and circling around, he suddenly brings the fish out onto dry land with a strong jerk. During this process, the unsuspecting fish thinks that it is breathing freely in the expanses of freedom!

3.10 THE SPIRIT OF ISLAM (SINCERITY)

عن عُمَرَ بْنَ الْخَطَّابِ ﵁ يَقُولُ: قَالَ رَسُولُ اللهِ ﷺ: إِنَّمَا الْأَعْمَالُ بِالنِّيَّاتِ، وَإِنَّمَا لِكُلِّ امْرِئٍ مَا نَوَى، فَمَنْ كَانَتْ هِجْرَتُهُ إِلَى اللهِ وَرَسُولِهِ فَهِجْرَتُهُ إِلَى اللهِ وَرَسُولِهِ، وَمَنْ كَانَتْ هِجْرَتُهُ لِدُنْيَا يُصِيبُهَا، أَوْ امْرَأَةٍ يَتَزَوَّجُهَا، فَهِجْرَتُهُ إِلَى مَا هَاجَرَ إِلَيْهِ. متفق عليه.

[19] On the authority of ʿUmar b. al-Khaṭṭāb, ﵁, who said: The Messenger of Allah ﷺ said, "Truly, actions are only by intentions; and truly, a man shall have only that which he intended. So he whose migration was to Allah and His Messenger, his migration is [actually] to Allah and His Messenger. And he whose migration was to the world for some benefit, or to a woman to marry her, his migration is [actually] to that which he migrated [by his intention]." Bukhārī and Muslim (*Mishkāt*, Book of Faith, *Ḥadīth* no. 1).

وعَنْ أَبِي مُوسَى ﵁ قَالَ: جَاءَ رَجُلٌ إِلَى النَّبِيِّ ﷺ، فَقَالَ: الرَّجُلُ يُقَاتِلُ لِلْمَغْنَمِ وَالرَّجُلُ يُقَاتِلُ لِلذِّكْرِ وَالرَّجُلُ يُقَاتِلُ لِيُرَى مَكَانُهُ، فَمَنْ فِي سَبِيلِ اللهِ؟ قَالَ: مَنْ قَاتَلَ لِتَكُونَ كَلِمَةُ اللهِ هِيَ الْعُلْيَا، فَهُوَ فِي سَبِيلِ اللهِ. متفق عليه.

[20] On the authority of Abū Mūsā ﵁, who said: A man came to the Prophet ﷺ and asked, "A man fights for booty, another

fights for fame, another fights to show off [his bravery]: which of these is [a warrior] in the way of Allah?" He replied, "He who fights such that the word of Allah is uppermost: only he is [the warrior] in the way of Allah." Bukhārī and Muslim (*Mishkāt*, Book of *Jihād*, *Ḥadīth* no. 3814).

عَنْ أَبِي هُرَيْرَةَ ۞ قَالَ: قَالَ رَسُولُ الله ﷺ: إِنَّ اللهَ لَا يَنْظُرُ إِلى صُوَرِكُمْ، وَأَمْوَالِكُمْ، وَلَكِنْ يَنْظُرُ إِلى قُلُوبِكُمْ وَأَعْمَالِكُمْ. رواه مسلم.

[21]   On the authority of Abū Hurayrah ۞, who said: The Messenger of Allah ﷺ said, "Truly, Allah does not look at your forms and wealth; rather, He looks at your hearts and deeds." Muslim (*Mishkāt*, Book of Heart-Softening Matters, *Ḥadīth* no. 5314).

عَنْ أَبِي أُمَامَةَ ۞، عَنْ رَسُولِ الله ﷺ أَنَّهُ قَالَ: مَنْ أَحَبَّ للهِ وَأَبْغَضَ للهِ وَأَعْطَى للهِ وَمَنَعَ للهِ، فَقَدِ اسْتَكْمَلَ الْإِيمَانَ. رواه أبو داود.

[22]   On the authority of Abū Umāmah ۞, who said: The Messenger of Allah ﷺ said, "He who loves [people] for the sake of Allah and hates for the sake of Allah, gives for the sake of Allah and withholds for the sake of Allah: such a person has advanced his faith to [the level of] perfection." Abū Dāwūd (*Mishkāt*, Book of Faith, *Ḥadīth* no. 30 and *Ṣaḥīḥ al-Jāmiʿ al-Ṣaghīr*, no. 5965).

3.11 MODERATION AND BALANCE

عَنْ عَائِشَةَ ۞ قالت: قال رَسُولِ الله ﷺ: خُذُوا مِنْ الْأَعْمَالِ مَا تُطِيقُونَ، فَإِنَّ اللهَ لَا يَمَلُّ حَتَّى تَمَلُّوا. رواه البخاري.

[23]   On the authority of ʿĀʾishah ۞, who said: The Messenger of Allah ﷺ said, "Take [upon yourself] as much work as you can bear, for truly Allah does not reduce His reward until you become weary." Bukhārī and Muslim (*Mishkāt*, Book of Prayer, *Ḥadīth* no. 1243).

Commentary

This means that Allah the Exalted does not close the door to His reward and forgiveness until a person deprives himself by his own lack of personal discipline.

عَنْ ابْنِ عَبَّاسٍ رضي الله عنه قَالَ: كَانَ أَهْلُ الْجَاهِلِيَّةِ يَأْكُلُونَ أَشْيَاءَ وَيَتْرُكُونَ أَشْيَاءَ تَقَذُّرًا، فَبَعَثَ اللهُ تَعَالَى نَبِيَّهُ ﷺ، وَأَنْزَلَ كِتَابَهُ، وَأَحَلَّ حَلَالَهُ، وَحَرَّمَ حَرَامَهُ، فَمَا أَحَلَّ فَهُوَ حَلَالٌ، وَمَا حَرَّمَ فَهُوَ حَرَامٌ، وَمَا سَكَتَ عَنْهُ فَهُوَ عَفْوٌ. رواه أبو داود.

[24] On the authority of Ibn ʿAbbās رضي الله عنه, who said, "The people of the Age of Ignorance used to eat certain foods and avoid other foods, regarding them as filthy until Allah sent His Prophet, revealed His Book, legalised the lawful and prohibited the unlawful. Thus, whatever He legalised is lawful, whatever He prohibited is unlawful, and whatever He was silent about is concessionary." Abū Dāwūd (*Mishkāt*, Book of Game and Slaughtered Meat, *Ḥadīth* no. 4146).

Commentary

This means that those matters about which there is neither explicit permission nor prohibition, it is not appropriate to question or probe them deeply, and there is no revulsion legally in employing them.

وعنْ حُذَيْفَةَ رضي الله عنه قَالَ :قَالَ رَسُولُ اللهِ ﷺ: ما أَحْسَنَ القَصْدَ فِي الغِنى مَا أَحْسَنَ القَصْدَ فِي الفَقْرِ، وَمَاأَحْسَنَ القَصْدَ فِي العِبَادَةِ . مسند البزار.

[25] On the authority of Ḥudhayfah رضي الله عنه, who said: The Messenger of Allah ﷺ said, "How excellent is moderation in prosperity! How excellent is moderation in poverty! How excellent is moderation in worship!" Musnad al-Bazzār (*Kanz al-ʿUmmāl*).

عَنْ أَبِي هُرَيْرَةَ ﴾، عَنِ النَّبِيِّ ﷺ، قَالَ: إِنَّ الدِّينَ يُسْرٌ، وَلَنْ يُشَادَّ الدِّينَ أَحَدٌ إِلَّا غَلَبَهُ، فَسَدِّدُوا وَقَارِبُوا وَأَبْشِرُوا، وَاسْتَعِينُوا بِالْغَدْوَةِ وَالرَّوْحَةِ، وَشَيْءٍ مِنَ الدُّلْجَةِ. رواه البخاري.

[26] On the authority of Abū Hurayrah ﴾, who said: The Messenger of Allah ﷺ said, "Truly, the religion is ease. Anyone who tries to outdo the religion in strictness, it will overcome him. So remain steadfast and be moderate, and seek help with journeys of the morning and evening and a part of the night." Bukhārī (*Mishkāt*, Book of Prayer, *Ḥadīth* no. 1246).

Commentary

Just as a traveller does not travel continuously, but rather proceeds during mild and cool times, using the remainder of the time to rest himself and his mount, thus should be the traveller on the path of Islam. Taking upon oneself more difficulty than one can bear and emphasising voluntary actions in a way opposed to the *Sunnah* are all deeds that open the door to extremism in the religion. Anyone who gets caught up in extremism and excessiveness and then tries to wrestle with the religion does not harm the religion at all; rather, he has to retreat in the end.

عَنْ حُذَيْفَةَ ﴾ قَالَ: قَالَ رَسُولُ الله ﷺ: لَا يَنْبَغِي لِلْمُؤْمِنِ أَنْ يُذِلَّ نَفْسَهُ. قَالُوا: وَكَيْفَ يُذِلُّ نَفْسَهُ؟ قَالَ: يَتَعَرَّضُ مِنَ الْبَلَاءِ لِمَا لَا يُطِيقُ. رواه الترمذي.

[27] On the authority of Ḥudhayfah ﴾, who said: The Messenger of Allah ﷺ said, "It does not befit a believer to humiliate himself." They asked, "How does he humiliate himself?" He replied, "He takes on burdens that he cannot bear." Tirmidhī, Ibn Mājah and Bayhaqī. Tirmidhī said that this *Ḥadīth* is *ḥasan gharīb* (*Mishkāt*, Book of Supplications, *Ḥadīth* no. 2503).

عَنْ أَنَسٍ ﴾، أَنَّ النَّبِيَّ ﷺ رَأَى شَيْخًا يُهَادِي بَيْنَ ابْنَيْهِ، فَقَالَ: مَا بَالُ هَذَا؟ قَالُوا: نَذَرَ أَنْ يَمْشِيَ إِلَى بَيْتِ الله. قَالَ: إِنَّ اللهَ عَزَّ وَجَلَّ عَنْ تَعْذِيبِ هَذَا نَفْسَهُ لَغَنِيٌّ. وَأَمَرَهُ أَنْ يَرْكَبَ. متفق عليه.

[28] On the authority of Anas ﵁ that the Prophet ﷺ saw an old man dragging himself on his feet, supported by his two sons. He asked, "What is the matter with this man?" They replied, "He vowed to walk to the House of Allah." He said, "Truly, Allah is not in need of this man's torturing himself," and he ordered him to ride [and complete his journey]. Bukhārī and Muslim (*Mishkāt*, Book of Oaths and Vows, *Ḥadīth* no. 3431).

Commentary

Here, this misconception has been corrected that the more a person puts himself to hardship and pain, the more Allah is pleased with him.

عَنْ عَبْدِ اللَّهِ بْنِ عَمْرِو بْنِ الْعَاصِ ﵄ قَالَ: قَالَ لِي رَسُولُ اللهِ ﷺ: يَا عَبْدَ اللهِ أَلَمْ أُخْبَرْ أَنَّكَ تَصُومُ النَّهَارَ وَتَقُومُ اللَّيْلَ. فَقُلْتُ: بَلى يَا رَسُولَ اللهِ. قَالَ: فَلا تَفْعَلْ، صُمْ وَأَفْطِرْ، وَقُمْ وَنَمْ، فَإِنَّ لِجَسَدِكَ عَلَيْكَ حَقًّا، وَإِنَّ لِعَيْنِكَ عَلَيْكَ حَقًّا، وَإِنَّ لِزَوْجِكَ عَلَيْكَ حَقًّا، وَإِنَّ لِزَوْرِكَ عَلَيْكَ حَقًّا، لا صَامَ مَنْ صَامَ الدَّهْرَ، صَوْمُ ثَلاثَةِ أَيَّامٍ مِّنْ كُلِّ شَهْرٍ، صَوْمُ الدَّهْرِ كُلِّهِ، صُمْ كُلَّ شَهْرٍ ثَلاثَةَ أَيَّامٍ. وَاقْرَأِ الْقُرْآنَ فِي كُلِّ شَهْرٍ. قُلْتُ: إِنِّي أُطِيقُ أَكْثَرَ مِنْ ذَلِكَ. قَالَ: صُمْ أَفْضَلَ الصَّوْمِ، صَوْمَ دَاوُدَ، صِيَامُ يَوْمٍ وَإِفْطَارُ يَوْمٍ، وَاقْرَأْ فِي كُلِّ سَبْعِ لَيَالٍ مَرَّةً وَلا تَزِدْ عَلَى ذَلِكَ. (بخاري – مشكاة – باب صيام التطوع).

[29] On the authority of ʿAbdullāh b. ʿAmr b. al-ʿĀṣ ﵄, who said: The Messenger of Allah ﷺ said to me, "O ʿAbdullāh! Have I not been informed that you fast every day and stand every night [in prayer]?" I replied, "Yes, O Messenger of Allah." He said, "Do not do so. Fast, and break your fast; stand [in prayer], and also sleep; for truly, your body has a right over you; and truly, your eyes have a right over you; and truly, your wife has a right over you; and truly, your visitors have a right over you. One who fasts every day has not fasted: fasting three days every month is [equivalent to] fasting for all time. So fast three days in every month, and recite the Qur'ān [completely] in every month." I said, "I can bear more than that." He said, "Then fast the best of

[voluntary] fasting, the fasting of [the Prophet] Dāwūd عليه السلام: fast one day and break the fast the next day; and recite [the Qur'ān] completely once in every seven nights, and do not increase upon that." Bukhārī and Muslim (*Mishkāt*, Book of Fasting, *Ḥadīth* no. 2054).

Commentary

By recitation of the Qur'ān is not meant parrot-fashion recitation, but recitation with understanding, contemplation, concentration and reflection. From another narration, it is known that the Qur'ān should not be completely recited in less than three days under any circumstances.

عَنْ سَعْدِ بْنِ أَبِي وَقَّاصٍ، عَنْ أَبِيهِ رضي الله عنه قَالَ: كَانَ رَسُولُ اللهِ ﷺ يَعُودُنِي عَامَ حَجَّةِ الْوَدَاعِ مِنْ وَجَعٍ اشْتَدَّ بِي، فَقُلْتُ: إِنِّي قَدْ بَلَغَ بِي مِنَ الْوَجَعِ وَأَنَا ذُو مَالٍ وَلَا يَرِثُنِي إِلَّا ابْنَةٌ، أَفَأَتَصَدَّقُ بِثُلُثَيْ مَالِي؟ قَالَ: لَا. فَقُلْتُ: بِالشَّطْرِ. فَقَالَ: لَا. ثُمَّ قَالَ: الثُّلُثُ وَالثُّلُثُ كَثِيرٌ، إِنَّكَ أَنْ تَذَرَ وَرَثَتَكَ أَغْنِيَاءَ خَيْرٌ مِنْ أَنْ تَذَرَهُمْ عَالَةً يَتَكَفَّفُونَ النَّاسَ. متفق عليه.

[30] On the authority of Sa'd b. Abī Waqqāṣ's father رضي الله عنه, who said: The Messenger of Allah ﷺ came to visit me in the year of the Farewell *Ḥajj*, due to a severe illness I had. I said, "O Messenger of Allah! The illness has affected me as much as you see. I have much wealth, but no-one inherits me except one daughter: should I then give two-thirds of my wealth in charity?" He said, "No." I said, "Then a half, O Messenger of Allah?" He said, "No." I said, "Then a third, O Messenger of Allah?" He said, "Yes, a third, but a third is a lot. That you leave your inheritors wealthy is better than leaving them poor, begging from the people." Bukhārī and Muslim (*Mishkāt*, Book of Inheritance and Wills, *Ḥadīth* no. 3071).

3.12 A COMPREHENSIVE CONCEPT OF VIRTUE

عَنِ الْمِقْدَامِ بْنِ مَعْدِي كَرِبَ رضي الله عنه قَالَ: قَالَ رَسُولُ اللهِ ﷺ: مَا أَطْعَمْتَ نَفْسَكَ فَهُوَ لَكَ صَدَقَةٌ، وَمَا أَطْعَمْتَ وَلَدَكَ فَهُوَ لَكَ صَدَقَةٌ، وَمَا أَطْعَمْتَ زَوْجَكَ فَهُوَ لَكَ صَدَقَةٌ، وَمَا أَطْعَمْتَ خَادِمَكَ فَهُوَ لَكَ صَدَقَةٌ. رَوَاهُ البخاري في الأدب المفرد.

[31]   On the authority of al-Miqdām b. Ma'dī Karib 🙵, that he heard the Messenger of Allah 🙵 saying, "What you feed yourself is charity for you. What you feed your child is charity for you. What you feed your wife is charity for you. What you feed your servant is charity for you." Bukhārī's *Al-Adab al-Mufrad*.

Commentary

This means that if a person earns his living through lawful means and thus feeds himself and his children, then he deserves reward and blessings from Allah for this.

عَنْ أَبِي ذَرٍّ 🙵 قَالَ: قَالَ رَسُولُ الله ﷺ: إِنَّ بِكُلِّ تَسْبِيحَةٍ صَدَقَةً، وَبِكُلِّ تَكْبِيرَةٍ صَدَقَةً، وَبِكُلِّ تَهْلِيلَةٍ صَدَقَةً، وَبِكُلِّ تَحْمِيدَةٍ صَدَقَةً، وَأَمْرٌ بِالْمَعْرُوفِ صَدَقَةٌ وَنَهْيٌ عَنِ الْمُنْكَرِ صَدَقَةٌ، وَفِي بُضْعِ أَحَدِكُمْ صَدَقَةٌ. قَالُوا: يَا رَسُولَ الله، يَأْتِي أَحَدُنَا شَهْوَتَهُ وَيَكُونُ لَهُ فِيهَا أَجْرٌ؟ فَقَالَ: أَرَأَيْتُمْ لَوْ وَضَعَهَا فِي الْحَرَامِ كَانَ عَلَيْهِ وِزْرٌ؟ فَكَذَلِكَ إِذَا وَضَعَهَا فِي الْحَلَالِ كَانَ لَهُ أَجْرٌ. (صحيح مسلم- مشكاة – باب فضل الصدقة).

[32]   On the authority of Abū Dharr 🙵, who said: The Messenger of Allah 🙵 said, "Truly, every glorification [of Allah] is charity. Every magnification [of Allah] is charity. Every praise [of Allah] is charity. Every declaration of Allah's Unity is charity. Enjoining goodness is charity. Forbidding evil is charity. Fulfilling your sexual desire is charity." They asked, "O Messenger of Allah 🙵! One of us fulfils his lust and is rewarded for it?" He replied, "Do you see that if he fulfilled it in a prohibited way, would it not be a sin upon him? Similarly, if he fulfils it in a lawful way, there will be reward for him." Muslim (*Mishkāt*, Book of *Zakāt*, *Ḥadīth* no. 1898).

3.13 THE BELIEVER'S VIEW OF THE WORLDLY LIFE

عَنْ أَبِي سَعِيدٍ الْخُدْرِيِّ 🙵، عَنِ النَّبِيِّ ﷺ قَالَ: إِنَّ الدُّنْيَا حُلْوَةٌ خَضِرَةٌ، وَإِنَّ اللهَ مُسْتَخْلِفُكُمْ فِيهَا، فَيَنْظُرُ كَيْفَ تَعْمَلُونَ. صحيح مسلم.

[33]   On the authority of Abū Saʿīd al-Khudrī ❀ from the Prophet ❀, who said, "Truly, the world is sweet and green, and Allah has placed you in it as vicegerents [trustees], in order to see what you do." Muslim (*Mishkāt*, Book of Marriage, *Ḥadīth* no. 3086; Book of Etiquette, *Ḥadīth* no. 5145.)

Commentary

The favours that Allah the Exalted has granted humanity: their real owner is Allah the Exalted. Man has only been given the post of vicegerent and deputy: his task is to fulfil the will of the real Master regarding the things he has been granted.

عَنْ أَبِي هُرَيْرَةَ ❀ قَالَ: قَالَ رَسُولُ الله ﷺ: الدُّنْيَا سِجْنُ الْمُؤْمِنِ، وَجَنَّةُ الْكَافِرِ. رواه مسلم.

[34]   On the authority of Abū Hurayrah ❀, who said: The Messenger of Allah ❀ said, "The world is the believer's prison and the unbeliever's garden." Muslim (*Mishkāt*, Book of Heart-Softening Matters, *Ḥadīth* no. 5158).

Commentary

The believer has to live his life confined within the four walls of the *Sharīʿah*, so the world for him is like a jail for the prisoner. On the contrary, the unbeliever thinks himself to be free of the restrictions of the *Sharīʿah*.

عَنْ شَدَّادِ بْنِ أَوْسٍ ❀، عَنِ النَّبِيِّ ﷺ، قَالَ: الْكَيِّسُ مَنْ دَانَ نَفْسَهُ وَعَمِلَ لِمَا بَعْدَ الْمَوْتِ، وَالْعَاجِزُ مَنْ أَتْبَعَ نَفْسَهُ هَوَاهَا وَتَمَنَّى عَلَى الله. رواه الترمذي.

[35]   On the authority of Shaddād b. Aws ❀ that the Prophet ❀ said, "The wise person is the one who calls himself to account, and works for what is after death. The incapable [unambitious] person is the one who allows his self to follow its desires, and maintains vain hopes [of bounty and generosity] of Allah." Tirmidhī and Ibn Mājah (*Mishkāt*, Book of Heart-Softening Matters, *Ḥadīth* no. 5289).

عَنْ أَبِي سَعِيدٍ الْخُدْرِيِّ ﷺ، عَنِ النَّبِيِّ ﷺ قَالَ: مَثَلُ الْمُؤْمِنِ وَمَثَلُ الإِيمَانِ كَمَثَلِ الْفَرَسِ فِي آخِيَّتِهِ يَجُولُ، ثُمَّ يَرْجِعُ إِلَى آخِيَّتِهِ، وَإِنَّ الْمُؤْمِنَ يَسْهُو، ثُمَّ يَرْجِعُ إِلَى الإِيمَانِ، فَأَطْعِمُوا طَعَامَكُمُ الأَتْقِيَاءَ، وَأَوْلُوا مَعْرُوفَكُمُ الْمُؤْمِنِينَ. مسند أحمد.

[36] On the authority of Abū Saʿīd al-Khudrī ﷺ that the Prophet ﷺ said, "The similitude of a believer and of faith is that of a horse tied to its post. He wanders around, and then returns to his post. Truly, the believer errs but then returns to faith. So feed your food to the pious, and benefit the believers with your kindness." Aḥmad (*Ḥadīth* no. 11526), Bayhaqī (*Branches of Faith*, *Ḥadīth* no. 10964) and Abū Nuʿaym (*Mishkāt*, Book of Food, *Ḥadīth* no. 4250).

عن ابْنِ عَبَّاسٍ ﷺ، أَنَّ رَسُولَ اللهِ ﷺ قَالَ: أَرْبَعٌ مَنْ أُعْطِيهُنَّ فَقَدْ أُعْطِيَ خَيْرَ الدُّنْيَا وَالآخِرَةِ: قَلْبٌ شَاكِرٌ، وَلِسَانٌ ذَاكِرٌ، وَبَدَنٌ عَلَى الْبَلاءِ صَابِرٌ، وَزَوْجَةٌ لاتَبْغِيهِ خَوْنًا فِي نَفْسِهَا وَلا مَالِهِ. رواه البيهقي.

[37] On the authority of Ibn ʿAbbās ﷺ, that the Messenger of Allah ﷺ said, "Four matters, if a person is granted them, he has been granted the goodness of the world and the Hereafter: (1) a grateful heart; (2) a remembering tongue; (3) a body patient upon trials; and (4) a wife who does not seek to betray him regarding herself or his wealth." Bayhaqī (*Mishkāt*, Book of Marriage, *Ḥadīth* no. 3273).

عَنْ ابْنِ عُمَرَ ﷺ، عَنِ النَّبِيِّ ﷺ قَالَ: الْمُسْلِمُ إِذَا كَانَ مُخَالِطًا النَّاسَ وَيَصْبِرُ عَلَى أَذَاهُمْ، أَفْضَلُ مِنَ الْمُسْلِمِ الَّذِي لا يُخَالِطُ النَّاسَ وَلا يَصْبِرُ عَلَى أَذَاهُمْ. رواه الترمذي.

[38] On the authority of Ibn ʿUmar ﷺ from the Prophet ﷺ, who said, "The Muslim who mixes with the people and endures their harms patiently is better than the one who neither mixes with them nor endures their harms patiently." Tirmidhī and Ibn Mājah (*Mishkāt*, Book of Etiquette, *Ḥadīth* no. 5087).

عَنْ أَبِي هُرَيْرَةَ ۞ قَالَ: قَالَ رَسُولُ الله ﷺ: الْمُسْلِمُ مَنْ سَلِمَ الْمُسْلِمُونَ مِنْ لِسَانِهِ وَيَدِهِ،
وَالْمُؤْمِنُ مَنْ أَمِنَهُ النَّاسُ عَلى دِمَائِهِمْ وَأَمْوَالِهِمْ. رواه الترمذي. وزاد البيهقي في شعب
الإيمان برواية فَضَالَةَ: وَالْمُجَاهِدُ مَنْ جَاهَدَ نَفْسَهُ فِي طَاعَةِ الله، وَالْمُهَاجِرُ مَنْ هَجَرَ الْخَطَايَا
وَالذُّنُوبَ.

[39]   On the authority of Abū Hurayrah ۞, who said: The
Messenger of Allah ﷺ said, "The Muslim [submitter] is he from
whose tongue and hand the Muslims are safe. The *Mu'min*
[believer] is the one whom people entrust with their blood and
wealth." Transmitted by Tirmidhī and Nasā'ī. Bayhaqī added in *The Branches
of Faith* from the narration of Faḍālah:

"The *Mujāhid* [warrior] is the one who strives against his self in
obeying Allah. The *Muhājir* [emigrant] is the one who leaves [the
path] of disobedience and sins." *Mishkāt*, Book of Faith, Ḥadīth nos.

4

Teachings of the Religion

4.1 VIRTUES OF KNOWLEDGE, WISDOM AND
TEACHING THE RELIGION

عَنْ عَبْدَ الله ابْنَ مَسْعُودٍ ﷺ قَالَ: قَالَ النَّبِيُّ ﷺ: لَا حَسَدَ إِلَّا فِي اثْنَتَيْنِ: رَجُلٌ آتَاهُ اللهُ مَالًا فَسُلِّطَ عَلَى هَلَكَتِهِ فِي الْحَقِّ، وَرَجُلٌ آتَاهُ اللهُ الْحِكْمَةَ فَهُوَ يَقْضِي بِهَا وَيُعَلِّمُهَا. البخاري ومسلم.

[40]   On the authority of Ibn Masʿūd ☙, who said: The Messenger of Allah ﷺ said, "Envy is only allowed in the case of two people: (1) a man to whom Allah has given wealth and enabled him to spend it in truth; (2) a man to whom Allah has given wisdom, so he decides amongst people by it and teaches it to them." Bukhārī and Muslim (*Mishkāt*, Book of Knowledge, *Ḥadīth* no. 202).

Commentary

By "envy" here is meant "jealousy", i.e. these two virtues are such that being jealous of those who have them is not only allowed but encouraged.

عَنْ ابْنَ عَبَّاسٍ ﷺ قَالَ: تَدَارُسُ الْعِلْمِ سَاعَةً مِنَ اللَّيْلِ خَيْرٌ مِنْ إِحْيَائِهَا. وقَالَ أَبُو هُرَيْرَةَ: إِنِّي لَأُجَزِّئُ اللَّيْلَ ثَلَاثَةَ أَجْزَاءٍ: فَثُلُثٌ أَنَامُ، وَثُلُثٌ أَقُومُ، وَثُلُثٌ أَتَذَكَّرُ أَحَادِيثَ رَسُولِ اللهِ ﷺ. رواه الدرامي.

[41] On the authority of Ibn ʿAbbās ﷺ, who said, "Studying and teaching knowledge for an hour of the night is better than staying awake [in prayer] for all of it." Abū Hurayrah said, "Truly, I split the night up into thirds: I sleep a third, I stand in prayer for a third and I recollect the teachings of the Messenger of Allah, ﷺ, for a third." Dārimī (*Mishkāt*, Book of Knowledge, *Ḥadīth* no. 256).

عَنْ أَبِي هُرَيْرَةَ ﵁ قَالَ: قَالَ رَسُولُ اللهِ ﷺ: كَلِمَةُ الْحِكْمَةِ ضَالَّةُ الْحَكِيمِ، فَحَيْثُ وَجَدَهَا فَهُوَ أَحَقُّ بِهَا. رواه الترمذي.

[42] On the authority of Abū Hurayrah ﵁, who said: The Messenger of Allah ﷺ said, "A word of wisdom is the lost property of the wise person: wherever he finds it, he has most right over it." Tirmidhī and Ibn Mājah (*Mishkāt*, Book of Knowledge, *Ḥadīth* no. 216.)

عَنْ ابْنِ مَسْعُودٍ ﵁ قَالَ: قَالَ رَسُوْلُ اللهِ ﷺ: نَضَّرَ اللهُ عَبْداً سَمِعَ مَقَالَتِي، فَحَفِظَهَا، وَوَعَاهَا وَأَدَّاهَا كَمَا سَمِعَهَا، فَرُبَّ مُبَلِّغٍ أَوعَى لَهَا مِنْ سَامِعٍ. (مشكاة ص ٣٥).

[43] On the authority of Ibn Masʿūd ﵁, who said: The Messenger of Allah ﷺ said, "May Allah brighten the face of a person who hears my teaching, preserves and understands it, and delivers it as he heard it, for sometimes one to whom it was conveyed may remember it better than the [initial] hearer." Shāfiʿī, Tirmidhī, Ibn Mājah and Bayhaqī (*Mishkāt*, Book of Knowledge, *Ḥadīth* nos. 228 and 230).

4.2 WISDOM IN PREACHING AND REFORM

عَنِ ابْنِ عَبَّاسٍ ﵁ قَالَ: قَالَ رَسُولُ اللهِ ﷺ: عَلِّمُوا وَيَسِّرُوا، عَلِّمُوا وَيَسِّرُوا، ثَلَاثَ مَرَّاتٍ، وَإِذَا غَضِبْتَ فَاسْكُتْ مَرَّتَيْنِ. (الأدب المفرد- باب يسكت اذا غضب ص ١٩١).

[44] On the authority of Ibn ʿAbbās ﷺ, who said: The Messenger of Allah ﷺ said, "Teach [the religion] and make things easy, teach [the religion] and make things easy," three times, "and when you become angry, be silent," twice. Bukhārī's *Al-Adab al-Mufrad*.

عَنْ شَقِيقٍ ﷺ قَالَ: كَانَ عَبْدُ اللهِ يُذَكِّرُ النَّاسَ فِي كُلِّ خَمِيسٍ، فَقَالَ لَهُ رَجُلٌ: يَا أَبَا عَبْدِ الرَّحْمَنِ لَوَدِدْتُ أَنَّكَ ذَكَّرْتَنَا كُلَّ يَوْمٍ. قَالَ: أَمَا إِنَّهُ يَمْنَعُنِي مِنْ ذَلِكَ، أَنِي أَكْرَهُ أَنْ أُمِلَّكُمْ، وَإِنِّي أَتَخَوَّلُكُمْ بِالْمَوْعِظَةِ كَمَا كَانَ النَّبِيُّ ﷺ يَتَخَوَّلُنَا بِهَا مَخَافَةَ السَّآمَةِ عَلَيْنَا. رواه البخاري و مسلم.

[45] On the authority of Shaqīq ⚄, who said: 'Abdullāh [b. Mas'ūd] used to remind the people every Thursday. A man said to him, "O 'Abū 'Abd al-Raḥmān! I would love that you reminded us every day." He replied, "What prevents me is that I dislike tiring you. I am considerate in admonishing you in the way that the Messenger of Allah ﷺ used to be considerate towards us regarding admonition, fearing boredom for us." Bukhārī and Muslim (*Mishkāt*, Book of Knowledge, *Ḥadīth* no. 207).

عَنْ أَنَسٍ ﷺ قَالَ: كَانَ النَّبِيُّ ﷺ قَلَّ مَا يُوَاجِهُ الرَّجُلَ بِشَيْءٍ يَكْرَهُهُ، فَدَخَلَ عَلَيْهِ يَوْمًا رَجُلٌ وَعَلَيْهِ أَثَرُ صُفْرَةٍ، فَلَمَّا قَامَ، قَالَ لِأَصْحَابِهِ: لَوْ غَيَّرَ أَوْ نَزَعَ هَذِهِ الصُّفْرَةَ. رواه أبو داود.

[46] On the authority of Anas ⚄, who said, "The Prophet ﷺ would rarely confront a man with something he disliked. A man came to him one day with a yellow stain [on his garment]. When the man left, he said to his Companions, 'If he were to change or remove this yellowness [it would be better]'." Bukhārī's *Al-Adab al-Mufrad* and Abū Dāwūd.

Commentary

If influential and responsible members of society correct people directly regarding every matter, then it is possible that, instead of positive effects, the diseases of obstinacy and stubbornness would appear. Thus, a wise approach should be taken in reform.

عَنْ عِكْرِمَةَ، عَنِ ابْنِ عَبَّاسٍ ﷺ قَالَ: حَدِّثِ النَّاسَ كُلَّ جُمُعَةٍ مَرَّةً، فَإِنْ أَبَيْتَ فَمَرَّتَيْنِ، فَإِنْ أَكْثَرْتَ فَثَلَاثَ مِرَارٍ، وَلَا تُمِلَّ النَّاسَ هَذَا الْقُرْآنَ، وَلَا أُلْفِيَنَّكَ تَأْتِي الْقَوْمَ وَهُمْ فِي حَدِيثٍ

مِنْ حَدِيثِهِمْ، فَتَقُصَّ عَلَيْهِمْ، فَتَقْطَعُ عَلَيْهِمْ حَدِيثَهُمْ، فَتُمِلُّهُمْ، وَلَكِنْ أَنْصِتْ فَإِذَا أَمَرُوكَ فَحَدِّثْهُمْ وَهُمْ يَشْتَهُونَهُ، فَانْظُرْ السَّجْعَ مِنْ الدُّعَاءِ. فَاجْتَنِبْهُ: فَإِنِي عَهِدْتُ رَسُولَ اللهِ ﷺ وَأَصْحَابَهُ لا يَفْعَلُونَ. صحيح البخاري.

[47] On the authority of ʿIkrimah that Ibn ʿAbbās ﵄ said, "Address the people once a week. If you must, then twice. If you wish more, then three times: do not make the people bored of this Qur'ān. Let me not find you coming to a people whilst they are in the midst of their conversation and you begin admonishing them, interrupting their conversation and making them resentful. Rather, keep silent until they request you: then speak to them when they desire it eagerly. Beware of rhyming prose in supplication and avoid it, for I have witnessed the Messenger of Allah ﷺ and his Companions: they did not do it." Bukhārī (*Mishkāt*, Book of Knowledge, *Ḥadīth* no. 252).

عَنْ ابْنِ عَبَّاسٍ ﵄ ، أَنَّ رَسُولَ اللهِ ﷺ بَعَثَ مُعَاذًا إِلَى الْيَمَنِ، فَقَالَ لَهُ: إِنَّكَ تَأْتِي قَوْمًا أَهْلَ كِتَابٍ، فَادْعُهُمْ إِلَى شَهَادَةِ أَنْ لا إِلَهَ إِلا اللهَ وَأَنِي رَسُولُ اللهِ، فَإِنْ هُمْ أَطَاعُوا لِذَلِكَ، فَأَعْلِمْهُمْ أَنَّ اللهَ افْتَرَضَ عَلَيْهِمْ خَمْسَ صَلَوَاتٍ فِي الْيَوْمِ وَاللَّيْلَةِ، فَإِنْ هُمْ أَطَاعُوا لِذَلِكَ، فَأَعْلِمْهُمْ أَنَّ اللهَ افْتَرَضَ عَلَيْهِمْ صَدَقَةً فِي أَمْوَالِهِمْ تُؤْخَذُ مِنْ أَغْنِيَائِهِمْ وَتُرَدُّ عَلَى فُقَرَائِهِمْ، فَإِنْ هُمْ أَطَاعُوا لِذَلِكَ، فَإِيَّاكَ وَكَرَائِمَ أَمْوَالِهِمْ، وَاتَّقِ دَعْوَةَ الْمَظْلُومِ، فَإِنَّهَا لَيْسَ بَيْنَهَا وَبَيْنَ اللهِ حِجَابٌ. رواه البخاري ومسلم.

[48] On the authority of Ibn ʿAbbās ﵄: The Messenger of Allah ﷺ sent Muʿādh [b. Jabal] to Yemen and said, "You will come to a nation who are people of Scripture. Therefore, invite them to bear witness that there is no god except Allah and that I am the Messenger of Allah. If they obey you in that, then inform them that Allah has made five prayers obligatory for them during the day and night. If they obey you in that, then inform them that Allah has obligated them to take alms from the rich amongst them and return it to their poor. If they obey you in that, then beware of their most precious wealth [i.e. avoid forcibly taking the best of their wealth in charity) and fear the

supplication of the oppressed, for there is no barrier between it and Allah." Bukhārī and Muslim (*Mishkāt*, Book of *Zakāt*, *Ḥadīth* no. 1772).

عَنْ أَنَسٍ ﵁، عَنِ النَّبِيِّ ﷺ، أَنَّهُ كَانَ إِذَا تَكَلَّمَ بِكَلِمَةٍ أَعَادَهَا ثَلاثًا حَتَّى تُفْهَمَ عَنْهُ، وَإِذَا أَتَى عَلَى قَوْمٍ، فَسَلَّمَ عَلَيْهِمْ سَلَّمَ عَلَيْهِمْ ثَلاثًا. رواه البخاري.

[49] On the authority of Anas ﵁, who said: "The Prophet ﷺ, when he stated something, would repeat it three times until it was understood. And when he came to a people and greeted them with peace, he would greet them three times."[34] Bukhārī (*Mishkāt*, Book of Knowledge, *Ḥadīth* no. 208).

4.3 RELIGIOUS EDUCATION AND UPBRINGING OF ONE'S CHILDREN AND FAMILY

عَنْ أَيُّوبَ بْنِ مُوسَى، عَنْ أَبِيهِ، عَنْ جَدِّهِ ﵁ قَالَ: قَالَ رَسُولُ اللهِ ﷺ: مَا نَحَلَ وَالِدٌ وَلَدَهُ مِنْ نَّحْلٍ أَفْضَلَ مِنْ أَدَبٍ حَسَنٍ. رواه أحمد والترمذي.

[50] On the authority of Ayyūb b. Mūsā from his father from his grandfather ﵁ that the Messenger of Allah ﷺ said, "No parent gave their child a gift better than beautiful manners." Aḥmad and Tirmidhī (*Mishkāt*, Book of Etiquette, *Ḥadīth* no. 4977).

Commentary

This means that the best gift and most valuable present for children from their parents is good manners and a sound upbringing.

عَنْ أَبِي هُرَيْرَةَ ﵁، أَنَّ رَسُولَ اللهِ ﷺ قَالَ: إِذَا مَاتَ الْإِنْسَانُ انْقَطَعَ عَنْهُ عَمَلُهُ إِلا مِنْ ثَلاثَةٍ: إِلا مِنْ صَدَقَةٍ جَارِيَةٍ، أَوْ عِلْمٍ يُنْتَفَعُ بِهِ، أَوْ وَلَدٍ صَالِحٍ يَدْعُو لَهُ. رواه مسلم.

34. One explanation as to why greeting with peace three times is part of the *Sunnah* is to greet when seeking permission to enter somewhere, then upon entry and finally upon leaving. Another explanation is that this applies solely to seeking permission to enter somewhere, for which a limit of three attempts is given in other *Aḥādīth*. – Trans. Note

[51] On the authority of Abū Hurayrah ﵁, who said: The Messenger of Allah ﷺ said, "When a man dies, his deeds cease except for three actions [that remain]: (1) continuous charity [i.e. such charity and benevolence that continues to benefit people for a long time], (2) knowledge by which people benefit, and (3) righteous children who pray for him." Muslim (*Mishkāt*, Book of Knowledge, *Ḥadīth* no. 203).

عَنْ عَمْرِو بْنِ شُعَيْبٍ، عَنْ أَبِيهِ، عَنْ جَدِّهِ ﵁ قَالَ: قَالَ رَسُولُ اللهِ ﷺ: مُرُوا أَوْلَادَكُمْ بِالصَّلَاةِ وَهُمْ أَبْنَاءُ سَبْعِ سِنِينَ ، وَاضْرِبُوهُمْ عَلَيْهَا وَهُمْ أَبْنَاءُ عَشْرٍ، وَفَرِّقُوا بَيْنَهُمْ فِي الْمَضَاجِعِ. رواه أبو داوُد.

[52] On the authority of ʿAmr b. Shuʿayb from his father from his grandfather ﵁, who said: The Messenger of Allah ﷺ said, "Command your children to pray when they are seven years old. Smack them upon [neglecting] it when they are ten years old,[35] and put them to sleep in separate beds." Abū Dāwūd (*Mishkāt*, Book of Prayer, *Ḥadīth* no. 572).

Commentary

This means that children should be familiarised with teachings of the religion from a young age. If after trying to making them understand and verbal warning, they do not become regular at prayer, then appropriate strict measures can also be taken. When children reach the age of ten, they should be made to sleep separately: it is not correct to put them to bed together.

4.4 FORBIDDANCE OF IRRESPONSIBLE TALK REGARDING THE RELIGION

عَنْ ابْنِ عَبَّاسٍ ﵄ قَالَ: قَالَ رَسُولُ اللهِ ﷺ: مَنْ قَالَ فِي الْقُرْآنِ برأيه فَلْيَتَبَوَّأْ مَقْعَدَهُ مِنْ النَّارِ. وفي رواية: مَنْ قَالَ فِي الْقُرْآنِ بِغَيْرِ عِلْمٍ، فَلْيَتَبَوَّأْ مَقْعَدَهُ مِنْ النَّارِ. رواه الترمذي.

35. "Smacking" is understood to be a last resort. The Prophet ﷺ *never* hit a woman, servant or child. – Trans. Note

[53] On the authority of Ibn ʿAbbās ﷺ, who said: The Messenger of Allah ﷺ said, "He who speaks about the Qur'ān with his own opinion, let him prepare his seat in the Fire." In one narration, "He who speaks about the Qur'ān without knowledge, let him prepare his seat in the Fire." Tirmidhī (*Mishkāt*, Book of Knowledge, *Ḥadīth* no. 234).

عَنْ عَبْدَ اللهِ بْنَ عَمْرٍ ﷺ قَالَ: هَجَّرْتُ إلى رَسُولِ اللهِ ﷺ يَوْمًا، قَالَ: فَسَمِعَ أَصْوَاتَ رَجُلَيْنِ اخْتَلَفَا فِي آيَةٍ، فَخَرَجَ عَلَيْنَا رَسُولُ اللهِ ﷺ يُعْرَفُ فِي وَجْهِهِ الْغَضَبُ، فَقَالَ: إِنَّمَا هَلَكَ مَنْ كَانَ قَبْلَكُمْ بِاخْتِلَافِهِمْ فِي الْكِتَابِ. رواه مسلم.

[54] On the authority of ʿAbdullāh b. ʿAmr ﷺ, who said: I went to the Messenger of Allah ﷺ one afternoon. He heard the voices of two men disputing about a verse [of the Qur'ān], so he came out to us with anger evident in his face and said, "Truly, those before you perished due to their disputing about the Scripture!" Muslim (*Mishkāt*, Book of Faith, *Ḥadīth* no. 152).

Commentary

This means that mutual discussion and exchange of views is allowed in understanding and studying the Qur'ān, but dispute and argumentation are opposed to the spirit of Islam.

عَنْ عَوْفِ بْنِ مَالِكٍ الْأَشْجَعِيِّ ﷺ قَالَ: سَمِعْتُ رَسُولَ اللهِ ﷺ يَقُولُ: لا يَقُصُّ إلا أَمِيرٌ، أَوْ مَأْمُورٌ، أَوْ مُخْتَالٌ. رواه أبو داوُد.

[55] On the authority of ʿAwf b. Mālik al-Ashjaʿī ﷺ, who said: The Messenger of Allah ﷺ said, "No-one speaks in public except the ruler, one appointed or one arrogant." Abū Dāwūd (*Mishkāt*, Book of Knowledge, *Ḥadīth* no. 240).

Commentary

"Speaking in public" refers to story-telling, conveying news and admonishing. The right of admonishing and public speaking and pronouncement belongs to the ruler or one appointed by him; otherwise these are the actions of an arrogant person. This means that in matters of religion and public responsibility, the right of addressing the public belongs to the ruler or one appointed by him. Apart from these two situations, a person who adopts this role is taking an irresponsible path that leads to corruption and the spread of mischief in society.

عَنْ ابْنِ أَبِي نُعْمٍ ﷺ قَالَ: كُنْتُ شَاهِدًا لِابْنِ عُمَرَ، وَسَأَلَهُ رَجُلٌ عَنْ دَمِ الْبَعُوضِ، فَقَالَ: مِمَّنْ أَنْتَ؟ فَقَالَ: مِنْ أَهْلِ الْعِرَاقِ. قَالَ: انْظُرُوا إِلَى هَذَا يَسْأَلُنِي عَنْ دَمِ الْبَعُوضِ، وَقَدْ قَتَلُوا ابْنَ النَّبِيِّ ﷺ، وَسَمِعْتُ النَّبِيَّ ﷺ يَقُولُ: هُمَا رَيْحَانَتَايَ مِنَ الدُّنْيَا. رواه البخاري.

[56] On the authority of Ibn Abī Nuʿm ﷺ, who said: I was a witness when Ibn ʿUmar was asked by a man about killing a mosquito. He asked, "From which people are you?" The man replied, "From the people of ʿIraq." He said, "Look at this one! He asks me about killing a mosquito, when they have killed the son of the Prophet ﷺ! I heard the Prophet ﷺ saying, 'These two [Ḥasan and Ḥusayn] are my sweet-basils [i.e. perfumed flowers] in this world'." Bukhārī (*Mishkāt*, Book of Virtues, *Ḥadīth* no. 6136).

Commentary

By "son of the Prophet" is meant his grandson Imām Ḥusayn here; i.e. this is an amazing irony that they spare the mosquito but "swallow the camel whole". What use is such piety and religiosity? Taking mountains upon one's head related to non-essential secondary matters but not even batting an eyelid upon seeing the foundations of Islam shaken!

عَنْ أَبِي هُرَيْرَةَ ﷺ قَالَ: قَالَ رَسُولُ اللَّهِ ﷺ: مَنْ أُفْتِيَ بِغَيْرِ عِلْمٍ كَانَ إِثْمُهُ عَلَى مَنْ أَفْتَاهُ، وَمَنْ أَشَارَ عَلَى أَخِيهِ بِأَمْرٍ يَعْلَمُ أَنَّ الرُّشْدَ فِي غَيْرِهِ، فَقَدْ خَانَهُ. رواه أبو داود.

[57] On the authority of Abū Hurayrah ﷺ, who said: The Messenger of Allah ﷺ said, "Whoever is given a legal opinion without knowledge, his sin [of acting on the legal opinion] is upon the one who gave the legal opinion. Whoever advises his [Muslim] brother on a matter when he knows that another way

is better and truer, he has betrayed him." Abū Dāwūd and Dārimī (*Mishkāt*, Book of Knowledge, *Ḥadīth* no. 242).

4.5 EVIL PEOPLE OF KNOWLEDGE

عَنْ أَبِي هُرَيْرَةَ ﷺ قَالَ: قَالَ رَسُولُ اللهِ ﷺ: مَنْ تَعَلَّمَ عِلْمًا مِمَّا يُبْتَغَى بِهِ وَجْهُ اللهِ عَزَّ وَجَلَّ لا يَتَعَلَّمُهُ إِلا لِيُصِيبَ بِهِ عَرَضًا مِنَ الدُّنْيَا، لَمْ يَجِدْ عَرْفَ الْجَنَّةِ يَوْمَ الْقِيَامَةِ. يَعْنِي: رِيحَهَا. رواه أحمد وأبو داود وابن ماجة.

[58] On the authority of Abū Hurayrah ﷺ, who said: The Messenger of Allah ﷺ said, "Whoever acquires some [sacred] knowledge by which the Countenance of Allah is sought, and yet he only learns it in order to attain a worldly gain, he will not [even] smell the fragrance of the Garden on the Day of Resurrection." Aḥmad, Abū Dāwūd and Ibn Mājah (*Mishkāt*, Book of Knowledge, *Ḥadīth* no. 227).

عَنْ أَبِي هُرَيْرَةَ ﷺ قَالَ: قَالَ رَسُولُ اللهِ ﷺ: مَنْ سُئِلَ عَنْ عِلْمٍ عَلِمَهُ، ثُمَّ كَتَمَهُ، أُلْجِمَ يَوْمَ الْقِيَامَةِ بِلِجَامٍ مِنْ نَارٍ. رواه أحمد وابو داود والترمذي.

[59] On the authority of Abū Hurayrah ﷺ, who said: The Messenger of Allah ﷺ said, "Whoever is asked about knowledge that he knew and then concealed it, will be bridled on the Day of Resurrection with a harness of fire." Aḥmad, Abū Dāwūd and Tirmidhī (*Mishkāt*, Book of Knowledge, *Ḥadīth* no. 223).

عن سُفْيَانَ ﷺ، أَنَّ عُمَرَ ﷺ، قَالَ لِكَعْبٍ ﷺ: مَنْ أَرْبَابُ الْعِلْمِ؟ قَالَ: الَّذِينَ يَعْمَلُونَ بِمَا يَعْلَمُونَ. قَالَ: فَمَا يَنْفِي الْعِلْمَ مِنْ صُدُورِ الرِّجَالِ؟ قَالَ: الطَّمَعُ. رواه الدارمي.

[60] On the authority of Sufyān ﷺ, that ʿUmar b. al-Khaṭṭāb ﷺ asked Kaʿb ﷺ, "Who are the masters of knowledge?" He replied, "Those who act by what they know." He asked, "So what expels [the blessing and light of] knowledge from the hearts of the people of knowledge?" He replied, "Greed [for this world]." Dārimī (*Mishkāt*, *Ḥadīth* no. 266).

عَنْ كَعْبِ بْنِ مَالِكٍ، عَنْ أَبِيهِ ﷺ قَالَ: سَمِعْتُ رَسُولَ اللهِ ﷺ يَقُولُ: مَنْ طَلَبَ الْعِلْمَ، لِيُجَارِيَ بِهِ الْعُلَمَاءَ، أَوْ لِيُمَارِيَ بِهِ السُّفَهَاءَ، أَوْ يَصْرِفَ بِهِ وُجُوهَ النَّاسِ إِلَيْهِ، أَدْخَلَهُ اللهُ النَّارَ. رواه الترمذي.

[61]   On the authority of Kaʿb b. Mālik's father ﷺ, who said: The Messenger of Allah ﷺ said, "Whoever seeks knowledge to compete with the people of knowledge, or to debate with fools, or to turn people's faces towards himself [i.e. to seek popularity], Allah will enter him into the Fire." Tirmidhī (*Mishkāt*, Book of Knowledge, *Ḥadīth* no. 225).

عَنِ ابْنِ عَبَّاسٍ ﷺ، عَنِ النَّبِيِّ ﷺ قَالَ: إِنَّ أُنَاسًا مِنْ أُمَّتِي سَيَتَفَقَّهُونَ فِي الدِّينِ، وَيَقْرَءُونَ الْقُرْآنَ، وَيَقُولُونَ نَأْتِي الْأُمَرَاءَ، فَنُصِيبُ مِنْ دُنْيَاهُمْ، وَنَعْتَزِلُهُمْ بِدِينِنَا، وَلَا يَكُونُ ذَلِكَ كَمَا لَا يُجْتَنَى مِنَ الْقَتَادِ إِلَّا الشَّوْكُ كَذَلِكَ لَا يُجْتَنَى مِنْ قُرْبِهِمْ إِلَّا الْخَطَايَا. رواه ابن ماجه.

[62]   On the authority of Ibn ʿAbbās ﷺ, who said: The Messenger of Allah ﷺ said, "Truly, groups of people from my nation will learn understanding of the religion and recite the Qurʾān. They will say, 'We shall go to the rulers and gain some of their worldly benefits, but we will stay apart from them with our religion.' That is not possible, for just as nothing is gained from a thorny tree except thorns, similarly, nothing is gained from approaching them except sins." Ibn Mājah (*Mishkāt*, Book of Knowledge, *Ḥadīth* no. 262).

عَنْ عَبْدِ اللهِ ابْنِ مَسْعُودٍ ﷺ قَالَ: لَوْ أَنَّ أَهْلَ الْعِلْمِ صَانُوا الْعِلْمَ وَوَضَعُوهُ عِنْدَ أَهْلِهِ، لَسَادُوا بِهِ أَهْلَ زَمَانِهِمْ، وَلَكِنَّهُمْ بَذَلُوهُ لِأَهْلِ الدُّنْيَا، لِيَنَالُوا بِهِ مِنْ دُنْيَاهُمْ، فَهَانُوا عَلَيْهِمْ، سَمِعْتُ نَبِيَّكُمْ ﷺ يَقُولُ: مَنْ جَعَلَ الْهُمُومَ هَمًّا وَاحِدًا هَمَّ آخِرَتِهِ، كَفَاهُ اللهُ هَمَّ دُنْيَاهُ، وَمَنْ تَشَعَّبَتْ بِهِ الْهُمُومُ فِي أَحْوَالِ الدُّنْيَا، لَمْ يُبَالِ اللهُ فِي أَيِّ أَوْدِيَتِهَا هَلَكَ. ابن ماجه.

[63]   On the authority of ʿAbdullāh b. Masʿūd ﷺ, who said: "Were the people of knowledge to protect knowledge and place it only before those who deserve it, they would be the leaders of the people of their time. However, they spend it for the people

of this world in order to gain something of their world, so they become humiliated in the eyes of the latter. I heard your Prophet ﷺ say, 'Whoever makes all his concerns into one concern, [by forgetting all concerns except] the concern of his Hereafter, Allah suffices him for his worldly concerns. Whoever is fully occupied by his concerns, with worldly affairs, Allah does not care in which valley of the world he perishes'." Ibn Mājah (*Mishkāt*, Book of Knowledge, *Ḥadīth* no. 263).

عَنْ أَبِي هُرَيْرَةَ رضي الله عنه قَالَ: قَالَ رَسُولُ اللهِ ﷺ: تَعَوَّذُوا بِاللَّهِ مِنْ جُبِّ الْحُزْنِ. قَالُوا: يَا رَسُولَ اللهِ وَمَا جُبُّ الْحُزْنِ؟ قَالَ: وَادٍ فِي جَهَنَّمَ تَعَوَّذُ مِنْهُ جَهَنَّمُ كُلَّ يَوْمٍ أَرْبَعَ مِائَةِ مَرَّةٍ. قِيلَ: يَا رَسُولَ اللهِ مَنْ يَدْخُلُهُ؟ قَالَ: أُعِدَّ لِلْقُرَّاءِ الْمُرَائِينَ بِأَعْمَالِهِمْ. رواه الترمذي، وكذا ابن ماجه— وَزَادَ فِيهِ: وَإِنَّ مِنْ أَبْغَضِ الْقُرَّاءِ إِلَى اللهِ الَّذِينَ يَزُورُونَ الأُمَرَاءَ. قَالَ الْمُحَارِبِيُّ: يعني: الْجَوَرَةَ.

[64] On the authority of Abū Hurayrah رضي الله عنه, who said: The Messenger of Allah ﷺ said, "Seek refuge with Allah from the Well of Grief." They asked, "O Messenger of Allah! What is the Well of Grief?" He replied, "A valley in Hell, from which Hell itself seeks refuge four hundred times every day." It was said, "O Messenger of Allah! Who will enter it?" He replied, "Those reciters [people of knowledge] who show off their actions." Tirmidhī and Ibn Mājah; the latter added:

"Amongst the most hated of reciters to Allah the Exalted are those who visit the rulers." Al-Muḥāribī [one of the narrators of the *Ḥadīth*] said, "This means the tyrannical rulers." *Mishkāt*, Book of Knowledge, *Ḥadīth* no. 275.

5

Establishing the Religion (*Dīn*)

5.1 THE EFFORT TO RENEW AND REVIVE THE RELIGION (*DĪN*)

عَنْ أَبِي هُرَيْرَةَ ﴾ قَالَ: قَالَ رَسُولُ الله ﷺ: بَدَأَ الإِسْلامُ غَرِيبًا وَسَيَعُودُ كَمَا بَدَأَ، فَطُوبَى لِلْغُرَبَاءِ. صحيح مسلم. وفي روايةٍ للترمذي: هُمُ الَّذِينَ يُصْلِحُونَ مَا أَفْسَدَ النَّاسُ مِنْ بَعْدِي مِنْ سُنَّتِي.

[65]   On the authority of Abū Hurayrah ﴾, who said: The Messenger of Allah ﷺ said, "Islam began as a stranger and will return as it began, so glad-tidings and congratulations to the strangers!" Muslim. In a narration of Tirmidhī, there is the addition:

"They are those who reform that which the people corrupt of my *Sunnah* after me." *Mishkāt*, Book of Faith, Ḥadīth nos. 159 and 170.

عَنْ أَبِي هُرَيْرَةَ ﴾ قَالَ: قَالَ رَسُولُ الله ﷺ: مَنْ تَمَسَّكَ بِسُنَّتِي عِنْدَ فَسَادِ أُمَّتِي، فَلَهُ أَجْرُ مَائَةِ شَهِيدٍ. رواه البيهقي.

[66]   On the authority of Abū Hurayrah ﴾, who said: The Messenger of Allah ﷺ said, "Whoever holds fast to my *Sunnah* when my nation becomes corrupt will have the reward of a hundred martyrs." Ibn ʿAdī, Ṭabarānī and Bayhaqī (*Mishkāt*, Book of Faith, Ḥadīth no. 176).

عَنْ أَنَسِ بْنِ مَالِكٍ ﴾ قَالَ: قَالَ رَسُولُ الله ﷺ: يَأْتِي عَلَى النَّاسِ زَمَانٌ الصَّابِرُ فِيهِمْ عَلَى دِينِهِ كَالْقَابِضِ عَلَى الْجَمْرِ. رواه الترمذي.

[67] On the authority of Anas ibn Malik ﷺ, who said: The Messenger of Allah ﷺ said, "There will come to the people a time when the one remaining steadfast on his religion will be like one holding a burning coal." Tirmidhī (*Mishkāt*, Book of Heart-Softening Matters, *Ḥadīth* no. 5367).

Commentary

Here, "religion" is meant in its broadest sense, i.e. that which applies to every branch of life. This is the same religion with whose rise unbelieving and corrupt powers are shaken. However, if religion is understood as being limited to the rulings on prayer, fasting, circumcision and funerals, then no power of falsehood feels any danger from it.

عَنْ ابْنِ عُمَرَ ﷺ، أَنَّ رَسُولَ اللهِ ﷺ قَالَ: إِقَامَةُ حَدٍّ مِنْ حُدُودِ اللهِ خَيْرٌ مِنْ مَطَرِ أَرْبَعِينَ لَيْلَةً فِي بِلَادِ اللهِ عَزَّ وَجَلَّ. رواه ابن ماجة .

[68] On the authority of Ibn 'Umar ﷺ, that the Messenger of Allah ﷺ said, "Establishing one of the limits [*ḥudūd*] of Allah is better than forty nights' rain in the lands of Allah, Mighty and Majestic." Ibn Mājah and Nasā'ī (*Mishkāt*, Book of Limits, *Ḥadīth* nos. 3588-9).

عَنْ أَبِي سَعِيدٍ الْخُدْرِيِّ ﷺ، أَنَّ النَّبِيَّ ﷺ قَالَ: أَفْضَلُ الْجِهَادِ مَنْ قَالَ كَلِمَةَ حَقٍّ عِنْدَ سُلْطَانٍ جَائِرٍ. رواه الترمذي وابوداود وابن ماجه.

[69] On the authority of Abū Sa'īd al-Khudrī ﷺ that the Prophet ﷺ said, "The best *Jihād* is to speak a word of truth before an oppressive, tyrannical ruler." Tirmidhī, Abū Dāwūd, Ibn Mājah, Aḥmad and Nasā'ī (*Mishkāt*, Book of Governance and Judgment, *Ḥadīth* nos. 3705-6).

عَنْ أَبِي سَعِيدٍ الْخُدْرِيِّ ﷺ، قَالَ: سَمِعْتُ رَسُولَ اللهِ ﷺ يَقُولُ: مَنْ رَأَى مِنْكُمْ مُنْكَرًا فَلْيُغَيِّرْهُ بِيَدِهِ، فَإِنْ لَمْ يَسْتَطِعْ فَبِلِسَانِهِ، فَإِنْ لَمْ يَسْتَطِعْ فَبِقَلْبِهِ، وَذٰلِكَ أَضْعَفُ الْإِيمَانِ. رواه مسلم.

[70] On the authority of Abū Saʿīd al-Khudrī ﵁, who said: I heard the Messenger of Allah ﷺ saying, "Whoever amongst you sees an evil must change it with his hand. If he is not able [to do so], then with his tongue. If he is not able [to do even this], then with his heart, and that is the weakest [level] of faith." Muslim (*Mishkāt*, Book of Etiquette, *Ḥadīth* no. 5137).

Commentary

Evil can only be removed by the hand, i.e. with power, when Allah-fearing leadership is in control. Otherwise, were every person to take the law into his own hands, there would be widespread corruption and anarchy in society, and the structure and fabric of the country would be reduced to ruin.

عَنْ النُّعْمَانَ بْنَ بَشِيرٍ ﵁، يَقُولُ: قَالَ النَّبِيُّ ﷺ: مَثَلُ الْمُدْهِنِ فِي حُدُودِ اللهِ وَالْوَاقِعِ فِيهَا، مَثَلُ قَوْمٍ اسْتَهَمُوا سَفِينَةً، فَصَارَ بَعْضُهُمْ فِي أَسْفَلِهَا وَصَارَ بَعْضُهُمْ فِي أَعْلَاهَا، فَكَانَ الَّذِي فِي أَسْفَلِهَا يَمُرُّونَ بِالْمَاءِ عَلَى الَّذِينَ فِي أَعْلَاهَا، فَتَأَذَّوْا بِهِ، فَأَخَذَ فَأْسًا، فَجَعَلَ يَنْقُرُ أَسْفَلَ السَّفِينَةِ، فَأَتَوْهُ، فَقَالُوا: مَا لَكَ. قَالَ: تَأَذَّيْتُمْ بِي وَلَا بُدَّ لِي مِنْ الْمَاءِ. فَإِنْ أَخَذُوا عَلَى يَدَيْهِ أَنْجَوْهُ وَنَجَّوْا أَنْفُسَهُمْ، وَإِنْ تَرَكُوهُ أَهْلَكُوهُ وَأَهْلَكُوا أَنْفُسَهُمْ. رواه البخاري.

[71] On the authority of al-Nuʿmān b. Bashīr ﵁: the Prophet ﷺ said, "The similitude of those who compromise the limits of Allah and those who exceed them is that of a people who drew lots to board a ship. Some of them ended up on the upper deck, others on the lower deck. One of those in the lower deck would pass by those on the upper deck to draw water and thus trouble them, so he took an axe and began chopping at the lower part of the ship. They came to him and said, 'What is the matter with you?' He said, 'You were troubled by me, and I must have water.' Therefore, if they prevent him forcibly, they will save him and save themselves; if they leave him as he is, they will destroy him and destroy themselves." Bukhārī (*Mishkāt*, Book of Etiquette, *Ḥadīth* no. 5138).

5.2 A RELIGIOUS SENSE OF HONOUR

عَنْ عَائِشَةَ رَضِيَ اللهُ عَنْهَا، أَنَّهَا قَالَتْ: مَا خُيِّرَ رَسُولُ اللهِ ﷺ بَيْنَ أَمْرَيْنِ إلا أَخَذَ أَيْسَرَهُمَا، مَا لَمْ يَكُنْ إِثْمًا، فَإِنْ كَانَ إِثْمًا كَانَ أَبْعَدَ النَّاسِ مِنْهُ، وَمَا انْتَقَمَ رَسُولُ اللهِ ﷺ لِنَفْسِهِ إلا أَنْ تُنْتَهَكَ حُرْمَةُ اللهِ فَيَنْتَقِمَ للهِ بِهَا عَزَّ وَجَلَّ. متفق عليه.

[72] On the authority of 'Āʾishah, ﷺ, who said: "Never was the Messenger of Allah ﷺ given a choice between two matters except that he chose the easier one, as long as it was not sinful. If it was sinful, he would be the most distant of men from it. The Messenger of Allah ﷺ never took revenge for himself: only if a sanctity [limit] of Allah was violated, he would take revenge for the sake of Allah, Mighty and Majestic." Bukhārī and Muslim (*Mishkāt*, Book of the Excellence and Virtues of the Messenger of Allah, *Ḥadīth* no. 5817).

عَنْ أَبِي هُرَيْرَةَ رَضِيَ اللهُ عَنْهُ قَالَ: خَرَجَ عَلَيْنَا رَسُولُ اللهِ ﷺ، وَنَحْنُ نَتَنَازَعُ فِي الْقَدَرِ، فَغَضِبَ حَتَّى احْمَرَّ وَجْهُهُ حَتَّى كَأَنَّمَا فُقِئَ فِي وَجْنَتَيْهِ حَبُّ الرُّمَّانُ، فَقَالَ: أَبِهَذَا أُمِرْتُمْ؟ أَمْ بِهَذَا أُرْسِلْتُ إِلَيْكُمْ؟ إِنَّمَا هَلَكَ مَنْ كَانَ قَبْلَكُمْ حِينَ تَنَازَعُوا فِي هَذَا الأَمْرِ، عَزَمْتُ عَلَيْكُمْ عَزَمْتُ عَلَيْكُمْ أَنْ لا تَتَنَازَعُوا فِيهِ. رواه الترمذي- مشكاة- باب القدر ص ١٤.

[73] On the authority of Abū Hurayrah ﷺ, who said: The Messenger of Allah ﷺ came out to us whilst we were arguing about predestination [*qadar*]. He became so angry that his face reddened as though pomegranate-seeds had been squeezed over his cheeks, saying, 'Is this what you were commanded to do? Is this what I have been sent with? Those before you were destroyed only when they began arguing about this matter [of predestination]. I urge you, I urge you: do not argue about this!'" Tirmidhī and Ibn Mājah (*Mishkāt*, Book of Faith, *Ḥadīth* nos. 98-99).

عَنْ مُجَاهِدٍ، عَنْ عَبْدِ اللهِ بْنِ عُمَرَ رَضِيَ اللهُ عَنْهُمَا، أَنَّ النَّبِيَّ ﷺ قَالَ: لا يَمْنَعَنَّ رَجُلٌ أَهْلَهُ أَنْ يَأْتُوا الْمَسَاجِدَ. فَقَالَ ابْنٌ لِعَبْدِ اللهِ بْنِ عُمَرَ: فَإِنَّا نَمْنَعُهُنَّ. قَالَ عَبْدُ اللهِ: أُحَدِّثُكَ عَنْ رَسُولِ اللهِ ﷺ، وَتَقُولُ هَذَا. قَالَ: فَمَا كَلَّمَهُ عَبْدُ اللهِ حَتَّى مَاتَ. رواه أحمد.

[74] On the authority of Mujāhid, from ʿAbdullāh b. ʿUmar ﵁ that the Prophet ﷺ said, "Let no man forbid his wife from attending mosques." A son of ʿAbdullāh b. ʿUmar said to him, "We certainly forbid our wives [from attending mosques]." ʿAbdullāh replied, "I narrate to you from the Messenger of Allah ﷺ and you say this?" and he refused to speak to him until he died. Aḥmad (*Mishkāt*, Book of Prayer, *Ḥadīth* no. 1084).

عَنْ عَلِيٍّ بْنِ أَبِي طَالِبٍ ﵁ قَالَ: مَرَّ النَّبِيُّ ﷺ عَلى قَوْمٍ، فِيهِمْ رَجُلٌ مُتَخَلِّقٌ بِخَلُوقٍ، فَنظَرَ إِلَيْهِمْ، وسَلَّمَ عَلَيْهِمْ، وَأَعْرَضَ عَنِ الرَّجُلِ، فَقَالَ الرَّجُلُ: أَعْرَضْتَ عَنِّي؟ قَالَ: بَيْنَ عَيْنَيْكَ جَمْرَةٌ. الأدب المفرد، باب ترك السلام على المتخلق واصحاب المعاصي.

[75] On the authority of ʿAlī ibn abī Ṭālib ﵁, who said: the Prophet ﷺ passed by a group of people that included a man with yellow perfume on his clothes. He looked at them and greeted them, but ignored the man. The man said, "You ignored me?" He replied, "Between your eyes there is a burning coal." Bukhārī's *Al-Adab al-Mufrad*, Chapter on Whoever Did Not Greet People of Disobedience). Ibn al-Athīr commented that the particular yellow perfume was customarily used by women, hence the Messenger's dislike of it for men (*Ṣaḥīḥ al-Adab al-Mufrad*, *Ḥadīth* no. 778).

Commentary

1. The perfume mentioned here is one that contains saffron and stains the garment yellow, a colour disliked by the Prophet ﷺ for men.
2. Avoiding giving greetings to people of sin is only appropriate when the duty of invitation and preaching has been fulfilled and a pious society has been created on the basis of this message.

عَنْ عَبْدِ اللهِ بْنِ عَمْرِو بْنِ الْعَاصِ ﵁ قَالَ: لا تَعُودُوا شُرَّابَ الْخَمْرِ إِذَا مَرِضُوا. الأدب المفرد، باب عيادة الفاسق.

[76]   On the authority of 'Abdullāh b. 'Amr b. al-'Āṣ ☙, who said, "Do not visit drinkers of wine when they fall ill." Bukhārī's *Al-Adab al-Mufrad*, Chapter on Visiting the Rebellious.

عَنْ عَائِشَةَ ﷺ زَوْجِ النَّبِيِّ ﷺ، أَنَّهُ بَلَغَهَا أَنَّ أَهْلَ بَيْتٍ فِي دَارِهَا كَانُوا سُكَّانًا فِيهَا، وَعِنْدَهُمْ نَرْدٌ، فَأَرْسَلَتْ إِلَيْهِمْ لَئِنْ لَمْ تُخْرِجُوهَا لَأُخْرِجَنَّكُمْ مِنْ دَارِي، وَأَنْكَرَتْ ذَلِكَ عَلَيْهِمْ. موطأ مالك، البيهقي.

[77]   On the authority of 'Ā'ishah ☙, wife of the Prophet ﷺ, who learnt that a family living in her house had backgammon pieces. She sent them the message, "If you do not turn these [instruments of gambling] out of the house, I shall turn you out of my house", and she scolded them severely. Bukhārī's *Al-Adab al-Mufrad* (Chapter on Expelling People of Falsehood), Mālik and Bayhaqī.

عَنْ أَسْلَمَ مَوْلَى عُمَرَ ﷺ قَالَ: لَمَّا قَدِمْنَا مَعَ عُمَرَ بْنِ الْخَطَّابِ الشَّامَ، أَتَاهُ الدِّهْقَانُ، قَالَ: يَا أَمِيرَ الْمُؤْمِنِينَ إِنِّي قَدْ صَنَعْتُ لَكَ طَعَامًا، فَأُحِبُّ أَنْ تَأْتِيَنِي بِأَشْرَافِ مَنْ مَعَكَ، فَإِنَّهُ أَقْوَى لِي فِي عَمَلِي وَأَشْرَفَ لِي، قَالَ: إِنَّا لَا نَسْتَطِيعُ أَنْ نَدْخُلَ كَنَائِسَكُمْ هَذِهِ مَعَ الصُّوَرِ الَّتِي فِيهَا. الادب المفرد، باب دعوة الذمي.

[78]   On the authority of Aslam, the freed-slave of 'Umar ☙, who said: when we came to Syria with 'Umar b. al-Khaṭṭāb, a village-elder came to him and said, "O Commander of the Believers! I have prepared some food for you and would like you to come to me along with the noblest people accompanying you, for this will be most supportive of me in my work and most honourable for me." He replied, "Truly, we are not able to enter these churches of yours containing images and statues." Bukhārī's *Al-Adab al-Mufrad*, Chapter on The Invitation of a Non-Muslim Subject.

Commentary

On the basis of this report, the question arises that during the Makkan era, the Messenger of Allah ﷺ wished to pray two *rak'ahs* inside the Ka'bah, even though there were hundreds of idols placed there. So did 'Umar ☙ have a greater sense of religious honour than the Prophet ﷺ? The reality of the matter is that during the Makkan era, the Messenger of Allah ﷺ was not in a position of control or authority: rather, he lived an extremely powerless and oppressed life. Under these conditions, there is no legal objection to putting up with such a situation. However, when 'Umar came to Syria, he was the man of authority, the unfettered ruler. In this situation, to tolerate such a great wrong would have been totally opposed to the spirit of Islam.

عن إبراهيم بن ميسرة رضي الله عنه قال: قال النَّبِيُّ ﷺ: مَنْ وَقَّرَ صَاحِبَ بِدْعَةٍ، فَقَدْ أَعَانَ عَلَى هَدْمِ الإِسْلاَمِ. مشكواة، باب الاعتصام.

[79] On the authority of Ibrāhīm b. Maysarah رضي الله عنه, who said: The Messenger of Allah ﷺ said, "Whoever honours a person of innovation has assisted in the demolition of Islam." Bayhaqī (*Mishkāt*, Book of Faith, *Ḥadīth* no. 189).

5.3 *JIHĀD* IN THE PATH OF ALLAH ﷻ

عَنْ أَبِي هُرَيْرَةَ رضي الله عنه قَالَ: قَالَ رَسُولُ اللهِ ﷺ: مَنْ مَاتَ وَلَمْ يَغْزُ وَلَمْ يُحَدِّثْ بِهِ نَفْسَهُ مَاتَ عَلَى شُعْبَةٍ مِنْ نِفَاقٍ. رواه مسلم- مشكاة- كتاب الجهاد.

[80] On the authority of Abū Hurayrah رضي الله عنه, who said: The Messenger of Allah ﷺ said, "Whoever dies, neither taking part in an expedition [of *Jihād*] nor having the thought of participating in his heart, dies upon a branch of hypocrisy." Muslim (*Mishkāt*, Book of *Jihād*, *Ḥadīth* no. 3813).

عَنْ ابْنِ عَبَّاسٍ رضي الله عنهما قَالَ: سَمِعْتُ رَسُولَ اللهِ ﷺ يَقُولُ: عَيْنَانِ لا تَمَسُّهُمَا النَّارُ: عَيْنٌ بَكَتْ مِنْ خَشْيَةِ اللهِ، وَعَيْنٌ بَاتَتْ تَحْرُسُ فِي سَبِيلِ اللهِ. رواه الترمذي.

[81] On the authority of Ibn 'Abbās رضي الله عنهما, who said: The Messenger of Allah ﷺ said, "Two eyes will not be touched by the Fire: (1) the eye that wept from the fear of Allah; and (2) the eye that spent the night keeping watch in the path of Allah." Tirmidhī (*Mishkāt*, Book of *Jihād*, *Ḥadīth* no. 3829).

6

Ritual Worship

6.1 THE IMPORTANCE OF PRAYER (*ṢALĀT*)

عَنْ ابْنِ عُمَرَ رضي الله عنه قَالَ: قَالَ رَسُولُ اللهِ ﷺ: لا إِيمَانَ لِمَنْ لا أَمَانَةَ لَهُ، ولا صَلاةَ لِمَنْ لاَ طُهورَ لَهُ، ولا دِينَ لِمَنْ لا صَلاةَ لَهُ، إِنَّما مَوْضِعُ الصَّلاةِ مِنَ الدِّينِ كَمَوْضِعِ الرَّأْسِ مِنَ الجَسَدِ. المعجم الصغير للطبراني.

[82] On the authority of Ibn ʿUmar رضي الله عنه, who said: the Messenger of Allah ﷺ said, "Whoever has no trustworthiness, has no faith. Whoever has no purity, has no prayer. Whoever has no prayer, has no religion: the position of prayer in the religion is none other than as the position of the head in the body." *Al-Muʿjam al-Ṣaghīr* of Ṭabarānī.

عَنْ أَبِي هُرَيْرَةَ رضي الله عنه قَالَ: قَالَ رَسُولَ اللهِ ﷺ: أَرَأَيْتُمْ لَوْ أَنَّ نَهرًا بِبَابِ أَحَدِكُمْ يَغْتَسِلُ فِيهِ كُلَّ يَوْمٍ خَمْسًا، هَلْ يُبْقِي مِنْ دَرَنِهِ؟ قَالُوا: لا يُبْقِي مِنْ دَرَنِهِ شَيْءٌ. قَالَ: فَذَلِكَ مِثْلُ الصَّلَوَاتِ الْخَمْسِ يَمْحُو اللهُ بِهِنَّ الْخَطَايَا. صحيح البخاري- كتاب مواقيت الصلاة.

[83] On the authority of Abū Hurayrah رضي الله عنه, who said: The Messenger of Allah ﷺ said, "Do you see that if there were a river at the door of one of you, and he was to bathe in it five times a day, would there be any dirt left upon him?" They replied, "No dirt would be left upon him." He said, "That is the example of the five prayers: Allah erases sins by way of them." Bukhārī and Muslim (*Mishkāt*, Book of Prayer, *Ḥadīth* no. 565).

عَنْ أَبِي هُرَيْرَةَ ﷺ أَنَّ رَسُولَ اللهِ ﷺ قَالَ: أَلَا أَدُلُّكُمْ عَلى مَا يَمْحُو اللهُ بِهِ الْخَطَايَا وَيَرْفَعُ
بِهِ الدَّرَجَاتِ. قَالُوا: بَلَى يَا رَسُولَ اللهِ. قَالَ: إِسْبَاغُ الْوُضُوءِ عَلَى الْمَكَارِهِ، وَكَثْرَةُ الْخُطَا
إِلَى الْمَسَاجِدِ، وَانْتِظَارُ الصَّلَاةِ بَعْدَ الصَّلَاةِ، فَذَلِكُمُ الرِّبَاطُ. وَفِي حَدِيثِ مَالِكٍ: فَذَلِكُمُ
الرِّبَاطُ فَذَلِكُمُ الرِّبَاطُ. رَدَّدَ مَرَّتَيْنِ. رواه مسلم.

[84]   On the authority of Abū Hurayrah ﷺ, who said: The
Messenger of Allah ﷺ said, "Shall I not point you to that by which
Allah erases [your] sins and raises [your] ranks?" They replied,
"Of course, O Messenger of Allah." He said, "(1) Performing the
ablution fully in adverse weather and conditions, (2) taking many
steps to the mosque [i.e. travelling a long distance to pray with
the congregation in the mosque], and (3) waiting for prayer after
prayer, for that is *ribāṭ* [guarding the frontier, i.e. the reward is
similar to that of watching the front in *Jihād*]."

In Malik's narration, "that is *ribāṭ*", is repeated twice. Malik,
Muslim and Tirmidhī (*Mishkāt*, Book of Purification, *Ḥadīth* nos. 282-3).

عَنْ أَبِي سَعِيدٍ الْخُدْرِيِّ ﷺ قَالَ: قَالَ رَسُولُ اللهِ ﷺ: إِذَا رَأَيْتُمُ الرَّجُلَ يَتَعَاهَدُ الْمَسْجِدَ،
فَاشْهَدُوا لَهُ بِالْإِيمَانِ، فَإِنَّ اللهَ تَعَالَى يَقُولُ: "إِنَّمَا يَعْمُرُ مَسَاجِدَ اللهِ مَنْ آمَنَ بِاللهِ وَالْيَوْمِ
الْآخِرِ وَأَقَامَ الصَّلَاةَ وَآتَى الزَّكَاةَ". رواه الترمذي.

[85]   On the authority of Abū Saʿīd al-Khudrī ﷺ, who said:
The Messenger of Allah ﷺ said, "When you see a man regularly
attending the mosque, bear witness that he has faith, for Allah
the Exalted truly says, '*It only becomes those who believe in Allah
and the Last Day and establish Prayer and pay* Zakāh [Alms-tax] *and
fear none but Allah to visit and tend the mosques of Allah*'".[36] Tirmidhī
(*Mishkāt*, Book of Prayer, *Ḥadīth* no. 723).

عَنْ بُرَيْدَةَ الْأَسْلَمِيِّ ﷺ، عَنِ النَّبِيِّ ﷺ قَالَ: بَشِّرِ الْمَشَّائِينَ فِي الظُّلَمِ إِلَى الْمَسَاجِدِ بِالنُّورِ
التَّامِّ يَوْمَ الْقِيَامَةِ. رواه الترمذي.

---

36.   *Sūrah al-Tawbah*, 9: 18.

[86] On the authority of Buraydah al-Aslamī ﷺ, who said: The Messenger of Allah ﷺ said, "Give glad-tidings of brilliant light on the Day of Resurrection to those who regularly walk to the mosques in darkness." Tirmidhī, Abū Dāwūd and Ibn Mājah (*Mishkāt*, Book of Prayer, *Ḥadīth* nos. 721-2).

6.2 *ZAKĀT* (GIVING ALMS)

عَنْ أَبِي هُرَيْرَةَ ﷺ قَالَ: قَالَ رَسُولَ الله ﷺ: مَثَلُ الْبَخِيلِ وَالْمُنْفِقِ كَمَثَلِ رَجُلَيْنِ عَلَيْهِمَا جُبَّتَانِ مِنْ حَدِيدٍ قَدْ اضطَرَّتْ أَيْدِهِمَا إلى ثَدِيِهِمَا وَتَرَاقِهِمَا، فَجَعَلَ الْمُتَصَدِقُ كُلَّمَا تَصَدَّقَ بِصَدَقَةٍ انْبَسَطَتْ عَنْهُ، وَجَعَلَ الْبَخِيلُ كُلَّمَا هَمَّ بِصَدَقَةٍ قَلَصَتْ وَأَخَذَتْ كُلُّ حَلَقَةٍ بِمَكَانِهَا. صحيح مسلم - كتاب الزكاة.

[87] On the authority of Abū Hurayrah ﷺ, who said: The Messenger of Allah ﷺ said, "The similitude of the miser and the giver is that of two men wearing iron suits of armour, with their arms pressed against their chests and necks. Whenever the benefactor gives charity, the armour loosens for him. Whenever the miser thinks of giving charity, the armour tightens and each link [of the chain-mail] remains firmly in its place." *Ṣaḥīḥ Muslim*, Book of *Zakāt*.

عَنْ عَائِشَةَ ﷺ قَالَتْ: سِمِعْتُ رَسُولَ اللهِ ﷺ يَقُولُ: مَا خَالَطَتِ الزَّكَاةُ مالاً قطُّ إلا أهلكته. مشكواة، كتاب الزكاة.

[88] On the authority of 'Ā'ishah ﷺ, who said: I heard the Messenger of Allah ﷺ saying, "Whenever *zakāt* wealth mixes with any wealth, it destroys it." Shāfi'ī, Hūmaydī, Bukhārī in his *Tārīkh* and Bayhaqī. (*Mishkāt*, Book of *Zakāt*, *Ḥadīth* no. 1793).

Commentary

The commentators on this *Ḥadīth* have given two meanings for the mixing of *zakāt* wealth.

1. For any wealth upon which *zakāt* is obligatory, if *zakāt* is not given from it, then the entire wealth becomes accursed and is deprived of blessing. Morally and legally, it does not

deserve to be used by a Muslim. Therefore, it is as though it has perished and been destroyed.

2. If a person takes *zakāt* from people despite being well-off and undeserving of *zakāt*, he makes all his wealth impure by mixing *zakāt* and charity with his lawful earnings.[37]

6.3 FASTING

عَنْ أَبِي هُرَيْرَةَ ﷺ قَالَ: قَالَ رَسُولُ اللهِ ﷺ: مَنْ لَمْ يَدَعْ قَوْلَ الزُّورِ وَالْعَمَلَ بِهِ، فَلَيْسَ لله حَاجَةٌ فِي أَنْ يَدَعَ طَعَامَهُ وَشَرَابَهُ. صحيح البخاري.

[89] On the authority of Abū Hurayrah ﷺ, who said: The Messenger of Allah ﷺ said, "Whoever does not give up speaking falsehood and acting upon it, Allah has no need of his [fasting and] giving up his food and drink."[38] Bukhārī (*Mishkāt*, Book of Fasting, *Ḥadīth* no. 1999).

6.4 *ḤAJJ* (PILGRIMAGE)

عَنْ أَبِي هُرَيْرَةَ ﷺ قَالَ: قَالَ رَسُولُ اللهِ ﷺ: مَنْ أَتَى هَذَا الْبَيْتَ، فَلَمْ يَرْفُثْ وَلَمْ يَفْسُقْ، رَجَعَ كَمَا وَلَدَتْهُ أُمُّهُ. صحيح مسلم.

[90] On the authority of Abū Hurayrah ﷺ, who said: The Messenger of Allah ﷺ said, "Whoever visits this House [of Allah] and does not become involved in obscenity and sinfulness, he returns [purified and clean] as the day his mother gave birth to him." *Ṣaḥīḥ Muslim*, Book of *Ḥajj*.

6.5 THE IMPORTANCE OF VOLUNTARY WORSHIP

عَنْ أَبِي هُرَيْرَةَ ﷺ قَالَ: قَالَ رَسُولُ اللهِ ﷺ: إِنَّ أَوَّلَ مَا يُحَاسَبُ بِهِ الْعَبْدُ يَوْمَ الْقِيَامَةِ مِنْ عَمَلِهِ صَلَاتُهُ، فَإِنْ صَلُحَتْ، فَقَدْ أَفْلَحَ وَأَنْجَحَ، وَإِنْ فَسَدَتْ فَقَدْ خَابَ وَخَسِرَ، فَإِنْ

---

37. This explanation of the *ḥadīth* is given by Imām Aḥmad b. Ḥanbal, as quoted in *Mishkāt*. – Trans. Note

38. This means that the reward of fasting is removed, but not its obligation. – Trans. Note

انْتَقَصَ مِنْ فَرِيضَتِهِ شَيْءٌ، قَالَ الرَّبُّ عَزَّ وَجَلَّ: انْظُرُوا هَلْ لِعَبْدِي مِنْ تَطَوُّعٍ فَيُكَمَّلَ بِهَا مَا انْتَقَصَ مِنَ الْفَرِيضَةِ، ثُمَّ يَكُونُ سَائِرُ عَمَلِهِ عَلَى ذَلِكَ. وفي رواية: ثُمَّ الزَّكَاةُ، ثُمَّ الأَعْمَالُ عَلَى حَسَبِ ذَلِكَ. رواه أبو داود.

[91] On the authority of Abū Hurayrah ﷺ, who said: The Messenger of Allah ﷺ said, "Truly, the first matter for which a servant [of Allah] will be taken to account on the Day of Resurrection will be his prayers. If these are sound, he will have succeeded; if they are corrupt, he will have failed and lost. If there is any shortcoming in his obligatory duties, the Lord, Blessed and Exalted, says, 'See: does my servant have any voluntary deeds by which the shortcoming in his obligatory duties may be rectified?' Next, all his deeds will be assessed in this manner." In one narration, "Next, the *zakāt* will be assessed similarly; then, all the deeds will be taken [account of] in this way." Aḥmad, Abū Dāwūd, Nasā'ī, Tirmidhī and Ḥākim (*Mishkāt*, Book of Prayer, *Ḥadīth* nos. 1330-1).

عَنْ أَبِي هُرَيْرَةَ ﷺ قَالَ: قَالَ رَسُولُ اللهِ ﷺ: رَحِمَ اللهُ رَجُلًا قَامَ مِنَ اللَّيْلِ، فَصَلَّى، وَأَيْقَظَ امْرَأَتَهُ، فَصَلَّتْ. فَإِنْ أَبَتْ، نَضَحَ فِي وَجْهِهَا الْمَاءَ. رَحِمَ اللهُ امْرَأَةً قَامَتْ مِنَ اللَّيْلِ، فَصَلَّتْ، وَأَيْقَظَتْ زَوْجَهَا. فَإِنْ أَبَى، نَضَحَتْ فِي وَجْهِهِ الْمَاءَ. رواه أبو داود.

[92] On the authority of Abū Hurayrah ﷺ, who said: The Messenger of Allah ﷺ said, "May Allah have mercy upon a man who wakes up at night and stands in prayer, then wakes his wife so that she may also pray. If she refuses, he sprinkles water on her face. May Allah have mercy upon a woman who wakes up at night and stands in prayer, then wakes her husband so that he may also pray. If he refuses, she sprinkles water on his face." Abū Dāwūd (*Mishkāt*, Book of Prayer, *Ḥadīth* no. 1230).

عَنْ مُعَاذِ بْنِ جَبَلٍ ﷺ، عَنِ النَّبِيِّ ﷺ قَالَ: مَا مِنْ مُسْلِمٍ يَبِيتُ عَلَى ذِكْرٍ طَاهِرًا، فَيَتَعَارُّ مِنَ اللَّيْلِ، فَيَسْأَلُ اللهَ خَيْرًا، إِلا أَعْطَاهُ اللهُ إِيَّاهُ. رواه أحمد.

[93] On the authority of Mu'ādh b. Jabal ﷺ, who said: The Messenger of Allah ﷺ said, "Any Muslim who goes to sleep

remembering Allah in a state of purity, then awakes at night and asks Allah for goodness and blessing, Allah answers [his supplication] and grants it to him." Aḥmad and Abū Dāwūd (*Mishkāt*, Book of Prayer, *Ḥadīth* no. 1215).

6.6 REMEMBRANCE AND RECITATION

وعَنْ أَبي سَعِيدٍ ﷺ قَالَ: جَاءَ رَجُلٌ إلى رَسُولِ اللهِ ﷺ، فَقَالَ: يا رَسُولَ اللهِ أَوْصِني. قال: عَلَيْكَ بتَقْوى اللهِ، فإنَّهَا جِمَاعُ كُلِّ خَيْرٍ، وعَلَيْكَ بالجِهَادِ في سَبيلِ الله، فإنَّها رَهْبَانِيَّةُ المُسْلِمِينَ، وَعَلَيْكَ بذِكْرِ اللهِ وَتلاوَةِ كِتَابِهِ، فإنَّهُ نُورٌ لَكَ في ألارْضِ، وذِكْرٌ لَكَ في السَّماءِ، واخْزُنْ لِسَانَكَ إلاَّ مِنْ خَيْرٍ، فَإنَّكَ بِذَلِكَ تَغْلِبُ الشَّيْطَانَ. رواه الطبراني وأبو يعلى في مسنده.

[94] On the authority of Abū Saʿīd ﷺ, who said: A man came to the Prophet ﷺ and said, "O Messenger of Allah! Advise me." He replied, "Make the *taqwā* [fear, consciousness] of Allah binding upon yourself, for it gathers every goodness. Make *Jihād* binding upon yourself, for it is the monasticism of the Muslims. Make the remembrance of Allah and the recitation of His Book binding upon yourself, for it is a light for you on the earth and a remembrance of you in the heavens. Withhold your tongue from everything except goodness, for then you will surely overcome Satan." *Al-Muʿjam al-Ṣaghīr* of Ṭabarānī and *Musnad* of Abū Yaʿlā.

عَنْ ابْنِ عُمَرَ ﷺ قَالَ: قَالَ رَسُولُ اللهِ ﷺ: إنَّ هذهِ الْقُلُوبَ تَصْدَأُ كَما يَصْدَأُ الْحَدِيدُ، إذَا أَصَابَهُ الْمَاءُ، قِيلَ: وَمَا جَلاؤُهَا؟ قَالَ: كَثْرَةُ ذِكْرِ الْمَوْتِ، وَتِلاوَةُ الْقُرْآنِ. رواه البيهقي.

[95] On the authority of Ibn ʿUmar ﷺ, who said: The Messenger of Allah ﷺ said, "Truly, these hearts rust the way iron rusts when touched by water." It was asked, "O Messenger of Allah! How can they be polished?" He replied, "By plentiful remembrance of death and recitation of the Qur'ān." Bayhaqī (*Mishkāt*, Book of the Virtues of the Qur'ān, *Ḥadīth* no. 2168).

عَنْ جُنْدَبِ بْنِ عَبْدِ اللهِ ﷺ، عَنِ النَّبِيِّ ﷺ قَالَ: اقْرَءُوا الْقُرْآنَ مَا ائْتَلَفَتْ عَلَيْهِ قُلُوبُكُمْ، فَإِذَا اخْتَلَفْتُمْ، فَقُومُوا عَنْهُ. متفق عليه.

[96] On the authority of Jundub b. ʿAbdullāh ﷺ, who said: The Messenger of Allah ﷺ said, "Recite the Qur'ān as long as your hearts are drawn towards it. When you feel drawn away from it, then [stop reciting and] get up." Bukhārī and Muslim (*Mishkāt*, Book of the Virtues of the Qur'ān, *Ḥadīth* no. 2190).

Commentary

The Majestic Qur'ān should be recited in a state of joy and enthusiasm. If one feels burdened by it, it is not appropriate to force oneself to recite the Qur'ān.

6.7 ABUNDANT REMEMBRANCE OF ALLAH ﷻ

وَعَنْ عَبْدِ الله بن بُسر ﷺ قَالَ: جاءَ أَعْرَابِيٌّ إِلى النبيِّ ﷺ، فقَالَ: أَيُّ النَّاسِ خيْرٌ؟ فَقَالَ: طُوبَى لِمَنْ طَالَ عُمُرُهُ، وحَسُنَ عمَلُهُ. قَالَ: يا رسولَ الله! أيُّ الأعمالِ أَفضلُ؟ قَالَ: أَنْ تُفارِقَ الدُّنْيَا وَلِسَانُكَ رَطْبٌ مِنْ ذِكْرِ الله. رواه أحمد والترمذي، مشكواة، باب ذكر الله.

[97] On the authority of ʿAbdullāh b. Busr ﷺ, who said: A Bedouin came to the Prophet ﷺ and asked, "Which of the people is best?" He replied, "Glad-tidings for the person whose life is long and his deeds beautiful." He asked, "O Messenger of Allah! Which deeds are most virtuous?" He replied, "That you depart from the world with your tongue moist with the remembrance of Allah." Aḥmad and Tirmidhī (*Mishkāt*, Book of Supplications, *Ḥadīth* no. 2270).

عَنْ أَبِي هُرَيْرَةَ ﷺ، عَنْ رَسُولُ الله ﷺ، أَنَّهُ قَالَ: مَنْ قَعَدَ مَقْعَدًا لَمْ يَذْكُرْ اللهَ فِيهِ كَانَتْ عَلَيْهِ مِنَ اللهِ تِرَةٌ، وَمَنْ اضْطَجَعَ مَضْجَعًا لا يَذْكُرُ اللهَ فِيهِ كَانَتْ عَلَيْهِ مِنَ اللهِ تِرَةٌ. أبو داود، مشكواة، باب ذكر الله.

[98] On the authority of Abū Hurayrah ﵁, who said: The Messenger of Allah ﷺ said, "Whoever sits somewhere without remembering Allah, will be punished by Allah. Whoever lies down somewhere without remembering Allah, will be punished by Allah." Abū Dāwūd (*Mishkāt*, Book of Supplications, *Ḥadīth* no. 2272).

6.8 SUPPLICATION AND ITS ETIQUETTE

عَنْ أَبِي هُرَيْرَةَ ﵁، عَنْ النَّبِيِّ ﷺ، أَنَّهُ قَالَ: لا يَزَالُ يُسْتَجَابُ لِلْعَبْدِ مَا لَمْ يَدْعُ بِإِثْم، أَوْ قَطِيعَةِ رَحِم مَا لَمْ يَسْتَعْجِلْ. قِيلَ: يَا رَسُولَ اللهِ مَا الاسْتِعْجَالُ؟ قَالَ: يَقُولُ قَدْ دَعَوْتُ وَقَدْ دَعَوْتُ، فَلَمْ أَرَ يَسْتَجِيبُ لِي، فَيَسْتَحْسِرُ عِنْدَ ذَلِكَ، وَيَدَعُ الدُّعَاءَ. رواه مسلم.

[99] On the authority of Abū Hurayrah ﵁, who said: The Messenger of Allah ﷺ said, "The servant's supplications continue to be answered as long as he does not ask for something sinful or for the severing of family relations, and as long as he is not hasty." He was asked, "O Messenger of Allah! What is meant by haste [here]?" He replied, "The person says, 'I have supplicated, I have supplicated, but my supplication has not been answered,' and he becomes weary and ceases supplicating." Muslim (*Mishkāt*, Book of Supplications, *Ḥadīth* no. 2227).

عَنْ أَبِي الزُّبَيْرِ ﵁ قَالَ سَمِعْتُ عَبْدَ اللهِ بْنَ الزُّبَيْرِ عَلى الْمِنْبَرِ، يَقُولُ: كَانَ النَّبِيُّ ﷺ إِذَا انْصَرَفَ مِنْ الصَّلَاةِ، يَقُولُ بِصَوْتِهِ الأَعْلَى: لا إِلَهَ إِلا اللهُ وَحْدَهُ لا شَرِيكَ لَهُ لَهُ الْمُلْكُ وَلَهُ الْحَمْدُ وَهُوَ عَلى كُلِّ شَيْءٍ قَدِيرٌ، لا حول ولا قوة الا با لله، لا إِلَهَ إِلا اللهُ ولا نعبد الا اياه، لَهُ النِّعْمَةُ وَلَهُ الفَضْلُ وله الثَّنَاءُ الحَسَنُ لا إِلَهَ إِلا اللهُ مُخْلِصِينَ لَهُ الدِّينَ وَلَوْ كَرِهَ الْكَافِرُونَ. رواه مسلم.

[100] On the authority of Abu'l-Zubayr ﵁, who said that he heard 'Abdullāh b. al-Zubayr saying, whilst preaching from the pulpit: When the Messenger of Allah ﷺ had invoked the greeting of peace at the end of his prayers, he would say at the top of his voice, "There is no god except Allah, alone. He has no partner. To Him belongs the Kingdom, and to Him belongs all Praise. He is

Powerful over all things. There is neither movement nor power except by Allah. There is no god except Allah, and we worship no-one but Him. To Him belongs all Grace, to Him belongs all Bounty, and to Him belongs all Beautiful Praise. There is no god except Allah, making the religion sincere for Him, even if the unbelievers detest this." Muslim (*Mishkāt*, Book of Prayer, *Ḥadīth* no. 963).

عَنْ أَبِي أَيُّوب الأَنْصَارِيِّ ﷺ قَالَ: كَانَ رَسُولُ الله ﷺ إِذَا أَكَلَ أَوْ شَرِبَ، قَالَ: الْحَمْدُ لله الَّذِي أَطْعَمَ وَسَقَى وَسَوَّغَهُ وَجَعَلَ لَهُ مَخْرَجًا. رواه أبوداود، مشكواة، كتاب الأطعمة.

[101] On the authority of Abū Ayyūb al-Ansārī ﷺ, who said: when the Messenger of Allah ﷺ had eaten or drunk something, he would say, "Praise be to Allah, Who enabled us to eat and drink, made the meal agreeable and provided a way out for it [i.e. for bodily waste]." Abū Dāwūd (*Mishkāt*, Book of Foodstuffs, *Ḥadīth* no. 4207).

عَنْ ابْنَ عُمَرَ ﷺ، أَنَّ رَسُولَ الله ﷺ كَانَ إِذَا اسْتَوَى عَلى بَعِيرِهِ خَارِجًا إِلى سَفَر، كَبَّرَ ثَلاثًا، ثُمَّ قَالَ: « **سُبْحَانَ الَّذِي سَخَّرَ لَنَا هَذَا وَمَا كُنَّا لَهُ مُقْرِنِينَ، وَإِنَّا إِلى رَبِّنَا لَمُنْقَلِبُونَ**» اللَّهُمَّ إِنَّا نَسْأَلُكَ فِي سَفَرِنَا هَذَا الْبِرَّ وَالتَّقْوَى وَمِنَ الْعَمَلِ مَا تَرْضَى، اللَّهُمَّ هَوِّنْ عَلَيْنَا سَفَرَنَا هَذَا وَاطْوِ عَنَّا بُعْدَهُ، اللَّهُمَّ أَنْتَ الصَّاحِبُ فِي السَّفَرِ وَالْخَلِيفَةُ فِي الأَهْلِ، اللَّهُمَّ إِنِّي أَعُوذُ بِكَ مِنْ وَعْثَاءِ السَّفَرِ وَكَآبَةِ الْمَنْظَرِ وَسُوءِ الْمُنْقَلَبِ فِي الْمَالِ وَالأَهْلِ. وَإِذَا رَجَعَ قَالَهُنَّ، وَزَادَ فِيهِنَّ: آيِبُونَ تَائِبُونَ عَابِدُونَ لِرَبِّنَا حَامِدُونَ. رواه مسلم.

[102] On the authority of Ibn 'Umar ﷺ that when the Messenger of Allah ﷺ sat on a camel intending a journey, he would magnify the glory of Allah[39] three times and then say, "*Glory be to Him Who has subjected this to us whereas we did not have the strength to subdue it. It is to our Lord that we shall eventually return.* [Qur'ān, 43: 13-14] O Allah! Truly, we ask of You in this

39. i.e. by saying *Allāhu akbar* ("Allah is the Greatest").

journey of ours: goodness and God-consciousness, and those deeds with which You are pleased. O Allah! Make this journey of ours easy for us, and fold up its distance for us. O Allah! You are our Companion during the journey, and our Trustee over our households. O Allah! Truly, I seek refuge with You from the hardship of travelling, from seeing sorrowful sights and from returning to find misfortune affecting wealth and family." When he began the return journey, he would also say these words and add, "[We are] returning, repentant, devoted: for our Lord, full of praise." Muslim (*Mishkāt*, Book of Supplications, *Ḥadīth* no. 2420).

عَنْ أَبِي هُرَيْرَةَ ﵁ قَالَ: كَانَ رَسُولُ اللهِ ﷺ يَقُولُ: اللَّهُمَّ أَصْلِحْ لِي دِينِي الَّذِي هُوَ عِصْمَةُ أَمْرِي، وَأَصْلِحْ لِي دُنْيَايَ الَّتِي فِيهَا مَعَاشِي، وَأَصْلِحْ لِي آخِرَتِي الَّتِي فِيهَا مَعَادِي، وَاجْعَلْ الْحَيَاةَ زِيَادَةً لِي فِي كُلِّ خَيْرٍ، وَاجْعَلْ الْمَوْتَ رَاحَةً لِي مِنْ كُلِّ شَرٍّ. رواه مسلم.

[103] On the authority of Abū Hurayrah ﵁, who said: The Messenger of Allah ﷺ used to say, "O Allah! Rectify my religion for me, for it is my protection. Rectify my worldly matters for me, for my livelihood is there. Rectify my Hereafter for me, for it is my destination. Increase life for me in every goodness, and make death an escape for me from every evil." Muslim (*Mishkāt*, Book of Supplications, *Ḥadīth* no. 2483).

عَنْ أَبِي سَعِيدٍ الْخُدْرِيِّ ﵁ قَالَ: دَخَلَ رَسُولُ اللهِ ﷺ ذَاتَ يَوْمٍ الْمَسْجِدَ، فَإِذَا هُوَ بِرَجُلٍ مِنْ الْأَنْصَارِ يُقَالُ لَهُ أَبُو أُمَامَةَ، فَقَالَ: يَا أَبَا أُمَامَةَ مَا لِي أَرَاكَ جَالِسًا فِي الْمَسْجِدِ فِي غَيْرِ وَقْتِ الصَّلَاةِ؟ قَالَ: هُمُومٌ لَزِمَتْنِي وَدُيُونٌ يَا رَسُولَ اللهِ. قَالَ: أَفَلَا أُعَلِّمُكَ كَلَامًا إِذَا أَنْتَ قُلْتَهُ أَذْهَبَ اللهُ عَزَّ وَجَلَّ هَمَّكَ وَقَضَى عَنْكَ دَيْنَكَ. قَالَ: قُلْتُ بَلَى يَا رَسُولَ اللهِ. قَالَ: قُلْ إِذَا أَصْبَحْتَ وَإِذَا أَمْسَيْتَ اللَّهُمَّ إِنِّي أَعُوذُ بِكَ مِنْ الْهَمِّ وَالْحَزَنِ وَأَعُوذُ بِكَ مِنْ الْعَجْزِ وَالْكَسَلِ وَأَعُوذُ بِكَ مِنْ الْجُبْنِ وَالْبُخْلِ وَأَعُوذُ بِكَ مِنْ غَلَبَةِ الدَّيْنِ وَقَهْرِ الرِّجَالِ. قَالَ: فَفَعَلْتُ ذَلِكَ، فَأَذْهَبَ اللهُ عَزَّ وَجَلَّ هَمِّي وَقَضَى عَنِّي دَيْنِي. رواه أبو داود.

[104] On the authority of Abū Sa'īd al-Khudrī ﵁, who said that the Messenger of Allah ﷺ entered the mosque one day and

found a man from the Anṣār there called Abū Umāmah. He asked him, "O Abū Umāmah! Why do I see you sitting in the mosque outside the times of prayer?" The man replied, "Worries and debts have taken hold of me, O Messenger of Allah!" He replied, "Should I not then teach you some words which, if you say them, Allah will remove your worries and enable you to repay your debts?" He said, "Of course." He said, "Every morning and every evening, say: O Allah! Truly, I seek refuge with You from worry and grief. I seek refuge with You from incapacity and laziness. I seek refuge with You from cowardice and miserliness. I seek refuge with You from being overcome by debt and overpowered by men." He said, "So I did that: Allah removed my worries and enabled the repayment of my debts." Abū Dāwūd (*Mishkāt*, Book of Supplications, *Ḥadīth* no. 2448).

عَنْ ابْنِ عَبَّاسٍ ﵄ قَالَ: قَالَ رَسُولُ اللهِ ﷺ: لَوْ أَنَّ أَحَدَكُمْ إِذَا أَرَادَ أَنْ يَأْتِيَ أَهْلَهُ، فَقَالَ بِاسْمِ اللهِ اللَّهُمَّ جَنِّبْنَا الشَّيْطَانَ وَجَنِّبْ الشَّيْطَانَ مَا رَزَقْتَنَا، فَإِنَّهُ إِنْ يُقَدَّرْ بَيْنَهُمَا وَلَدٌ فِي ذَلِكَ لَمْ يَضُرَّهُ شَيْطَانٌ أَبَدًا. متفق عليه.

[105] On the authority of Ibn 'Abbās ﵄, who said: The Messenger of Allah ﷺ said, "When you wish to make love to your spouse, were you to say, 'With the Name of Allah. O Allah! Keep us away from Satan, and keep Satan away from that which You bestow upon us [i.e. children],' then if a child is decreed for the two of you, Satan will never harm the child." Bukhārī and Muslim (*Mishkāt*, Book of Supplications, *Ḥadīth* no. 2416).

عَنْ أَبِي مَالِكٍ الْأَشْعَرِيِّ ﵁ قَالَ: قَالَ رَسُولُ اللهِ ﷺ: إِذَا وَلَجَ الرَّجُلُ بَيْتَهُ، فَلْيَقُلْ: اللَّهُمَّ إِنِي أَسْأَلُكَ خَيْرَ الْمَوْلَجِ وَخَيْرَ الْمَخْرَجِ، بِسْمِ اللهِ وَلَجْنَا، وَبِسْمِ اللهِ خَرَجْنَا، وَعَلَى اللهِ رَبِّنَا تَوَكَّلْنَا، ثُمَّ لِيُسَلِّمْ عَلَى أَهْلِهِ. رواه ابو داود.

[106] On the authority of Abū Mālik al-Ash'arī ﵁, who said: The Messenger of Allah ﷺ said, "When a man enters his house he should say, 'O Allah! I ask of You goodness when entering and goodness when leaving. With the Name of Allah we enter,

with the Name of Allah we exit, and upon Allah, our Lord, we rely.' He should then greet his family." Abū Dāwūd (*Mishkāt*, Book of Supplications, *Ḥadīth* no. 2444).

وعَنْ أُمِّ مَعْبَدٍ ﵁ قَالَتْ: سَمِعْتُ رَسُول الله ﷺ يَقُول: اللَّهُمَّ طَهِّرْ قَلْبِي مِنَ النفَاق، وَعَمَلِي مِنَ الرِّيَاءِ، وَلِسَانِي مِنَ الْكَذِبِ، وَعَيْنِي مِنَ الْخِيَانَة، فَإِنَّكَ تَعْلَمُ خَائِنَةَ الأَعْيُنِ وَمَا تُخْفِي الصُّدُورُ. رواه البيهقي.

[107] On the authority of Umm Ma'bad ﵁, who said: I heard the Messenger of Allah ﷺ saying, "O Allah! Purify my heart from hypocrisy, my deeds from ostentation, my tongue from lying and my eye from treachery; for truly, You know the treachery of the eyes and what the hearts conceal." Bayhaqī (*Mishkāt*, Book of Supplications, *Ḥadīth* no. 2501).

7

Morality and Character

7.1 THE IMPORTANCE OF MORALITY IN ISLAM

عَنْ مَالِك ﷺ، أَنَّهُ قَدْ بَلَغَهُ أَنَّ رَسُولَ الله ﷺ قَالَ: بُعِثْتُ لِأُتَمِّمَ مَكَارِمَ الأَخْـلَاقِ. موطأ مالك.

[108] On the authority of Mālik ﷺ, whom it reached that the Messenger of Allah ﷺ said, "I was [only] sent to complete the noblest ethics." Mālik and Aḥmad, who transmitted it on the authority of Abū Hurayrah (*Mishkāt*, Book of Etiquette, *Ḥadīth* nos. 5096-7).

Commentary

By *makārim al-akhlāq* (the noblest ethics) is meant the best concepts, principles and qualities of morality, upon which a pure human life and a righteous human society may be based. By completion of the *makārim al-akhlāq* is meant that previous prophets ﷺ and their righteous followers upheld various aspects of virtuous morality through their teachings amongst different nations and lands at different times. Further, they continued to present outstanding manifestations of this morality in their practical lives. However, no all-embracing personality appeared during that time to explain completely the correct principles of morality related to all aspects of human life. Further, no such person had manifested these principles in his own life on the one hand, and built and maintained a society and system of government based on these principles on the other hand. This task remained outstanding, and it was precisely to fulfil it that the Prophet ﷺ was sent.

The Prophet ﷺ is himself referring to this task as the real objective of his mission. We learn from this that it was not some secondary task, i.e. that the Prophet's real mission was something else and that he accomplished this task along the way. Rather, this was the real task for which he was sent.

7.2 THE RELATIONSHIP BETWEEN FAITH AND MORALITY

عَـنْ أَبِي هُرَيْرَةَ ﷺ قَالَ: قَـالَ رَسُولُ اللهِ ﷺ: أَكْمَلُ الْمُؤْمِنِينَ إِيمَانًا أَحْسَنُهُمْ خُلُقًا. ابو داود.

[109] On the authority of Abū Hurayrah ﷺ, who said: The Messenger of Allah ﷺ said, "The most complete of the believers in faith are those with the best character [and morals]." Abū Dāwūd, Tirmidhī and Dārimī (*Mishkāt*, Book of Etiquette, *Ḥadīth* no. 5101; Book of Marriage, *Ḥadīth* no. 3264).

Commentary

In this narration, good morals and character have been made the measure of faith.

عَنْ أَبِي أُمَامَةَ ﷺ، أَنَّ رَجُلا سَأَلَ رَسُولَ اللهِ ﷺ: مَا الْإِيمَانُ؟ قَالَ: إِذَا سَرَّتْكَ حَسَنَتُكَ وَسَاءَتْكَ سَيِّئَتُكَ، فَأَنْتَ مُؤْمِنٌ. قَالَ: يَا رَسُولَ اللهِ فَمَا الْإِثْمُ؟ قَالَ: إِذَا حَاكَ فِي نَفْسِكَ شَيْءٌ فَدَعْهُ. رواه أحمد.

[110] On the authority of Abū Umāmah ﷺ: that a man asked the Messenger of Allah ﷺ, "What is faith?" He replied, "When your good deeds please you and your evil deeds grieve you, then you are a person of faith." The man asked, "O Messenger of Allah! Then what is sin?" He replied, "When something causes uncertainty in your heart, leave it." Aḥmad (*Mishkāt*, Book of Faith, *Ḥadīth* no. 45).

Commentary

This criterion of good and evil can only be considered when one's conscience is alive and the original natural state (*fiṭrah*) has not been disfigured by the negative effects of one's environment and evil deeds.

8

The Foundations of the Noblest Ethics

8.1 PIETY

عَـنْ عَطِيَّةَ السَّعْدِيِّ ﷺ، وَكَانَ مِـنْ أَصْـحَابِ النَّبِيِّ ﷺ، قَالَ: قَالَ رَسُولُ اللهِ ﷺ: لا يَبْلُغُ الْعَبْدُ أَنْ يَكُونَ مِـنْ الْمُتَّقِينَ حَتَّى يَـدَعَ مَا لا بَأْسَ بِـهِ حَذَرًا لِمَا بِهِ الْبَأْسُ. رواه الترمذي.

[111] On the authority of ʿAṭiyyah al-Saʿdī ﷺ, one of the Companions of the Prophet, who said: The Messenger of Allah ﷺ said, "A person does not reach the stage of being amongst the pious unless he leaves that which [apparently] has no sin, being wary of falling into that which is sinful." Tirmidhī and Ibn Mājah (*Mishkāt*, Book of Transactions, *Ḥadīth* no. 2775).

Commentary

Sometimes, lawful matters can also lead to prohibited matters. This is why the believer should not only look at whether something is lawful, but should always be alert in case a lawful action leads to the prohibited.

عَنْ عَائِشَةَ ﷺ، أَنَّ رَسُولَ اللهِ ﷺ قَالَ: يَا عَائِشَةُ إِيَّاكِ وَمُحَقَّرَاتِ الذُّنُوبِ، فَإِنَّ لَهَا مِنْ اللهِ طَالِبًا. رواه ابن ماجه.

[112] On the authority of ʿĀ'ishah ﵂ that the Messenger of Allah ﷺ said, "O ʿĀ'ishah! Beware of trivial sins, for truly there will be accountability before Allah regarding them." Ibn Mājah, Dārimī and Bayhaqī (*Mishkāt*, Book of Heart-Softening Matters, *Ḥadīth* no. 5356).

Commentary

Just as major sins endanger the salvation of a Muslim, minor sins are no less dangerous. A minor sin apparently seems small, but if it is committed over and over again, the heart becomes rusty and the hatred of major sins vanishes. Ḥāfiẓ Ibn al-Qayyim has written, "Do not look at how small the sin is. Bear in mind the Greatness of the Lord Who is being disobeyed." If the Majesty of the Master of the Day of Judgment and the terrors of His punishment were always kept in mind, a person would not dare to incline towards the smallest of sins.

8.2 PURITY OF METHODS AND MEANS OF LIVELIHOOD

وَعَنْ ابْنِ مَسْعُودٍ ﵁ قَالَ: قَالَ رَسُولُ الله ﷺ: إِنَّ نَفْساً لَنْ تَمُوتَ حَتَّى تَسْتَكمِلَ رِزْقَهَا، أَلا فَاتَّقُوا اللهَ، وأَجْمِلُوا في الطَلَبِ، ولا يَحْمِلَنَّكُمْ اسْتِبْطاءُ الرِّزْقِ أَنْ تَطْلُبُوهُ بِمَعاصي الله، فإِنَّهُ لا يُدرَكُ ما عِنْدَ الله إلاَّ بِطَاعتِهِ. رواه البغوي والبيهقي.

[113] On the authority of Ibn Masʿūd ﵁, who said: The Messenger of Allah ﷺ said, "No soul dies until it acquires all its livelihood [decreed by Allah]. Therefore, fear Allah and seek livelihood beautifully [i.e. lawfully]. Do not let a delay in acquiring livelihood prompt you to seek it through disobeying Allah, for what is with Him can only be acquired through obeying Him." Baghawī and Bayhaqī (*Mishkāt*, Book of Heart-Softening Matters, *Ḥadīth* no. 5300).

Commentary

This narration unveils some basic realities of the religion:

1. If a person experiences failure or delay in earning a livelihood, he should not despair. The livelihood that Allah has decreed for him will reach him all the same, sooner or later.

2. A person may disobey Allah and apparently be content and comfortable. However, this is actually a respite from Allah, after which the Divine Punishment lashes him. The real happiness and tranquillity is that gained by obeying Allah.

عَنْ عَبْدِ اللهِ ابْنِ مَسْعُودٍ ﵁، عَنْ رَسُولِ اللهِ ﷺ قَالَ: لا يَكْسِبُ عَبْدٌ مالا مِنْ حَرَام فَيَتَصَدَّقُ مِنْهُ، فَيُقْبَلُ مِنْهُ، فَيُبَارِكُ لَهُ فِيهِ، ولا يَتْرُكُهُ خَلْفَ ظَهْرِهِ إلاَّ كانَ زَادُهُ إلى النَّارِ، إنَّ اللهَ لا يَمْحُو السَّيِّئَ بالسَّيِّئِ ولَكِنْ يَمْحُو السَّيِّئَ بالحَسَنِ، إنَّ الخَبِيثَ لا يَمْحُو الخَبِيثَ.

رواه أحمد والبغوي.

[114] On the authority of ʿAbdullāh b. Masʿūd ﵁ that the Messenger of Allah ﷺ said, "If a person earns unlawful wealth and gives it in charity, it is not accepted from him and he is not blessed in it. If he leaves it accumulated, it is [only] his provision towards the Fire [i.e. it cannot become a means to happiness and success in the Hereafter]. Truly, Allah does not remove evil with evil: rather, He removes evil with goodness. Truly, the impure does not remove the impure." Aḥmad and Baghawī (*Mishkāt*, Book of Transactions, *Ḥadīth* no. 2771).

8.3 THE SEAT OF PIETY

عَنْ أَبِي هُرَيْرَةَ ﵁ قَالَ: قَالَ رَسُولُ اللهِ ﷺ: لا تَحَاسَدُوا وَلا تَنَاجَشُوا وَلا تَبَاغَضُوا وَلَا تَدَابَرُوا وَلا يَبِعْ بَعْضُكُمْ عَلى بَيْعِ بَعْضٍ وَكُونُوا عِبَادَ اللهِ إِخْوَانًا، الْمُسْلِمُ أَخُو الْمُسْلِمِ لَا يَظْلِمُهُ وَلا يَخْذُلُهُ وَلا يَحْقِرُهُ، التَّقْوَى هَاهُنَا، وَيُشِيرُ إِلى صَدْرِهِ ثَلَاثَ مَرَّاتٍ، بِحَسْبِ امْرِئٍ مِنَ الشَّرِّ أَنْ يَحْقِرَ أَخَاهُ الْمُسْلِمَ، كُلُّ الْمُسْلِمِ عَلَى الْمُسْلِمِ حَرَامٌ دَمُهُ وَمَالُهُ وَعِرْضُهُ.

رواه مسلم.

[115] On the authority of Abū Hurayrah ﵁, who said: The Messenger of Allah ﷺ said, "Do not envy one another. Do not inflate prices over each other. Do not hate each other. Do not turn your backs on each other. Do not undercut one another in business transactions. Be servants of Allah, as brothers. The Muslim is the brother of the Muslim. He should not oppress him. He should not disgrace him [by leaving him helpless]. He

should not regard him with contempt. Piety is here" – and he pointed to his chest, repeating the last sentence three times. "It is enough evil for a person to regard his brother Muslim with contempt. Every Muslim is totally inviolable for all Muslims: his blood, his wealth, his dignity." Muslim (*Mishkāt*, Book of Etiquette, *Ḥadīth* no. 4959).

Commentary

In this *Ḥadīth*, several matters have been indicated:

1. It is a requirement of Islamic brotherhood that a Muslim must neither oppress another Muslim nor hand him over to oppressors. He must not regard anyone else with contempt due to his own superiority in wealth, family, physique or knowledge.
2. The real seat of *taqwā* (piety) is the heart. If the seed of *taqwā* takes root in the heart, a person's exterior will remain evergreen and fresh with the sprouting of righteous actions. However, if there is not even a trace of *taqwā* in the heart, then external pious forms and actions will neither improve a person's character nor save him in the Hereafter.
3. In a Muslim society, to violate any Muslim's life, wealth or dignity is an extremely despicable act. The punishment for this is severe in this world, and the perpetrator cannot easily escape Allah's punishment in the Hereafter.

8.4 SIGNS OF PIETY

عَنْ الْحَسَنِ بْنِ عَلِيٍّ ﷺ قَالَ: حَفِظْتُ مِنْ رَسُولِ اللهِ ﷺ: دَعْ مَا يَرِيبُكَ إِلى مَا لا يَرِيبُكَ، فَإِنَّ الصِّدْقَ طُمَأْنِينَةٌ، وَإِنَّ الْكَذِبَ رِيبَةٌ. رواه الترمذي.

[116] On the authority of al-Ḥasan b. ʿAlī ﷺ, who said: I preserved this from the Messenger of Allah ﷺ, "Leave that which gives you doubt for that which does not give you doubt, for truthfulness is calmness [and tranquillity] whilst falsehood is uncertainty [and doubt]." Aḥmad, Tirmidhī and Nasāʾī (*Mishkāt*, Book of Transactions, *Ḥadīth* no. 2773).

Commentary

If a matter is doubtful on the basis of direct and circumstantial evidence and there is no obvious indication of lawfulness or prohibition, then instead of becoming involved in uncertainty and doubt, such a course of action should be taken that is based on certainty or at least on a strong likelihood. However, this does not mean that one becomes unnecessarily involved in speculation, creating doubts and misconceptions.

عَنْ أَسْمَاءَ بِنْتِ يَزِيدَ ﵂، أَنَّهَا سَمِعَتْ رَسُولَ اللهِ ﷺ يَقُولُ: أَلَا أُنَبِّئُكُمْ بِخِيَارِكُمْ؟ قَالُوا: بَلَى يَا رَسُولَ اللهِ. قَالَ: خِيَارُكُمْ الَّذِينَ إِذَا رُءُوا ذُكِرَ اللهُ عَزَّ وَجَلَّ. رواه ابن ماجه.

[117] On the authority of Asmā' bint Yazīd ﵂ that she heard the Messenger of Allah ﷺ saying, "Shall I not inform you of the best among you?" They replied, "Of course, O Messenger of Allah!" He said, "The best of you are those who, when they are seen, Allah the Mighty and Majestic is remembered." Aḥmad, Ibn Mājah and Bayhaqī (*Mishkāt*, Book of Etiquette, *Ḥadīth* nos. 4871-2, 5023).

Commentary

When the joy of *taqwā* appears in the heart, its effects become manifest externally. The insight and intelligence of a believer become so perceptive that no matter what, he remains a person of Truth whose fear of Allah affects all that is around him.

8.5 EXTREMISM IN PIETY

عَنْ أَبِي هُرَيْرَةَ ﵁ قَالَ: قَالَ رَسُولُ اللهِ ﷺ: إِذَا دَخَلَ أَحَدُكُمْ عَلَى أَخِيهِ الْمُسْلِمِ، فَأَطْعَمَهُ طَعَامًا، فَلْيَأْكُلْ مِنْ طَعَامِهِ، وَلَا يَسْأَلْهُ عَنْهُ، فَإِنْ سَقَاهُ شَرَابًا مِنْ شَرَابِهِ، فَلْيَشْرَبْ مِنْ شَرَابِهِ وَلَا يَسْأَلْهُ عَنْهُ. رواه أحمد والبيهقي.

[118] On the authority of Abū Hurayrah ﵁, who said: The Prophet ﷺ said, "When one of you visits his Muslim brother, he should eat from his food and not enquire about it, and drink

from his drink and not enquire about it." Transmitted by Aḥmad, Bayhaqī, and *Mishkāt*, Book of Marriage, *Ḥadīth* no. 3228.

Commentary

A person should keep a good opinion of other Muslims, so when he receives a gift of food or an invitation to a meal, he should not ask detailed questions about the origin of the food. The expectation should be maintained that other Muslims eat what is lawful and feed their friends and loved ones only that which is lawful and pure.[40]

8.6 TRUST IN GOD

عَنْ أَنَسِ بْنَ مَالِكٍ ﷺ يَقُولُ: قَالَ رَجُلٌ: يَا رَسُولَ اللهِ ﷺ أَعْقِلُهَا وَأَتَوَكَّلُ أَوْ أُطْلِقُهَا وَأَتَوَكَّلُ؟ قَالَ: اعْقِلْهَا وَتَوَكَّلْ. رواه الترمذي.

[119] On the authority of Anas b. Mālik ﷺ, who said that a man asked, "O Messenger of Allah ﷺ! Shall I tie my camel and trust [in Allah] or release it and trust [in Him]?" He replied, "Tie it and trust [in Allah]." Transmitted by Tirmidhī.

عَنْ عُمَرَ بْنَ الْخَطَّابِ ﷺ يَقُولُ: إِنَّهُ سَمِعَ نَبِيَّ اللهِ ﷺ يَقُولُ: لَوْ أَنَّكُمْ تَتَوَكَّلُونَ عَلَى اللهِ حَقَّ تَوَكُّلِهِ لَرَزَقَكُمْ كَمَا يَرْزُقُ الطَّيْرَ، تَغْدُو خِمَاصًا وَتَرُوحُ بِطَانًا. رواه الترمذي.

[120] On the authority of ʿUmar b. al-Khaṭṭāb ﷺ, who said: I heard the Messenger of Allah ﷺ saying, "Were you to place your trust [totally] in Allah as it should be placed, He would give you sustenance the way He sustains the birds: they go out in the morning hungry and return in the evening with bellies full." Tirmidhī and Ibn Mājah (*Mishkāt*, Book of Heart-Softening Matters, *Ḥadīth* no. 5299).

---

40. This commentary endorses Imām Bayhaqī's own explanation of this *Ḥadīth*. – Trans. Note

Commentary

By this comparison with the birds, the Messenger of Allah ﷺ has unveiled the reality that *tawakkul* (trust in God) is not that a person sits at home with his hands and feet inactive: rather, *tawakkul* is to employ God-given methods and means whilst entrusting the results to Allah.

عَنْ عَوْفِ بْنِ مَالِك ﵁: أَنَّ النَّبِيَّ ﷺ قَضى بَيْنَ رَجُلَيْن، فَقَالَ الْمَقْضِيُّ عَلَيْهِ لَمَّا أَدْبَرَ: حَسْبِيَ اللهُ وَنِعْمَ الْوَكِيلُ. فَقَالَ النَّبِيُّ ﷺ: إِنَّ اللهَ يَلُومُ عَلى الْعَجْزِ، وَلَكِنْ عَلَيْكَ بِالْكَيْسِ، فَإِذَا غَلَبَكَ أَمْرٌ، فَقُلْ: حَسْبِيَ اللهُ وَنِعْمَ الْوَكِيلُ. رواه أبو داود.

[121] On the authority of ʿAwf b. Mālik ﵁ that the Prophet ﷺ passed judgment between two men. The one against whom the verdict went said, "Allah is sufficient for me and what an excellent Guardian He is!", as he turned to go. The Prophet ﷺ said, "Lacking aspiration is blameworthy before Allah. Have ambition and determination, but if a matter overpowers you, then say, 'Allah is sufficient for me and what an excellent Guardian He is!'" Abū Dāwūd (*Mishkāt*, Book of Governance and Judgment, *Ḥadīth* no. 3784).

8.7 A MODEL OF TRUST IN GOD

عَنْ ابْنِ عَبَّاس ﵄ قَالَ: حَسْبُنَا اللهُ وَنِعْمَ الْوَكِيلُ قَالَهَا إِبْرَاهِيمُ عَلَيْهِ السَّلَام حِينَ أُلْقِيَ فِي النَّار، وَقَالَهَا مُحَمَّدٌ ﷺ حِينَ قَالُوا إِنَّ النَّاسَ قَدْ جَمَعُوا لَكُمْ فَاخْشَوْهُمْ فَزَادَهُمْ إِيمَانًا وَقَالُوا حَسْبُنَا اللهُ وَنِعْمَ الْوَكِيلُ. صحيح البخاري.

[122] On the authority of Ibn ʿAbbās ﵄ who said: "Enough for us is Allah, an excellent Protector!" was said by Ibrāhīm ﵇ when he was thrown into the fire, and by Muḥammad ﷺ when they said, "*Behold, a host has gathered around you and you should fear them.*" But it only increased them in faith, and they said: "*Allah is sufficient for us; and what an excellent Guardian He is!*" [Qur'ān, *Āl ʿImrān*, 3: 173] Bukhārī.

8.8 GRATITUDE

عَنْ أَبِي هُرَيْرَةَ ﵁، عَنِ النَّبِيِّ ﷺ قَـــالَ: الطَّاعِمُ الشَّاكِرُ بِمَنْزِلَةِ الصَّائِمِ الصَّابِرِ. رواه الترمذي.

[123] On the authority of Abū Hurayrah ﵁, who said: The Messenger of Allah ﷺ said, "One who eats gratefully is at the same level as one who fasts patiently." Tirmidhī, Ibn Mājah and Dārimī (*Mishkāt*, Book of Foodstuffs, *Ḥadīth* nos. 4205-6).

Commentary

This means that the one who shows patience and fasts optionally and the one who shows gratitude and eats of God-given lawful earnings during the day are equal in rank before Allah. The *Ḥadīth* gives some idea of the exalted status of gratitude before Allah.

عَنْ أَبِي هُرَيْرَةَ ﵁، أَنَّ رَسُولَ الله ﷺ قَالَ: انْظُرُوا إِلَى مَنْ هُوَ أَسْفَلَ مِنْكُمْ، وَلَا تَنْظُرُوا إِلَى مَنْ هُوَ فَوْقَكُمْ فَهُوَ أَجْدَرُ أَنْ لَا تَزْدَرُوا نِعْمَةَ الله عَلَيْكُمْ. رواه مسلم، وقال: إِذَا نَظَرَ أَحَدُكُمْ إِلَى مَنْ فُضِّلَ عَلَيْهِ فِي الْمَالِ وَالْخَلْقِ، فَلْيَنْظُرْ إِلَى مَنْ هُوَ أَسْــفَلَ مِنْهُ. متفق عليه.

[124] On the authority of Abū Hurayrah ﵁, who said: The Messenger of Allah ﷺ said, "Look at those below you [in wealth, power and reputation] and do not look at those above you [in these respects], for that will lead you to not belittle Allah's favours upon you."

In one narration, "If one of you looks at someone who has been favoured over him in wealth and power, then he should look at someone who is below him [in these respects]." Bukhārī and Muslim (*Mishkāt*, Book of Heart-Softening Matters, *Ḥadīth* no. 5242).

8.9 ṢABR (PATIENCE, PERSEVERANCE, STEADFASTNESS)

عَنْ صُهَيْبٍ ﵁ قَالَ: قَالَ رَسُولُ الله ﷺ: عَجَبًا لِأَمْرِ الْمُؤْمِنِ إِنَّ أَمْرَهُ كُلَّهُ خَيْرٌ، وَلَيْسَ ذَاكَ لِأَحَدٍ إِلَّا لِلْمُؤْمِنِ، إِنْ أَصَابَتْهُ سَرَّاءُ شَكَرَ، فَكَانَ خَيْرًا لَهُ، وَإِنْ أَصَابَتْهُ ضَرَّاءُ صَبَرَ، فَكَانَ خَيْرًا لَهُ. رواه مسلم.

[125]   On the authority of Ṣuhayb ☼, who said: The Messenger of Allah ☼ said, "Wonderful is the situation of the believer: all his matters are good for him, and this is only for the believer. If good fortune befalls him, he shows gratitude, so that is good for him. If misfortune afflicts him, he has patience, and that is also good for him." Muslim (*Mishkāt*, Book of Heart-Softening Matters, *Ḥadīth* no. 5297).

Commentary

In other words, he gains goodness in every situation.

8.10 PATIENCE IN DIFFICULTY

عَنْ أَنَسِ بْنِ مَالِكٍ ☼ قَالَ: مَرَّ النَّبِيُّ ﷺ بِامْرَأَةٍ تَبْكِي عِنْدَ قَبْرٍ، فَقَالَ: اتَّقِي اللهَ وَاصْبِرِي. فَقَالَتْ: إِلَيْكَ عَنِّي فَإِنَّكَ لَمْ تُصَبْ بِمُصِيبَتِي. قَالَ: فَجَاوَزَهَا، وَلَمْ تَعْرِفْهُ، فَمَرَّ بِهَا رَجُلٌ، فَقِيلَ لَهَا: أَنَّهُ النَّبِيُّ صَلَّى اللهُ عَلَيْهِ وَسَلَّمَ. فَأَتَتْ بَابَ النَّبِيِّ صَلَّى اللهُ عَلَيْهِ وَسَلَّمَ، فَلَمْ تَجِدْ عِنْدَهُ بَوَّابَيْنِ، فَقَالَتْ: لَمْ أَعْرِفْكَ. فَقَالَ النَّبِيُّ ﷺ: إِنَّمَا الصَّبْرَ عِنْدَ الصَّدْمَةِ الأُولَى.(رواه البخاري ومسلم– مشكاة– كتاب البكاء على الميت ص١٤٢).

[126]   On the authority of Anas ibn Mālik ☼, who said: The Prophet ☼ passed by a woman weeping at the side of a grave. He said, "Fear Allah, and have patience." She said, "Get away from me, for you have not been afflicted with my difficulty", for she had not recognised him. She was told that this was actually the Prophet ☼, so she came [hurriedly] to his door and, finding no door-keepers, said, "I did not recognise you." He said, "Patience is only that which is shown at the first strike of calamity." Bukhārī and Muslim (*Mishkāt*, Book of Funerals, *Ḥadīth* no. 1728).

8.11 PATIENCE IN OBEYING ALLAH ☼

عَنْ أَبِي هُرَيْرَةَ ☼ قَالَ: قَالَ رَسُولُ اللهِ ﷺ: حُفَّتِ الْجَنَّةُ بِالْمَكَارِهِ، وَحُفَّتِ النَّارُ بِالشَّهَوَاتِ. رواه أحمد.

[127] On the authority of Abū Hurayrah ﷺ, who said: The Messenger of Allah ﷺ said, "The Garden is surrounded by hardships [i.e. those things disliked by the self], while the Fire is surrounded by lusts [i.e. those things desired by the self]." Muslim (*Mishkāt*, Book of Heart-Softening Matters, *Ḥadīth* no. 5160).[41]

Commentary

This means that a Muslim cannot deserve the Garden without sacrificing his or her desires and comfort. Similarly, the doors of the Fire are wide upon for those who become worshippers of the self without discriminating between the lawful and the prohibited.

8.12 PATIENCE IN ONE'S PRINCIPLES: A PRINCIPLED LIFE

عَنْ حُذَيْفَةَ ﷺ قَالَ: قَالَ رَسُولُ اللهِ ﷺ: لا تَكُونُوا إِمَّعَةً تَقُولُونَ إِنْ أَحْسَنَ النَّاسُ أَحْسَنَّا، وَإِنْ ظَلَمُوا ظَلَمْنَا، وَلَكِنْ وَطِّنُوا أَنْفُسَكُمْ إِنْ أَحْسَنَ النَّاسُ أَنْ تُحْسِنُوا وَإِنْ أَسَاءُوا فَلَا تَظْلِمُوا. رواه الترمذي.

[128] On the authority of Ḥudhayfah ﷺ, who said: The Messenger of Allah ﷺ said, "[O people!] Do not be unprincipled, saying, 'If the people behave well we also will treat them well, but if they behave badly, we will also be unjust.' Rather, train yourselves: if people behave well, treat them well; if they behave badly, do not be unjust." Tirmidhī (*Mishkāt*, Book of Etiquette, *Ḥadīth* no. 5129).

Commentary

This means that we should always choose the path of justice and kindness, no matter what path society follows.

41. In the narration of Bukhārī there occurs, "veiled" (*ḥujibat*) instead of "surrounded" (*ḥuffat*). Hence, the Garden and Fire are respectively veiled from us by hardships and lusts. – Trans. Note

8.13 STEADFASTNESS IN FACING THE ENEMY

عَنْ عَبْدِ اللهِ بْنُ أَبِي أَوْفَى ﷺ، أَنَّ رَسُولَ اللهِ ﷺ في بَعْضِ أَيَّامِهِ الَّتِي لَقِيَ فِيهَا العَدُوَّ، انْتَظَرَ حَتَّى مَالَتْ الشَّمْسُ، ثُمَّ قَامَ فِي النَّاسِ خَطِيبًا، قَالَ: أَيُّهَا النَّاسُ لا تَتَمَنَّوْا لِقَاءَ الْعَدُوِّ وَسَلُوا اللهَ الْعَافِيَةَ، فَإِذَا لَقِيتُمُوهُمْ فَاصْبِرُوا وَاعْلَمُوا أَنَّ الْجَنَّةَ تَحْتَ ظِلَالِ السُّيُوفِ.

البخاري ومسلم، رياض الصالحين.

[129] On the authority of ʿAbdullāh b. Abī Awfā ﷺ that during one of the days that he faced the enemy, the Messenger of Allah ﷺ waited until the sun passed its zenith and then stood amongst the people and addressed them, saying, "O people! Do not wish to meet the enemy, but rather, pray to Allah for safety. However, if you do meet them, then remain steadfast and know that the Garden lies beneath the shade of swords." Bukhārī and Muslim (*Riyāḍ al-Ṣāliḥīn* and *Mishkāt*, Book of *Jihād*, *Ḥadīth* no. 3930).

Commentary

It is known from this *Ḥadīth* that it is not approved to wish to meet the enemy in combat and to boast about chivalry. However, if the enemy is stubborn then they should be fought with all one's might.

8.14 PATIENCE IN POVERTY AND DESTITUTION

عَنْ أَبِي سَعِيدٍ الْخُدْرِيِّ ﷺ، أَنَّ نَاسًا مِنْ الْأَنْصَارِ سَأَلُوا رَسُولَ اللهِ ﷺ، فَأَعْطَاهُمْ، ثُمَّ سَأَلُوهُ، فَأَعْطَاهُمْ، ثُمَّ سَأَلُوهُ، فَأَعْطَاهُمْ حَتَّى نَفِدَ مَا عِنْدَهُ، فَقَالَ: مَا يَكُونُ عِنْدِي مِنْ خَيْرٍ، فَلَنْ أَدَّخِرَهُ عَنْكُمْ، وَمَنْ يَسْتَعْفِفْ يُعِفَّهُ اللهُ، وَمَنْ يَسْتَغْنِ يُغْنِهِ اللهُ، وَمَنْ يَتَصَبَّرْ يُصَبِّرْهُ اللهُ، وَمَا أُعْطِيَ أَحَدٌ عَطَاءً خَيْرًا وَأَوْسَعَ مِنْ الصَّبْرِ. رواه البخاري ومسلم.

[130] On the authority of Abū Saʿīd al-Khudrī ﷺ that some people of the Anṣār presented their needy situation to the Messenger of Allah ﷺ, so he gave them wealth to fulfil their need. They then asked him again and he fulfilled their need, until all that he had was exhausted. When he had given them everything,

he said, "Any wealth there is, I will not hoard it [and keep it] away from you. Whoever seeks contentment, Allah makes him content. Whoever seeks independence, Allah enriches him. Whoever seeks patience, Allah grants him steadfastness. Of all the qualities that a person is given in his character, no one has been given a quality better and broader [in terms of results and fruits] than patience." Bukhārī and Muslim (*Mishkāt*, Book of *Zakāt*, *Ḥadīth* no. 1844).

8.15 DISCIPLINE AGAINST THE DESIRE FOR REVENGE

عَنْ ابْنَ عَبَّاسٍ ﷺ قَالَ: دَخَلَ عُيَيْنَةُ بْنُ حِصْنِ بْنِ حُذَيْفَةَ بْنِ بَدْرٍ على عُمَرَ ابْنَ الْخَطَّاب، وقَالَ: هِيْ يَا ابْنَ الْخَطَّاب، فَوَ اللهِ مَا تُعْطِينَا الْجَزْلَ، وَلا تَحْكُمُ بَيْنَنَا بِالْعَدْلِ. فَغَضِبَ عُمَرُ حَتَّى هَمَّ أَنْ يُوقِعَ بِهِ. فَقَالَ لَهُ: الْحُرُّ يَا أَمِيرَ الْمُؤْمِنِينَ، إِنَّ اللهَ تَعَالى قَالَ لِنَبِيِّهِ ﷺ: »خُذْ الْعَفْوَ وَأْمُرْ بِالْعُرْفِ وَأَعْرِضْ عَنْ الْجَاهِلِينَ"، وَإِنَّ هَذَا مِنْ الْجَاهِلِينَ. وَاللهِ مَا جَـاوَزَهَا عُمَرُ حِينَ تَلَاهَا عَلَيْهِ، وَكَانَ وَقَّـافًا عِنْدَ كِتَابِ اللهِ. صحيح البخاري، رياض الصالحين.

[131] On the authority of Ibn 'Abbās ﷺ, who said: 'Uyaynah b. Ḥiṣn b. Hudhayfah b. Badr came to 'Umar b. al-Khaṭṭāb and said, "Hey, son of al-Khaṭṭāb! By Allah, you neither give to us with generosity nor judge between us with justice." 'Umar became so angry that he was about to jump upon him, when Ḥurr ['Uyaynah's nephew] said, "O Commander of the Believers! Truly, Allah has said to His Prophet, '*Show forgiveness, enjoin what is good, and avoid the ignorant*'[42] and truly, this man is amongst the ignorant." By Allah, 'Umar did not go any further when he recited this verse to him. 'Umar would always stop at the Book of Allah [i.e. at Allah's Command]. Bukhārī and *Riyāḍ al-Ṣāliḥīn*.

عَنْ أَبِي هُرَيْرَةَ ﷺ قَالَ: أَخْبَرَنِي عُبَيْدُ اللهِ بْنُ عِيَاضٍ، أَنَّ بِنْتَ الْحَارِثِ أَخْبَرَتْهُ: أَنَّهُمْ حِينَ اجْتَمَعُوا، اسْتَعَارَ خُبَيْبٌ مِنْهَا مُوسىً، يَسْتَحِدُّ بِهَا فَأَعَارَتْهُ، فَأَخَذَ ابْنًا لِي، وَأَنَا غَافِلَةٌ حِينَ

42. *Sūrah al-A'rāf* (The Heights), 7: 199.

أَتَاهُ، قَالَتْ: فَوَجَدْتُهُ مُجْلِسَهُ عَلَى فَخِذِهِ وَالْمُوسَى بِيَدِهِ، فَفَزِعْتُ فَزْعَةً عَرَفَهَا خُبَيْبٌ فِي وَجْهِي. فَقَالَ: تَخْشَيْنَ أَنْ أَقْتُلَهُ، مَا كُنْتُ لِأَفْعَلَ ذَلِكَ. وَاللهِ مَا رَأَيْتُ أَسِيرًا قَطُّ خَيْرًا مِنْ خُبَيْبٍ. صحيح البخاري.

[132] On the authority of Abū Hurayrah ﵁, who said: 'Ubaydullāh b. 'Iyāḍ informed me that the daughter of al-Ḥārith informed him that when the polytheists gathered, Khubayb borrowed a razor from her in order to shave [parts of his body]. She continued, "He took one of my sons [in his lap] whilst I was unaware. When I came to him, I found my son sitting on Khubayb's thigh, with the razor in Khubayb's hand. I became so worried that Khubayb recognised the anxiety on my face and said, 'Do you fear that I will kill him? I would never do that!' By Allah, I never saw a prisoner better than Khubayb." Bukhārī, Book of *Jihād*.

Commentary

This incident happened when some polytheists deceived some Companions from Madīnah and captured them, bringing them to Makkah where they were imprisoned in various houses. Later, they were hanged.

Even though Khubayb knew for certain that the polytheists would kill him after a while, he did not think of allowing himself to be overcome by the desire for revenge and to kill the child. Had he done so, this would have certainly been against the *Sharī'ah*. It is transmitted in a *ḥadīth* that the Messenger of Allah ﷺ has said, "Do not kill women and children." Khubayb ﵁ has set the most excellent example of character for all Muslim prisoners and captives until the Day of Judgment.

9

Personal Character

9.1 SELF-CONTROL

عَنْ أَبِي هُرَيْرَةَ ﵁، أَنَّ رَسُولَ اللهِ ﷺ قَالَ: لَيْسَ الشَّدِيدُ بِالصُّرَعَةِ، إِنَّمَا الشَّدِيدُ الَّذِي يَمْلِكُ نَفْسَهُ عِنْدَ الْغَضَبِ. صحيح مسلم.

[133] On the authority of Abū Hurayrah ﵁, who said: The Messenger of Allah ﷺ said, "The strong man is not the one who wrestles another to the ground: the strong man is the one who controls himself when angry." Bukhārī and Muslim (*Mishkāt*, Book of Etiquette, *Ḥadīth* no. 5105).

عَنْ أَبِي هُرَيْرَةَ ﵁، أَنَّ رَجُلا قَالَ لِلنَّبِيِّ ﷺ: أَوْصِنِي. قَالَ: لا تَغْضَبْ. فَرَدَّدَ مِرَارًا. قَالَ: لا تَغْضَبْ. رواه البخاري.

[134] On the authority of Abū Hurayrah ﵁ that a man said to the Prophet ﷺ, "Advise me." He replied, "Do not become angry." The man repeated this question several times, each time receiving the answer, "Do not become angry." Bukhārī (*Mishkāt*, Book of Etiquette, *Ḥadīth* no. 5104).

Commentary

The Prophet ﷺ would point out that weakness by which the person was most afflicted. It seems that this person was extremely prone to being overcome by anger, so he ﷺ impressed upon him repeatedly to avoid this weakness.

عَنْ أَنَسٍ ﷺ، أَنَّ النَّبِيَّ ﷺ قَالَ: ثَلاثٌ مِنْ أَخْلاقِ الإِيمَانِ: مَنْ إِذَا غَضِبَ لَمْ يُدْخِلْهُ
غَضَبُهُ فِي بَاطِلٍ، وَمَنْ إِذَا رَضِيَ لَمْ يُخْرِجْهُ رِضَاهُ مِنْ حَقٍّ، وَمَنْ إِذَا قَدَرَ لَمْ يَتَعَاطَ مَا لَيْسَ
لَهُ. المعجم الصغير للطبراني.

[135]   On the authority of Anas ﷺ that the Messenger of Allah ﷺ
said, "Three matters are from the character of faith: (1) when a
person is angry, his anger does not land him in falsehood; (2)
when he is pleased, his pleasure does not take him outside the
truth; (3) despite having the power [to do so], he does not take
that which does not belong to him." *Al-Muʿjam al-Ṣaghīr* of Ṭabarānī.

Commentary

By "character of faith" is meant that these three matters are
among the fundamental requirements of faith; without them,
the essential substance of faith itself no longer remains.

9.2 FORGIVENESS AND FORBEARANCE

عَنْ عَائِشَةَ ﵂، أَنَّهَا قَالَتْ: مَا انْتَقَمَ رَسُولُ اللهِ ﷺ لِنَفْسِهِ إِلا أَنْ تُنْتَهَكَ حُرْمَةُ اللهِ، فَيَنْتَقِمَ
اللهُ بِهَا. متفق عليه.

[136]   On the authority of ʿĀʾishah ﵂, who said: "The Messenger
of Allah ﷺ never took revenge for himself about anything at all.
It was only if one of the sanctities of Allah [sacred symbols or
limits set by Allah] were violated, that he would take revenge for
the sake of Allah." Bukhārī and Muslim (*Riyāḍ al-Ṣāliḥīn*).

9.3 MAGNANIMITY

وَعَنْ أَبِي الأَحْوَصِ الجُشَمِي، عَنْ أَبِيهِ ﵁، قال قُلْتُ يا رَسُولَ اللهِ ﷺ أَرَأَيْتَ إِنْ مَرَرْتُ
بِرَجُلٍ، فَلَمْ يُقْرِنِي، وَلَمْ يُضَيِّفْنِي، ثُمَّ مَرَّ بَعْدَ ذَلِكَ أَقْرِيهِ أَمْ أَجْزِيهِ؟ قَالَ: بَلْ أَقْرِهِ. رواه
الترمذي.

[137]   On the authority of Abū'l-Aḥwaṣ al-Jushamī from his
father ﵁, who said: I asked, "O Messenger of Allah! If I visit a

man who does not show me hospitality or treat me appropriately as his guest, and then he later visits me: should I show him hospitality or recompense him [i.e. treat him as he treated me, inhospitably and stingily]?" He answered, "Nay, show him hospitality." Tirmidhī (*Mishkāt*, Book of Food, *Ḥadīth* no. 4248).

9.4 ḤAYĀʾ (MODESTY, SHAME, SHYNESS)

عَنْ ابْنِ عُمَرَ ﷺ أَنَّ رَسُولَ الله ﷺ مَرَّ عَلَى رَجُلٍ مِنَ الْأَنْصَارِ، وَهُوَ يَعِظُ أَخَاهُ فِي الْحَيَاءِ، فَقَالَ رَسُولُ الله ﷺ: دَعْهُ، فَإِنَّ الْحَيَاءَ مِنَ الْإِيمَانِ. (متفق عليه -مشكاة - باب الرفق - ص ٤٢٣).

[138]   On the authority of Ibn ʿUmar ﷺ that the Messenger of Allah ﷺ passed by a man from the Anṣār who was admonishing [i.e. scolding] his brother about his shyness. The Messenger of Allah ﷺ said, "Leave him, for shyness is part of faith." Bukhārī and Muslim (*Mishkāt*, Book of Etiquette, *Ḥadīth* no. 5070).

عَنْ أَنَسٍ ﷺ، قَالَ: كَانَ النَّبِيُّ ﷺ إِذَا أَرَادَ الْحَاجَةَ، لَمْ يَرْفَعْ ثَوْبَهُ حَتَّى يَدْنُوَ مِنَ الْأَرْضِ. رواه الترمذي.

[139]   On the authority of Anas ﷺ, who said: When the Prophet ﷺ intended to answer the call of nature, he would not raise his garment until he was [crouched down] near the ground. Tirmidhī, Abū Dāwūd and Dārimī (*Mishkāt*, Book of Purification, *Ḥadīth* no. 346).

عَنْ ابْنِ عُمَرَ ﷺ، أَنَّ رَسُولَ الله ﷺ قَالَ: إِيَّاكُمْ وَالتَّعَرِّيَ، فَإِنَّ مَعَكُمْ مَنْ لَا يُفَارِقُكُمْ إِلَّا عِنْدَ الْغَائِطِ، وَحِينَ يُفْضِي الرَّجُلُ إِلَى أَهْلِهِ، فَاسْتَحْيُوهُمْ وَأَكْرِمُوهُمْ. رواه الترمذي.

[140]   On the authority of Ibn ʿUmar ﷺ, who said: The Messenger of Allah ﷺ said, "Beware of nudity, for truly there are with you those [angels] who only leave you at the time of the toilet and sexual relations; therefore, feel shy of them and respect them." Tirmidhī (*Mishkāt*, Book of Marriage, *Ḥadīth* no. 3115).

9.5 DIGNITY AND SOLEMNITY

عَنْ أَبِي هُرَيْرَةَ ﷺ، عَنِ النَّبِيِّ ﷺ قَالَ: إِذَا سَمِعْتُمُ الْإِقَامَةَ، فَامْشُوا إِلَى الصَّلَاةِ، وَعَلَيْكُمْ بِالسَّكِينَةِ وَالْوَقَارِ، وَلَا تُسْرِعُوا. صحيح البخاري.

[141] On the authority of Abū Hurayrah ﷺ, who said: The Messenger of Allah ﷺ said, "When you hear the *iqāmah* [the call immediately before prayer], then walk to the prayer [i.e. to the mosque] with tranquillity and dignity: do not rush." Bukhārī and Muslim (*Mishkāt*, Book of Prayer, *Ḥadīth* no. 686).

9.6 KEEPING SECRETS

عَنْ مُعَاذِ بْنِ جَبَلٍ ﷺ قَالَ: قَالَ رَسُولُ اللهِ ﷺ: اسْتَعِينُوا عَلَى قَضَاءِ حَوَائِجِكُمْ بِالْكِتْمَانِ، فَإِنَّ كُلَّ ذِي نِعْمَةٍ مَحْسُودٌ. المعجم الصغير للطبراني.

[142] On the authority of Mu'ādh b. Jabal ﷺ, who said: The Messenger of Allah ﷺ said, "Help yourselves to fulfil your needs successfully by concealing your secrets, for every possessor of grace is envied [i.e. he becomes the target of jealousy and envy]." *Al-Mu'jam al-Ṣaghīr* of Ṭabarānī (*Ṣaḥīḥ al-Jāmi' al-Ṣaghīr*, *Ḥadīth* no. 943).

Commentary

A person should not be so naïve as to tell people all about his intentions before the appropriate time, otherwise he will not be safe from the poisonous effects of the envious and their plots.

عَنْ عَمْرِو بْنِ العَاصِ ﷺ قال: عَجِبْتُ مِنَ الرَّجُلِ يَفِرُّ مِنَ القَدَرِ، وهُوَ مُوَاقِعُهُ، ويَرَى القَذَاةَ فِي عَيْنِ أَخِيهِ، ويَدَعُ الجِذْعَ فِي عَيْنِهِ، ويُخْرِجُ الضَغَنَ مِنْ نَفْسِ أَخِيهِ، وَيَدَعُ الضَغَنَ فِي نَفْسِهِ، ومَا وَضَعْتُ سِرِّي عِنْدَ أَحَدٍ فَلُمْتُهُ على إِفْشَائِهِ، وكَيْفَ أَلُومُهُ وقَدْ ضِقْتُ بِهِ ذَرْعًا. الأدب المفرد، صحيح الإسناد.

[143] On the authority of 'Amr b. al-'Āṣ ﷺ, who said, "I am amazed at the man who flees from his destiny when he will surely meet it [one day], who sees the speck in his brother's eye

but forgets the log in his own eye, and who wishes to remove rancour from his brother's heart but leaves the rancour [and hatred towards others] in his own heart. I have never entrusted my secret to another person and then condemned him for spreading it: how can I blame him when I was bursting with it myself?" Bukhārī's *Al-Adab al-Mufrad*, Chapter on Revealing Secrets (*Ṣaḥīḥ al-Adab al-Mufrad*, *Ḥadīth* no. 681).

9.7 HUMILITY

وعَــنْ عُمَرَ ﵁ قَـالَ وهُوَ عَلى المِنْبَرِ: يَا أَيُّهَا النَّاسُ! تَوَاضَعُوا، فَإِني سَمِعْتُ رَسُـوْلَ الله ﷺ يَقُولُ: مَنْ تَوَاضَعَ لله رَفَعَهُ اللهُ، فَهُوَ فِي نَفْسِهِ صَغِيرٌ، وفي أَعْيُنِ النَّاسِ عَظِيمٌ، وَمَنْ تَكَبَّرَ وَضَعَهُ اللهُ، فَهُوَ فِي أَعْيُنِ النَّاسِ صَغِيرٌ، وَفِي نَفْسِهِ كَبِيرٌ، حَتَّى لَـهُوَ أَهْوَنُ عَلَيْهِمْ مِنْ كَلْبٍ أَوْ خِنْزِيرٍ. رواه البيهقي.

[144] On the authority of 'Umar ﵁, who said whilst upon the pulpit, "O people! Be humble, for I heard the Messenger of Allah saying, 'Whoever humbles himself for [the sake of] Allah, Allah elevates him such that he feels small in himself but is great in the eyes of the people. Whoever is arrogant, Allah lowers him such that he becomes small in the eyes of the people but feels great in himself, to the extent that he is worse than a dog or a pig in their view.'" Bayhaqī (*Mishkāt*, Book of Etiquette, *Ḥadīth* no. 5119).

عَنْ عَبْدِ اللَّهِ بْنِ عَمْرٍو ﵁ قَالَ: مَا رُئِيَ رَسُولُ اللهِ ﷺ يَأْكُلُ مُتَّكِئًا قَطُّ، وَلا يَطَأُ عَقِبَهُ رَجُلَانِ. راوه ابو داود، مشكواة، كتاب الأطعمة.

[145] On the authority of 'Abdullāh b. 'Amr ﵁, who said, "The Messenger of Allah ﷺ was never at all seen eating whilst reclining, and he was never seen with two people walking behind him." Abū Dāwūd (*Mishkāt*, Book of Food, *Ḥadīth* no. 4212).

Commentary

The Prophet ﷺ had such humility and self-effacement that he never ate whilst resting against a pillow, and it was not his way to walk ahead of people with them following behind. He did not even approve of walking ahead of two people: even this was regarded as pomposity. Both of these matters are regarded as characteristics of those who seek fame and reputation and are arrogant.

9.8 HUMILITY AND SELF-EFFACEMENT

عَنْ أُمِّ سَلَمَةَ رضي الله عنها قَالَتْ: رَأَى النَّبِيُّ ﷺ غُلَامًا لَنَا، يُقَالُ لَهُ أَفْلَحُ، إِذَا سَجَدَ نَفَخَ، فَقَالَ: يَا أَفْلَحُ تَرِّبْ وَجْهَكَ. رواه الترمذي.

[146] On the authority of Umm Salamah رضي الله عنها, who said: The Prophet ﷺ saw a servant of ours called Aflah blowing [on the ground to clean it] when prostrating, so he said, "O Aflah! Rub your face in the dust!" Tirmidhī (*Mishkāt*, Book of Prayer, *Ḥadīth* no. 1002).

9.9 AVOIDING FAME

عَنْ سَعْدٍ رضي الله عنه قَالَ: قَالَ رَسُولَ اللهِ ﷺ: إِنَّ اللهَ يُحِبُّ الْعَبْدَ التَّقِيَّ الْغَنِيَّ الْخَفِيَّ. رواه مسلم.

[147] On the authority of Sa'd رضي الله عنه, who said: The Messenger of Allah ﷺ said, "Truly, Allah loves the pious, rich [or content], obscure servant." Muslim (*Mishkāt*, Book of Heart-Softening Matters, *Ḥadīth* no. 5284).

Commentary

By "rich" in this *Ḥadīth* can be meant self-sufficiency and contentment, or affluence can also be intended. If affluence and richness is accompanied by *taqwā*, then this is also a great favour from Allah, especially when the person is not hungry for fame and reputation. The latter quality is what is meant by "obscure."

9.10 CONTENTMENT

عَنْ عَبْدِ الله بْنِ عَمْرِو بْنِ الْعَاصِ ﵁، أَنَّ رَسُولَ الله ﷺ قَالَ: قَدْ أَفْلَحَ مَنْ أَسْلَمَ وَرُزِقَ كَفَافًا وَقَنَّعَهُ اللهُ بِمَا آتَاهُ. رواه مسلم، مشكواة، كتاب الرقاق.

[148] On the authority of ʿAbdullāh b. ʿAmr b. al-ʿĀṣ ﵁, who said: The Messenger of Allah ﷺ said, "He has truly succeeded: the one who embraces Islam, is given sufficient livelihood to meet his needs and Allah makes him contented with what He has bestowed upon him." Muslim (*Mishkāt*, Book of Heart-Softening Matters, *Ḥadīth* no. 5165).

عن ابنِ الفَرَاسِيِّ، أَنَّ الفَرَاسِيَّ ﵁، قَالَ: قُلْتُ لِرَسُولِ الله: أَسْأَلُ يا رَسُولَ الله؟ فَقَالَ النَّبِيُّ: لَا، وإِنْ كُنْتَ لا بُدَّ فَسَلِ الصَّالِحِيْنَ. رواه أبو داود والنسائي.

[149] On the authority of the son of al-Farāsī, that al-Farāsī ﵁ said: I asked the Messenger of Allah ﷺ, "May I beg, O Messenger of Allah?" The Prophet ﷺ replied, "No! But if you have no other option, then beg from the righteous." Abū Dāwūd (*Mishkāt*, Book of *Zakāt*, *Ḥadīth* no. 1853) and Nasāʾī (no. 2587).

Commentary

The permission is given to beg from the righteous in a situation of necessity because such people will neither want recompense for themselves nor remind the beggar of their kindness, thus damaging his self-respect.

عَنْ أَنَسِ بْنِ مَالِكٍ ﵁ قَالَ: قَالَ رَسُولُ الله ﷺ: إِنَّ الْمَسْأَلَةَ لا تَصْلُحُ إِلا لِثَلَاثَةٍ: لِذِي فَقْرٍ مُـدْقِعٍ، أَوْ لِذِي غُـرْمٍ مُفْظِعٍ، أَوْ لِذِي دَمٍ مُـوجِعٍ. رواه أبو داود والترمذي وابن ماجه.

[150] On the authority of Anas b. Mālik ﵁, who said: The Messenger of Allah ﷺ said, "Begging is not lawful, except for three types of people: (1) one in desperate poverty, (2) one facing

overwhelming debt, or (3) one responsible for painful blood-money." Abū Dāwūd, Tirmidhī and Ibn Mājah (*Mishkāt*, Book of *Zakāt*, *Ḥadīth* nos. 1850-1).

Commentary

One of the Anṣār came begging to the Prophet ﷺ. He asked, "Do you have any possessions in your house?" He replied, "We have a blanket: we use part of it to spread on the floor and part of it to cover ourselves, and we have a bowl in which we drink water." The Prophet ﷺ called for the two items and sold them for two dirhams, which he gave to the man, saying, "Buy food with one dirham and an axe with the other. Then come to me." When he did so, the Prophet ﷺ fitted a piece of wood to the axe with his own blessed hand and said, "Go to the wilderness and chop firewood. Do not return to me in less than fifteen days." The Anṣārī began chopping firewood and selling it, and when he returned to the Prophet ﷺ after fifteen days he had a pouch of ten dirhams, with which he bought food and clothing. The Prophet ﷺ said, "This [working for a living] is better for you than [the humiliation of] begging appearing on your face on the Day of Resurrection in the form of specks and blotches."

عَنْ أُمِّ سَلَمَةَ رضي الله عنها قَالَتْ: قَالَ رَسُولُ اللهِ ﷺ: مَا نَقَصَ مَالٌ مِنْ صَدَقَةٍ، ولا عَفَا رَجُلٌ عنْ مَظْلَمَةٍ إلاَّ زادَهُ اللهُ بها عِزًّا، فاعْفُوا يُعِزَّكُمُ اللهُ، ولا فتحَ رَجُلٌ على نَفْسِهِ بَابَ مَسْئَلَةٍ إلاَّ فَتَحَ اللهُ عَلَيهِ بَابَ فَقْرٍ. رواه الطبراني في المعجم الصغير وروى أحمد ومسلم والترمذي مثله عن أبي هريرة.

[151] On the authority of Umm Salamah رضي الله عنها, who said: The Messenger of Allah ﷺ said, "(1) Never did wealth decrease because of charity. (2) Never did a man forgive an injustice, except that Allah increased him in honour by it, so forgive – Allah will honour you! (3) Never did a man open the door to begging for himself, except that Allah opened upon him the door of poverty." *Al-Mu'jam al-Ṣaghīr* of Ṭabarānī. A similar *Ḥadīth* is transmitted by Muslim, Aḥmad and Tirmidhī on the authority of Abū Hurayrah (*Ṣaḥīḥ al-Jāmi' al-Ṣaghīr*, *Ḥadīth* no. 5809).

Commentary

In this *Ḥadīth*, attention has been drawn to three issues of morality:

1. Wealth does not decrease because of *zakāt* or charity: rather, the Qur'ān explicitly states that in fact wealth increases in this way.

   "As for the *zakāt*, that you give, seeking with it Allah's good pleasure, that is multiplied manifold." (*Sūrah al-Rūm*, 30: 39)

   Through charity and *zakāt*, a person's wealth apparently decreases. However, the reality is that in this way the communal capital of society increases. Simultaneously, the giver of *zakāt* is purified from undesirable qualities such as greed, miserliness and selfishness.
2. Usually, not taking revenge upon one's enemy is regarded as humiliation and cowardice. However, this *Ḥadīth* teaches that by forgiving oppression and injustice, a person increases in honour and achieves leadership in character and acceptance amongst people.
3. Begging apparently increases a person's wealth. However, he loses self-independence and dignity, and is degraded in the eyes of the people.

9.11 SIMPLICITY IN LIFESTYLE

عَنْ عَبْدِ اللهِ ابْنِ مَسْعُودٍ ﷺ قَالَ: قَالَ رَسُولُ اللهِ ﷺ: لا تَتَّخِذُوا الضَّيْعَةَ فَتَرْغَبُوا فِي الدُّنْيَا. رواه الترمذي – مشكواة، كتاب الرقاق.

[152] On the authority of ʿAbdullāh b. Masʿūd ﷺ, who said: The Messenger of Allah ﷺ said, "Do not collect much possessions or property, lest you become desirous of the world." Tirmidhī (*Mishkāt*, Book of Softening the Hearts, *Ḥadīth* no. 5178).

Commentary

From another narration, it is known that it is not a sin to acquire land and build houses within lawful limits. The matter that is forbidden here is that which leads to a person's attitude becoming confined to material progress and neglecting the real purpose of life.

عَنْ عَبْدِ اللهِ الرُّومِي ﷺ قَالَ: دَخَلْتُ عَلى أُمِّ طَلْق، فَقُلْتُ: مَا أَقْصَرَ سَقفَ بَيتِك هَذَا! قَالت: يَا بُني إِنَّ أَمِيرَ الْمُؤْمِنِيْنَ عُمَرَ بْنِ الْخَطَّابِ رَضِيَ اللهُ عَنْهُ كَتَبَ إِلى عُمَّالِهِ أَنْ لا تُطِيلُوا بِنَاءَكُمْ، فَإِنَّهُ مِنْ شَرِّ أَيَّامِكُمْ .الأدب المفرد.

[153] On the authority of 'Abdullāh al-Rūmī ﷺ who said: I visited Umm Ṭalq and said to her, "How low the roof of your house is!" She replied, "O my son! The Commander of the Believers, 'Umar b. al-Khaṭṭāb, wrote to his governors, 'Do not build your buildings up high, for that is [a sign] of the worst of times.'" Bukhārī's *Al-Adab al-Mufrad*, *Ḥadīth* no. 452.

عَــنْ أَبِي أُمَامَةَ ﷺ قَالَ: ذَكَرَ أَصْحَابُ رَسُولِ اللهِ ﷺ يَوْمًا عِنْدَهُ الدُّنْيَا، فَقَالَ رَسُــولُ اللهِ ﷺ: أَلا تَسْمَعُونَ، أَلا تَسْمَعُونَ إِنَّ الْبَذَاذَةَ مِنْ الْإِيمَانِ، إِنَّ الْبَذَاذَةَ مِنْ الْإِيمَانِ. ابو داود، مشكواة، كتاب اللباس.

[154] On the authority of Abū Umāmah ﷺ, who said: One day, the companions of the Messenger of Allah mentioned the world in his presence. The Messenger of Allah ﷺ said, "Do you not listen? Do you not listen? Truly, simplicity is part of faith! Truly, simplicity is part of faith!" Abū Dāwūd (*Ḥadīth* no. 4161; *Mishkāt*, Book of Dress, *Ḥadīth* no. 4145).

Commentary

By "simplicity" is meant a lifestyle that is not polluted by contrived behaviour and artificial appearances. Islam does not prohibit neat appearances and presentability, but these considerations exceed the bounds, if a person wastes his wealth in extravagance, futile spending, pomposity and show. Based on this, Islam teaches a path in between the extremes of extravagant, luxurious living and monastic renunciation of the world. This is what is denoted by the term "simplicity" in this narration.

عَنْ أَبِي هُرَيْرَةَ ﷺ قال: قَالَ رَسُولُ اللهِ ﷺ: مَا اسْتَكْبرَ مَن أَكَلَ مَعَهُ خَادِمُهُ، وَرَكِبَ الحِمَارَ بِالأَسْوَاقِ، وَاعْتَقَلَ الشَّاةَ فَحَلَبَهَا. حسن، الأدب المفرد.

[155] On the authority of Abū Hurayrah ﷺ, who said: The Messenger of Allah ﷺ said, "He is free from pride and arrogance: the one whose servant eats with him, who rides a donkey in the marketplaces, and who keeps a ewe and milks it himself." Bukhārī's *Al-Adab al-Mufrad*, Chapter on Pride, *Ḥadīth* no. 550.

عَنْ عَائِشَةَ ﷺ قَالَتْ: سُئِلَتْ مَا كَانَ رَسُولُ اللهِ ﷺ فِي بَيْتِهِ، قَالَتْ: كَانَ بَشَرًا مِنْ الْبَشَرِ يَفْلِي ثَوْبَهُ وَيَحْلُبُ شَاتَهُ وَيَخْدُمُ نَفْسَهُ. رواه أحمد، الأدب المفرد، باب ما يعمل الرجل في بيته.

[156] On the authority of 'Ā'ishah ﷺ that she was asked, "What did the Messenger of Allah ﷺ use to do in his house?" She replied, "He was a human being like anyone else: he would remove insects from his clothes, milk his ewe, and do his own chores." Bukhārī's *Al-Adab al-Mufrad*, Chapter on What a Man Does at Home, *Ḥadīth* no. 541. It is also transmitted by Aḥmad and Tirmidhī in his *Shamā'il*.

عَن مُعَاذِ بْنِ جَبَلٍ ﷺ، انَّ رَسُولِ اللهِ ﷺ، لَمَّا بَعَثَهُ إِلى الْيَمَنِ، قَالَ: إِيَّاكَ وَالتَّنَعُّمَ، فَإِنَّ عِبَادَ اللهِ لَيْسُوا بِالْمُتَنَعِّمِينَ. رواه أحمد، مشكواة، باب فضل الفقراء.

[157] On the authority of Mu'ādh b. Jabal ﷺ, that when the Messenger of Allah ﷺ sent him to Yemen, he said, "Beware of luxurious living, for the servants of Allah do not live in luxury." Aḥmad (*Mishkāt*, Book of the Virtue of the Poor, *Ḥadīth* no. 5262).

Commentary

There is a difference between beautification [caring about cleanliness, tidiness and presentability] and luxury [love of extravagance and excessive comfort]. Beautification is established from the Prophet ﷺ himself, as occurs in the *Ḥadīth* that when the Prophet ﷺ would wear a new garment, his supplication included the words, "By which I may beautify myself in this life ...." Another narration states that "he would wear nice garments when receiving delegations."

However, excessiveness in beautification borders on luxuriant living whilst neglecting beautification leads to monastic life. All that remains is the specification of the limits of excessiveness and neglect: the *Sharī'ah* leaves this to the live and perceptive conscience of a believer. The instruction, "Consult your heart for a verdict",[43] is applicable to this kind of situation.

عَنْ عَمْرِو بْنِ شُعَيْبٍ، عَنْ أَبِيهِ، عَنْ جَدِّهِ ﷺ قَالَ: قَالَ رَسُولُ اللهِ ﷺ: كُلُوا واشْرَبُوا وَتَصَدَّقُوا وَالْبَسُوا، مَا لَمْ يُخَالِطْ إِسْرَافٌ وَلا مَخِيلَةٌ. رواه احمد والنسائي وابن ماجة، مشكواة، كتاب اللباس.

[158] On the authority of 'Amr b. Shu'ayb from his father from his grandfather ﷺ, who said: The Messenger of Allah ﷺ said, "Eat, drink, give in charity and wear garments – as long as neither extravagance nor pride is involved." Aḥmad, Nasā'ī and Ibn Mājah (*Mishkāt*, Book of Dress, *Ḥadīth* no. 4381).

9.12 MODERATION

عَنْ عَبْدِ اللهِ بْنِ سَرْجِسَ الْمُزَنِيِّ ﷺ، أَنَّ النَّبِيَّ ﷺ قَالَ: السَّمْتُ الْحَسَنُ وَالتُّؤَدَةُ وَالاقْتِصَادُ جُزْءٌ مِنْ أَرْبَعَةٍ وَعِشْرِينَ جُزْءًا مِنَ النُّبُوَّةِ. رواه الترمذي.

[159] On the authority of 'Abdullāh b. Sarjis al-Muzanī ﷺ, that the Prophet ﷺ said, "Beautiful conduct [i.e. righteous behaviour], gentleness and moderation constitute one of twenty-four parts of Prophethood." Tirmidhī, *Ḥadīth* no. 2010 (*Mishkāt*, *Ḥadīth* no. 5059).

---

43. This instruction is part of an authentic *Ḥadīth* transmitted by Imām Nawawī in his famous collection of forty *Aḥādīth*. – Trans. Note

Commentary

This means that:

1. These qualities are prominent in the lives of the noble prophets. As far as a person adopts these qualities, to that extent he is following the way of the prophets.
2. Moderation means that a person should adopt a balanced way in all matters of life, rather than excessiveness or shortcomings, examples of which are extravagance and miserliness, respectively; between them, a path of generosity should be followed. The *Sharī'ah* gives importance to moderation in all areas of life.

عَنْ عَمَّارٍ ﷺ قَالَ: سَمِعْتُ رَسُولَ اللهِ ﷺ يَقُولُ: إِنَّ طُولَ صَلَاةِ الرَّجُلِ وَقِصَرَ خُطْبَتِهِ مَئِنَّةٌ مِنْ فِقْهِهِ، فَأَطِيلُوا الصَّلَاةَ وَاقْصُرُوا الْخُطْبَةَ وَإِنَّ مِنَ الْبَيَانِ لَسِحْرًا. رواه مسلم، مشكواة، باب الخطبة.

[160] On the authority of 'Ammār ﷺ, who said: I heard the Messenger of Allah ﷺ saying, "Truly, the lengthy nature of a man's prayer and the brevity of his sermon are a sign of his wisdom. Therefore, lengthen the prayer and shorten the sermon. Truly, rhetoric can work magic [i.e. bewitch]." Muslim (*Mishkāt*, Chapter on the Sermon, *Ḥadīth* no. 1406).

9.13 CONSTANCY

عَنْ عَائِشَةَ ﷺ قَالَتْ: كَانَ رَسُولُ اللهِ ﷺ يَقُولُ: إِنَّ أَحَبَّ الدِّينِ إِلَى اللهِ مَا دَاوَمَ عَلَيْهِ صَاحِبُهُ. متفق عليه.

[161] On the authority of 'Ā'ishah ﷺ, who said: The Messenger of Allah ﷺ said, "Truly, the most beloved [aspects] of religion to Allah are the acts that a person does regularly [even if they are few]." Bukhārī and Muslim (*Mishkāt*, Chapter on Moderation in Works, *Ḥadīth* no. 1242).

Commentary

If even a small number of good actions is done regularly and constantly, the end results are much better than those of sudden energetic activity carried out in a fit of passion followed by a long period of inaction.

عَنْ عَبْدِ اللهِ بْنُ عَمْرِو بْنِ الْعَاصِ ﷺ قَالَ: قَالَ لِي رَسُولُ اللهِ ﷺ: يَا عَبْدَ اللهِ لا تَكُنْ مِثْلَ فُلَانٍ، كَانَ يَقُومُ اللَّيْلَ، فَتَرَكَ قِيَامَ اللَّيْلِ. رواه البخاري ومسلم، مشكواة، باب التحريض على قيام الليل.

[162] On the authority of ʿAbdullāh b. ʿAmr b. al-ʿĀṣ ﷺ, who said: The Messenger of Allah ﷺ advised me, "O ʿAbdullah! Do not be like so-and-so, who used to stand in prayer at night but later abandoned the practice." Bukhārī and Muslim (*Mishkāt*, Chapter on Encouraging Prayer at Night, *Ḥadīth* no. 1234).

Commentary

Constancy and consistency are a must in compulsory and mandatory duties, but are also important in voluntary works.

عَنْ نَافِعٍ ﷺ، عَنْ عَائِشَةَ ﷺ قَالَتْ: سَمِعْتُ رَسُولَ اللهِ ﷺ يَقُولُ: إِذَا سَبَّبَ اللهُ لِأَحَدِكُمْ رِزْقًا مِنْ وَجْهٍ، فَلا يَدَعْهُ حَتَّى يَتَغَيَّرَ لَهُ، أَوْ يَتَنَكَّرَ لَهُ. سنن أبن ماجه ومسند أحمد، مشكواة، باب الكسب.

[163] On the authority of Nāfiʿ from ʿĀ'ishah ﷺ, who said: I heard the Messenger of Allah ﷺ saying, "When Allah provides a means of sustenance for one of you, he should not abandon it unless it changes [with harmful consequences] or becomes [morally] repulsive to him." Aḥmad (*Mishkāt*, Chapter on Earning, *Ḥadīth* no. 2785) and Ibn Mājah (no. 2148).

Commentary

The background of this narration is that Nāfiʿ ﷺ used to send goods for trade to Syria and Egypt. Later, he changed the destination to Iraq for no reason. ‘Ā’ishah ﷺ admonished him for this change and quoted to him the above-mentioned Prophetic saying. From this *Ḥadīth*, we learn that a believer should be constant and consistent in matters of transactions as well as those of ritual worship: it does not befit him to continually change his ways and mind.

عَنْ جَابِرٍ ﷺ قَالَ: قَالَ رَسُولُ اللهِ ﷺ: اسْتِتْمَامُ الْمَعْرُوفِ أَفْضَلُ مِنْ ابْتِدَائِهِ. المعجم الصغير للطبراني.

[164]   On the authority of Jābir ﷺ, who said: The Messenger of Allah ﷺ said, “Completing good works is better than beginning them.” Ṭabarānī’s *Al-Muʿjam al-Ṣaghīr*.

Commentary

This means that if one shows goodness and kindness to someone, they should see this act through to completion, otherwise half-finished kind actions are not regarded as being from good character; rather, these usually lead to negative complaints and the good that has been done is also often forgotten.

9.14 GENEROSITY

عَنْ عَبْدِ اللهِ بن الزُّبَيْرِ ﷺ قَالَ: مَا رَأَيْتُ امْرَأَتَيْنِ أَجْوَدَ مِن عَائِشَةَ وَأَسْمَاءَ، وجُودُهُمَا مُخْتَلِفٌ، أَمَّا عَائِشَةُ فَكَانَتْ تَجْمَعُ الشَّيءَ إلى الشَّيْءِ حَتَّى إِذَا كَانَ اجْتَمَعَ عِنْدَهَا قَسَمَتْ، وَأَمَّا أَسْمَاءُ فَكَانَت لا تُمْسِكُ شيئاً لِغَدٍ. الأدب المفرد، باب سخاوة النفس.

[165]   On the authority of ‘Abdullāh b. al-Zubayr ﷺ, who said, “I have not seen two women more generous than ‘Ā’ishah and Asmā’.[44] Their generosity was of different kinds: ‘Ā’ishah would save wealth until it reached a sizeable amount, when she would distribute it [amongst the needy]; Asmā’ would not

---

44.   ‘Abdullāh b. al-Zubayr was the son of Asmā’, sister of ‘Ā’ishah, both of whom were daughters of Abū Bakr ﷺ, the first caliph of Islam.

keep anything for the following day [i.e. she would distribute it immediately]." Bukhārī's *Al-Adab al-Mufrad*, Chapter on Generous-Heartedness, *Ḥadīth* no. 280.

9.15 HONESTY AND TRUSTWORTHINESS

عَنْ عَبْدِ اللهِ بْنِ عَمْرٍو ﴾، أَنَّ رَسُولَ اللهِ ﷺ قَالَ، أَرْبَعٌ إِذَا كُنَّ فِيكَ فَلَا عَلَيْكَ مَا فَاتَكَ مِنَ الدُّنْيَا: حِفْظُ أَمَانَةٍ، وَصِدْقُ حَدِيثٍ، وَحُسْنُ خَلِيقَةٍ، وَعِفَّةٌ فِي طُعْمَةٍ. رواه أحمد، مشكواة، كتاب الرقاق.

[166] On the authority of 'Abdullāh b. 'Amr ﴾, that the Messenger of Allah ﷺ said, "There are four qualities such that, if you have them, it will not harm you to be deprived of anything in the world: (1) safeguarding trusts, (2) truthfulness in speech, (3) good character and (4) purity of livelihood." Aḥmad (*Mishkāt*, Book of Softening the Hearts, *Ḥadīth* no. 5222 and *Ṣaḥīḥ al-Jāmi'*, *Ḥadīth* no. 873).

عَنْ أَبِي هُرَيْرَةَ ﴾ قَالَ: قَالَ النَّبِيُّ ﷺ: أَدِّ الْأَمَانَةَ إِلَى مَنِ ائْتَمَنَكَ، وَلَا تَخُنْ مَنْ خَانَكَ. رواه الترمذي، مشكواة، باب الشركة.

[167] On the authority of Abū Hurayrah ﴾ that the Prophet ﷺ said, "If someone entrusts you with something, safeguard the trust. Do not betray the one who betrays you." Tirmidhī, Abū Dāwūd and Dārimī (*Mishkāt*, Book of Partnership, *Ḥadīth* no. 2934).

10

Despicable Qualities

10.1 NARCISSISM (SELF-ADMIRATION)

وعَنْ أَبِي هُرَيْرَةَ ﵁، أَنَّ رَسُولَ الله ﷺ قالَ: ثَلاثٌ مُنْجِياتٌ، وَثَلاثٌ مُهْلِكاتٌ؛ فأَمَّا الْمُنْجِيَاتُ: فَتَقْوَى الله فِي السرِّ وَالعَلانِيةِ، وَالقولُ بِالْحَقِّ فِي الرِّضى وَالسَّخَطِ، وَالقَصْدُ فِي الغِنَى وَالفَقْرِ. وَأَمَّا الْمُهْلِكَاتُ: فَهَوًى مُتَّبَعٌ، وَشُحٌّ مُطاعٌ، وَإعْجَابُ الْمَرْءِ بِنَفْسِهِ، وَهِيَ أَشَدُّهُنَّ. رواه البيهقي.

[168] On the authority of Abū Hurayrah ﵁, who said: The Messenger of Allah ﷺ said, "There are three qualities that earn salvation, and three that cause destruction. Those that earn salvation are *taqwā* of Allah, in private and in public, speaking the truth in happiness and anger [i.e. in every situation], and moderation in poverty and affluence [i.e. in every situation]. Those that cause destruction are desire that enslaves the person following it, greed that is obeyed, and a person's self-admiration, [the third] being the most dangerous of the three." Bayhaqī's Branches of Faith (*Mishkāt*, *Ḥadīth* no. 5122).

Commentary

A person's becoming proud about his knowledge, wealth, physical prowess or even his renunciation of the world and piety, is a moral disease. If one becomes afflicted by it, he becomes infected by self-deception, neither admitting his mistakes nor having a desire to seek the truth.

10.2 PREVENTING SELF-ADMIRATION

عَنْ المِقدادِ ﷺ قَالَ: قَالَ رَسُولُ اللهِ ﷺ: إِذا رَأَيْتُمُ الْمَدَّاحِينَ فَاحْثُوْا فِي وجُوهِهِمُ التُّرابَ.
صحيح مسلم، مشكواة- ص ٤١٢.

[169] On the authority of al-Miqdād ﷺ, who said: The Messenger of Allah ﷺ said, "When you see those who flatter others, throw sand in their faces."[45] Muslim (*Mishkāt, Ḥadīth* no. 4826).

Commentary

This means that one should prevent them from attaining their objective of flattery and excessive praise.

10.3 AVOIDING SELF-ADMIRATION

عَنْ عَدِيٍّ بْنِ أَرْطَأَةَ ﷺ، قَالَ: كَانَ الرَّجُلُ مِنْ أَصْحابِ النَّبِيِّ ﷺ، إِذا زُكِّيَ، قال: اللَّهُمَّ لا تُؤاخِذْنِي بِما يَقولُونَ وَاغْفِرْ لِي مَا لا يَعْلَمُوْنَ. صحيح الإسناد،الأدب المفرد، باب الرجل إذا زكى.

[170] On the authority of ʿAdī b. Arṭāh ﷺ, who said: When a Companion of the Prophet ﷺ was praised, he would say, "O Allah! Punish me not for what they say; forgive me what they know not!"[46] Bukhārī's *Al-Adab al-Mufrad*, Chapter on What Should a Man Say If He is Praised, *Ḥadīth* no. 761.

Commentary

Usually, a person's listening to flattery of himself leads to his being afflicted with self-deception and self-admiration. This is why in such a situation, the noble Companions would turn in supplication to Allah in order to be saved from this evil. On the

45. Another tradition of Muslim provides some interesting context about the transmission of this teaching. On the authority of Abū Maʿmar, who said: A man stood up and praised one of the governors, upon which al-Miqdād began throwing dust at him, and said, "The Messenger of Allah ﷺ ordered us to throw sand in the faces of those who indulge in flattery." – Trans. Note

46. Bayhaqī's transmission of this prayer in his *Branches of Faith* adds the sentence, "Make me better than what they think about me." (*Ṣaḥīḥ al-Adab al-Mufrad, Ḥadīth* no. 585/761) – Trans. Note

one hand, they would ask not to be punished for the flattery; on the other hand, dreading that their ego may be inflated by listening to praise, they would ask Allah's forgiveness, bringing to mind their own defects and weaknesses.

10.4 LOVE OF FAME

عَنْ ابْنِ عُمَرَ ﷺ قَالَ: قَالَ رسولُ الله ﷺ: مَنْ لَبِسَ ثَوْبَ شُهْرَةٍ فِي الْدُنيَا، أَلْبَسَهُ الله ثَوْبَ مَذَلَّةٍ يَوْمَ الْقِيَامَةِ. رواه ابو داود، مشكواة، كتاب اللباس .

[171] On the authority of Ibn ʿUmar ﷺ, who said: The Messenger of Allah ﷺ said, "Whoever wears a garment of fame in this world, Allah will make him wear a garment of humiliation on the Day of Resurrection." Aḥmad, Abū Dāwūd and Ibn Mājah (*Mishkāt*, Book of Dress, *Ḥadīth* no. 4346).

Commentary

A "garment of fame and show" is of two types:

1. That people of authority and wealth wear colourful and dazzling costumes so that their air of prestige and authority is emphasised in the minds of the general public.
2. Religious figures, monks and renouncers of the world wear dervish-costumes in order to convey a sense of holy sanctity and pure spirituality.

In an Islamic society, there is neither a specific form of dress for the rich and powerful, nor is there any religious elite that can show its spiritual holiness through a particular style of clothing.

10.5 ARROGANCE

عَنْ عَبْدِ اللهِ ابْنِ مَسْعُودٍ ﷺ، عَنْ النَّبِيِّ ﷺ، قَالَ: لا يَدْخُلُ الْجَنَّةَ مَنْ كَانَ فِي قَلْبِهِ مِثْقَالُ ذَرَّةٍ مِنْ كِبْرٍ. قَالَ رَجُلٌ: إِنَّ الرَّجُلَ يُحِبُّ أَنْ يَكُونَ ثَوْبُهُ حَسَنًا وَنَعْلُهُ حَسَنًا. قَالَ: إِنَّ اللهَ جَمِيلٌ يُحِبُّ الْجَمَالَ الْكِبْرُ بَطَرُ الْحَقِّ وَغَمْطُ النَّاسِ. صحيح مسلم.

[172]   On the authority of 'Abdullāh b. Mas'ūd ⁕, who said: The Messenger of Allah ⁕ said, "Whoever has an atom's weight of pride in his heart will not enter the Garden." A man asked, "What if a person likes to have nice clothes and nice sandals?" He replied, "Truly, Allah is Beautiful and loves beauty. Pride is to be obstinate against truth, and to be contemptuous of people." Muslim (*Mishkāt, Ḥadīth* no. 5108).

Commentary

If a person chooses beautiful clothing and a standard of living in accordance with his means and status and within lawful limits, he cannot be accused of pride and arrogance. Pride and arrogance is to be so obsessed with worldly delights and pleasures that a person neither fulfils the rights of Allah nor cares about the rights of His servants.

10.6 SELF-ABASEMENT

عَنْ أَبِي الأَحْوَصِ، عَنْ أَبِيهِ ﷺ قَالَ: أَتَيْتُ النَّبِيَّ ﷺ فِي ثَوْبٍ دُونٍ، فَقَالَ: أَلَكَ مَالٌ؟ قلتُ: نَعَمْ. قَالَ: مِنْ أَيِّ الْمَالِ؟ قُلْتُ: مِنْ كُلِّ الْمَالِ قَدْ أَعْطَانِيَ اللهُ ،مِنَ الإِبِلِ وَالْغَنَمِ وَالْخَيْلِ وَالرَّقِيقِ، قال: فَإِذَا أَتَاكَ اللهُ مَالاً، فَلْيُرَ أَثَرُ نِعْمَةِ اللهِ عَلَيْكَ وَكَرَامَتِهِ. رواه أحمد والنسائي.

[173]   On the authority of Abū'l-Aḥwaṣ from his father ⁕, who said: I came to the Messenger of Allah ⁕, wearing simple clothing. He asked me, "Do you have wealth?" I replied, "Yes." He asked, "What kind of wealth?" I replied, "Every kind of wealth. Allah has bestowed upon me camels, cattle, sheep, horses and slaves." He said, "If He has bestowed wealth upon you, the traces of Allah's Bounty and Favour should be visible upon you." Aḥmad and Nasā'ī (*Mishkāt, Ḥadīth* no. 4352).

Commentary

This *Ḥadīth* forbids self-abasement or a lowly mentality that can lead to ingratitude towards the Divine favours. However, the manifestation of such favours should not be pursued to such an extreme that becomes pride and show, extravagance and the wasting of wealth.

10.7 TIGHT-FISTEDNESS

عَنْ ابْنِ عَبَّاسٍ رَضِيَ اللَّهُ عَنْهُ، قَالَ: قَالَ النَّبِيُّ ﷺ: الْعَائِدُ فِي هِبَتِهِ كَالْكَلْبِ يَعُودُ فِي قَيْئِهِ لَيْسَ لَنَا مَثَلُ السَّوْءِ. صحيح البخاري.

[174]   On the authority of Ibn 'Abbās ☙, who said: The Messenger of Allah ﷺ said, "One who takes his gift back is like the dog who licks up his [own] vomit. There is no worse example than that!" Bukhārī (*Mishkāt*, Chapter on Gifts, *Ḥadīth* no. 3018).

10.8 SELFISHNESS

عَنْ أَبِي هُرَيْرَةَ ☙ قَالَ: قَالَ رَسُولُ الله ﷺ: لَا تَسْأَلْ الْمَرْأَةُ طَلَاقَ أُخْتِهَا، لِتَسْتَفْرِغَ صَحْفَتَهَا، وَلْتَنْكِحْ، فَإِنَّ لَهَا مَا قُدِّرَ لَهَا. صحيح البخاري.

[175]   On the authority of Abū Hurayrah ☙, who said: The Messenger of Allah ﷺ said, "A woman must not ask for the divorce of her sister [in Islam] to empty her plate. She should [simply] marry, for she shall have what has been determined for her." Bukhārī and Muslim (*Mishkāt*, *Ḥadīth* no. 3145).

Commentary

If a man intends to marry a second wife, the second wife-to-be should not ask him to divorce his first wife before marrying her, in order for her to receive, in place of the first wife, whatever the latter was receiving.

10.9 MISERLINESS AND NARROW-MINDEDNESS

عن ابْنِ عَبَّاسٍ رَضِيَ اللَّهُ عَنْهُ، قَالَ النَّبِيُّ ﷺ: لَيْسَ الْمُؤْمِنُ بِالَّذِي يَشْبَعُ وَجَارُهُ جَائِعٌ إِلَى جَنْبِهِ. رواه البيهقي في شعب الإيمان.

[176] On the authority of Ibn ʿAbbās ﵁, who said: The Prophet ﷺ said, "The believer is not the one who eats his fill while his next-door neighbour goes hungry." Bayhaqī's *Branches of Faith* and Bukhārī's *Al-Adab al-Mufrad* (*Mishkāt*, *Ḥadīth* no. 4991).

10.10 DISHONOURABLE AND MEAN BEHAVIOUR

عَنْ عَبْدِ اللّٰهِ بْنِ عُمَرَ ﵄، قَالَ رَسُولُ الله ﷺ: مَنْ دُعِيَ، فَلَمْ يُجِبْ، فَقَدْ عَصى الله وَرَسُولَهُ، وَمَنْ دَخَلَ عَلى غَيْرِ دَعْوَةٍ دَخَلَ سَارِقًا وَخَرَجَ مُغِيرًا. رواه أبو داود.

[177] On the authority of ʿAbdullāh b. ʿUmar ﵄, who said: The Messenger of Allah ﷺ said, "Whoever is invited [to a meal] and does not accept, has disobeyed Allah and His Messenger. Whoever attends without invitation enters as a thief and leaves as a bandit." Abū Dāwūd (*Ḥadīth* no. 3741; *Mishkāt*, *Ḥadīth* no. 3222)

Commentary

1. In order to maintain and develop the brotherly relations of Islam, it is necessary that people should exchange presents and gifts and be concerned about inviting and hosting others. A person who does not accept the invitation of his Muslim brother is actually severing these ties of brotherhood that Islam wishes to maintain.
2. Attending a meal without being invited is a sign of meanness and a dishonourable nature. However, if the host is very welcoming and informal, then there is no harm in such a visit. Similarly, if a person does not accept the invitation of his Muslim brother due to a legally-valid excuse, he does not fall under the threat explained in this *Ḥadīth*.

10.11 GREED

عَنْ عَمْرِو بْنِ عَوْفٍ ﵁ أَنَّ رَسُولَ الله ﷺ، قَالَ: فَوَاللهِ لا الْفَقْرَ أَخْشَى عَلَيْكُمْ، وَلَكِنْ أَخْشَى عَلَيْكُمْ أَنْ تُبْسَطَ عَلَيْكُمْ الدُّنْيَا كَمَا بُسِطَتْ عَلَى مَنْ كَانَ قَبْلَكُمْ، فَتَنَافَسُوهَا كَمَا تَنَافَسُوهَا، وَتُهْلِكَكُمْ كَمَا أَهْلَكَتْهُمْ. رواه البخاري ومسلم.

[178]   On the authority of 'Amr b. 'Awf ☙, who said: The Messenger of Allah ﷺ said, "By Allah! It is not poverty that I fear for you: rather, I fear for you that the world will be opened up to you as it was opened up to those before you, so that you seek it earnestly as they sought it earnestly. Thus it would destroy you as it destroyed them." Bukhārī and Muslim (*Mishkāt*, Book of Softening the Hearts, Ḥadīth no. 6163).

Commentary

Islam teaches moderation in this matter. One should neither reject totally the pleasures and delights of the world like monks, nor be so consumed by them that the original purpose of life is wasted. In this narration, the abundance of wealth has been declared as being more dangerous than the situation of poverty and need. The undesirable effects of poverty and need are relatively limited: they do not lead to a wicked and corrupt system, caused by an abundance of wealth, that uproots and discards all principles of character and morality.

10.12 ARTIFICIALITY AND UNNATURAL BEHAVIOUR

عَنْ ابْنِ عَبَّاسٍ ﵁ قَالَ: لَعَنَ رَسُولُ الله ﷺ الْمُتَشَبِّهِينَ مِنْ الرِّجَالِ بِالنِّسَاءِ وَالْمُتَشَبِّهَاتِ مِنْ النِّسَاءِ بِالرِّجَالِ. صحيح البخاري.

[179]   On the authority of Ibn 'Abbās ☙, who said: The Prophet ﷺ said: "Allah has cursed men who imitate women and women who imitate men." Bukhārī (*Mishkāt*, Chapter on Combing the Hair, Ḥadīth no. 4429).

Commentary

Here, imitation of the other sex is not being forbidden in specific or general matters; rather, the meaning is that men and women should not allow their appearances to deteriorate to such an extent that it becomes difficult to distinguish between them outwardly.

10.13 ARTIFICIALITY AND AFFECTATION IN CONVERSATION

عَنْ أَبِي ثَعْلَبَةَ الْخُشَنِيِّ ﷺ، أَنَّ رَسُولَ اللهِ ﷺ، قَالَ: إِنَّ أَحَبَّكُمْ إِلَيَّ وَأَقْرَبَكُمْ مِنِّي يَوْمَ الْقِيَامَةِ أَحَاسِنُكُمْ أَخْلَاقًا، وَإِنَّ أَبْغَضَكُمْ إِلَيَّ وَأَبْعَدَكُمْ مِنِّي مَسَاوِيكُمْ أَخْلَاقًا الثَّرْثَارُونَ الْمُتَفَيْهِقُونَ الْمُتَشَدِّقُونَ. رواه البيهقي في شعب الإيمان.

[180] On the authority of Abū Tha'labah al-Khushanī ﷺ that the Messenger of Allah ﷺ said, "Truly, the most beloved and nearest of you to me on the Day of Resurrection will be the best among you in character. Truly, the most hateful to me and furthest from me will be the worst among you in character, whose tongues move like scissors, who puff up their mouths in contrived speech, and are arrogant." Bayhaqī's *Branches of Faith*, Tirmidhī, Aḥmad, Ibn Ḥibbān and Ṭabarānī (*Mishkāt*, *Ḥadīth* nos. 4797-8).

Commentary

There are many qualities associated with immoral people. One of these is that they are expert in inventing and exaggerating stories. Turning falsehood into truth with their quick tongues is child's play for them.

10.14 FALSE FORMALITY

عَنْ أَسْمَاءَ بِنْتِ عُمَيْسٍ ﷺ قَالَتْ: زَفَفْنَا إِلَى رَسُولِ اللهِ ﷺ بَعْضَ نِسَائِهِ، فَلَمَّا دَخَلْنَا عَلَيْهِ أَخْرَجَ عُسًّا مِنْ لَبَنٍ، فَشَرِبَ مِنْهُ، ثُمَّ نَاوَلَهُ امْرَأَتَهُ، فَقَالَتْ: لا أَشْتَهِيهِ، فَقَالَ: لَا تَجْمَعِي جُوعًا وَكَذِبًا. رواهُ ابن ماجه والطبراني.

[181] On the authority of Asmā' bint 'Umays ﷺ, who said: We presented one of the Messenger of Allah's wives ﷺ to him as a bride. When we entered upon him, he took out a bowl of milk and drank from it. He then passed it to his wife, upon which she said, "I do not desire it." He replied, "Do not combine hunger and lying!" Ṭabarānī's *Al-Mu'jam al-Ṣaghīr* and Ibn Mājah (*Mishkāt*, Chapter on Hospitality, *Ḥadīth* no. 4256).

Commentary

Generally, it has become a fashion nowadays that if a friend or colleague presents some food or drink, one rejects it despite being hungry, protesting that one is not actually hungry. In the above-mentioned narration, it is precisely this kind of lie, induced by excessive formality, that is forbidden.

10.15 EXTRAVAGANCE AND EXAGGERATED FORMALITY

عَنْ جَابِرِ بْنِ عَبْدِ الله ﷺ، أَنَّ رَسُولَ الله ﷺ قَالَ لَهُ: فِرَاشٌ لِلرَّجُلِ، وَفِرَاشٌ لِامْرَأَتِهِ، وَالثَّالِثُ لِلضَّيْفِ، وَالرَّابِعُ لِلشَّيْطَانِ. رواه مسلم، مشكواة، كتاب اللباس.

[182] On the authority of Jābir b. ʿAbdullāh ﷺ, that the Messenger of Allah ﷺ said to him, "There is [in a house] one bed for the man [head of the household], one bed for his wife, a third for the guest, and a fourth for Satan." Muslim (*Mishkāt*, Book of Dress, *Ḥadīth* no. 4310).

Commentary

A Muslim's house should contain furniture and other possessions only according to the need. Having lots of furniture and household items for the purposes of excessive formality and ostentation is a satanic code of behaviour that is extremely displeasing to Allah. The objective of this *Ḥadīth* is not to specify the number of beds in a household; rather, it is to erase the mentality that gives rise to a love of luxurious and extravagant living.

عَـنْ عَبْدِ الله بْنِ عَمْرِو بْنِ الْعَاصِ ﷺ، أَنَّ النَّبِيَّ ﷺ مَرَّ بِسَـعْدٍ وَهُوَ يَتَوَضَّأُ، فَقَالَ: مَا هَذَا السَّـرَفُ يَا سَعْدُ. قَالَ: أَفِي الْوُضُوءِ سَرَفٌ؟ قَالَ: نَعَمْ، وَإِنْ كُنْتَ عَلَى نَهْرٍ جَارٍ.

رواه أحمد.

[183] On the authority of ʿAbdullāh b. ʿAmr b. al-ʿĀṣ ﷺ, that the Prophet ﷺ passed by Saʿd, who was performing his ablution,

and said to him, "What is this extravagance, O Saʿd?" He asked, "Can there be extravagance in ablution?" He replied, "Yes, even if you were on the bank of a flowing river." Aḥmad and Ibn Mājah (*Mishkāt*, Chapter on the Etiquette of Ablution, *Ḥadīth* no. 427).

Commentary

The purpose of this style of instruction is to prevent an extravagant mentality. In some situations, even though extravagance may not have any outward harmful effects, this kind of behaviour must still be avoided, for otherwise it is likely that extravagant habits on other occasions may lead to perdition in this world and the Hereafter. Again, it is made clear here that extravagance is not only forbidden in worldly transactions, but it is also a sin in acts of ritual worship.

عَنْ أَبِي هُرَيْرَةَ ﴿، أَنَّ رَسُولَ الله ﷺ، قَالَ: لا يَنْظُرُ اللهُ يَوْمَ الْقِيَامَةِ إلى مَنْ جَرَّ إِزَارَهُ بَطَرًا. صحيح البخاري، مشكواة، كتاب اللباس.

[184]   On the authority of Abū Hurayrah ☙, that the Prophet ﷺ said, "On the Day of Resurrection, Allah will not look at the one who drags his lower garment [along the ground] out of pride." Bukhārī and Muslim (*Mishkāt*, Book of Dress, *Ḥadīth* no. 4311).

Commentary

Pride and pomp, arrogance and self-delusion are totally repugnant to Allah. This is why in Islam all actions and attitudes that can lead to pride and self-delusion are prohibited.

10.16 EXTRAVAGANCE AND LUXURY

وَعَنْ بِنِ عُمَرَ ﴿، أَنَّ النَّبِيَّ ﷺ قَالَ: مَنْ شَرِبَ فِي إِنَاءٍ مِنْ ذَهَبٍ، أَوْ فِضَّةٍ، أَوْ إِنَاءٍ فِيهِ شَيْءٌ مِنْ ذَلِكَ فَإِنَّمَا يُجَرْجِرُ فِي بَطْنِهِ نَاراً مِنْ جَهَنَّمَ. (رواه الدار قطني – مشـــكاة – باب الأشربة).

[185] On the authority of Ibn ʿUmar ﵄, that the Prophet ﷺ said, "If anyone drinks from a utensil of gold or silver, or from a utensil containing any amount of gold or silver, he is only pouring [or gulping] into his belly the Fire of Hell." Darāquṭnī (*Mishkāt*, Chapter on Drinks, *Ḥadīth* no. 4285). Bukhārī and Muslim (*Mishkāt*, *Ḥadīth* no. 4271) transmit a similar narration on the authority of Umm Salamah.

Commentary

The idea here is that Islam seeks to guard Muslim society against alien formalities and ostentation in wealth. Only drinking is mentioned in the *Ḥadīth*. However, the reality is that it applies to all such utensils of eating and drinking by which wealth is flaunted.

10.17 DESPAIR AND LOSS OF ASPIRATION

عَنْ أَنَس بْنِ مَالِك ﵁، قَالَ النَّبِيُّ ﷺ: لا يَتَمَنَّيَنَّ أَحَدُكُمْ الْمَوْتَ مِنْ ضُرٍّ أَصَابَهُ، فَإِنْ كَانَ لا بُدَّ فَاعِلاً، فَلْيَقُلْ: اللَّهُمَّ أَحْيِنِي مَا كَانَتْ الْحَيَاةُ خَيْرًا لِي، وَتَوَفَّنِي إِذَا كَانَتْ الْوَفَاةُ خَيْرًا لِي. متفق عليه.

[186] On the authority of Anas b. Mālik ﵁, who said: The Messenger of Allah ﷺ said, "None of you should wish for death due to an affliction that befalls him. If you must do, then you should say, 'O Allah! Grant me life as long as life is better for me, and take me when death is better for me.'" Bukhārī and Muslim (*Mishkāt*, Chapter: Wishing for Death, *Ḥadīth* no. 1600).

Commentary

In Islam, wishing for death is not allowed, let alone committing suicide! The reason for this is that amongst the countless favours of Allah, life itself is a great favour. Therefore, to hope for the cessation or removal of this favour is actually ingratitude and lack of appreciation towards it. Thus, it is obviously sinful.

10.18 SELF-DELUSION

عَنْ أَبِي هُرَيْرَةَ ﷺ قَالَ: قَالَ رَسُولُ اللهِ ﷺ: إِذَا وَجَدَ أَحَدُكُمْ فِي بَطْنِهِ شَيْئًا، فَأَشْكَلَ عَلَيْهِ، أَخَرَجَ مِنْهُ شَيْءٌ أَمْ لَا، فَلَا يَخْرُجَنَّ مِنَ الْمَسْجِدِ حَتَّى يَسْمَعَ صَوْتًا، أَوْ يَجِدَ رِيحًا.

رواه مسلم.

[187] On the authority of Abū Hurayrah ﷺ, who said: The Messenger of Allah ﷺ said, "If one of you feels something in his stomach, and then is unsure as to whether or not anything has escaped from it, he should not leave the mosque unless he hears a sound or smells an odour." Muslim (*Mishkāt*, Chapter: What Necessitates Ablution, *Ḥadīth* no. 306).

Commentary

This means that prayer should not be abandoned purely out of doubt or conjecture, but rather only when there is certainty.

II

Virtuous Living

II.1 UNDERSTANDING AND INTELLIGENCE

عَنْ أَبِي هُرَيْرَةَ رضي الله عنه قَالَ: سَمِعْتُ أَبَا الْقَاسِمِ ﷺ يَقُولُ: خَيْرُكُمْ إِسْلَامًا أَحَاسِنُكُمْ أَخْلَاقًا إِذَا فَقُهُوا. رواه أحمد والبخاري في الأدب المفرد.

[188] On the authority of Abū Hurayrah ﵁, who said: I heard Abū'l-Qāsim ﷺ saying, "The best of you in Islam are the best of you in character, if they have understanding [of the religion]." Aḥmad and Bukhārī's *Al-Adab al-Mufrad*, *Ḥadīth* no. 285.

عَنْ أَبِي مَسْعُودٍ الأَنْصَارِيِّ رضي الله عنه قَالَ: كَانَ رَسُولُ اللهِ ﷺ يَمْسَحُ مَنَاكِبَنَا فِي الصَّلَاةِ، وَيَقُولُ: اسْتَوُوا وَلَا تَخْتَلِفُوا، فَتَخْتَلِفَ قُلُوبُكُمْ، لِيَلِنِي مِنْكُمْ أُولُو الأَحْلَامِ وَالنُّهَى، ثُمَّ الَّذِينَ يَلُونَهُمْ، ثُمَّ الَّذِينَ يَلُونَهُمْ. صحيح مسلم.

[189] On the authority of Abū Mas'ūd al-Anṣārī ﵁, who said: The Messenger of Allah ﷺ used to touch our shoulders [to straighten our rows] for the prayer and say, "Be level [in the row]: do not step out of line, otherwise there will be dissension amongst your hearts. The people of maturity and understanding should be closest to me, followed by those next to them, followed by those next to them."[47] Muslim (*Mishkāt*, Chapter on the Congregation, *Ḥadīth* no. 1088).

---

47. The narrator, Abū Mas'ūd, remarked after transmitting this tradition to the next generation, "Today, you are divided far more." – Trans. Note

Commentary

This means that those who possess intelligence, wisdom, understanding and awareness of the religion should stand closest to the Imām in prayer. After that, the rows of the people should be formed according to their ranks in this regard.

11.2 INTELLIGENCE AND EXPERIENCE

عَنْ أَبِي هُرَيْرَةَ ﵁، عَنِ النَّبِيِّ ﷺ، قَالَ: لا يُلْدَغُ الْمُؤْمِنُ مِنْ جُحْرٍ وَاحِدٍ مَرَّتَيْنِ. صحيح البخاري وصحيح مسلم.

[190] On the authority of Abū Hurayrah ﵁, who said: The Messenger of Allah ﷺ said, "The believer is not bitten from the same [snake's or scorpion's] hole twice." Bukhārī and Muslim (*Mishkāt*, *Ḥadīth* no. 5053).

Commentary

A believer remains so alert and perceptive that even if he is deceived once, he does not fall into a trap again. However, since out of the fear of Allah he is content with lawful earnings, no matter how little, he does not even raise his glance towards the opposing stacks of unlawful wealth piled up. Therefore, worldly people regard him as foolish, and it is on this basis that some narrations describe the believer as *ghirr karīm* (naïve and noble) whilst the hypocrite is described as *khabb la'īm* (deceptive and despicable). This meaning is also transmitted in the narration that says that, "Truly, the People of the Garden are simple folk."

عَنْ أَبِي سَعِيدٍ ﵁ قَالَ: قَالَ رَسُولُ اللهِ ﷺ: لا حَلِيمَ إِلا ذُو عَثْرَةٍ، وَلا حَكِيمَ إِلا ذُو تَجْرِبَةٍ. سنن الترمذي ومسند أحمد.

[191] On the authority of Abū Sa'īd ﵁, who said: The Messenger of Allah ﷺ said, "Only one who has endured tribulation can be forbearing. Only one who has experience can be wise." Aḥmad and Tirmidhī (*Mishkāt*, Book of Warning, *Ḥadīth* no. 5056).

11.3 PURIFICATION AND CLEANLINESS

عَــنْ أَبِي مَالِكٍ الْأَشْعَرِيِّ ﷺ قَالَ: قَــالَ رَسُولُ اللهِ ﷺ: الطُّهُورُ شَــطْرُ الْإِيمَانِ.
صحيح مسلم.

[192] On the authority of Abū Mālik al-Ashʿarī ﷺ, who said: The Messenger of Allah ﷺ said, "Purification is half of faith." Muslim (*Mishkāt*, Book of Purification, *Ḥadīth* no. 281).

Commentary

Islam does not only teach spiritual and moral purification and cleanliness, but it also simultaneously emphasises physical hygiene and purity and a sense of presentability. On this basis, physical purification and cleanliness is declared as being half of faith in this *Ḥadīth*.

عَنْ عَائِشَةَ ﷺ قَالَتْ: كَانَتْ يَدُ رَسُولِ اللهِ ﷺ الْيُمْنَى لِطُهُورِهِ وَطَعَامِهِ، وَكَانَتْ يَدُهُ الْيُسْرَى لِخَلَائِهِ وَمَا كَانَ مِنْ أَذًى. سنن أبي داود.

[193] On the authority of ʿĀ'ishah ﷺ, who said: The Messenger of Allah ﷺ would use his right hand for purification [i.e. ablution] and eating, and his left hand for the toilet and other such matters involving dirt." Abū Dāwūd (*Mishkāt*, Chapter: Toilet Etiquette, *Ḥadīth* no. 348).

Commentary

"Matters involving dirt" means that the Prophet ﷺ would use his left hand for things such as nasal discharge. Conversely, he would perform clean acts with his right hand.

عَنْ عَبْدِ اللَّهِ بْنِ مُغَفَّلٍ ﷺ قَالَ: قَالَ رَسُولُ اللهِ ﷺ: لا يَبُولَنَّ أَحَدُكُمْ فِي مُسْتَحَمِّهِ، ثُمَّ يَغْتَسِلُ فِيهِ، أَوْ قَالَ ثُمَّ يَتَوَضَّأُ فِيهِ. رواه أبو داود، مشكواة، باب آداب الخلاء.

[194] On the authority of ʿAbdullāh b. Mughaffal ﷺ, who said: The Messenger of Allah ﷺ said, "None of you should urinate in

his place of washing and then bathe or perform ablution there." Abū Dāwūd, Tirmidhī and Nasā'ī (*Mishkāt*, Chapter: Toilet Etiquette, *Ḥadīth* no. 353).

Commentary

This means that there should be separate places for urination and washing. If such matters are not given due consideration, one's purification and cleanliness become dubious.

عَنْ أَبِي مُوسَى ﷺ قَالَ: كُنْتُ مَعَ رَسُولِ اللهِ ﷺ ذَاتَ يَوْمٍ، فَأَرَادَ أَنْ يَبُولَ، فَأَتَى دَمِثًا فِي أَصْلِ جِدَارٍ، فَبَالَ، ثُمَّ قَالَ ﷺ: إِذَا أَرَادَ أَحَدُكُمْ أَنْ يَبُولَ، فَلْيَرْتَدْ لِبَوْلِهِ مَوْضِعًا. سنن أبو داود.

[195] On the authority of Abū Mūsā ﷺ, who said: I was with the Prophet ﷺ one day, when he needed to urinate. He found a soft patch of ground at the base of a wall and urinated there. He then said, "When one of you needs to urinate, he should find an appropriate place for it." Abū Dāwūd (*Mishkāt*, Chapter: Toilet Etiquette, *Ḥadīth* no. 345).

عَنْ عُمَرَ ﷺ قَالَ رَآنِي النَّبِيُّ ﷺ، وَأَنَا أَبُولُ قَائِمًا، فَقَالَ: يَا عُمَرُ لا تَبُلْ قَائِمًا، فَمَا بُلْتُ قَائِمًا بَعْدُ. رواه الترمذي وابن ماجه.

[196] On the authority of 'Umar ﷺ, who said: The Prophet ﷺ saw me urinate standing, so he said, "O 'Umar, do not urinate standing!" I never did it again. Tirmidhī and Ibn Mājah (*Mishkāt*, Chapter: Toilet Etiquette, *Ḥadīth* no. 363).

Commentary

One can urinate standing due to an excuse or if it is unavoidable, otherwise the ruling given in this *Ḥadīth* must be followed.

عَنْ أَبِي هُرَيْرَةَ ﷺ قَالَ: قَالَ رَسُولُ اللهِ ﷺ: إِنَّمَا أَنَا لَكُمْ مِثْلُ الْوَالِدِ لِوَلَدِهِ، أُعَلِّمُكُمْ إِذَا أَتَيْتُمُ الْغَائِطَ، فَلا تَسْتَقْبِلُوا الْقِبْلَةَ وَلا تَسْتَدْبِرُوهَا. وَأَمَرَ بِثَلَاثَةِ أَحْجَارٍ، وَنَهَى عَنِ الرَّوْثِ وَالرِّمَّةِ، وَنَهَى أَنْ يَسْتَطِيبَ الرَّجُلُ بِيَمِينِهِ. رواه ابو داود والنسائي وابن ماجه.

[197] On the authority of Abū Hurayrah ﷺ, who said: The Messenger of Allah ﷺ said, "Truly, I am only to you like a father to his children. I teach you that when you answer the call of nature, neither face the *qiblah* nor turn your back to it." He commanded the use of three stones, and forbade the use of dung and bones [for purification]. He also forbade that a man should clean himself with his right hand. Abū Dāwūd, Nasā'ī and Ibn Mājah (*Mishkāt*, Chapter: Toilet Etiquette, *Ḥadīth* no. 347).

Commentary

1. There is disagreement amongst the jurists and Imāms regarding the issue of facing towards or away from the *qiblah* when answering the call of nature. From all the legal evidences, the position of Imām Shāfiʿī seems to be the strongest one, i.e. that the restriction applies to open areas, but not to built-up areas (where there is a wall between the person and the *qiblah*).
2. There are three ways of purification after answering the call of nature: (a) the use of three stones or clods of earth; (b) the use of water; and (c) a combination of the two methods.[48]

عَنْ عَائِشَةَ رضي الله عنها قَالَتْ: سَمِعْتُ رَسُولَ اللهِ ﷺ يَقُولُ: لا صَلَاةَ بِحَضْرَةِ الطَّعَامِ، وَلا هُوَ يُدَافِعُهُ الأَخْبَثَانِ. صحيح مسلم، مشكواة باب الجماعة.

[198] On the authority of 'Ā'ishah رضي الله عنها that she said: I heard the Messenger of Allah ﷺ saying, "There should be no prayer when food has been served, or when either of the two calls of nature are troubling a person." Muslim (*Mishkāt*, Chapter: The Congregation, *Ḥadīth* no. 1057).

Commentary

1. If one is hungry and food is ready, then one should eat to one's satisfaction first, so that one can offer the prayer with

48. As Imām Ibn al-Qayyim argued, the use of cotton, bark or leaves is analogous to that of stones and earth, and therefore perfectly acceptable. In our times, this ruling can easily be seen to extend to the use of toilet paper. – Trans. Note

full concentration and focus of the heart. However, if one is not too hungry, it is better to perform the prayer first.

2. It is never appropriate to pray whilst resisting the basic calls of nature.

عَنْ مُعَاذِ بْنِ جَبَلٍ ﷺ قَالَ: قَالَ رَسُولُ اللهِ ﷺ: اتَّقُوا الْمَلَاعِنَ الثَّلَاثَةَ: الْبَرَازَ فِي الْمَوَارِدِ، وَقَارِعَةِ الطَّرِيقِ، وَالظِّلِّ. سنن أبي داود، مشكواة باب آداب الخلاء.

[199] On the authority of Muʿādh b. Jabal ﷺ, who said: The Messenger of Allah ﷺ said, "Beware of three accursed places [when answering the call of nature]: (1) river-banks, (2) public paths and (3) shady spots." Abū Dāwūd and Ibn Mājah (*Mishkāt*, Chapter: Toilet Etiquette, *Ḥadīth* no. 355).

Commentary

This means that if a person answers the call of nature in any of these three places, he deserves Divine curses. Two matters are learnt from this ruling:

1. That those who are inclined towards cleanliness find such disgusting behaviour to be revolting; and
2. To answer the call of nature in such places where the general public pass by and take rest is a proof of utter shamelessness and extreme selfishness.

عَنْ مُعَاوِيَةَ بْنِ قُرَّةَ، عَنْ أَبِيهِ ﷺ، أَنَّ النَّبِيَّ ﷺ نَهَى عَنْ هَاتَيْنِ الشَّجَرَتَيْنِ، وَقَالَ: مَنْ أَكَلَهُمَا فَلَا يَقْرَبَنَّ مَسْجِدَنَا، وَقَالَ: إِنْ كُنْتُمْ لَا بُدَّ آكِلِيهِمَا، فَأَمِيتُوهُمَا طَبْخًا. قَالَ: يَعْنِي الْبَصَلَ وَالثُّومَ. سنن أبي داود، مشكواة، باب المساجد.

[200] On the authority of Muʿāwiyah b. Qurrah from his father ﷺ, that the Messenger of Allah ﷺ forbade the produce of these two plants, i.e. onion and garlic, and said, "Whoever eats these must not come near our mosque." He also said, "If you really must eat them, then kill their odour by cooking them." Abū Dāwūd (*Mishkāt*, Chapter: The Mosques, *Ḥadīth* no. 736).

Commentary

There is so much attention given to cleanliness and social etiquette in Islam that it is forbidden to enter the mosque after eating things whose odour is usually regarded as repulsive. We learn two matters from this ruling:

1. that one should avoid eating and using such things that give off extremely repulsive odours;
2. that at the time of public gatherings and social occasions, one should respect one's companions.

11.4 ETIQUETTE OF EATING

عَنْ عُمَرَ بْنَ أَبِيْ سَلَمَةَ ﵁ قَالَ: كُنْتُ غُلَامًا فِي حِجْرِ رَسُولِ اللهِ ﷺ، وَكَانَتْ يَدِيْ تَطِيْشُ فِي الصَّحْفَةِ، فَقَالَ لِيْ رَسُولُ اللهِ ﷺ: سَمِّ اللهَ وَكُلْ بِيَمِيْنِكَ وَكُلْ مِمَّا يَلِيْكَ. رواه البخاري ومسلم، مشكواة، كتاب الأطعمة.

[201] On the authority of 'Umar b. Abī Salamah ﵁, who said: I was a young boy being brought up in the household of the Messenger of Allah ﷺ. At mealtimes, my hand would rove all around the dish, so he ﷺ said to me, "Mention the Name of Allah, eat with your right hand and eat from [the side of the dish] that is nearest to you." Bukhārī and Muslim (*Mishkāt*, Chapter: Foodstuffs, *Ḥadīth* no. 4159).

Commentary

This habit of 'Umar b. Abī Salamah may seem to be trivial, but nevertheless the Prophet ﷺ advised him and taught him the basic etiquette of eating. This teaches us that parents or guardians should be extremely concerned about teaching children even seemingly trivial matters.

It should be remembered that 'Umar b. Abī Salamah was the step-son of the Prophet ﷺ, being the son of Mother of the Believers Umm Salamah and her first husband, Abū Salamah. Thus, the Prophet ﷺ took care of his upbringing just as he would take care of his own child.

عَنْ أَبِي هُرَيْرَةَ ﷺ قَالَ: مَا عَابَ النَّبِيُّ ﷺ طَعَامًا قَطُّ، إِنْ اشْتَهَاهُ أَكَلَهُ، وَإِلا تَرَكَهُ. صحيح البخاري ومسلم، مشكواة ، كتاب الأطعمة.

[202] On the authority of Abū Hurayrah ﷺ, who said: The Prophet ﷺ never criticised food at all. If he desired it, he would eat it; if he disliked it, he would leave it. Bukhārī and Muslim (*Mishkāt*, Chapter: Foodstuffs, *Ḥadīth* no. 4172).

Commentary

The essential thing is to eat in order to live, and not to live in order to eat. This is why one who keeps the highest objectives in mind, neither finds fault in food and drink nor causes conflict within his household by criticising every small matter.

عَنْ وَحْشِيِّ بْنِ حَرْبٍ، عَنْ أَبِيهِ، عَنْ جَدِّهِ ﷺ، أَنَّ أَصْحَابَ النَّبِيِّ ﷺ، قَالُوا: يَا رَسُولَ اللهِ ﷺ إِنَّا نَأْكُلُ وَلَا نَشْبَعُ. قَالَ: فَلَعَلَّكُمْ تَفْتَرِقُونَ. قَالُوا: نَعَمْ. قَالَ: فَاجْتَمِعُوا عَلَى طَعَامِكُمْ، وَاذْكُرُوا اسْمَ اللهِ عَلَيْهِ يُبَارَكْ لَكُمْ فِيهِ. سنن أبي داود، مشكواة، باب الضيافة.

[203] On the authority of Waḥshī b. Ḥarb from his father from his grandfather ﷺ, that the Companions of the Messenger of Allah ﷺ said, "O Messenger of Allah! Truly, we eat but are not satisfied." He replied, "Perhaps you eat separately?" They said, "Yes." He said, "Then come together over your meals and mention the name of Allah: you will be blessed in your food." Abū Dāwūd (*Mishkāt*, Chapter: Hospitality, *Ḥadīth* no. 4252).

Commentary

It is legally permissible to eat separately, but eating communally is more approved and brings goodness and blessing. Since the communal way in the matter of eating can be so effective, we can gain some idea of the results and fruits of collective work in every aspect of life.

عَنْ أَبِي هُرَيْرَةَ ﷺ قَالَ: قَالَ رَسُولُ اللهِ ﷺ: مَنْ بَاتَ وَفِي يَدِهِ رِيحُ غَمَرٍ، فَأَصَابَهُ شَيْءٌ، فَلا يَلُومَنَّ إِلا نَفْسَهُ. سنن الترمذي، مشكواة ، كتاب الأطعمة.

[204] On the authority of Abū Hurayrah ﵁, who said: The Messenger of Allah ﷺ said, "Whoever spends the night with his hand sticky, not having washed it, should only blame himself if he is afflicted with some harm." Tirmidhī, Abū Dāwūd and Ibn Mājah (*Mishkāt*, Chapter: Foodstuffs, *Ḥadīth* no. 4219).

Commentary

This means that it is necessary to wash the hands after eating, especially when they are sticky.

11.5 DIGNITY

عَنْ يَعْلى بْنِ مَمْلَكٍ ﵁ أَنَّهُ سَأَلَ أُمَّ سَلَمَةَ ﵂ زَوْجَ النَّبِيِّ ﷺ، عَنْ قِرَاءَةِ النَّبِيِّ ﷺ، فَإِذَا هِيَ تَنْعَتُ قِرَاءَةً مُفَسَّرَةً حَرْفًا حَرْفًا. سنن الترمذي، مشكواة، كتاب فضائل القرآن.

[205] On the authority of Ya'la b. Mamlak ﵁, that he asked Umm Salamah about the recitation of the Prophet ﷺ, so she described it as being lucid, clearly articulating each letter. Tirmidhī (*Ḥadīth* no. 2923), Abū Dāwūd and Nasā'ī (*Mishkāt*, Chapter: Virtues of the Qur'ān, *Ḥadīth* no. 2204).

Commentary

Therefore, the Prophet's recitation was neither hurried nor nervous but rather it was firm and clear, distinguishing each letter, manifesting the greatest dignity and confidence.

11.6 BEAUTY OF VOICE

عَنْ أَبِي هُرَيْرَةَ ﵁ قَالَ: قَالَ رَسُولُ اللهِ ﷺ: لَيْسَ مِنَّا مَنْ لَمْ يَتَغَنَّ بِالْقُرْآنِ. صحيح البخاري، مشكواة، كتاب فضائل القرآن.

[206] On the authority of Abū Hurayrah ﵁, who said: The Messenger of Allah ﷺ said, "He who does not recite the Qur'ān melodiously is not one of us ." Bukhārī (*Mishkāt*, Chapter: Virtues of the Qur'ān, *Ḥadīth* no. 2194).

Commentary

Reciting the Qur'ān melodiously with a beautiful voice without contrived artificiality is a recommended matter. Reciting the Qur'ān with a contrived, artificial or monotonous voice is displeasing to Allah.

11.7 CLARITY OF DISCOURSE

عَنْ عَائِشَةَ رضي الله عنها قَالَتْ: إنَّ رسولَ الله ﷺ لَمْ يَكُنْ يَسْرُدُ الْحَدِيثَ كَسَرْدِكُمْ، كان يُحدِّثُ حديثاً لو عَدَّهُ العادُّ لأحصاه. متفق عليه، مشكواة، باب أخلاق النبيّ ﷺ.

[207] On the authority of 'Ā'ishah ﷺ, who said, "Truly, the Messenger of Allah ﷺ would not speak quickly the way you do. He would speak in such a way that if someone were to count his words, he would be able to do so." Bukhārī and Muslim (*Mishkāt*, Chapter: Character of the Prophet, ﷺ, *Ḥadīth* no. 5815).

11.8 PURITY OF TONGUE

عَنْ أَنَس رضي الله عنه قَالَ: لَمْ يَكُنْ رَسُولُ الله ﷺ فَاحِشًا وَلا لَعَّانًا وَلَا سَبَّابًا ، كَانَ يَقُولُ عِنْدَ الْمَعْتَبَةِ مَا لَهُ تَرِبَ جَبِينُهُ. صحيح البخاري، مشكواة، باب في أخلاق النبي ﷺ.

[208] On the authority of Anas ﷺ, who said, "The Messenger of Allah ﷺ would not engage in obscene talk, constant cursing or hurling insults. When he wished to criticise someone, he would simply say, 'What is the matter with him? May his forehead be rubbed in dust!'" Bukhārī (*Mishkāt*, Chapter: Character of the Prophet, ﷺ, *Ḥadīth* no. 5811).

11.9 CORRECTING UNDIGNIFIED APPEARANCES

وَعنَ جَابِرٍ رضي الله عنه، أَنَّ النَّبِيَ ﷺ، أَبصرَ رَجُلاً ثَائِرَ الرَأْسِ، فقال: لِمَ يُشَوِّهُ أَحَدُكُمْ نَفْسَهُ. وأشَارَ بِيَدِه أيْ :خُذْ مِنْهُ. المعجم الصغير للطبراني.

[209] On the authority of Jabir ﷺ, that the Prophet ﷺ, upon seeing a man with unruly hair, said, "Why does one of you disfigure himself?" and he indicated with his hand that the man should trim his hair. Ṭabarānī's *Al-Mu'jam al-Ṣaghīr*.

11.10 GOOD-NATUREDNESS

عَنْ عَبْدِ اللهِ بْنِ الْحَارِثِ بْنِ جَزْءٍ ﷺ قَالَ: مَا رَأَيْتُ أَحَدًا أَكْثَرَ تَبَسُّمًا مِنْ رَسُولِ اللهِ ﷺ.
رواه الترمذي، مشكواة، باب في أخلاق النبي ﷺ.

[210] On the authority of 'Abdullāh b. al-Ḥārith b. Jaz' ﷺ, who said, "I never saw anyone smiling more than the Messenger of Allah, ﷺ." Tirmidhī (*Mishkāt*, Chapter: Character of the Prophet, ﷺ, *Ḥadīth* no. 5829).

Commentary

The temperament of the Prophet ﷺ was such that it was neither extremely dry and uninspiring nor so jolly that he would burst out laughing at the smallest things; rather, his demeanour was balanced and moderate.

11.11 AVOIDING EXCESSIVE LAUGHTER

عَنْ عَائِشَةَ ﷺ قَالَتْ: مَا رَأَيْتُ النَّبِيَّ ﷺ، مُسْتَجْمِعًا قَطُّ ضَاحِكًا حَتَّى أَرَى مِنْهُ لَهَوَاتِهِ، إِنَّما كَانَ يَتَبَسَّمُ. صحيح البخاري، مشكواة، باب في أخلاق النبي ﷺ.

[211] On the authority of 'Ā'ishah ﷺ, who said, "I never saw the Prophet ﷺ burst out laughing such that his uvula became visible. He would only smile."[49] Bukhārī (*Mishkāt*, Chapter: Character of the Prophet, ﷺ, *Ḥadīth* no. 5814).

49. The uvula is a fleshy lobe at the back of the throat. – Trans. Note

11.12 ETIQUETTE OF TRAVELLING

عَنْ أَبِي هُرَيْرَةَ ﷺ قَالَ: قَالَ رَسُولُ اللَّهِ ﷺ: السَّفَرُ قِطْعَةٌ مِنَ الْعَذَابِ يَمْنَعُ أَحَدَكُمْ نَوْمَهُ وَطَعَامَهُ وَ شَرَابَهُ، فَإِذَا قَضَى نَهْمَتَهُ مِنْ وَجْهِهِ، فَلْيُعَجِّلْ إِلَى أَهْلِهِ. صحيح البخاري، مشكواة، باب آداب السفر.

[212] On the authority of Abū Hurayrah ﷺ, who said: The Messenger of Allah ﷺ said, "Travelling is a piece of punishment: it prevents you from your sleep, food and drink. Therefore, when you have finished your business, hurry back to your family." Bukhārī and Muslim (*Mishkāt*, Chapter: Etiquette of Travelling, *Ḥadīth* no. 3899).

عَنْ جَابِرِ بْنِ عَبْدِ الله ﷺ قَالَ: قَالَ رَسُولُ الله ﷺ: إِذَا أَطَالَ أَحَدُكُمْ الْغَيْبَةَ، فَلا يَطْرُقْ أَهْلَهُ لَيْلًا. صحيح البخاري ومسلم، مشكواة، باب آداب السفر.

[213] On the authority of Jābir b. ʿAbdullāh ﷺ, who said: The Messenger of Allah ﷺ said, "When one of you is away for a long time, he should not return to his family at night." Bukhārī and Muslim (*Mishkāt*, Chapter: Etiquette of Travelling, *Ḥadīth* no. 3903).

Commentary

The instruction given in this *Ḥadīth* must be put into practice when a person is returning home after a long absence without prior notice. However, if he informs his family beforehand, the purpose of the *Ḥadīth* is fulfilled and he may return whenever is convenient for him.

عَنْ كَعْبِ بْنِ مَالِكٍ ﷺ، أَنَّ رَسُولَ الله ﷺ، كَانَ لا يَقْدَمُ مِنْ سَفَرٍ إِلا نَهَارًا فِي الضُّحَى، فَإِذَا قَدِمَ بَدَأَ بِالْمَسْجِدِ، فَصَلَّى فِيهِ رَكْعَتَيْنِ. صحيح مسلم، مشكواة، باب آداب السفر.

[214] On the authority of Kaʿb b. Mālik ﷺ, who said, "The Prophet ﷺ would only return from journeys in the morning [before noon]. Upon arrival, he would first proceed to the mosque, where he would pray two *rakʿahs*." Bukhārī (*Mishkāt*, Chapter: Etiquette of Travelling, *Ḥadīth* no. 3906).

Commentary

Offering a two-*rak'ah* prayer is the best and most effective way to express gratitude for returning safe and sound from a journey, especially from a long journey.

11.13 TAKING PRECAUTIONS

عَنْ رَجُلٍ مِنْ أَصْحَابِ النَّبِيِّ ﷺ قَالَ: قَالَ رَسُولُ الله ﷺ: مَنْ بَاتَ عَلَى أَنْجَارٍ، فَوَقَعَ مِنْهُ، فَمَاتَ،وَمَنْ رَكِبَ الْبَحْرَ حِينَ يَرْتَجُّ، فَهَلَكَ، فَقَدْ بَرِئَتْ مِنْهُ الذِّمَّةُ. مسند أحمد، الأدب المفرد، باب من بات على سطح ليس له ستره- ص ١٢٤ .

[215] On the authority of one of the Companions of the Prophet ﷺ that he said, "If someone sleeps near the edge of a roof and falls off, or travels by sea when it is stormy, and perishes, then no-one is liable." Aḥmad and Bukhārī's *Al-Adab al-Mufrad*, Chapter on Whoever Sleeps on an Unfenced Roof, *Ḥadīth* no. 1194.

Commentary

Life is also one of Allah's great favours, and therefore to lose or harm it through heedlessness or lack of caution is forbidden for a believer.

عَنْ عَبْدِ اللهِ بْنِ سَرْجِسَ رضي الله عنه، أَنَّ نَبِيَّ الله ﷺ، قَالَ: لا يَبُولَنَّ أَحَدُكُمْ فِي جُحْرٍ. رواه ابو داود والنسائي.

[216] On the authority of 'Abdullāh b. Sarjis رضي الله عنه, who said: The Messenger of Allah ﷺ said, "None of you should urinate into a [snake's or scorpion's] hole." Abū Dāwūd and Nasā'ī (*Mishkāt*, Chapter: Toilet Etiquette, *Ḥadīth* no. 354).

11.14 ETIQUETTE OF SLEEPING

عَنْ أَبِي أُمَامَةَ رضي الله عنه قَالَ: مَرَّ النَّبِيُّ ﷺ عَلى رَجُلٍ نَائِمٍ فِي الْمَسْجِدِ مُنْبَطِحٍ عَلى وَجْهِهِ، فَضَرَبَهُ بِرِجْلِهِ، وَقَالَ: قُمْ وَاقْعُدْ فَإِنَّهَا نَوْمَةٌ جَهَنَّمِيَّةٌ. سنن أبن ماجه، الأدب المفرد، باب الضجعة على وجه.

[217]   On the authority of Abū Umāmah ☺, that the Messenger of Allah ﷺ passed by a man lying face-down in the mosque so he prodded him with his foot and said, "Get up! This is a hellish sleeping posture." Bukhārī's *Al-Adab al-Mufrad*, Chapter on Lying Face-Down, *Ḥadīth* no. 1188.

II.15 PROTECTING HEALTH

عَنْ أَبِي قَيْسٍ ☺، أَنَّهُ جَاءَ وَرَسُولُ الله ﷺ يَخْطُبُ، فَقَامَ فِي الشَّمْسِ، فَأَمَرَهُ، فَتَحَوَّلَ إِلَى الظِّلِّ. سنن أبي داود، الأدب المفرد.

[218]   On the authority of Abū Qays ☺ that he came [to the mosque] while the Messenger of Allah ﷺ was delivering a sermon and stood in the sun, so the Prophet ﷺ ordered him to move into the shade. Bukhārī's *Al-Adab al-Mufrad*, Chapter on One Should Not Sit in the Sun, *Ḥadīth* no. 1174.

Commentary

We can gain an idea of the love and concern that the Prophet ﷺ had for his people. In even very small matters, he would take care that no-one was harmed.

II.16 ETIQUETTE OF WALKING

عَنْ أَبِي هُرَيْرَةَ ☺، أَنَّ رَسُولَ الله ﷺ، قَالَ: لَا يَمْشِ أَحَدُكُمْ فِي نَعْلٍ وَاحِدَةٍ، لِيُنْعِلْهُمَا جَمِيعًا، أَوْ لِيَخْلَعْهُمَا جَمِيعًا. صحيح البخاري، مشكواة، باب النعال.

[219]   On the authority of Abū Hurayrah ☺, who said: The Messenger of Allah ﷺ said, "None of you should walk wearing one sandal: you should either remove both or wear both." Bukhārī (*Mishkāt*, Chapter on Sandals, *Ḥadīth* no. 4411).

12

A Virtuous Society

12.1 RIGHTS OF PARENTS

عَنْ أَبُو أُسَيْدٍ ﷺ قَالَ: بَيْنَما أَنَا جَالِسٌ عِنْدَ رَسُولِ اللهِ ﷺ، إِذْ جَاءَهُ رَجُلٌ مِنَ الْأَنْصَارِ، فَقَالَ: يَا رَسُولَ اللهِ هَلْ بَقِيَ عَلَيَّ مِنْ بِرِّ أَبَوَيَّ شَيْءٌ بَعْدَ مَوْتِهما أَبَرُّهُمَا بِهِ؟ قَالَ: نَعَمْ، خِصَالٌ أَرْبَعَةٌ: الصَّلَاةُ عَلَيْهِمَا، وَالاسْتِغْفَارُ لَهُمَا، وَإِنْفَاذُ عَهْدِهِمَا، وَإِكْرَامُ صَدِيقِهِمَا، وَصِلَةُ الرَّحِمِ الَّتِي لا رَحِمَ لَكَ إِلا مِنْ قِبَلِهِمَا. مسند أحمد، الأدب المفرد.

[220] On the authority of Abū Usayd ﷺ, who said: I was sitting with the Messenger of Allah ﷺ when a man of the Anṣār came to him and asked, "O Messenger of Allah! Is there anything left after the death of my parents by which I may show kindness to them?" He replied, "Yes, there are four activities: (1) supplicating and praying for forgiveness for them, (2) implementing their promises and bequests, (3) treating their friends kindly and (4) maintaining your parental family ties." Aḥmad and Bukhārī's *Al-Adab al-Mufrad*, *Ḥadīth* no. 35.

Commentary

The last instruction means that one should show due care and respect towards one's paternal and maternal uncles and aunts.

عَنْ عَبْدِ اللهِ بْنِ عَمْرِو بْنِ الْعَاصِ ﷺ قَالَ: جَاءَ رَجُلٌ إِلَى النَّبِيِّ ﷺ، يُبَايِعُهُ. قَالَ: جِئْتُ لِأُبَايِعَكَ عَلَى الْهِجْرَةِ، وَتَرَكْتُ أَبَوَيَّ يَبْكِيَانِ. قَالَ: فَارْجِعْ إِلَيْهِمَا، فَأَضْحِكْهُمَا كَمَا أَبْكَيْتَهُمَا. مسند أحمد، والأدب المفرد.

[221] On the authority of ʿAbdullāh b. ʿAmr b. al-ʿĀṣ ﵄, who said: A man came to the Prophet ﷺ, leaving his parents weeping, in order to pledge his allegiance after having performed *hijrah*, so the Prophet ﷺ said to him, "Return to them and make them laugh as you made them weep." Aḥmad and Bukhārī's *Al-Adab al-Mufrad*, *Ḥadīth* no. 13.

Commentary

If one's parents are weak and in need of their children's help, then in this situation, to stay with them and serve them is more virtuous than even an action as great as *hijrah* (emigration for the sake of God).

عَنْ ابْنِ عَبَّاسٍ ﵄، أَخْبَرَهُ أَنَّ سَعْدَ بْنَ عُبَادَةَ الْأَنْصَارِيَّ اسْتَفْتَى النَّبِيَّ ﷺ فِي نَذْرٍ كَانَ عَلَى أُمِّهِ، فَتُوُفِّيَتْ قَبْلَ أَنْ تَقْضِيَهُ، فَأَفْتَاهُ أَنْ يَقْضِيَهُ عَنْهَا. صحيح البخاري ومسلم.

[222] On the authority of Ibn ʿAbbās ﵄, that Saʿd b. ʿUbādah sought a legal verdict from the Prophet ﷺ regarding fulfilment of a vow that was incumbent upon his mother, but she had died before fulfilling it. He gave the verdict that Saʿd should fulfil it on her behalf. Bukhārī and Muslim (*Mishkāt*, Chapter on Vows, *Ḥadīth* no. 3433).

12.2 MAINTAINING FAMILY TIES

عَنْ بَكَّارِ بن عَبْدِ العَزِيزِ، عَنْ أَبِيهِ، عَنْ جَدِّهِ ﵁، عَنِ النَّبِيِّ ﷺ قَالَ: كُلُّ ذُنُوبٍ يُؤَخِّرُ اللهُ مِنْهَا مَا شَاءَ إِلَى يَوْمِ القِيَامَةِ إلا البَغْيَ وَعُقُوقَ الْوَالِدَيْنِ أَوْ قَطِيْعَةَ الرَّحِمْ يُعجِلُ لِصَاحِبِهَا فِي الدُّنْيَا قَبْلَ الْمَوْتِ. الأدب المفرد، باب في النهي عن البغي.

[223] On the authority of Bakkār ibn ʿAbd al-ʿAzīz, from his father from his grandfather ﵁, that the Prophet ﷺ said, "Allah will delay the punishment of every sin, if He wishes, until the Day of Resurrection, except for (1) sedition and rebellion, (2) disobedience to parents and (3) severing family ties. For these sins, the person will be punished in this world before his death." Bukhārī's *Al-Adab al-Mufrad*, Chapter on Sedition and Rebellion, *Ḥadīth* no. 591 (*Mishkāt*, *Ḥadīth* no. 4945).

12.3 OBEYING THE HUSBAND

عَنْ أَبِي سَعِيدٍ ﷺ قَالَ: قَالَ رَسُولُ اللهِ ﷺ: لا تَصُومُ امْرَأَةٌ إِلا بِإِذْنِ زَوْجِهَا. سنن أبي داود وابن ماجه.

[224] On the authority of Abū Saʿīd ﷺ, who said: The Messenger of Allah ﷺ said, "A woman must not fast unless it is with her husband's permission." Abū Dāwūd and Ibn Mājah (*Mishkāt*, Chapter: Treatment and Rights of Women, *Ḥadīth* no. 3269).

Commentary

This *Ḥadīth* refers to voluntary fasting. For an obligatory fast, she must fast irrespective of her husband's approval, as another *Ḥadīth* states that, "There is no obedience to the created in disobedience to the Creator." However, a voluntary fast should not be performed without the husband's permission.[50]

12.4 THE VIRTUOUS WIFE

عَنْ أَبِي هُرَيْرَةَ ﷺ، عَنْ النَّبِيِّ ﷺ قَالَ: تُنْكَحُ الْمَرْأَةُ لِأَرْبَعٍ: لِمَالِهَا وَلِحَسَبِهَا وَلِجَمَالِهَا وَلِدِينِهَا، فَاظْفَرْ بِذَاتِ الدِّينِ تَرِبَتْ يَدَاكَ. صحيح البخاري ومسلم، مشكواة، كتاب النكاح.

[225] On the authority of Abū Hurayrah ﷺ, who said: The Messenger of Allah ﷺ said, "A woman is married for four things: (1) her wealth, (2) her family lineage, (3) her beauty and (4) her religion. Choose the one possessing religion, may your hands be full of dust [i.e. may you be happy and content]!" Bukhārī and Muslim (*Mishkāt*, Book of Marriage, *Ḥadīth* no. 3082).

عَنْ عَبْدِ اللهِ بْنِ عَمْرِو بْنِ الْعَاصِ ﷺ، أَنَّ رَسُولَ اللهِ ﷺ، قَالَ: إِنَّ الدُّنْيَا كُلَّهَا مَتَاعٌ، وَخَيْرُ مَتَاعِ الدُّنْيَا الْمَرْأَةُ الصَّالِحَةُ. صحيح مسلم، مشكواة، كتاب النكاح.

50. Sexual intercourse is forbidden during fasting, which also reduces sexual appetite. This teaching aims to protect the importance of conjugal rights in marriage. – Trans. Note

[226] On the authority of ʿAbdullāh b. ʿAmr b. al-ʿĀṣ ﵄, who said: The Messenger of Allah ﷺ said, "The world, all of it, is for enjoyment, and the best worldly enjoyment is a righteous wife." Muslim (*Mishkāt*, Book of Marriage, *Ḥadīth* no. 3083).

Commentary

It is a reality that no matter how pious and righteous a man may be, if his wife is not virtuous then he will never live in peace and tranquillity in this world.

12.5 THE IMPORTANCE OF ACCEPTING PROPOSALS FROM THE VIRTUOUS

عَنْ أَبِي هُرَيْرَةَ ﵁ قَالَ: قَالَ رَسُولُ اللهِ ﷺ: إِذَا خَطَبَ إِلَيْكُمْ مَنْ تَرْضَوْنَ دِينَهُ وَخُلُقَهُ فَزَوِّجُوهُ، إِلا تَفْعَلُوا تَكُنْ فِتْنَةٌ فِي الْأَرْضِ وَفَسَادٌ عَرِيضٌ. سنن الترمذي، مشكواة، كتاب النكاح.

[227] On the authority of Abū Hurayrah ﵁, who said: The Messenger of Allah ﷺ said, "When a marriage proposal is made by someone whose religion and character you approve of, accept the proposal. Unless you do so, there will be much tribulation and comprehensive corruption in the land." Tirmidhī (*Mishkāt*, Book of Marriage, *Ḥadīth* no. 3090).

Commentary

To reject or stall proposals from appropriate suitors on the basis of tribal considerations or cultural restrictions mostly causes severe tribulation within society. Hence, it is described as "comprehensive corruption" in this *Ḥadīth*.

12.6 A HAPPY MARRIED LIFE

عَنْ أَبِي هُرَيْرَةَ ﵁ قَالَ: قَالَ رَسُولُ اللهِ ﷺ: لا يَفْرَكْ مُؤْمِنٌ مُؤْمِنَةً إِنْ كَرِهَ مِنْهَا خُلُقًا رَضِيَ مِنْهَا آخَرَ. صحيح مسلم، مشكواة.

[228] On the authority of Abū Hurayrah ﷺ, who said: The Messenger of Allah ﷺ said, "A believing man [i.e. a husband] must not hate a believing woman [i.e. his wife]. If he dislikes one of her qualities, he will like another." Muslim (*Mishkāt*, Chapter: Treatment and Rights of Women, *Ḥadīth* no. 3240).

Commentary

It is impossible for a woman to be perfect in every way. If she has a bad quality or weakness, she will also have good qualities. Thus, a believer should keep in mind both sides of the coin.[51]

12.7 THE IMPORTANCE OF A HAPPY MARRIED LIFE

عَنْ أَبِي هُرَيْرَةَ ﷺ، أَنَّ النَّبِيَّ ﷺ، كَانَ إِذَا رَفَّأَ الْإِنْسَانَ إِذَا تَزَوَّجَ، قَالَ: بَارَكَ اللهُ لَكَ، وَبَارَكَ عَلَيْكَ، وَجَمَعَ بَيْنَكُمَا فِي الْخَيْرِ. سنن الترمذي، أبي داود، مسند أحمد، مشكواة، باب الدعوات.

[229] On the authority of Abū Hurayrah ﷺ, that when the Prophet ﷺ would congratulate a person on marrying, he would say, "May Allah bless you, may He shower His blessings upon the two of you, and join you together in a relationship of goodness." Aḥmad, Tirmidhī, Abū Dāwūd and Ibn Mājah (*Mishkāt*, Chapter on Supplications, *Ḥadīth* no. 2445).

12.8 AN EASY-GOING RELATIONSHIP

عَنْ عَائِشَةَ ﷺ، أَنَّهَا كَانَتْ مَعَ النَّبِيِّ ﷺ فِي سَفَرٍ، قَالَتْ: فَسَابَقْتُهُ، فَسَبَقْتُهُ عَلَى رِجْلَيَّ، فَلَمَّا حَمَلْتُ اللَّحْمَ سَابَقْتُهُ، فَسَبَقَنِي، فَقَالَ: هَذِهِ بِتِلْكَ السَّبْقَةِ. سنن أبي داود، مسند أحمد.

[230] On the authority of 'Ā'ishah ﷺ, that she was with the Messenger of Allah ﷺ on a journey. She said, "I ran a race against him and won. Later, when I had put on weight, I raced him again

51. Cf. Qur'ān, *Sūrah al-Nisā'* (Chapter: Women), 4: 19, "*If you dislike them* [your wives], *it may be that you dislike something in which Allah has placed much good for you.*" – Trans. Note

but he won this time and said, 'This win is in return for that one'." Aḥmad and Abū Dāwūd (*Mishkāt*, Chapter on the Treatment and Rights of Women, *Ḥadīth* no. 3251).

Commentary

This *Ḥadīth* contains a nice example of a happy married life. A man should not be dry and formal with his family, but be extremely informal and good-natured.

12.9 WINNING THE WIFE'S HEART

عَنْ عَائِشَةَ رضي الله عنها قَالَتْ: كُنْتُ أَلْعَبُ بِالْبَنَاتِ عِنْدَ النَّبِيِّ ﷺ، وَكَانَ لِي صَوَاحِبُ يَلْعَبْنَ مَعِي، فَكَانَ رَسُولُ اللهِ ﷺ إِذَا دَخَلَ يَتَقَمَّعْنَ مِنْهُ، فَيُسَرِّبُهُنَّ إِلَيَّ، فَيَلْعَبْنَ مَعِي. رواه البخاري ومسلم.

[231] On the authority of 'Ā'ishah رضي الله عنها, who said, "I used to play with dolls in the house of the Prophet ﷺ, and I had friends who would play with me. When the Messenger of Allah ﷺ would enter, they would hide from him so he would [find them] and send them to me so that they could play with me."[52] Bukhārī and Muslim (*Mishkāt*, Chapter on the Treatment and Rights of Women, *Ḥadīth* no. 3243).

12.10 TREATING ONE'S WIVES EQUALLY

عَنْ عَائِشَةَ رضي الله عنها قَالَتْ: كَانَ رَسُولُ اللهِ ﷺ إِذَا أَرَادَ سَفَرًا أَقْرَعَ بَيْنَ نِسَائِهِ، فَأَيَّتُهُنَّ خَرَجَ سَهْمُهَا خَرَجَ بِهَا مَعَهُ. رواه البخاري ومسلم.

[232] On the authority of 'Ā'ishah رضي الله عنها, who said, "When the Messenger of Allah ﷺ intended to undertake a journey, he would draw lots among his wives. Whoever's name turned up, he would

52. The Prophet ﷺ married 'Ā'ishah whilst she was still very young, but the marriage was certainly only consummated when she was an adult. – Trans. Note

travel in her company." Bukhārī and Muslim (*Mishkāt*, Chapter: Sharing, *Ḥadīth* no. 3232).

Commentary

A number of matters are learnt from this *Ḥadīth*:

1. A man who has more than one wife should treat his wives equally and justly: he should not even prefer one particular wife when travelling.
2. In some disputed issues, the matter can be resolved by drawing lots.
3. The Messenger of Allah ﷺ would care so much about the education and heartfelt happiness of his purified wives that he would take one of them with him when travelling. This is an ideal example of a good husband.

عَنْ ابْنِ عُمَرَ رضي الله عنه، عَنْ النَّبِيِّ ﷺ، قَالَ: أَبْغَضُ الْحَلَالِ إِلَى اللهِ تَعَالَى الطَّلَاقُ. سنن أبي داود، مشكواة، باب فضل الصدقة.

[233] On the authority of Ibn ʿUmar رضي الله عنه, that the Prophet ﷺ said, "To Allah the most hated of the lawful acts is divorce." Abū Dāwūd (*Mishkāt*, Chapter: Divorce, *Ḥadīth* no. 3280).

Commentary

This has been taught so that the matter of divorce does not become one of play and sport within Muslim society. Divorce is only allowed when all possibilities of reconciliation have been exhausted.

12.11 THE RIGHTS OF FAMILY

عَنْ أَبِي هُرَيْرَةَ رضي الله عنه، أَنَّهُ قال: يَارَسُولَ اللهِ ﷺ أَيُّ الصَّدَقَةِ أَفْضَلُ؟ قَالَ: جُهْدُ الْمُقِلِّ، وَابْدَأْ بِمَنْ تَعُولُ. سنن أبي داود.

[234] On the authority of Abū Hurayrah رضي الله عنه, who asked, "O Messenger of Allah! Which charity is best?" He replied, "That

which results from the efforts of the poor and destitute. Begin with your dependants." Abū Dāwūd (*Ḥadīth* no. 1677 – *Mishkāt*, Chapter: The Virtues of Charity, *Ḥadīth* no. 1938).

Commentary

Two matters are learnt from this *Ḥadīth*.

1. Any charity that is given on a sincere basis reaches the station of acceptance with Allah. However, the charity that is given by a poor or destitute Muslim after laborious efforts has a more beloved and virtuous rank with Allah.
2. A person must first care for his dependants (i.e. charity begins at home). It often happens that in pursuit of fame and reputation, needy relatives are overlooked and charity and donations are showered upon others.

عَنْ أَبِي هُرَيْرَةَ ﷺ، عَنْ النَّبِيِّ ﷺ، قَالَ: خَيْرُ الصَّدَقَةِ مَا كَانَ عَنْ ظَهْرِ غِنًى، وَابْدَأْ بِمَنْ تَعُولُ. صحيح البخاري، مشكواة، باب فضل الصدقة.

[235] On the authority of Abū Hurayrah ﷺ who said: The Messenger of Allah said, "The best charity is that which still leaves one in a state of affluence. Begin with your dependants." Bukhārī (*Mishkāt*, Chapter: The Virtues of Charity, *Ḥadīth* no. 1929).

Commentary

These two *Aḥādīth* apparently seem to contradict. However, the reality is that the first *Ḥadīth* seeks to remove the feeling of inferiority because of which a poor man may think that his humble contribution is worthless compared to the charity and donations of the wealthy. The point is that Allah the Exalted grants reward according to the sincerity of the heart, not according to the outward amount of charity. The purpose of the second *Ḥadīth* is to teach that a person should not distribute his wealth so freely in charity that he is forced to beg from others to provide for himself and his children.

عَنْ ابْنِ عُمَرَ رضي الله عنه، أَنَّ رَجُلاً كَانَ عِنْدَهُ وَلَهُ بَنَاتٌ، فتمنَّى مَوْتَهُنَّ، فَغَضِبَ ابْنُ عُمَرَ، فقال: أَنْتَ تَرْزُقُهُنَّ. الأدب المفرد.

[236] On the authority of Ibn 'Umar ﷺ, that there was a man in his presence who had several daughters. The man expressed the wish that they would die, upon which Ibn 'Umar became very angry and said, "Are you the one who provides for them?" Bukhārī's *Al-Adab al-Mufrad, Ḥadīth* no. 83.

عَنْ نَبِيطِ بنِ شُرَيْطٍ رضي الله عنه قَالَ: سَمِعْتُ رَسُوْلَ اللهِ ﷺ، يَقُوْلُ: إِذَا وُلِدَ لِلرَّجُلِ ابنَةٌ بَعثَ اللهُ ـ عَزَّ وَجَلَّ ـ مَلاَئِكَةٌ يَقُولُونَ: السَّلاَمُ عَلَيْكُمْ أَهْلَ البَيْتِ. يَكْتَنِفُونَهَا بِأَجْنِحَتِهِمْ، وَيَمْسَحُونَ ايْدِيهِمْ عَلى رَأْسِهَا، وَيَقُولُونَ: ضَعِيْفَةٌ خَرَجَتْ مِنْ ضَعِيفَةٍ، القَيِّمُ عَلَيْهَا مُعَانٌ إِلى يَوْمِ القِيَامَةِ. المعجم الصغير للطبراني.

[237] On the authority of Nabīṭ b. Shurayṭ ﷺ, who said: I heard the Messenger of Allah ﷺ saying, "When a daughter is born to a person, Allah sends angels who say, 'Peace be upon you, O people of the house!' They shade her with their wings and caress her head with their hands, saying, 'A weak one, born of a weak one. The one who looks after her will be helped until the Day of Resurrection'." Ṭabarānī's *Al-Mu'jam al-Ṣaghīr*.

Commentary

Generally, the Arabs used to despise the birth of a girl; some tribes would even bury her alive. Even now there are many people who turn their noses up at the birth of a girl. In order to overturn this mentality, there are plenty of exhortations in the *Aḥādīth* encouraging the care, education and upbringing of daughters.

عَنْ عَائِشَةَ رضي الله عنها قَالَتْ: جَاءَتْنِي امْرَأَةٌ وَمَعَهَا ابْنَتَانِ لَهَا تَسْأَلُنِي، فَلَمْ تَجِدْ عِنْدِي غَيْرَ تَمْرَةٍ وَاحِدَةٍ، فَأَعْطَيْتُهَا إِيَّاهَا، فَأَخَذَتْهَا،فَقَسَمَتْهَا باثْنَيْنِ بَيْنَ ابْنَتَيْهَا، وَلَمْ تَأْكُلْ مِنْهَا شَيْئًا، ثُمَّ قَامَتْ، فَخَرَجَتْ، فَدَخَلَ النَّبِيُّ ﷺ، فَحَدَّثْتُهُ، فَقَال : مَنْ ابْتُلِيَ مِنْ هَذِهِ الْبَنَاتِ بِشَيْءٍ، فَأَحْسَنَ إِلَيْهِنَّ، كُنَّ لَهُ سِتْرًا مِنْ النَّارِ. متفق عليه – مشكاة – باب الشفقة– ص ٤١٣ .

[238] On the authority of ʿĀʾishah ﵂, who said: A woman came to me begging, and she had two daughters with her. I only had one date, so I gave it to her and she divided it between her daughters without eating any of it. She then stood up and left. When the Prophet ﷺ came, I narrated this incident to him, upon which he said, "Whoever is tested by [being blessed with] daughters and treats them kindly, they will be a barrier for him or her from the Fire." Bukhārī and Muslim (*Mishkāt*, Chapter on Compassion, *Ḥadīth* no. 4949).

12.12 EQUAL TREATMENT OF CHILDREN

عَنْ النُّعْمَانَ بْنَ بَشِيرٍ ﵄، وَهُوَ عَلى الْمِنْبَرِ يَقُولُ: أَعْطَانِي أَبِي عَطِيَّةً، فَقَالَتْ عَمْرَةُ بِنْتُ رَوَاحَةَ: لا أَرْضى حَتَّى تُشْهِدَ رَسُولَ الله ﷺ، فَأَتَى رَسُولَ الله ﷺ، فَقَالَ: إِني أَعْطَيْتُ ابْنِي مِنْ عَمْرَةَ بِنْتِ رَوَاحَةَ عَطِيَّةً، فَأَمَرَتْنِي أَنْ أُشْهِدَكَ يَا رَسُولَ الله. قَالَ: أَعْطَيْتَ سَائِرَ وَلَدِكَ مِثْلَ هَذَا. قَالَ: لَا. قَالَ: فَاتَّقُوا اللهَ وَاعْدِلُوا بَيْنَ أَوْلَادِكُمْ. قَالَ: فَرَجَعَ، فَرَدَّ عَطِيَّتَهُ. صحيح البخاري ومسلم، وَفِي رِوَايَةٍ: قَالَ: إِنِّي لَآ أَشْهَدُ عَلَى جُورٍ.

[239] On the authority of al-Nuʿmān b. Bashīr ﵄, who narrated whilst upon the pulpit: My father gave me a gift, upon which [my mother] ʿAmrah bint Rawāḥah said, "I will not approve of this until you ask the Messenger of Allah ﷺ to bear witness over it." My father came to the Messenger of Allah ﷺ and said, "Truly, I have given a gift to my son from ʿAmrah, and she has asked me to seek your witness over it, O Messenger of Allah!" He asked, "Have you given all your children something like it?" He replied, "No." He said, "Then fear Allah, and deal justly amongst your children!" So he returned and recalled his gift.

In another narration, the Prophet ﷺ said, "Truly, I do not bear witness to injustice." Bukhārī and Muslim (*Mishkāt*, Chapter on Gifts).

Commentary

Children have the right over their parents that they treat their children justly and equally. Regarding this, the Imāms disagree as to whether sons and daughters have to be treated equally, or whether they should inherit according to the ratio of inheritance. Some of the people of knowledge hold that sons should be given twice as much as daughters, based on the principles of the share of inheritance. However, the correct position in this regard is that there is no need for differentiation in this matter: sons and daughters should be given gifts in equal proportions.

12.13 MAINTAINING FAMILY TIES

عَنْ مَيْمُونَةَ بِنْتَ الْحَارِثِ ﵂، أَنَّهَا أَعْتَقَتْ وَلِيدَةً فِي زَمَانِ رَسُوْلِ اللهِ ﷺ، فَذَكَرَتْ ذَلِكَ لِرَسُوْلِ اللهِ ﷺ، فَقَالَ: لَوْ أَعْطَيْتِهَا أَخْوَالَكِ كَانَ أَعْظَمَ لِأَجْرِكِ. صحيح البخاري ومسلم، مشكواة، باب فضل الصدقة.

[240] On the authority of Maymūnah bint al-Ḥārith ﵂ that she freed a slave-girl during the era of the Messenger of Allah ﷺ and mentioned this to him, upon which he said, "Had you presented her to your maternal uncles, your reward would have been greater." Bukhārī and Muslim (*Mishkāt*, Chapter: The Virtue of Charity, *Ḥadīth* no. 1935).

Commentary

This charity is a good act of worship in its own right. However, if needy relatives benefit from the charity, it attracts a two-fold reward: one reward for the charity, the other for treating one's relatives well.[53]

12.14 SERVING HUMANITY

عن أَنَس،وعن عَبْدِ الله ﵄ قَالَ :قَالَ رسولُ الله ﷺ: الْخَلْقُ عِيَالُ الله، فَأَحَبُّ الْخَلْقِ إِلَى اللهِ مَنْ أَحْسَنَ إِلى عِيَالِهِ. رواه البيهقي، مشكواة، باب الشفقة.

53. This means that to present the slave-girl as a gift to needy relatives who would treat her well in their possession would have been better than freeing her and thus leaving her with no support at all. The Prophet's advice was for the mutual benefit of the slave as well as his wife's relatives. – Trans. Note

[241] On the authority of Anas and ʿAbdullāh ﷺ, who said: The Messenger of Allah ﷺ said, "All of creation is Allah's family [i.e. dependants], and the most beloved of creation to Allah are those who show kindness to His family [i.e. dependants]." Bayhaqī (*Mishkāt*, Chapter on Compassion, *Ḥadīth* nos. 4998-9).

Commentary

If there is any action in Islam that is most important after the worship of the Creator, it is serving His creation, i.e. helping and caring for the weak and unsupported individuals in the society. Actually, this is also a kind of worship of Allah.

عن سَهْلِ بن سَعْدٍ ﷺ قَالَ: قَالَ رَسُولُ اللهِ ﷺ: سيِّدُ القومِ في السَّفَرِ خادمُهم، فمنْ سبَقَهُم بخدمةٍ لم يسبِقوهُ بعملٍ إلاَّ الشَّهادةَ. رواه البيهقي، مشكواة، باب آداب السفر.

[242] On the authority of Sahl b. Saʿd ﷺ, who said: The Messenger of Allah ﷺ said, "The leader of a people in a journey is their servant. They cannot overtake the one who becomes foremost by serving them with any achievement except martyrdom [i.e. the martyr's status is higher than the one engaged in the *Jihād* of serving humanity]." Bayhaqī (*Mishkāt*, Etiquette of Travelling, *Ḥadīth* no. 3925).

12.15 GOOD NEIGHBOURLINESS

عَنْ نَافِعِ بْنِ عَبْدِ الْحَارِثِ ﷺ قَالَ: قَالَ رَسُولُ اللهِ ﷺ: مِنْ سَعَادَةِ الْمَرْءِ: الْجَارُ الصَّالِحُ، وَالْمَرْكَبُ الْهَنِيءُ، وَالْمَسْكَنُ الْوَاسِعُ. مسند أحمد، الأدب المفرد.

[243] On the authority of Nāfiʿ b. ʿAbdul Ḥārith ﷺ that the Prophet ﷺ said, "The signs of a person's happiness and good fortune are (1) a good neighbour, (2) a comfortable riding-beast and (3) a spacious dwelling." Aḥmad and Bukhārī's *Al-Adab al-Mufrad*, *Ḥadīth* nos. 116 and 457.

عَنْ عَبْدِ اللهِ ابْنِ مَسْعُودٍ ﵁ قَالَ: قَالَ رَجُلٌ لِرَسُولِ اللهِ ﷺ: كَيْفَ لِي أَنْ أَعْلَمَ إِذَا أَحْسَنْتُ وَإِذَا أَسَأْتُ؟ فَقَالَ النَّبِيُّ ﷺ: إِذَا سَمِعْتَ جِيرَانَكَ يَقُولُونَ قَدْ أَحْسَنْتَ فَقَدْ أَحْسَنْتَ، وَإِذَا سَمِعْتَهُمْ يَقُولُونَ قَدْ أَسَأْتَ فَقَدْ أَسَأْتَ. مسند أحمد، وابن ماجه، مشكواة، باب الشفقة.

[244] On the authority of ʿAbdullāh b. Masʿūd ﵁, who said: A man asked the Messenger of Allah ﷺ, "How can I know whether I am doing good works or bad deeds?" The Prophet ﷺ replied, "When you hear your neighbours saying that you are doing good works, then you really are doing good works. When you hear your neighbours saying that you are doing bad deeds, then you really are doing bad deeds." Aḥmad and Ibn Mājah (*Mishkāt*, Chapter on Compassion, *Ḥadīth* no. 4988).

Commentary

By "neighbours" here is meant every person who has a close association in some way, whether a neighbour of one's house, a colleague at the office or a companion during a journey – this *Ḥadīth* includes all of them. In other words, it refers to those people who live nearby and those who can observe one's public actions and movements. Their witness is more worthy of consideration in this regard, with the condition that the thinking of the one bearing witness has not been corrupted by evil and sinful influences.

12.16 RIGHTS OF THE GUEST

عَنْ أَبِي شُرَيْحٍ الْعَدَوِيِّ ﵁ قَالَ: سَمِعَتْ أُذُنَايَ وَأَبْصَرَتْ عَيْنَايَ حِينَ تَكَلَّمَ النَّبِيُّ ﷺ، فَقَالَ: مَنْ كَانَ يُؤْمِنُ بِاللَّهِ وَالْيَوْمِ الْآخِرِ، فَلْيُكْرِمْ جَارَهُ، وَمَنْ كَانَ يُؤْمِنُ بِاللَّهِ وَالْيَوْمِ الْآخِرِ، فَلْيُكْرِمْ ضَيْفَهُ جَائِزَتَهُ. قِيلَ: وَمَا جَائِزَتُهُ يَا رَسُولَ اللهِ؟ قَالَ: يَوْمٌ وَلَيْلَةٌ وَالضِّيَافَةُ ثَلَاثَةُ أَيَّامٍ، فَمَا كَانَ وَرَاءَ ذَلِكَ فَهُوَ صَدَقَةٌ عَلَيْهِ، وَلَا يَحِلُّ لَهُ يَثْوِيَ عِنْدَهُ حَتَّى يُحْرِجَهُ. وَمَنْ كَانَ يُؤْمِنُ بِاللهِ وَالْيَوْمِ الْآخِرِ، فَلْيَقُلْ خَيْرًا أَوْ لِيَصْمُتْ. الأدب المفرد.

[245] On the authority of Abū Shurayḥ al-ʿAdawī ﷺ, who said: I heard with my own two ears and saw with my own two eyes, the Prophet ﷺ saying, "Whoever believes in Allah and the Last Day must honour his neighbour. Moreover, whoever believes in Allah and the Last Day must honour his guest with the required hospitality." He was asked, "What is the required hospitality, O Messenger of Allah?" He replied, "The [minimum] required hospitality is a day and night; full hospitality is for three days; anything more than that is charity on behalf of the host. It is not permitted for the guest to stay for so long as to trouble his host. And whoever believes in Allah and the Last Day must speak goodness or remain silent." Bukhārī's *Al-Adab al-Mufrad*, Chapter: The Guest Must Not Stay So Long As To Trouble His Host, *Ḥadīth* no. 741.

Commentary

In this *Ḥadīth*, two requirements of faith in Allah and the Hereafter have been explained:

1. Guarding the tongue, i.e. shunning backbiting, bad language and idle chatter, and using the tongue instead in beneficial ways.
2. Generosity and magnanimity. One form of this is that if a traveller wishes to stay the night at one's house, one should not be selfish and miserly of heart, but should magnanimously see to his food, drink and stay. At the same time, the guest is reminded to be responsible enough not to impose upon his host for more than three days. In this way, if hosts display such generosity and guests show such responsibility, the social life of the nation will be extremely pleasant.

12.17 RIGHTS OF SLAVES AND SERVANTS

عَنْ أَبِي ذَرٍّ ﷺ قَالَ: قَالَ رَسُولُ اللهِ ﷺ: هُمْ إِخْوَانُكُمْ جَعَلَهُمْ اللهُ تَحْتَ أَيْدِيكُمْ، فَمَنْ جَعَلَ اللهُ أَخَاهُ تَحْتَ يَدِهِ، فَلْيُطْعِمْهُ مِمَّا يَأْكُلُ، وَلْيُلْبِسْهُ مِمَّا يَلْبَسُ، وَلا يُكَلِّفْهُ مِنْ الْعَمَلِ مَا يَغْلِبُهُ، فَإِنْ كَلَّفَهُ مَا يَغْلِبُهُ فَلْيُعِنْهُ عَلَيْهِ. صحيح البخاري وصحيح مسلم، مشكواة، باب النفقات.

[246]   On the authority of Abū Dharr ☙, who said: The
Messenger of Allah ﷺ said, "Your [slaves are your] brothers,
whom Allah has placed under your authority. A brother whom
Allah has placed under your authority, you must feed him with
the food you eat yourself and clothe him with the garments you
wear yourself. Moreover, you must not burden him with so much
work that it oppresses him. If you burden him with more than
he can bear, then you must assist him with the task." Bukhārī and
Muslim (*Mishkāt*, Chapter on Spending, *Ḥadīth* no. 3345).

عَنْ عَلِيٍّ ☙ قَالَ: كَانَ آخِرُ كَلَامِ رَسُولِ اللهِ ﷺ، الصَّلَاةَ الصَّلَاةَ، اتَّقُوا اللهَ فِيَما مَلَكَتْ
أَيْمَانُكُمْ. سنن أبي داود، الأدب المفرد.

[247]   On the authority of 'Alī ☙, who said: The last words of
the Prophet ﷺ were, "The prayer, the prayer! Fear Allah regarding
those whom your right hands possess." Bukhārī's *Al-Adab al-Mufrad*,
Ḥadīth no. 158.

Commentary

This means, "Be mindful of observing the prayer and treat your
slaves kindly: do not oppress or mistreat them." This *Ḥadīth*
combines emphasis upon the importance of prayer and the kind
treatment of slaves, and indicates that when a person's heart is
overcome by the awe and fear of Allah through the performance
of prayer, he will not dare to violate the rights of the weakest
sections of society.[54]

12.18 KIND TREATMENT OF PRISONERS

وَعَنْ أَبِي عَزِيزِ بْنِ عُمَيْرٍ، أَخِي مُصْعَبِ بْنِ عُمَيْرٍ ☙، قَالَ: كُنْتُ فِي الأَسْرَى يَوْمَ بَدْرٍ،
فَقَالَ رَسُولُ اللهِ ﷺ: اسْتَوْصُوا بِالأُسَارَى خَيْرًا، وَكُنْتُ فِي نَفَرٍ مِنَ الأَنْصَارِ، فَكَانُوا إِذَا

---

54.   As pointed out by one of the commentators, this glorious and final
Prophetic teaching combines the duty of direct prayer to the highest being
(Allah) and the treatment of the most vulnerable amongst society, i.e. slaves. In
a sense, therefore, it also includes duties to all beings in between. – Trans. Note

قَدَّمُوا غَدَاءَهُمْ وَعَشَاءَهُمْ، أَكَلُوا التَّمْرَ وَأَطْعَمُونِي الْخُبْزَ بِوَصِيَّةِ رسولِ الله ﷺ. المعجم الصغير للطبراني.

[248] On the authority of Abū ʿAzīz b. ʿUmayr ﵁, brother of Muṣʿab b. ʿUmayr, who said: I was amongst the captives on the Day of Badr. The Messenger of Allah ﷺ said, "Treat the captives well." I was held by a group of the Ansar, and whenever they brought out their lunch and supper, they would themselves eat dates whilst giving me bread to eat because of the instruction of the Messenger of Allah ﷺ to them. Ṭabarānī's *Al-Muʿjam al-Ṣaghīr*.

Commentary

This *Ḥadīth* gives us an indication of Islam's care for the rights of the weak, Muslim or non-Muslim. Even an enemy non-Muslim captive deserves kind treatment in a Muslim society.

قَالَ رَسُولُ الله ﷺ: إِنَّ اللهَ لا يُقَدِّسُ أُمَّةً لا يُؤْخَذُ لِلضَّعِيفِ فِيهِمْ حَقُّهُ. رواه البغوي في شرح السنة.

[249] The Messenger of Allah ﷺ said, "Truly, Allah does not purify a nation in which the rights of the weak are not granted." Transmitted by Baghawī in *Sharḥ al-Sunnah* (*Mishkāt*, Chapter: Reviving Dead Land, *Ḥadīth* no. 3004).

Commentary

The Messenger of Allah ﷺ once granted ʿAbdullāh b. Masʿūd some land in Madīnah. This land was adjacent to some dwellings and date-orchards belonging to the Anṣār. One of the families of the Anṣār, the Banū ʿAbd b. Zuhrah, asked Ibn Masʿūd to move from there, upon which the Prophet ﷺ said, "Then why did Allah send me as a Messenger?" Or, in other words, the objective of the Prophet's mission was to liberate the weak and oppressed from the injustices of the strong and powerful. However, if the weak were still oppressed and ejected from their lands after his appearance, then what would have been the point of his mission?

12.19 CARING FOR THE POOR

عَـنْ مُصْـعَبِ بْنِ سَـعْدٍ ﷺ قَـالَ: رَأَى سَـعْدٌ ﷺ، أَنَّ لَـهُ فَضْلا عَلى مَـنْ دُونَـهُ. فَقَالَ النَّبِيُّ ﷺ: هَلْ تُنْصَرُونَ وَتُرْزَقُونَ إِلا بِضُعَفَائِكُم. صحيح البخاري، مشكواة، باب فضل الفقراء.

[250] On the authority of Muṣʿab b. Saʿd ﷺ, who said: Saʿd thought that he was better than people less well-off than him, so the Messenger of Allah ﷺ said, "Are you helped and sustained [by Allah] for any reason other than the presence of the weak amongst you?" Bukhārī (*Mishkāt*, Chapter: Virtues of the Poor, *Ḥadīth* no. 5232).

Commentary

This means that people who are physically or financially strong should not treat those who are physically or financially weak with contempt. This affluence and strength is actually a test from Allah, that well-off people should not become so decadent in Allah's blessings that they despise the weaker sections of humanity.

12.20 THE RIGHTS OF THE POOR OVER THE WEALTH OF THE RICH

عَنْ أَبِي سَعِيدٍ الْخُدْرِيِّ ﷺ قَالَ: بَيْنَما نَحْنُ فِي سَفَرٍ مَعَ النَّبِيِّ ﷺ، إِذْ جَاءَ رَجُلٌ عَلى رَاحِلَةٍ لَهُ، قَالَ: فَجَعَلَ يَصْرِفُ بَصَرَهُ يَمِيشًا وَشِمَالًا، فَقَالَ رَسُولُ الله ﷺ: مَنْ كَانَ مَعَهُ فَضْلُ ظَهْرٍ فَلْيَعُدْ بِهِ عَلى مَنْ لا ظَهْرَ لَهُ، وَمَنْ كَانَ لَهُ فَضْلٌ مِنْ زَادٍ فَلْيَعُدْ بِهِ عَلى مَنْ لا زَادَ لَهُ، قَالَ: فَذَكَرَ مِنْ أَصْنَافِ الْمَالِ مَا ذَكَرَ حَتَّى رَأَيْنَا أَنَّهُ لا حَقَّ لِأَحَدٍ مِنَّا فِي فَضْلٍ. رواه مسلم، مشكواة، باب آداب السفر.

[251] On the authority of Abū Saʿīd al-Khudrī ﷺ, who said: Whilst we were on a journey with the Messenger of Allah ﷺ, a man came to him on a riding-beast, looking right and left [i.e. he was anxious because his mount was not a good one]. The

Messenger of Allah ﷺ said, "Whoever has a spare mount must give it to one who does not have a mount. Whoever has spare provisions must give them to one who does not have provisions ..." He continued to mention other types of wealth in this way, until we thought that we had no right to own any spare wealth at all. Muslim (*Mishkāt*, Chapter: Etiquette of Travelling, *Ḥadīth* no. 3898).

Commentary

This occurred during a battle situation. In such critical times, the *amīr* is legally permitted to impose a tax, besides *zakāt*, on the wealthy or to distribute their spare possessions amongst the deserving poor.

12.21 HELPING THOSE AFFLICTED BY TRIBULATIONS

عَنْ عَبْدِ اللَّهِ بْنِ جَعْفَرٍ رضي الله عنه قَالَ: لَمَّا جَاءَ نَعْيُ جَعْفَرٍ، قَالَ: النَّبِيُّ ﷺ اصْنَعُوا لِأَهْلِ جَعْفَرٍ طَعَامًا فَإِنَّهُ قَدْ جَاءَهُمْ مَا يُشْغِلُهُمْ. سنن الترمذي وأبن ماجه وأحمد، مشكواة، باب البكاء على الميت.

[252] On the authority of ʿAbdullāh b. Jaʿfar رضي الله عنه, who said: When the news of Jaʿfar's death was announced, the Prophet ﷺ said, "Prepare food for the family of Jaʿfar, for there has come to them that which distracts them [from worldly matters]." Abū Dāwūd, Tirmidhī and Ibn Mājah (*Mishkāt*, Chapter: Weeping Over the Dead, *Ḥadīth* no. 1739).

12.22 RESPECT FOR ELDERS

عَنْ عَبْدَ اللَّهِ بْنَ عُمَرَ رضي الله عنه أَنَّ رَسُولَ اللهِ ﷺ قَالَ: أَرَانِي فِي الْمَنَامِ أَتَسَوَّكُ بِسِوَاكٍ، فَجَذَبَنِي رَجُلَانِ أَحَدُهُمَا أَكْبَرُ مِنْ الْآخَرِ، فَنَاوَلْتُ السِّوَاكَ الْأَصْغَرَ مِنْهُمَا، فَقِيلَ لِي: كَبِّرْ فَدَفَعْتُهُ إِلَى الْأَكْبَرِ. صحيح البخاري وصحيح مسلم، مشكواة، باب السواك.

[253] On the authority of ʿAbdullāh b. ʿUmar رضي الله عنه that the Prophet ﷺ said, "I saw myself in a dream cleaning my teeth with a tooth-stick, when two men of unequal age came to me. I offered the tooth-stick to the younger of them, upon which I was told,

'The elder!' So I gave it to the elder of the two." Bukhārī and Muslim (*Mishkāt*, Chapter: The Tooth-Stick, *Ḥadīth* no. 385).

12.23 SOCIAL ETIQUETTE

عَنْ عَائِشَةَ ﵂ قَالَتْ: قَالَ رَسُولُ الله ﷺ: أَنْزِلُوا النَّاسَ مَنَازِلَهُمْ. أبو داود، مشكواة، باب الشفقة.

[254] On the authority of 'Ā'ishah ﵂ that the Prophet ﷺ said, "Treat people according to their positions [in society]." Abū Dāwūd (*Mishkāt*, Chapter: Compassion, *Ḥadīth* no. 4949).

Commentary

Whether rich or poor, righteous or wicked, elder or younger, all people are equal in the eyes of the law: in the matter of the limits of Allah, not even an atom's weight of allowance may be made for the sake of any of them. However, in general social dealings, it is necessary to take account of knowledge, piety and other approved distinguishing characteristics. This is the reality expressed by the words, "Treat people according to their positions."

12.24 RIGHTS OF FRIENDSHIP AND COMPANIONSHIP

عَنْ ابْنِ عُمَرَ ﵄ أَنَّ النَّبِيَّ ﷺ، إِذا أَوْدَعَ رجُلا أَخَذَ بيدِه، فلا يَدَعُها حتَّى يَكونَ الرَّجُلُ هو يَدَعُ يَدَ النَّبِيِّ، ويقولُ: أَسْتَوْدِعُ الله دِينَكَ وَأَمَانَتَكَ وَآخِرَ عَمَلِكَ. وفي رواية خَوَاتِيمَ عَمَلِكَ. رواه الترمذي، مشكواة، باب الدعوات.

[255] On the authority of Ibn 'Umar ﵄, who said: When the Prophet ﷺ would bid farewell to a person, he would take his hand and not let go of it until the man released his hand himself. He would say [upon bidding farewell], "I place your religion, trust and your last actions [in one narration, "... the seal of your actions"] in the care of Allah." Tirmidhī (*Mishkāt*, Chapter: Supplications, *Ḥadīth* no. 2435).

12.25 INFORMALITY WITH CLOSE FRIENDS

عَنْ بَكْرِ بْنِ عَبْدِ اللهِ ﵁ قَالَ: كَانَ أَصْحَابُ النَّبِيِّ ﷺ يَتَبَادَحُونَ بالبَطِّيخِ، فَإِذَا كَانَتِ الْحَقَائِقُ كَانُوا هُمُ الرِّجَالَ. الأدب المفرد، باب المزاح.

[256] On the authority of Bakr b. ʿAbdullāh ﵁, who said, "The Companions of the Prophet ﷺ would throw watermelon at each other [when playing and joking], but when real situations [of war and battle] occurred, the same people were real men [for the occasion]." Bukhārī's *Al-Adab al-Mufrad*, Chapter on Joking, *Ḥadīth* no. 266).

عَنْ مُحَمَّد بْنِ زِيادٍ ﵁ قَالَ: أَدْرَكْتُ السَّلَفَ وَإِنَّهُمْ لَيَكُوْنُوْنَ فِي الْمَنْزِلِ الْوَاحِدِ بِأَهَالِيهِمْ، فَرُبَّمَا نَزَلَ عَلى بَعْضِهِمْ الضَّيْفَ، وَقِدْرُ أَحَدِهِمْ عَلى النَّارِ، فيَأْخُذَهَا صَاحِبُ الضَّيْفِ لِضَيْفِهِ، فَيَفْقِدَ القِدْرَ صَاحِبُهَا، فَيَقُوْلُ: مَنْ أَخَذَ القِدْرَ؟ فَيَقُوْلُ صَاحِبُ الضَّيْفِ: نَحْنُ أَخَذْنَاهَا لِضَيْفِنَا، فَيَقُوْلُ صَاحِبُ الْقِدْرِ: بَارَكَ اللهُ لَكُمْ فِيْهَا، أَوْ كَلِمَةً نَحْوَهَا، قَالَ بَقِيَّةٌ: وَقَالَ مُحَمَّدٌ: وَالْخُبْزَ إِذَا خَبَزُوْا مِثْلَ ذَلِكَ وَلَيْسَ بَيْنَهُم إِلَّا جُدُرُ القَصَبِ، قَالَ بَقِيَّةٌ: وأَدْرَكْتُ أَنَا ذَلِكَ. مُحَمَّدَ بْنَ زِيَادٍ وَأَصْحَابُهُ.

[257] On the authority of Muḥammad b. Ziyād ﵁, who said: I experienced the way of the previous generations. Several of them would stay with their families in the same house. Often a guest would visit one of them, while another's cooking-pot would be over the fire, so the guest's host would take the pot for his guest. The pot's owner would find it missing and ask after it, so the guest's host would say that he had taken it for his guest. The pot's owner would say, "May Allah put blessings in the pot for you." Similar would be the situation when one of them was baking bread. Only walls of reeds would separate the families.

Baqiyyah b. al-Walīd said that he found Muḥammad b. Ziyād behaving similarly with his companions. Bukhārī's *Al-Adab al-Mufrad*, *Ḥadīth* no. 739.

Commentary

This can only happen when there is a high level of mutual trust and sincerity, otherwise in general such informality can also create strife.

12.26 MODERATION IN CHEERFULNESS

عَنْ عَبْدِ الرَّحْمنِ ﷺ قَالَ: لَمْ يَكُنْ أَصْحَابُ رَسُولِ اللهِ ﷺ مُتَحَزِّقِينَ، وَلا مُتَمَاوِتِينَ، وَكَانُوْا يَتَنَاشَدُوْنَ الشِعْرَ فِي مَجَالِسِهِمْ وَيَذْكُرُونَ أَمْرَ جَاهِلِيَّتِهِمْ، فَإِذَا أُرِيدَ أَحَدٌ مِنْهُمْ عَلَى شَيْءٍ مِنْ أَمْرِ اللهِ دَارَتْ حَمَالِيقُ عَينَيهِ كَأَنَّهُ مَجْنُونٌ. الأدب المفرد، باب الكبر.

[258] On the authority of ʿAbd al-Raḥmān ﷺ, who said: The Companions of the Messenger of Allah ﷺ were neither dry-natured nor morbid. They would chant poetry to each other in their gatherings, and mention some of the matters of their Days of Ignorance [*Jāhiliyyah*]. However, if any of them was asked to do something against the command of Allah, the pupils of his eyes would revolve as though he were mad. Bukhārī's *Al-Adab al-Mufrad*, Chapter on Pride, *Ḥadīth* no. 555.

Commentary

This means that the Noble Companions learnt a balanced nature from the company of the Prophet ﷺ: they were neither dry-natured like monks and ascetics nor totally obsessed with amusement and story-telling like those captivated by this world. Rather, as well as having sweet temperaments, their hearts were also full of religious honour and zeal.

12.27 CONCERN FOR THE WEAK AND DISADVANTAGED

عَنْ أَبِي هُرَيْرَةَ ﷺ أَنَّ رَسُولَ اللهِ ﷺ قَالَ: إِذَا صَلى أَحَدُكُمْ لِلنَّاسِ فَلْيُخَفِّفْ، فَإِنَّ مِنْهُمْ الضَّعِيفَ وَالسَّقِيمَ وَالْكَبِيرَ- وَفِي رِوَايَةٍ وَذَ الحَاْجَةِ - وَإِذَا صَلى أَحَدُكُمْ لِنَفْسِهِ فَلْيُطَوِّلْ مَا شَاءَ. صحيح البخاري ومسلم، مشكواة ،باب ما جاء على الامام.

[259] On the authority of Abū Hurayrah ﷺ, who said: The Messenger of Allah ﷺ said, "When one of you leads the people in prayer, he must shorten the prayer, for there are amongst them the weak, the sick and the elderly." In another narration, "... and those with needs to attend to. When you pray by yourself, then you may lengthen the prayer as much as you wish." Bukhārī and Muslim (*Mishkāt*, Chapter: Duties of the Imām, *Ḥadīth* no. 1131).

Commentary

Shortening the prayer means that the recitation, bowing and prostration must not be lengthened more than is established in the *Sunnah*. It does not mean that the prayer should be so hurried that dignity, calmness and tranquillity disappear from the prayer.

عَنْ أَبِي سَعِيدٍ الْخُدري ﷺ قَالَ: انْتَظَرْنَا رَسُولَ الله ﷺ لَيْلَةَ صَلَاةَ الْعِشَاءِ حَتَّى ذَهَبَ نَحْوٌ مِنْ شَطْرِ اللَّيْلِ، قَالَ: فَجَاءَ فَصَلَّى بِنَا، ثُمَّ قَالَ: خُذُوا مَقَاعِدَكُمْ، فَإِنَّ النَّاسَ قَدْ أَخَذُوا مَضَاجِعَهُمْ، وَإِنَّكُمْ لَنْ تَزَالُوا فِي صَلَاةٍ مُنْذُ انْتَظَرْتُمُوهَا، وَلَوْلَا ضَعْفُ الضَّعِيفِ وَسَقَمُ السَّقِيمِ وَحَاجَةُ ذِي الْحَاجَةِ لَأَخَّرْتُ هَذِهِ الصَّلَاةَ إِلَى شَطْرِ اللَّيْلِ. سنن النسائي وأبي داود ومسند أحمد، مشكواة، باب تعجيل الصلاة.

[260] On the authority of Abū Saʿīd al-Khudrī ﷺ, who said: We waited for the *ʿIshāʾ* prayer with the Messenger of Allah ﷺ one night, but he only came out for the prayer after almost half the night had passed. He instructed us to sit down, and we did so. He then said, "Truly, many people have prayed and gone to bed. You are in [the state of] prayer as long as you are waiting for it. Were it not for the weakness of the weak, the people's pressing needs and the illness of the sick, I would have delayed this prayer until the middle of the night." Aḥmad, Abū Dāwūd and Nasāʾi (*Mishkāt*, Chapter: Offering the Prayer Early, *Ḥadīth* no. 618).

12.28 CONCERN FOR WORKERS

عَنْ جَابِرٍ ﷺ قَالَ: كَانَ مُعَاذٌ يُصَلِّي مَعَ النَّبِيِّ ﷺ، ثُمَّ يَأْتِي فَيَؤُمُّ قَوْمَهُ، فَصَلَّى لَيْلَةً مَعَ النَّبِيِّ ﷺ الْعِشَاءَ، ثُمَّ أَتَى قَوْمَهُ فَأَمَّهُمْ، فَافْتَتَحَ بِسُورَةِ الْبَقَرَةِ، فَانْحَرَفَ رَجُلٌ، فَسَلَّمَ، ثُمَّ صَلَّى وَحْدَهُ وَانْصَرَفَ، فَقَالُوا لَهُ: أَنَافَقْتَ يَا فُلَانُ. قَالَ: لَا وَاللهِ وَلَآتِيَنَّ رَسُولَ اللهِ ﷺ، فَلَأُخْبِرَنَّهُ، فَأَتَى رَسُولَ اللهِ ﷺ، فَقَالَ يَا رَسُولَ اللهِ: إِنَّا أَصْحَابُ نَوَاضِحَ نَعْمَلُ بِالنَّهَارِ وَإِنَّ مُعَاذًا صَلَّى مَعَكَ الْعِشَاءَ، ثُمَّ أَتَى، فَافْتَتَحَ بِسُورَةِ الْبَقَرَةِ، فَأَقْبَلَ رَسُولُ اللهِ ﷺ عَلَى مُعَاذٍ، فَقَالَ: يَا مُعَاذُ أَفَتَّانٌ أَنْتَ، اقْرَأْ وَالشَّمْسِ وَضُحَاهَا وَاللَّيْلِ إِذَا يَغْشَى وَسَبِّحِ اسْمَ رَبِّكَ. رواه البخاري ومسلم.

[261] On the authority of Jābir ﵁, who said: Muʿādh [b. Jabal] used to pray with the Prophet ﷺ and then come and lead his people in prayer. One night, he prayed the *ʿIshā'* prayer with the Prophet ﷺ and then came to his people and led them in prayer. He began to recite *Sūrah al-Baqarah*, so one man separated from the congregation, completed the prayer by himself and went away. The people asked him, "Have you become a hypocrite?" He replied, "No, by Allah! I will go to the Messenger of Allah ﷺ." He did so and said, "O Messenger of Allah! We tend camels that water the fields: we work all day. Muʿādh prayed *ʿIshā'* with you and then came to his people and began reciting *Sūrah al-Baqarah*!" The Messenger of Allah ﷺ turned to Muʿādh and said, "O Muʿādh! Are you one determined to put people through tribulation? You should recite [short or medium-length] *sūrahs* [such as] *al-Shams*, *al-Layl* and *al-Aʿlā* [nos. 91, 92, and 87 respectively]." Bukhārī and Muslim (*Mishkāt*, Chapter: Recitation in Prayer).

12.29 CONCERN FOR POOR OR UNINFLUENTIAL PERSONS

عَنْ أَبِي هُرَيْرَةَ ﵁ أَنَّ امْرَأَةً سَوْدَاءَ كَانَتْ تَقُمُّ الْمَسْجِدَ (أَوْ شَابًّا)، فَفَقَدَهَا (أَوْ فَقَدَهُ) رَسُولُ اللهِ ﷺ، فَسَأَلَ عَنْهَا (أَوْ عَنْهُ)، فَقَالُوا ماتت (أو مَاتَ). قَالَ: أَفَلا كُنْتُمْ آذَنْتُمُونِي، قَالَ: فَكَأَنَّهُمْ صَغَّرُوا أَمْرَهَا (أَوْ أَمْرَهُ)، فَقَالَ: دُلُّونِي عَلَى قَبْرِهَا (أَو قَبْرِهِ)، فَدَلُّوهُ، فَصَلَّى عَلَيْهَا (أَوْ عَلَيهِ) . رواه البخاري ومسلم، مشكواة، باب المشى بالجنازه.

[262] On the authority of Abū Hurayrah ﵁, that a black woman [or man] used to sweep the mosque. One day, the Prophet ﷺ missed her [or him], so he asked about her [or him]. They informed him that the person had died, so he replied, "Why did you not inform me?" It was as though they regarded the matter as unimportant. He said, "Show me the grave." They pointed out the grave to him, so he prayed [the funeral prayer] over the person. Bukhārī and Muslim (*Mishkāt*, Chapter: Walking with the Funeral).

Commentary

A number of matters are learnt from this *Ḥadīth*:

1. Usually, many people are overlooked in society due to their lack of knowledge, wealth or fame. The Prophet ﷺ used to be extremely concerned about such people too.
2. If a person is unable to participate in a funeral prayer for some reason, he can go and perform the prayer at the person's graveside.

12.30 HELPING THE NEEDY

عَنْ أَبِي هُرَيْرَةَ ﷺ قَالَ: قَالَ رَسُولُ اللهِ ﷺ: السَّاعِي عَلَى الأَرْمَلَةِ وَالْمِسْكِينِ، كَالْمُجَاهِدِ فِي سَبِيلِ اللهِ، وَأَحْسِبُهُ قَالَ: كَالْقَائِمِ لا يَفْتُرُ وَكَالصَّائِمِ لا يُفْطِرُ. صحيح البخاري ومسلم، مشكواة، باب الشفقة.

[263] On the authority of Abū Hurayrah ﷺ, who said: The Messenger of Allah ﷺ said, "One who strives to help a widow or a poor person is like one striving [in *Jihād*] in the way of Allah." One narrator added that he thought that the Prophet added, "... and like one who stands in prayer permanently or fasts continuously." Bukhārī and Muslim (*Mishkāt*, Chapter on Compassion, *Ḥadīth* no. 4951).

12.31 KIND TREATMENT OF ORPHANS

عَنْ جَابِرٍ ﷺ قَالَ: قُلْتُ يَا رَسُولَ اللهِ ﷺ: مِمَّ أَضْرِبُ مِنْهُ يَتِيمِي؟ قَالَ: مِمَّ كُنْت ضَارِبًا مِنْهُ وَلَدَكَ غَيْرَ وَاقٍ مَالَكَ بِمَالِهِ وَلا مُتَأَثِّلاً مِنْ مَالِهِ مَالاً. المعجم الصغير للطبراني.

[264] On the authority of Jābir ﷺ, who said: I asked, "O Messenger of Allah! In which situations am I allowed to smack the orphan under my care?" He replied, "In the same situations that you smack your own child." He added, "You must neither save your wealth at the expense of his wealth, nor embezzle any of his wealth." Ṭabarānī's *Al-Mu'jam al-Ṣaghīr*.

12.32 KIND TREATMENT OF SERVANTS

عَنْ أَبِي هُرَيْرَةَ ﷺ قَالَ: قَالَ رَسُولُ اللهِ ﷺ: إِذَا صَنَعَ لِأَحَدِكُمْ خَادِمُهُ طَعَامَهُ، ثُمَّ جَاءَهُ بِهِ وَقَدْ وَلِيَ حَرَّهُ وَدُخَانَهُ، فَلْيُقْعِدْهُ مَعَهُ فَلْيَأْكُلْ، فَإِنْ كَانَ الطَّعَامُ مَشْفُوهًا قَلِيلًا، فَلْيَضَعْ فِي يَدِهِ مِنْهُ أُكْلَةً أَوْ أُكْلَتَيْنِ. صحيح مسلم، مشكواة، باب النفقات.

[265] On the authority of Abū Hurayrah ﷺ, who said: The Messenger of Allah ﷺ said, "When your servant endures heat and smoke to prepare and serve your meal, you must sit him down with you, and he should eat [without feeling embarrassed]. If the food is little, you should [at least] place one or two morsels in his hand." Muslim (*Mishkāt*, Chapter: Spending, *Ḥadīth* no. 3347).

12.33 COMPASSION TOWARDS ANIMALS

عَنْ أَبِي هُرَيْرَةَ ﷺ قَالَ: سَمِعْتُ رَسُولَ اللهِ ﷺ يَقُولُ: قَرَصَتْ نَمْلَةٌ نَبِيًّا مِنَ الْأَنْبِيَاءِ، فَأَمَرَ بِقَرْيَةِ النَّمْلِ فَأُحْرِقَتْ، فَأَوْحَى اللهُ إِلَيْهِ أَنْ قَرَصَتْكَ نَمْلَةٌ أَحْرَقْتَ أُمَّةً مِنَ الْأُمَمِ تُسَبِّحُ. صحيح البخاري ومسلم، مشكواة، باب ما يحل أكله.

[266] On the authority of Abū Hurayrah ﷺ, who said: The Messenger of Allah ﷺ said, "An ant bit one of the Prophets, so he ordered that the whole colony of ants be burned, upon which Allah revealed to him, 'Because one ant bit you, you burned a whole community that glorified [Me]?'" Bukhārī and Muslim (*Mishkāt*, Chapter: What is Lawful to Eat, *Ḥadīth* no. 4122).[55]

Commentary

We know from another *Ḥadīth* that the Prophet ﷺ has forbidden punishing with fire. Based on this, the people of knowledge do not allow the killing of harmful creatures such as poisonous beetles using boiling water, and rule that the method mentioned in this *Ḥadīth* (i.e. a Prophet's use of fire) has been abrogated

55. Interestingly, a similar story occurs in *Aesop's Fables*. – Trans. Note

for the nation of Muḥammad. The best resolution of this issue is that the *Ḥadīth* prohibiting the use of fire for such purposes should rule in general. However, if a critical situation arises, even the method mentioned in this *Ḥadīth* can be used.

عَنْ سَهْلِ ابْنِ الْحَنْظَلِيَّةِ ﷺ قَالَ: مَرَّ رَسُولُ اللهِ ﷺ بِبَعِيرٍ قَدْ لَحِقَ ظَهْرُهُ بِبَطْنِهِ، فَقَالَ: اتَّقُوا اللهَ فِي هَذِهِ الْبَهَائِمِ الْمُعْجَمَةِ، فَارْكَبُوهَا صَالِحَةً وَأَتْرُكُوهَا صَالِحَةً. سنن أبي داود.

[267] On the authority of Sahl b. al-Ḥanẓaliyyah ﷺ, who said: The Messenger of Allah ﷺ passed by a camel so emaciated that its back was touching its stomach, so he said, "Fear Allah regarding these dumb animals. Ride them when they are healthy [i.e. suitable for riding] and leave them healthy (i.e. with some strength)." Abū Dāwūd (*Mishkāt*, Chapter on Spending, *Ḥadīth* no. 3370).

Commentary

This means that one should not work them so much that one leaves them utterly exhausted, but should release them so that they are suitable for more work in future.

12.34 SHOWING MERCY TO PEOPLE IN GENERAL

عَنْ جَرِيرِ بْنِ عَبْدِ اللهِ ﷺ قَالَ: قَالَ رَسُولُ اللهِ ﷺ: لا يَرْحَمُ اللهُ مَنْ لا يَرْحَمُ النَّاسَ. صحيح البخاري ومسلم، مشكواة، باب الشفقة.

[268] On the authority of Jarīr b. ʿAbdullāh ﷺ, who said: The Messenger of Allah ﷺ said, "Allah does not show mercy to the one who does not show mercy to people." Bukhārī and Muslim (*Mishkāt*, Chapter on Compassion, *Ḥadīth* no. 4947).

13

Social Virtues

13.1 SINCERE ADVICE

عَنْ أَبِي هُرَيْرَةَ ﷺ قَالَ: قَالَ رَسُولُ اللهِ ﷺ: الْمُسْلِمُ أَخُو الْمُسْلِمِ لا يَخُونُهُ وَلا يَكْذِبُهُ وَلَا يَخْذُلُهُ وَلا يَظْلِمُهُ ،وَإِنَّ أَحَدَكُمْ مِرْآةُ أَخِيهِ، فَإِنْ رَأَى أَذَىً فَلْيُمِطْ عَنْهُ. سنن الترمذي.

[269] On the authority of Abū Hurayrah ﷺ, who said: The Messenger of Allah ﷺ said, "The Muslim is the brother of the Muslim: he does not betray him, speak lies to him, disgrace him [leaving him needy and helpless] or oppress him. Each of you is the mirror of his brother: if he sees a fault, he should remove it from him." Tirmidhī (*Ḥadīth* nos. 1927 and 1929; *Mishkāt*, *Ḥadīth* nos. 4959 and 4985).

Commentary

In this *Ḥadīth*, a Muslim has been declared to be the mirror of another Muslim. This is a profoundly meaningful comparison. Keeping this comparison in mind, the following aspects of a Muslim's relationship with another Muslim become apparent:

1. A mirror reflects only those spots and stains that actually exist. It neither reduces nor enlarges them.
2. The mirror only reveals spots and stains when the face is present. If the person goes away, the tongue of the mirror is silenced.

3. We have never heard of anyone becoming annoyed or angry at seeing their spots and stains in the mirror. On the contrary, we see that people gratefully keep the mirror in a safe place so that it may be used when needed later.
4. The mirror only reveals the spots and stains when it is level with the person's face. If the mirror is above or below the face, it does not serve its essential purpose.

Instead of simile and metaphor, it can be stated in plain words that through the comparison with the mirror, the Messenger of Allah ﷺ has given us four pieces of guidance:

1. If there is a need to mention a Muslim's defect, it should only be described as far as it exists.
2. The defect should be mentioned in the person's presence, not behind their back.
3. If someone informs us of a defect or criticises us, we should be grateful to them instead of being annoyed with them.
4. When a sincere adviser or critic criticises, he should neither show himself as greater and higher, nor use flattery and sycophancy.

13.2 PREVENTING OPPRESSION

عَنْ أَنَس رضي الله عنه قَالَ: قَالَ رَسُولُ الله ﷺ: اُنْصُرْ أَخَاكَ ظَالِمًا أَوْ مَظْلُومًا، فَقَالَ رَجُلٌ: يَا رَسُولَ الله ﷺ أَنْصُرُهُ إِذَا كَانَ مَظْلُومًا، أَفَرَأَيْتَ إِذَا كَانَ ظَالِمًا كَيْفَ أَنْصُرُهُ؟ قَالَ: تَحْجُزُهُ، أَوْ تَمْنَعُهُ مِنْ الظُّلْمِ، فَإِنَّ ذَلِكَ نَصْرُهُ. صحيح البخاري ومسلم، مشكواة، باب الشفقة.

[270] On the authority of Anas رضي الله عنه, who said: The Messenger of Allah ﷺ said, "Help your brother, whether he is an oppressor or oppressed." A man asked, "I can help him when he is oppressed, but how can I help him when he is an oppressor?" He replied, "Prevent him from oppressing others – that will be your helping him." Bukhārī and Muslim (*Mishkāt*, Chapter on Compassion, *Ḥadīth* no. 4957).

13.3 LOVE AND COMPASSION

عَنْ أَبِي مُوسَى ﵁، عَنِ النَّبِيِّ ﷺ، قَالَ: إِنَّ الْمُؤْمِنَ لِلْمُؤْمِنِ كَالْبُنْيَانِ يَشُدُّ بَعْضُهُ بَعْضًا. وَشَبَّكَ أَصَابِعَهُ. صحيح البخاري ومسلم، مشكواة، باب الشفقة.

[271] On the authority of Abū Mūsā ﵁, that the Prophet ﷺ said, "Believers are like parts of a building that strengthen each other [in their mutual conduct]." He then interlocked his fingers. Bukhārī and Muslim (*Mishkāt*, Chapter on Compassion, *Ḥadīth* no. 4955).

Commentary

This means that Muslims should live together in such a way that they support and assist each other in times of misfortune.

عَنْ النُّعْمَانِ بْنِ بَشِيرٍ ﵁ قَالَ: قَالَ رَسُولُ اللهِ ﷺ: الْمُسْلِمُونَ كَرَجُلٍ وَاحِدٍ، إِنْ اشْتَكَى عَيْنُهُ اشْتَكَى كُلُّهُ، وَإِنْ اشْتَكَى رَأْسُهُ اشْتَكَى كُلُّهُ. صحيح مسلم، مشكواة، باب الشفقة.

[272] On the authority of al-Nuʿmān b. Bashīr ﵁, who said: The Messenger of Allah ﷺ said, "The believers are like a single person: if his eye hurts, his whole body hurts; if his head hurts, his whole body hurts." Muslim (*Mishkāt*, Chapter on Compassion, *Ḥadīth* no. 4954).

عَنْ أَبِي هُرَيْرَةَ ﵁، أَنَّ النَّبِيَّ ﷺ، قَالَ: الْمُؤْمِنُ مَأْلَفٌ وَلَا خَيْرَ فِيمَنْ لَا يَأْلَفُ وَلَا يُؤْلَفُ. مسند أحمد، مشكواة، باب الشفقة.

[273] On the authority of Abū Hurayrah ﵁, that the Messenger of Allah ﷺ said, "The believer is loving and caring. There is no good in one who does not love and care for others and is not loved and cared for by others." Aḥmad (*Mishkāt*, Chapter on Compassion, *Ḥadīth* no. 4995).

13.4 GENEROSITY IN DEALINGS

عَنْ أَبِي قَتَادَةَ ﷺ قال: سَمِعْتُ رَسُولَ الله ﷺ يَقُولُ: مَنْ أَنْظَرَ مُعْسِراً، أَوْ وَضَعَ عَنْهُ، أَنْجَاهُ اللهُ مِنْ كُرَبِ يَوْمَ الْقِيَامَةِ. رواه مسلم.

[274] On the authority of Abū Qatādah ﷺ, who said: The Messenger of Allah ﷺ said, "Whoever gives respite to a debtor in hardship or waives the debt, Allah will save him from the hardships of the Day of Resurrection." Muslim (*Mishkāt*, *Ḥadīth* no. 2903).

عَنْ جَابِرِ بْنِ عَبْدِ اللهِ ﷺ، أَنَّ رَسُولَ الله ﷺ قَالَ: رَحِمَ اللهُ رَجُلا سَمْحًا إِذَا بَاعَ، وَإِذَا اشْتَرَى، وَإِذَا اقْتَضَى. صحيح البخاري، مشكواة، باب المسائلة.

[275] On the authority of Jābir b. ʿAbdullāh ﷺ, who said: The Messenger of Allah ﷺ said, "May Allah have mercy on a person who is gentle and generous when he sells, buys or demands the settlement of a debt." Bukhārī (*Mishkāt*, Chapter on Mutual Flexibility, *Ḥadīth* no. 2790).

عَنْ أَبِي سَعِيدٍ ﷺ، عَنْ النَّبِيِّ ﷺ، قَالَ: التَّاجِرُ الصَّدُوقُ الأَمِينُ مَعَ النَّبِيِّينَ وَالصِّدِّيقِينَ وَالشُّهَدَاءِ. سنن الترمذي، مشكواة، باب المسائلة.

[276] On the authority of Abū Saʿīd ﷺ, who said: The Messenger of Allah ﷺ said, "The honest trader will be [raised] with the Prophets, the truthful ones and martyrs." Tirmidhī (*Mishkāt*, Chapter on Mutual Flexibility, *Ḥadīth* nos. 2796-7).

Commentary

This *Ḥadīth* makes it clear that Islam is not merely a few rituals of worship; rather, honesty and integrity in trade are also important parts of the religion, without which the performance of worship rituals have no weight with Allah.

13.5 DEFENDING A MUSLIM BROTHER

عَنْ أَسْمَاءَ بِنْتِ يَزِيدَ ﵂، عَنْ النَّبِيِّ ﷺ قَالَ: مَنْ ذَبَّ عَنْ لَحْمِ أَخِيهِ بِالْغِيبَةِ كَانَ حَقًّا عَلَى اللهِ أَنْ يُعْتِقَهُ مِنْ النَّارِ. مسند أحمد، رواه البيهقي، مشكواة، باب الشفقة.

[277] On the authority of Asmā' bint Yazīd ﵂, who said: The Messenger of Allah ﷺ said, "Whoever defends his brother's flesh in his absence, it will be binding upon Allah to liberate him from the Fire." Aḥmad, Ṭabarānī and Bayhaqī (*Mishkāt*, Chapter on Compassion, *Ḥadīth* no. 4981).

Commentary

This means that if a Muslim is being backbitten, the audience should not remain silent; rather, they should fully defend their oppressed brother or sister. The metaphor here, "his brother's flesh", is taken from the Qur'ānic *āyah*, "*Would any of you like to eat the flesh of his dead brother?*" (*Sūrah al-Ḥujurāt*, 49: 12)

13.6 THINKING WELL OF OTHERS

عَنْ أَبِي هُرَيْرَةَ ﵁ قَالَ: قَالَ رَسُولُ اللهِ ﷺ: حُسْنُ الظَّنِّ مِنْ حُسْنِ العِبَادَةِ. سنن أبي داود وأحمد.

[278] On the authority of Abū Hurayrah ﵁, who said: The Messenger of Allah ﷺ said, "Thinking well of others is part of worshipping [Allah] in the best manner." Aḥmad and Abū Dāwūd (*Mishkāt*, *Ḥadīth* no. 5048).

Commentary

The relationship between one Muslim and another should be on the basis of a positive view of each other. This optimistic view should remain until a person proves himself to be unworthy of it.

13.7 ETIQUETTE OF SOCIAL INTERACTION

عَنْ عَبْدِ اللهِ ابْنِ مَسْعُودٍ ﷺ، قَالَ النَّبِيُّ ﷺ: إِذَا كُنْتُمْ ثَلَاثَةً فَلا يَتَنَاجَى رَجُلَانِ دُونَ الثَّالِثِ، فَإِنَّهُ يُحْزِنُهُ فِي ذٰلِكَ. وَفِي رِوَايَةٍ: قُلْنَا فَإِنْ كَانُوْا أَرْبَعَةً، قَالَ: لَايَضُرُّهُ. الأدب المفرد، باب إذا كانوا اربعة.

[279] On the authority of ʿAbdullāh b. Masʿūd ﷺ, who said: The Prophet ﷺ said, "When there are three of you, two of you should not speak privately to the exclusion of the third, for that will cause him grief." In one narration: We asked, "What if there are four of us?" He replied, "Then there is no harm." Bukhārī's *Al-Adab al-Mufrad*, Chapter on When There Are Four, *Ḥadīth* nos. 891-3 (*Mishkāt*, *Ḥadīth* no. 4965).

عَنْ سَعِيدٍ الْمَقْبُرِيِّ ﷺ قَالَ: مَرَرْت عَلَى ابْنِ عُمَرَ وَمَعَهُ رَجُل يَتَحَدَّثُ، فَقُمْتُ إِلَيْهِمَا فَلَطَمَ صَدْرِي، وَقَالَ: إِذَا وَجَدْت اثْنَيْنِ يَتَحَدَّثَانِ فَلا تَقُمْ مَعَهُما حَتَّى تَسْتَأْذِنَهُمَا. فَقُلْتُ: أَصْلَحَكَ اللهُ يَا أَبَا عَبْدِ الرَّحْمٰنِ، إِنَّما رَجَوْتُ أَنْ أَسْمَعَ مِنْكُما خَيْرًا. الأدب المفرد، باب اذا رأى قوما يتناجون فلا يدخل عليهم.

[280] On the authority of Saʿīd al-Maqbūrī ﷺ, who said: I passed by Ibn ʿUmar, who was talking to another man. I joined the two of them, upon which Ibn ʿUmar slapped my chest and said, "When you find two people conversing, do not join them or sit with them without asking their permission." I replied, "May Allah give you righteousness, O Abū ʿAbd al-Raḥmān! I expected nothing but hearing some goodness from you." Bukhārī's *Al-Adab al-Mufrad*, Chapter on When Someone Sees People Speaking Privately, He Should Not Join Them, *Ḥadīth* no. 889.

عَنْ أَبِي هُرَيْرَةَ ﷺ قَالَ: إِذَا تَنَخَّعَ بَيْنَ يَدَيْ الْقَوْمِ، فَلْيُوارِ بِكَفَّيْهِ حَتَّى تَقَعَ نُخَاعَتُهُ إِلَى الْأَرْضِ، وَإِذَا صَامَ فَلْيَدَّهِنْ لاَ يُرَى عَلَيْهِ أَثَرُ الصَّوْمِ. الأدب المفرد، باب اذا تَنَخَّعَ وهُوَ مع القَوْم.

[281] On the authority of Abū Hurayrah ﷺ, who said, "If someone needs to blow his nose in the presence of others, he should

cover it with both his palms such that his nasal discharge falls to the ground. If someone fasts, he should apply oil to himself so that the effects of fasting are not apparent." Bukhārī's *Al-Adab al-Mufrad*, Chapter on Blowing One's Nose in the Company of Others, *Ḥadīth* no. 1303.

13.8 ETIQUETTE OF ENTERING AND LEAVING HOUSES

عَنْ جَابِرٍ ﵁ قَالَ: يَسْتَأْذِنُ الرَّجُلُ عَلى وَلَدِهِ وَأُمِّهِ وَإِنْ كَانَتْ عَجُوزًا وَأَخِيهِ وَأُخْتِهِ وَأَبِيهِ. الأدب المفرد، باب يستأذن على ابيه وولده.

[282] On the authority of Jābir ﵁, who said, "A person should seek permission to enter the houses or rooms of his children, his mother, even if she is an old woman, his brothers, his sisters and his father." Bukhārī's *Al-Adab al-Mufrad*, Chapter on Seeking Permission to Enter Upon One's Parents and Children, *Ḥadīth* no. 1062.

13.9 ETIQUETTE OF FRIENDSHIP

عَنْ أَبِي هُرَيْرَةَ ﵁ قَالَ: قَالَ رَسُولُ اللهِ ﷺ: الْمَرْءُ عَلى دِينِ خَلِيلِهِ، فَلْيَنْظُرْ أَحَدُكُمْ مَنْ يُخَالِلُ. مسند أحمد، مشكواة، باب الحب.

[283] On the authority of Abū Hurayrah ﵁, who said: The Messenger of Allah ﷺ said, "A person follows the way of life [or religion] of his close friend. Therefore, each of you must be careful about whom you befriend." Aḥmad, Tirmidhī and Abū Dāwūd (*Mishkāt*, Chapter on Love, *Ḥadīth* no. 5019).

عَنْ الْمِقْدَامِ بْنِ مَعْدِي كَرِبَ ﵁، عَنْ النَّبِيِّ ﷺ قَالَ: إِذَا أَحَبَّ الرَّجُلُ أَخَاهُ فَلْيُخْبِرْهُ أَنَّهُ يُحِبُّهُ. رواه أبو داود، مشكواة، باب الحب.

[284] On the authority of Al-Miqdām b. Maʿdī Karib ﵁ that the Prophet ﷺ said, "If a man loves his brother, he should tell him that he loves him." Abū Dāwūd and Tirmidhī (*Mishkāt*, Chapter on Love, *Ḥadīth* no. 5016).

عَنْ أَبِي سَعِيدٍ ﷺ، أَنَّهُ سَمِعَ رَسُولَ اللهِ ﷺ يَقُولُ: لَا تُصَاحِبْ إِلَّا مُؤْمِنًا، وَلَا يَأْكُلْ طَعَامَكَ إِلَّا تَقِيٌّ. رواه الترمذي، مشكواة، باب الحب.

[285] On the authority of Abū Saʿīd ﷺ that he heard the Prophet ﷺ saying, "Only befriend a believer. Only a righteous person should share your food." Aḥmad, Abū Dāwūd, Tirmidhī and Dārimī (*Mishkāt*, Chapter on Love, Ḥadīth no. 5018).

Commentary

This Ḥadīth does not mean that one should not have any contacts with unbelievers or sinners: the essential meaning of this Ḥadīth is that deep bonds of friendship and everyday relationships should only be maintained with people whose character and behaviour is fully trusted.

13.10 EFFECTS OF FRIENDSHIP

عَنْ أَبِي مُوسَى ﷺ قَالَ: قَالَ رَسُولُ اللهِ ﷺ: مَثَلُ الْجَلِيسِ الصَّالِحِ وَالسَّوْءِ كَحَامِلِ الْمِسْكِ وَنَافِخِ كِيرٍ، فَحَامِلُ الْمِسْكِ إِمَّا أَنْ يُحْذِيَكَ وَإِمَّا أَنْ تَبْتَاعَ مِنْهُ وَإِمَّا أَنْ تَجِدَ مِنْهُ رِيحًا طَيِّبَةً، وَنَافِخُ الْكِيرِ إِمَّا أَنْ يُحْرِّقَ بَدَنَكَ أَوْ ثِيَابَكَ وَإِمَّا أَنْ تَجِدَ مِنْهُ رِيحًا خَبِيثَةً. صحيح البخاري.

[286] On the authority of Abū Mūsā ﷺ, who said: The Messenger of Allah ﷺ said, "The parable of a righteous companion and an evil companion is that of the perfumer and the iron-monger. The perfumer may present you with a gift, you may buy something from him or [at the very least] you will smell a beautiful fragrance from him. The iron-monger will either burn your [body and] clothes or you will smell a disgusting odour from him." Bukhārī and Muslim (*Mishkāt*, Chapter on Love, Ḥadīth no. 5010).

13.11 MODERATION IN FRIENDSHIP AND ENMITY

عَنْ أَسْلَمَ، عَنْ عُمَرَ بْنِ الْخَطَّابِ ﷺ قَالَ: لَا يَكُنْ حُبُّكَ كَلَفًا وَلَا بُغْضُكَ تَلَفًا. فَقُلْتُ كَيْفَ ذَاكَ؟ قَالَ: إِذَا أَحْبَبْتَ كَلِفْتَ كَلَفَ الصَّبِيِّ، وَإِذَا أَبْغَضْتَ أَحْبَبْتَ لِصَاحِبِكَ التَّلَفَ. الأدب المفرد.

[287] On the authority of Aslam that ʿUmar b. al-Khaṭṭāb ﷺ said, "Let not your love become obsession. Let not your hatred become destruction." I asked, "How is that?" He replied, "When your love becomes obsession like that of a child, and when your hatred leads you to wish for the destruction of [life and property belonging to] another person." Bukhārī's *Al-Adab al-Mufrad*, *Ḥadīth* no. 1322.

عَنْ عُبَيْدِ الكِنْدِي، عَنْ عَلِيٍّ ﷺ قَالَ: أَحْبِبْ حَبِيْبَكَ هَوْنَاً مَا عَسَى أَنْ يَكُوْنَ بَغِيْضَكَ يَوْماً مَا، وَأَبْغِضْ بَغِيْضَكَ هَوْناً مَا عَسَى أَنْ يَكُونَ حَبِيْبَكَ يَوْماً مَا. الأدب المفرد، باب أحبب حبيبك.

[288] On the authority of ʿUbayd al-Kindī ﷺ, who said: I heard ʿAlī ﷺ saying, "Love your friend a little less [i.e. in moderation]: he may be your enemy one day. Hate your enemy a little less [i.e. in moderation]: he may be your friend one day." Bukhārī's *Al-Adab al-Mufrad*, Chapter on Loving Your Beloved, *Ḥadīth* no. 1321.

13.12 BEING GOOD-NATURED

وَعَنْ أَنَس ﷺ، عَنْ النَّبِيِّ ﷺ، قَالَ لامْرَأَةٍ عَجُوز: إِنَّهُ لا تَدْخُلُ الْجَنَّةَ عَجُوزٌ. فقالتْ: وَمَا لَهُنَّ؟ وَكَانَتْ تَقْرَأُ القُرآنَ. فَقَالَ لَهَا: أَمَا تَقْرَئِينَ القرآنَ؟ **﴿ إِنَّا أَنْشَأْنَاهُنَّ إِنْشَاءً فَجَعَلْنَاهُنَّ أَبْكَاراً عُرُباً أَتْرَاباً ﴾**. مشكواة، باب المزاح.

[289] On the authority of Anas ﷺ, that the Prophet ﷺ said to an elderly lady: "Old women will not enter the Garden." She was a reciter of the Qur'ān and asked, "What is their sin?" He replied, "Do you not recite the Qur'ān? '*And their spouses We shall have brought them into being afresh, and shall have made them virgins, intensely loving and of matching age.*' (*Sūrah al-Wāqiʿah*, 56: 35-37)." Razīn and Baghawī (*Mishkāt*, Chapter on Humour, *Ḥadīth* no. 4888).

Commentary

Old women will enter the Garden, but without the infirmities, furrows and facial wrinkles of old age. Rather, they will be radiant with youthfulness as they enjoy this eternal bliss from Allah.

عَنْ أَبِى هُرَيْرَةَ ﷺ قَالَ: أَخَذَ النَّبِيُّ ﷺ بِيَدِ الحَسَنِ أَوِ الْحُسَيْنِ رَضِيَ اللهُ عَنْهُمَا، ثُمَّ وَضَعَ قَدَمَيْهِ عَلى قَدَمَيْهِ، ثُمَّ قَالَ: تَرَقَّ. الأدب المفرد، باب المزاح مع الصبي.

[290] On the authority of Abū Hurayrah ﷺ, who said: The Prophet ﷺ once took the hand of Ḥasan or Ḥusayn and placed the child's feet on his own feet, saying, "Climb up!" Bukhārī's *Al-Adab al-Mufrad*, Chapter on Humour with Children, *Ḥadīth* no. 249.

Commentary

Being good-humoured towards children does not negate piety and renunciation of the world. However, if this humour goes out of bounds, bad and dangerous habits may develop in children.

14

Social Ills

14.1 HAVING A CARELESS TONGUE

عَنْ سَهْلِ بْنِ سَعْدٍ ﷺ، عَنْ رَسُولِ اللهِ ﷺ، قَالَ: مَنْ يَضْمَنْ لِي مَا بَيْنَ لَحْيَيْهِ وَمَا بَيْنَ رِجْلَيْهِ أَضْمَنْ لَهُ الْجَنَّةَ. صحيح البخاري.

[291] On the authority of Sahl b. Saʿd ﷺ, who said: The Messenger of Allah ﷺ said, "Whoever guarantees to me what is between his jaws [i.e. his tongue] and what is between his legs [i.e. his chastity], I guarantee the Garden for him." Bukhārī (*Mishkāt*, *Ḥadīth* no. 4812).

14.2 IRRESPONSIBLE TALK

عَنْ أَبِي هُرَيْرَةَ ﷺ قَالَ: قَالَ رَسُولُ اللهِ ﷺ: كَفَى بِالْمَرْءِ كَذِبًا أَنْ يُحَدِّثَ بِكُلِّ مَا سَمِعَ.

صحيح مسلم، مشكواة، باب الاعتصام.

[292] On the authority of Abū Hurayrah ﷺ, who said: The Messenger of Allah ﷺ said, "It is enough to make a person a liar that he narrates everything he hears [without investigation]." Muslim (*Mishkāt*, Chapter on Holding Fast, *Ḥadīth* no. 156).

عَنِ ابْنِ مَسْعُودٍ ﷺ قَالَ: إِنَّ الشَّيْطَانَ لَيَتَمَثَّلُ فِي صُورَةِ الرَّجُلِ، فَيَأْتِي الْقَوْمَ، فَيُحَدِّثُهُمْ بِالْحَدِيثِ مِنَ الْكَذِبِ، فَيَتَفَرَّقُونَ، فَيَقُولُ الرَّجُلُ مِنْهُمْ: سَمِعْتُ رَجُلاً أَعْرِفُ وَجْهَهُ وَلَا أَدْرِي مَا اسْمُهُ يُحَدِّثُ. صحيح مسلم.

[293] On the authority of Ibn Masʿūd ﷺ, who said, "Truly, Satan takes the form of men, coming to people and narrating untrue stories to them. After he has done this, the people disperse, one of them saying, 'I heard a man narrating this; I recognise him by face but do not know his name.'" Muslim (*Mishkāt*, *Ḥadīth* no. 4863).

Commentary

From this narration, we learn that spreading false rumours and believing them without investigation are both diabolical actions.

عَنْ عَائِشَةَ رَضِيَ اللهُ عَنْهَا قَالَتْ: قُلْتُ لِلنَّبِيِّ ﷺ: حَسْبُكَ مِنْ صَفِيَّةَ كَذا وَكَذَا، تَعْنِي قَصِيرَةً ، فَقَالَ: لَقَدْ قُلْتِ كَلِمَةً لَوْ مُزِجَ بِهَا الْبَحْرُ لَمَزَجَتْهُ. سنن الترمذي.

[294] On the authority of ʿĀ'ishah ﷺ, who said: I said to the Prophet ﷺ, "It is enough for you regarding Ṣafiyyah that she is such-and-such", meaning that she was short in height. He replied, "You have said a word that would turn the ocean sour, were it mixed with it." Aḥmad, Abū Dāwūd and Tirmidhī (*Mishkāt*, *Ḥadīth* no. 4853).

Commentary

A number of matters are learnt from this *Ḥadīth*:

1. Jealousy amongst co-wives is of such a nature that a woman, even if she reaches the summit of piety, will be affected by it to some extent; this emotion cannot be totally eliminated. However, her bitterness can be minimised through education and instruction. This is why the Messenger of Allah ﷺ censured his wife on this occasion.
2. It is a heavy responsibility upon a husband that he does not neglect the religious education and moral reform of his household for even one moment.
3. Extreme caution is needed when using the tongue. Even slight negligence in this matter can lead to very dangerous consequences, both in this world and the Hereafter.

14.3 VULGARITY

عَنْ عَائِشَةَ ﵂: رَجُلاً إِسْتَأْذَنَ عَلى النَبيِّ ﷺ فَقَالَ: ائْذَنُوا لَهُ بِئْسَ أَخُو الْعَشِيرَةِ، فَلَمَّا جَلَسَ، تَطَلَّقَ النَبيِّ ﷺ فِي وَجهِهِ وَانْبَسَطَ إِلَيْهِ، فَلَمَّا انْطَلَقَ الرَجُلُ، قَالَتْ عَائِشَةَ: يَا رَسُولَ اللهِ قُلْتَ لَهُ كَذَا وَكَذَا، ثُمَّ تَطَلَّقْتَ فِي وَجْهِهِ وَانْبَسَطْتَّ إِلَيْهِ. فَقَالَ رَسُولُ اللهِ ﷺ: مَتَى عَاهَدْتِّنِيْ فَحَاشَا، إِنَّ شَرَّ النَّاسِ مَنْزِلَةً يَوْمَ القِيَامَةِ مَنْ يَتْرُكُهُ النَّاسُ اتِّقَاءَ شَرِّهِ أَوْ اتِّقَاءَ فُحْشِهِ. صحيح البخاري، مشكاة – ص٤١٢.

[295] On the authority of 'Ā'ishah ﵂, that a man sought permission to meet the Prophet ﷺ. He said, "Give him permission to enter, what a bad member of his tribe!" When the man entered and sat down, the Prophet ﷺ smiled in his face and was pleasant towards him. When the man left, 'Ā'ishah said, "O Messenger of Allah! You said such-and-such about him and then you smiled in his face and were pleasant to him?" The Messenger of Allah ﷺ replied, "When have you ever found me to be vulgar? Truly, the worst of the people on the Day of Resurrection will be one who is avoided by people because of his evil or vulgarity." Bukhārī (*Miskhāt*, *Ḥadīth* no. 4829).

Commentary

1. Generally, a Muslim should meet another Muslim with a cheerful, smiling face. Irritability, bad moods and vulgar talk are extremely displeasing to Allah.
2. If a person is intent on spreading corruption in society, he can be condemned in his absence in order to save people from his mischief.

14.4 FREQUENT SWEARING OF OATHS

عَنْ أَبِي قَتَادَةَ الأَنْصَارِيِّ ﵁، أَنَّهُ سَمِعَ رَسُولَ اللهِ ﷺ يَقُولُ: إِيَّاكُمْ وَكَثْرَةَ الْحَلَفِ فِي الْبَيْعِ، فَإِنَّهُ يُنَفِّقُ ثُمَّ يَمْحَقُ. رواه مسلم، مشكواة، باب المسائله في المعاملة.

[296] On the authority of Abū Qatādah al-Anṣārī ﵁, that he heard the Messenger of Allah ﷺ saying, "Beware of frequent oaths

in buying and selling, for this [initially] facilitates business but then deprives it [of blessing]." Muslim (*Mishkāt*, Chapter: Flexibility in Transactions, *Ḥadīth* no. 2793).

14.5 RIDICULING OTHERS

عَنْ عَائِشَةَ ﵂ قَالَتْ: مَرَّ رَجُلٌ مُصَابٌ عَلى نِسْوَةٍ فَتَضَاحَكْنَ بِهِ يَسْخَرْنَ، فأُصِيْبَ بَعْضُهُنَّ. الأدب المفرد، باب السخرية.

[297] On the authority of ʿĀ'ishah ﵂, who said, "A man with an affliction passed by a group of women who began laughing amongst themselves, making a mockery of him. Later, some of them were afflicted with the same condition." Bukhārī's *Al-Adab al-Mufrad*, Chapter on Ridicule, *Ḥadīth* no. 887.

Commentary

It seems that the affliction mentioned in this *Ḥadīth* was epilepsy.

14.6 BEING SUSPICIOUS OF OTHERS

عَنْ أَبِي هُرَيْرَةَ ﵁، أَنَّ رَسُولُ اللهِ ﷺ قَالَ: إِيَّاكُمْ وَالظَّنَّ، فَإِنَّ الظَّنَّ أَكْذَبُ الْحَدِيثِ. متفق عليه.

[298] On the authority of Abū Hurayrah ﵁, who said: The Messenger of Allah ﷺ said, "Beware of suspicion and baseless speculation, for they are the most false kinds of speech." Bukhārī and Muslim (*Mishkāt*, *Ḥadīth* no. 5028).

عَنْ بِلَالِ بْنِ سَعْدِ الْأَشْعَرِيِّ ﵁ أَنَّ مُعَاوِيَةَ كَتَبَ إِلى أَبِي الدَرْدَاءِ: أُكْتُبْ إِلَيَّ فُسَّاقَ دِمَشْقَ، فَقَالَ: مَا لِي وَفُسَّاقُ دِمَشْقَ وَمِنْ أَيْنَ أَعْرِفُهُمْ؟ فَقَالَ ابْنُهُ بِلَالٌ :أَنَا أَكْتُبُهُمْ، فَكَتَبَهُمْ. قَالَ: مِنْ أَيْنَ عَلِمْتَ؟ مَا عَرَفتَ أَنَّهُمْ فُسَّاقٌ إِلا وَأَنْتَ مِنْهُمْ، اِبْدَأْ بِنَفْسِكَ، وَلَمْ يُرْسِلْ بِأَسْمَائِهِمْ. الأدب المفرد، باب الظن.

[299] On the authority of Bilāl b. Saʿd al-Ashʿarī ﵁, that Muʿāwiyah wrote to Abū'l-Dardā', "Write to me the names of

the mischief-makers of Damascus." Abū'l-Dardā' said, "What have I to do with the mischief-makers of Damascus? How will I know them?" His son, Bilāl, said, "I shall write their names", and did so. Abū'l-Dardā' said, "How did you know these names? You only recognised them as mischief-makers because you are one of them! Begin the list with yourself!" He did not send the names to Muʿāwiyah. Bukhārī's *Al-Adab al-Mufrad*, Chapter on Suspicion, *Ḥadīth* no. 1290.

14.7 SPYING AND FAULT-FINDING

عَنْ أَنَسِ بْنِ مَالِكٍ ﷺ، أَنَّ أَعْرَابِيًّا أَتَى بَيْتَ رَسُولِ اللهِ ﷺ، فَأَلْقَمَ عَيْنَهُ خَصَاصَ الْبَابِ فَأَخَذَ سَهْمًا، أَوْ عُوْدًا مُحَدَّدًا، فَتَوَخَّى لِيَفْقَأَ عَيْنَ الْأَعْرَابِيَّ، فَذَهَبَ، فَقَالَ: أَمَا إِنَّكَ لَوْ ثَبَتَّ لَفَقَأْتُ عَيْنَكَ. الأدب المفرد، باب الظن.

[300] On the authority of Anas b. Mālik ﷺ, that a Bedouin came to the house of the Messenger of Allah ﷺ and pressed his eye against a gap in the doorway [to peep inside]. The Prophet picked up an arrow or pointed stick and proceeded towards the man in order to pierce his eye, so that the latter fled. The Prophet ﷺ said, "Truly, if you had stayed where you were, I would have pierced your eye!" Bukhārī, Muslim and Bukhārī's *Al-Adab al-Mufrad*, Chapter on Peering into Houses, *Ḥadīth* no. 1069).

Commentary

Spying is forbidden in Islam. The type of behaviour described in this *Ḥadīth* is only practised by those who enjoy looking for others' faults.

14.8 CARRYING TALES

عَنْ عَبْدِ اللهِ ابْنِ مَسْعُودٍ ﷺ قَالَ: قَالَ رَسُولُ اللهِ ﷺ: لَا يُبَلِّغُنِي أَحَدٌ عَنْ أَحَدٍ مِنْ أَصْحَابِي شَيْئًا، فَإِنِي أُحِبُّ أَنْ أَخْرُجَ إِلَيْكُمْ وَأَنَا سَلِيمُ الصَّدْرِ. سنن الترمذي وأبي داود، رياض الصالحين، باب حفظ اللسان.

[301]   On the authority of ʿAbdullāh b. Masʿūd ☼, who said: The Messenger of Allah ﷺ said, "None of my Companions should convey to me anything about another, for I love to come out to you with a clean heart [i.e. with no grudge or ill-feeling towards anyone]." Abū Dāwūd and Tirmidhī (Nawawī, *Riyāḍ al-Ṣāliḥīn*, Chapter on Guarding the Tongue; *Mishkāt*, *Ḥadīth* no. 4852).

عَنْ أَبِي هُرَيْرَةَ ﷜، أَنَّ رَسُولَ الله ﷺ قَالَ: أَتَدْرُونَ مَا الْغِيبَةُ؟ قَالُوا: اللهُ وَرَسُولُهُ أَعْلَمُ. قَالَ: ذِكْرُكَ أَخَاكَ بِمَا يَكْرَهُ. قِيلَ أَفَرَأَيْتَ إِنْ كَانَ فِي أَخِي مَا أَقُولُ؟ قَالَ: إِنْ كَانَ فِيهِ مَا تَقُولُ فَقَدِ اغْتَبْتَهُ، وَإِنْ لَمْ يَكُنْ فِيهِ فَقَدْ بَهَتَّهُ. صحيح مسلم.

[302]   On the authority of Abū Hurayrah ☼, that the Messenger of Allah ﷺ asked, "Do you know what backbiting is?" They replied, "Allah and His Messenger know best." He said, "It is to mention something about your brother that he dislikes." Someone asked, "What if that thing is true about my brother?" He replied, "If it is true about him, you have backbitten him. If you say something untrue about him, you have slandered him." Muslim (*Mishkāt*, *Ḥadīth* no. 4828).

عَنْ فَاطِمَةَ بِنْتِ قَيْسٍ ﷞ قَالَتْ: أَتَيْتُ النَّبِيَّ ﷺ، فَقُلْتُ: إِنَّ أَبَا جَهْمٍ وَ مُعَاوِيَةَ خَطَبَانِي. فَقَالَ رَسُولُ الله ﷺ: ، أَمَّا مُعَاوِيَةُ فَصُعْلُوكٌ وَ أَمَّا أَبُو جَهْمٍ فَلَا يَضَعُ عَصَاهُ عَنْ عَاتِقِهِ. متفق عليه، رياض الصالحين،

[303]   On the authority of Fāṭimah bint Qays ☼, who said: I came to the Prophet ﷺ and told him that Abū Jahm and Muʿāwiyah had asked for my hand in marriage. The Messenger of Allah ﷺ replied, "As for Muʿāwiyah, he is a very poor man. As for Abū Jahm, his stick never leaves his shoulder [i.e. he beats his wives]." Bukhārī, Muslim, and *Riyāḍ al-Ṣāliḥīn*.

Commentary

We learn from this *Ḥadīth* that if a person of responsibility mentions people's faults where required upon being consulted, this will not be regarded as backbiting. In view of the public benefit, to do so is not only permissible but may, in some situations, be necessary.

عَنْ عَائِشَةَ ﵂، أَنَّ هِنْدَ بِنْتَ عُتْبَةَ، قَالَتْ: يَا رَسُولَ اللهِ ﷺ إِنَّ أَبَا سُفْيَانَ رَجُلٌ شَحِيحٌ وَلَيْسَ يُعْطِينِي مَا يَكْفِينِي وَوَلَدِي إِلا مَا أَخَذْتُ مِنْهُ وَهُوَ لا يَعْلَمُ. فَقَالَ: خُذِي مَا يَكْفِيكِ وَوَلَدَكِ بِالْمَعْرُوفِ. صحيح البخاري، رياض الصالحين.

[304] On the authority of ʿĀ'ishah ﵂, who said: Hind bint ʿUtbah, [wife of Abū Sufyān,] said, "O Messenger of Allah! Truly, Abū Sufyān is a miserly person. He does not give me enough to suffice me and my children, unless I take from his wealth without his knowledge." He replied, "Take what will reasonably suffice you and your children." Bukhārī (*Riyāḍ al-Ṣāliḥīn* and *Mishkāt*, *Ḥadīth* no. 3242).

Commentary

1. In general, backbiting is not permitted. However if a matter is being referred to a person of knowledge and a person's fault is mentioned in order to clarify the essential issue, this does not fall under prohibited backbiting.
2. If a husband does not meet the necessary living expenses of his wife and children, it is allowed for the wife to take what is necessary from her husband's wealth without his permission.
3. The phrase "reasonably" (*bi'l-maʿrūf*) shows that in these kinds of social transactions, the prevailing custom (*ʿurf*) and practice is to be considered unless this conflicts with an unequivocal revealed text of the *Sharīʿah*.

14.9 THE LIMITS OF BACKBITING

عَنْ عَائِشَةَ ﵂ قَالَتْ: قَالَ النَّبِيُّ ﷺ: مَا أَظُنُّ فُلَانًا وَفُلَانًا يَعْرِفَانِ مِنْ دِينِنَا شَيْئًا. صحيح البخاري، رياض الصالحين.

[305] On the authority of ʿĀ'ishah ﵂, who said: The Messenger of Allah ﷺ said, "I do not think that so-and-so and so-and-so know anything about our religion." Bukhārī and *Riyāḍ al-Ṣāliḥīn*.

Commentary

This seems outwardly to be a form of backbiting. However, on the basis of public religious benefit, a Muslim's fault or weakness can be explained behind his back, as long as the objective is neither to satisfy a desire for personal revenge nor to derive personal enjoyment from backbiting. Rather, the aim should be to safeguard other Muslims from this person's evil or to prevent them from having a false idea of his knowledge and piety.

14.10 SPEAKING ILL OF THE DEAD

عَنْ عَائِشَةَ رضي الله عنها قَالَتْ: قَالَ النَّبِيُّ ﷺ: لا تَسُبُّوا الْأَمْوَاتَ، فَإِنَّهُمْ قَدْ أَفْضَوْا إِلَى مَا قَدَّمُوا.
صحيح البخاري، مشكواة، باب المشي بالجنازة.

[306] On the authority of ʿĀ'ishah ﷺ, who said: The Messenger of Allah ﷺ said, "Do not abuse the deceased, for they have found what they sent forth." Bukhārī (*Mishkāt*, Chapter: Walking with the Funeral, *Ḥadīth* no. 1664).

Commentary

This means that it is not permissible to talk about a person's faults after his death. He is already tasting the consequences of his bad deeds with Allah. What benefit is there in unnecessarily ruining one's own register of deeds by criticising him?

14.11 BEING TWO-FACED

عَـنْ أَبِي هُرَيْرَةَ رضي الله عنه، يَبْلُغُ بِـهِ النَّبِيَّ ﷺ قَالَ: تَجِدُونَ مِـنْ شَـرِّ النَّاسِ يَـومَ القِيامَةِ ذَا الْوَجْهَيْنِ، الَّذِي يَأْتِي هَؤُلَاءِ بِوَجْهٍ وَهَؤُلَاءِ بِوَجْهٍ. متفق عليه.

[307] On the authority of Abū Hurayrah ﷺ, who said: The Prophet ﷺ said, "On the Day of Resurrection, you will find the worst of people to be the two-faced one: he appears to some people with one face and to others with another." Bukhārī and Muslim (*Mishkāt*, *Ḥadīth* no. 4822).

Commentary

This means that the person appears here and there with different "colours". In other words, he keeps changing his hypocritical stances according to the situation.

14.12 ENMITY AND HATRED

عَنْ الزُّبَيْرَ بْنَ الْعَوَّام ﷺ، أَنَّ النَّبِيَّ ﷺ قَالَ: دَبَّ إِلَيْكُمْ دَاءُ الْأُمَمِ قَبْلَكُمْ، الْحَسَدُ وَالْبَغْضَاءُ هِيَ الْحَالِقَةُ، لا أَقُولُ تَحْلِقُ الشَّعْرَ، وَلَكِنْ تَحْلِقُ الدِّينَ. سنن الترمذي وأحمد.

[308] On the authority of al-Zubayr b. al-ʿAwwām ﷺ, who said: The Prophet ﷺ said, "The diseases of previous nations have crept [imperceptibly] amongst you: envy and hatred. These shave everything. I do not mean that they shave hair; rather, they shave [i.e. eradicate] the religion." Aḥmad and Tirmidhī (*Mishkāt*, Chapter: What is Forbidden, *Ḥadīth* no. 5039).

عَنْ أَبِي هُرَيْرَةَ ﷺ، أَنَّ النَّبِيَّ ﷺ قَالَ: إِيَّاكُمْ وَالْحَسَدَ، فَإِنَّ الْحَسَدَ يَأْكُلُ الْحَسَنَاتِ كَمَا تَأْكُلُ النَّارُ الْحَطَبَ. سنن أبي داود، مشكواة، باب ما ينهى.

[309] On the authority of Abū Hurayrah ﷺ, who said: The Messenger of Allah ﷺ said, "Beware of envy, for envy devours good deeds the way fire devours wood." Abū Dāwūd (*Mishkāt*, Chapter: What is Forbidden, *Ḥadīth* no. 5040).

14.13 MUTUAL SEVERING OF RELATIONS

عَنْ أَبِي أَيُّوبَ الْأَنْصَارِيِّ ﷺ، أَنَّ رَسُولَ الله ﷺ قَالَ: لا يَحِلُّ لِرَجُلٍ أَنْ يَهْجُرَ أَخَاهُ فَوْقَ ثَلَاثِ لَيَالٍ يَلْتَقِيَانِ فَيُعْرِضُ هَذَا وَيُعْرِضُ هَذَا، وَخَيْرُهُمَا الَّذِي يَبْدَأُ بِالسَّلَامِ. رواه البخاري ومسلم، مشكواة، باب النهي.

[310] On the authority of Abū Ayyūb al-Anṣārī ﷺ, who said: The Messenger of Allah ﷺ said, "It is not lawful for a man to shun his brother for more than three nights: when they meet,

each turns his face away from the other. The better of the two is the first one to give the other the greeting of peace." Bukhārī and Muslim (*Mishkāt*, Chapter: What is Forbidden, *Ḥadīth* no. 5027).

Commentary

On another occasion, the Prophet ﷺ declared, "The first to give the greeting of peace is absolved of pride and arrogance."

عَنْ عِمْرَانَ بْنِ أَبِي أَنَسٍ رضي الله عنه، أَنَّ رَجُلاً مِنْ أَسْلَمَ مِنْ أَصْحَابِ النَّبِيِّ ﷺ، حَدَّثُهُ عَنِ النَّبِيِّ ﷺ، قَالَ: هِجْرَةُ الْمُؤْمِنِ سَنَةً كَسَفْكِ دَمِهِ. الأدب المفرد، باب من هجر أخاه سنه.

[311] On the authority of ʿImrān b. Abī Anas رضي الله عنه from a Companion from the tribe of Aslam, that the Prophet ﷺ said, "To shun a believer for a whole year is like shedding his blood." Bukhārī's *Al-Adab al-Mufrad*, Chapter on Whoever Boycotts His Brother for a Year, *Ḥadīth* no. 404.

14.14 HAUGHTINESS

عَنْ جَابِرٍ رضي الله عنه، عَنْ رَسُولِ اللهِ ﷺ قَالَ: مَنْ اعْتَذَرَ إِلَى أَخِيهِ ، فَلَمْ يَعْذِرْهُ، كَانَ عَلَيْهِ مِثْلُ خَطِيئَةِ صَاحِبِ مَكْسٍ. رواه البيهقي، مشكواة، باب ما ينهى عنه من التهاجر.

[312] On the authority of Jābir رضي الله عنه that the Prophet ﷺ said, "If someone apologises to his brother [for a mistake] but the latter does not excuse him, the latter will incur a sin like that of a tax-collector." Bayhaqī (*Mishkāt*, Chapter: What is Forbidden of Mutual Boycotting, *Ḥadīth* no. 5052).

Commentary

By "tax-collector" is meant an official who collects taxes or other dues and commits injustice and excesses whilst doing so, or lines his pockets with bribes.

14.15 BEING UNSCRUPULOUS

عَنْ أَبِي أُمَامَةَ ﷺ، أَنَّ رَسُولَ اللهِ ﷺ قَالَ: مِنْ شَرِّ النَّاسِ مَنْزِلَةً عِنْدَ اللهِ يَوْمَ الْقِيَامَةِ عَبْدٌ أَذْهَبَ آخِرَتَهُ بِدُنْيَا غَيْرِهِ. سنن ابن ماجه، مشكواة، باب الظلم.

[313] On the authority of Abū Umamah ﷺ that the Messenger of Allah ﷺ said, "Amongst the worst of people on the Day of Resurrection will be a person who destroyed his Hereafter for another's worldly gain." Ibn Mājah (*Mishkāt*, Chapter on Injustice, *Ḥadīth* no. 5132).

Commentary

This means that the person does everything possible, whether lawful or unlawful, in order to please others and obtain worldly benefit for them. As a result, he himself becomes the object of punishment in the Hereafter.

14.16 HARMFUL AND FRIVOLOUS POETRY

عَنْ أَبِي هُرَيْرَةَ ﷺ قَالَ: قَالَ رَسُولُ اللهِ ﷺ: لَأَنْ يَمْتَلِئَ جَوْفُ رَجُلٍ قَيْحًا يَرِيهِ خَيْرٌ مِنْ أَنْ يَمْتَلِئَ شِعْرًا. صحيح البخاري ومسلم وأحمد، الأدب المفرد، باب من الشعر حكمة.

[314] On the authority of Abū Hurayrah ﷺ, who said: The Messenger of Allah ﷺ said, "That a man's stomach be filled with pus is better than it being filled with poetry." Bukhārī, Muslim and Bukhārī's *Al-Adab al-Mufrad*, Chapter on Some Poetry is Wisdom (*Mishkāt*, *Ḥadīth* no. 4794).

Commentary

Here, morally-corrupting and frivolous poetry is being condemned. However, there is no harm in indulging in beneficial poetry when needed.[56]

56. This *Ḥadīth* and the principle mentioned in it apply also to songs, *nashīds*, etc. – Trans. Note

14.17 BREAKING PROMISES

عَنْ عَبْدِ اللهِ ابْنِ مَسْعُودٍ ﷺ قَالَ: لا يَصْلُحُ الكَذِبُ فِي جِدٍّ وَلا هَزلٍ، وَلا أَنْ يَعِدَ أَحَدُكُمْ وَلَدَهُ شَيْئًا ثُمَّ لا يُنْجِزُ لَهُ. الأدب المفرد.

[315] On the authority of ʿAbdullāh b. Masʿūd ﷺ, who said, "Lying is never good, whether it is done seriously nor jokingly. It is also not good that you promise your child something and then fail to fulfil the promise." Bukhārī's *Al-Adab al-Mufrad, Ḥadīth* no. 387.

14.18 THE CORRUPTION OF HYPOCRISY

عَنْ أَبِي هُرَيْرَةَ ﷺ قَالَ: قَالَ رَسُولُ اللهِ ﷺ: خَصْلَتَانِ لا تَجْتَمِعَانِ فِي مُنَافِقٍ: حُسْنُ سَمْتٍ، وَلا فِقْهٌ فِي الدِّينِ. سنن الترمذي.

[316] On the authority of Abū Hurayrah ﷺ, who said: The Messenger of Allah ﷺ said, "There are two qualities that never combine in a hypocrite: good character and understanding of the religion." Tirmidhī (*Mishkāt, Ḥadīth* no. 219).

Commentary

This means that hypocrisy is such an affliction that those affected by it can never enjoy the blessings of good character or understanding of Islam.

عَنْ عَبْدِ اللَّهِ بْنِ عَمْرٍو ﷺ، أَنَّ النَّبِيَّ ﷺ قَالَ: أَرْبَعٌ مَنْ كُنَّ فِيهِ كَانَ مُنَافِقًا خَالِصًا، وَمَنْ كَانَتْ فِيهِ خَصْلَةٌ مِنْهُنَّ كَانَتْ فِيهِ خَصْلَةٌ مِنَ النِّفَاقِ حَتَّى يَدَعَهَا: إِذَا اؤْتُمِنَ خَانَ، وَإِذَا حَدَّثَ كَذَبَ، وَإِذَا عَاهَدَ غَدَرَ، وَإِذَا خَاصَمَ فَجَرَ. صحيح البخاري ومسلم.

[317] On the authority of ʿAbdullāh b. ʿAmr ﷺ, who said: The Messenger of Allah ﷺ said, "There are four qualities which, if found in a person, mean that he is a pure hypocrite. If he possesses one of them, he possesses a characteristic of hypocrisy until he abandons it. They are: (1) when he is entrusted, he betrays; (2) when he speaks, he lies; (3) when he promises, he breaks

his promise; (4) when he quarrels, he behaves in a wicked manner [i.e. with obscene talk, abuse and insults]." Bukhārī and Muslim (*Mishkāt*, *Ḥadīth* no. 56).

14.19 INCONSISTENCY OF SPEECH AND ACTION

وَعَنْ عُمَرَ بْنِ الخَطَّابِ ﷺ، عَنِ النَّبِيِّ ﷺ قال: إِنَّمَا أَخَافُ عَلَى هَذِهِ الْأُمَةِ كُلَّ مُنَافِقٍ يَتَكَلَّمُ بِالْحِكْمَةِ وَيَعْمَلُ بِالْجَوْرِ. رواه البيهقي، مشكواة، باب الرياء.

[318] On the authority of ʿUmar b. al-Khaṭṭāb ﷺ that the Prophet ﷺ said, "I only fear for this nation every hypocrite who speaks with wisdom but behaves with tyranny." Bayhaqī (*Mishkāt*, Chapter on Ostentation, *Ḥadīth* no. 5337).

Commentary

Here, a reference is made towards such leaders who invoke the name of Islam in every matter but when the time comes for action, they are far ahead of everyone in violating the limits of Islam.

عَنْ جَابِرِ بْنِ عَبْدِ اللهِ ﷺ، أَنَّ رَسُولَ اللهِ ﷺ قَالَ: اتَّقُوا الظُّلْمَ فَإِنَّ الظُّلْمَ ظُلُمَاتٌ يَوْمَ الْقِيَامَةِ، وَاتَّقُوا الشُّحَّ فَإِنَّ الشُّحَّ أَهْلَكَ مَنْ كَانَ قَبْلَكُمْ حَمَلَهُمْ عَلَى أَنْ سَفَكُوا دِمَاءَهُمْ وَاسْتَحَلُّوا مَحَارِمَهُمْ. صحيح مسلم، مشكواة، باب الانفاق.

[319] On the authority of Jābir b. ʿAbdullāh ﷺ, that the Messenger of Allah ﷺ said, "Beware of injustice and oppression [*ẓulm*], for it will be layers of darkness [*ẓulumāt*] on the Day of Resurrection. Beware of avarice and greed, for it destroyed those before you: it led them to the shedding of blood and the violation of sanctities." Muslim (*Mishkāt*, Chapter on Spending, *Ḥadīth* no. 1865).

14.20 SUPPORTING THE OPPRESSOR

عَنْ ابْنِ عَبَّاسٍ ﷺ، قال: قال رسولُ الله ﷺ: مَنْ أَعَانَ ظَالِمًا بِبَاطِلٍ لِيُدْحِضَ بِبَاطِلِهِ حقًّا فَقَدْ بَرِئَ مِنْ ذِمَّةِ اللهِ عَزَّ وَجَلَّ وذِمَّةِ رَسُولِهِ ﷺ، وَمَنْ أَكَلَ دِرْهَمًا مِنْ رِبًا فَهُوَ مِثْلُ ثَلَاثَةٍ وَثَلَاثِينَ زِنْيَةٍ، وَمَنْ نَبَتَ لَحْمُهُ مِنْ سُحْتٍ فَالنَّارُ أَوْلَى بِهِ. المعجم الصغير للطبراني.

[320] On the authority of Ibn ʿAbbās ﵄, who said: The Messenger of Allah ﷺ said, "Whoever supports an oppressor with falsehood such that his falsehood defeats truth, he is excluded from the protection of Allah and the protection of His Messenger ﷺ. Whoever devours a *dirham* of *ribā* [usury], it is like thirty-three acts of *zinā* [unlawful sexual intercourse]. One whose flesh is nourished from unlawful earnings, the Fire has most right to it." Ṭabarānī's *Al-Muʿjam al-Ṣaghīr*.

Commentary

The protection of Allah and His Messenger that is mentioned here includes the responsibility and protection of an Islamic government.

14.21 USURPING THE RIGHTS OF OTHERS

عَنْ عَلِيٍّ ﵁ قَالَ: قَالَ رَسُولُ اللهِ ﷺ: إِيَّاكَ وَدَعْوَةُ الْمَظْلُومِ، فَإِنَّمَا يَسْئَلُ اللهَ تَعَالَى حَقَّهُ وَإِنَّ اللهَ لَا يَمْنَعُ ذَا حَقٍّ حَقَّهُ. رواه البيهقي، مشكواة، باب الظلم.

[321] On the authority of ʿAlī ﵁, who said: The Messenger of Allah ﷺ said, "Beware of the supplication of the oppressed, for he only asks Allah for his right. Truly, Allah does not prevent someone's right from reaching him." Bayhaqī (*Mishkāt*, Chapter on Oppression, *Ḥadīth* no. 5134).

14.22 USURPING PROPERTY

عَنْ سَعِيدِ بْنِ زَيْدٍ ﵁ قَالَ: سَمِعْتُ رَسُولَ اللهِ ﷺ يَقُولُ: مَنْ أَخَذَ شِبْرًا مِنَ الْأَرْضِ ظُلْمًا فَإِنَّهُ يُطَوَّقُهُ يَوْمَ الْقِيَامَةِ مِنْ سَبْعِ أَرْضِينَ. صحيح البخاري ومسلم، مشكواة، باب الغصب.

[322] On the authority of Saʿīd b. Zayd ﵁, who said: The Messenger of Allah ﷺ said, "Whoever usurps a handspan of land will be made to wear a collar as wide as seven Earths on the Day of Resurrection." Bukhārī and Muslim (*Mishkāt*, Chapter on Usurpation, *Ḥadīth* no. 2938).

عَنْ عَبْدِ اللهِ بْنِ عُمَرَ رضي الله عنهما، أَنَّ رَسُولَ اللهِ ﷺ قَالَ: لا يَحْلُبَنَّ أَحَدٌ مَاشِيَةَ امْرِئٍ بِغَيْرِ إِذْنِه، أَيُحِبُّ أَحَدُكُمْ أَنْ تُؤْتَى مَشْرُبَتُهُ، فَتُكْسَرَ خِزَانَتُهُ، فَيُنْتَقَلَ طَعَامُهُ؟ فَإِنَّمَا تَخْزُنُ لَهُمْ ضُرُوعُ مَوَاشِيهِمْ أَطْعِمَاتِهِمْ. صحيح البخاري ومسلم، مشكواة، باب الغصب.

[323] On the authority of ʿAbdullāh b. ʿUmar ﷺ, who said: The Messenger of Allah ﷺ said, "None of you should milk another's animal without his permission. Would any of you like someone to come to your food-store, break in and take your food away? The udders of livestock store sustenance for their owners." Muslim (*Mishkāt*, Chapter on Usurpation, *Ḥadīth* no. 2939).

14.23 TREACHERY

عَنْ عُبَادَةَ بْنِ الصَّامِتِ رضي الله عنه، عَنِ النَّبِيِّ ﷺ قَالَ: أَدُّوا الْخَيْطَ وَالْمَخِيطَ، وَإِيَّاكُمْ وَالْغُلُولَ، فَإِنَّهُ عَارٌ عَلَى أَهْلِهِ يَوْمَ الْقِيَامَةِ. مسند أحمد والنسائي والدرامي، مشكواة، باب قسمة الغنائم.

[324] On the authority of ʿUbādah b. al-Ṣāmit ﷺ that the Prophet ﷺ used to say, "Return [trusts, even if they be] a needle or thread. Beware of treachery, for it is a disgrace for its practitioners on the Day of Resurrection." Nasāʾī and Dārimī (*Mishkāt*, Chapter: Distribution of Booty, *Ḥadīth* nos. 4023-4).

عَنْ عَبْدِ اللَّهِ بْنِ عَمْرٍو رضي الله عنه قَالَ: كَانَ عَلَى ثَقَلِ النَّبِيِّ ﷺ رَجُلٌ يُقَالُ لَهُ كَرْكَرَةٌ، فَمَاتَ، فَقَالَ رَسُولُ اللهِ ﷺ: هُوَ فِي النَّارِ. فَذَهَبُوا يَنْظُرُونَ إِلَيْهِ، فَوَجَدُوا عَبَاءَةً قَدْ غَلَّهَا. صحيح البخاري، مشكواة، باب قسمة الغنائم.

[325] On the authority of ʿAbdullāh b. ʿAmr ﷺ, who said: There was a man named Karkarah appointed to look after the possessions of the Prophet ﷺ. He died, and the Messenger of Allah ﷺ said about him, "He is in the Fire." The people went to investigate him and found that he had stolen a cloak. Bukhārī (*Mishkāt*, Chapter: Distribution of Booty, *Ḥadīth* no. 3998).

Commentary

This incident occurred during a military expedition. From this we learn that even an important act of worship such as *Jihād* will carry no weight with Allah if it is accompanied by treachery and dishonesty. Rather, the person will be afflicted with a severe punishment.

14.24 BRIBERY

عَنْ عَبْدِ اللَّهِ بْنِ عَمْرٍو ﵄ قَالَ: لَعَنَ رَسُولُ اللهِ ﷺ الرَّاشِيَ وَالْمُرْتَشِيَ. سنن الترمذي وأبي داود وابن ماجه وأحمد، مشكواة، باب الولاة وهداياهم.

[326] On the authority of ʿAbdullāh b. ʿAmr ﵄, who said, "The Messenger of Allah ﷺ cursed the one who pays a bribe[57] and the one who accepts it." Abū Dāwūd and Ibn Mājah (*Mishkāt*, Chapter: Governors and Gifts Presented to Them, *Ḥadīth* nos. 3753-4).

عَنْ عَمْرِو بْنِ الْعَاصِ ﵁ قَالَ: سَمِعْتُ رَسُولَ اللهِ ﷺ يَقُولُ: مَا مِنْ قَوْمٍ يَظْهَرُ فِيهِمُ الرِّبَا إِلا أُخِذُوا بِالسَّنَةِ، وَمَا مِنْ قَوْمٍ يَظْهَرُ فِيهِمُ الرُّشَا إِلا أُخِذُوا بِالرُّعْبِ. مسند أحمد، مشكواة، كتاب الحدود.

[327] On the authority of ʿAmr b. al-ʿĀṣ ﵁, who said: I heard the Messenger of Allah ﷺ saying, "Any people amongst whom usury [*ribā*][58] becomes widespread will be afflicted with famine. Any people amongst whom bribery becomes widespread will be afflicted with fear and terror." Aḥmad (*Mishkāt*, Book of Criminal Punishments, *Ḥadīth* no. 3582).

57. This refers to paying a bribe in order to gain something to which the person is not entitled. – Trans. Note

58. In some versions of this tradition, *zinā* (unlawful sexual intercourse) is mentioned instead of *ribā* (usury). – Trans. Note

14.25 BLOCKING THE HIDDEN AVENUES TO BRIBERY

عَنْ أَبِي حُمَيْدٍ السَّاعِدِيِّ ﷺ قَالَ: اسْتَعْمَلَ النَّبِيُّ ﷺ رَجُلًا مِن الأَزْدِ يُقَالُ له ابْنَ اللَّتَبِيَّةِ، عَلَى الصَّدقة، فَلَما قدمَ حَاسَبَهُ، قَالَ: هَذَا لَكُمْ وَهَذَا أُهْدِيَ لِيَّ. فَخَطَبَ النَّبِيُّ ﷺ فحَمِدَ اللهَ وأثْنَى عَلَيْهِ ثُمَّ قَالَ: أَمَّا بَعْدُ: فَإِنِّي أَسْتَعْمِلُ رَجُلاً عَلى أُمُور ولَّاني الله، فَيَأْتِي فَيَقُولُ هَذَا لَكُمْ وَهَذِهِ هَدِيَّةٌ أُهْدِيَتْ لِي، فَهَلا جَلَسَ فِي بَيْتِ أَبِيهِ وَأُمِّهِ، فَيَنْظُرَ أَيُهدَى لَهُ أَمْ لَا. والَّذِيْ نَفْسِي بِيَدِهِ لا يَأْخُذُ أَحَدٌ مِنْه شَيْئًا إلا جَاءَ بِهِ يومَ القِيَامَةِ يَحْمِلُهُ عَلَى رَقَبَتِهِ، إِنْ كَانَ بَعِيرًا لَهُ رُغَاءٌ أَوْ بَقَرَةً لَهَا خُوَارٌ أَوْ شَاةً تَيْعِرُ، ثُمَّ رَفَعَ يَدَهُ حَتَّى رَأَيْنَا عُفْرَةَ إِبْطَيْهِ ، ثُمَّ قَالَ: اللَّهُمَّ هَلْ بَلَّغْتُ، اللَّهُمَّ هَلْ بَلَّغْتُ. صحيح البخاري ومسلم، مشكواة، باب الزكاة.

[328] On the authority of Abū Ḥumayd al-Sāʿidī ﷺ, who said: The Prophet ﷺ appointed a man from the tribe of Azd called Ibn al-Lutbiyyah to collect charity [*zakāt*]. When he came with the *zakāt* he said, "This is for you [i.e. the *Bayt al-Māl* or Treasury] and this was a gift for me." The Prophet ﷺ addressed the people. After praising and glorifying Allah, he said, "To proceed: I appoint people over matters which Allah has entrusted to me. [I then see that] one of them comes and says, 'This is for you, and this is a gift presented to me.' Why does he not sit in his parents' house and see whether or not he is presented with any gifts! By the One in whose Hand is my life, no-one takes anything from this wealth except that he will bring it on the Day of Resurrection, carrying it on his neck. If it is a camel, it will be snorting; if a cow, it will be lowing; if a lamb, it will be bleating." He then raised his hands until we could see the whiteness of his armpits and said, "O Allah! [Bear witness:] Have I conveyed [Your judgment]? O Allah! Have I conveyed?" Bukhārī and Muslim.

عَنْ أَبِي أُمَامَةَ ﷺ، عَنْ النَّبِيِّ ﷺ قَالَ: مَنْ شَفَعَ لِأَخِيهِ بِشَفَاعَةٍ فَأَهْدَى لَهُ هَدِيَّةً عَلَيْهَا فَقَبِلَهَا، فَقَدْ أَتَى بَابًا عَظِيمًا مِنْ أَبْوَابِ الرِّبَا. سنن أبي داود.

[329] On the authority of Abū Umāmah ﷺ that the Messenger of Allah ﷺ said, "Whoever intercedes for his brother [in Islam or humanity] and the latter presents him with a gift and he accepts

it, has truly approached one of the major doors of *ribā* [usury]." Abū Dāwūd (*Mishkāt*, Chapter: Governors and Gifts Presented to Them, *Ḥadīth* no. 3757).

14.26 BLOCKING THE HIDDEN AVENUES TO USURY

عَنْ أَنَسَ بْنَ مَالِكٍ ﷺ قَالَ: قَالَ رَسُولُ اللهِ ﷺ: إِذَا أَقْرَضَ أَحَدُكُمْ قَرْضًا، فَأَهْدَى لَهُ أَوْ حَمَلَهُ عَلى الدَّابَّةِ، فَلا يَرْكَبْهَا، وَلا يَقْبَلْهُ، إِلا أَنْ يَكُونَ جَرَى بَيْنَهُ وَبَيْنَهُ قَبْلَ ذَلِكَ. سنن ابن ماجه، مشكواة، باب الربا.

[330] On the authority of Anas b. Mālik ﷺ, who said: The Messenger of Allah ﷺ said, "When one of you gives a loan and the debtor presents him with a gift or offers him a ride on his animal, he should neither ride the mount nor accept the gift unless the two of them were accustomed to doing so beforehand." Ibn Mājah (*Mishkāt*, Chapter on Usury, *Ḥadīth* no. 2831).

Commentary

Where Islam has prohibited usury, it has also closed all doors to it so that it may not pollute the Muslim society at all.

14.27 PREVENTING THE CAUSES OF DISPUTES AND FIGHTS

عَنْ أَبِي مُوسَى ﷺ، عَنْ النَّبِيِّ ﷺ قَالَ: إِذَا مَرَّ أَحَدُكُمْ فِي مَسْجِدِنَا، أَوْ فِي سُوقِنَا، وَمَعَهُ نَبْلٌ، فَلْيُمْسِكْ عَلى نِصَالِهَا أَنْ يُصِيبَ أَحَدًا مِنْ الْمُسْلِمِينَ مِنْهَا شَيْءٌ. صحيح البخاري ومسلم وأبي داود وابن ماجه وأحمد، مشكواة، باب مالا يضمن من الجنايات.

[331] On the authority of Abū Mūsā ﷺ, that the Prophet ﷺ said, "When one of you passes through our mosque or market holding an arrow, he must cover its head lest any Muslim be hurt by it." Bukhārī and Muslim (*Mishkāt*, Chapter on Injuries That Are Not Indemnified, *Ḥadīth* no. 3517).

Commentary

In places of public gathering, one must be extremely careful when carrying weapons or dangerous instruments.

14.28 DISSENSION AND DISPUTE

عَنْ جَابِرٍ ﷺ قَالَ: سَمِعْتُ النَّبِيَّ ﷺ يَقُولُ: إِنَّ الشَّيْطَانَ قَدْ أَيِسَ أَنْ يَعْبُدَهُ الْمُصَلُّونَ فِي جَزِيرَةِ الْعَرَبِ، وَلَكِنْ فِي التَّحْرِيشِ بَيْنَهُمْ. صحيح مسلم، مشكواة، باب في الوسوسة.

[332] On the authority of Jābir ﷺ, who said: I heard the Prophet ﷺ saying, "Truly, Satan has despaired of being worshipped by the people of prayer [i.e. Muslims] in the Arabian peninsula, but not of stoking dissension amongst them." Muslim (*Mishkāt*, Chapter on Satan's Whispering, *Ḥadīth* no. 72).

Commentary

Here, by "worship" is not meant the ritual sort, for we have never heard of anyone making a statue or image of Satan and then worshipping it. Rather, a wider meaning is intended, i.e. that Satan's wishes are obeyed in all branches of life. This understanding is supported by the *āyah* of the Qur'ān, "*Father, do not serve Satan, for Satan has indeed been a persistent rebel against the Most Compassionate Lord.*" (*Sūrah Maryam*, 19: 44)

It should be remembered that "people of prayer" are mentioned here, i.e. such people who are regular at prayer and therefore their hearts are full of the love and fear of Allah. Satan's magic does not work on such people who do not bow to his wishes. However, it is possible that he creates mutual misunderstandings amongst them, stoking disagreements and dissension.

14.29 KILLING A MUSLIM

عَنْ عَبْدِ اللهِ بْنِ عَمْرٍو ﷺ، أَنَّ النَّبِيَّ ﷺ قَالَ: لَزَوَالُ الدُّنْيَا أَهْوَنُ عَلَى اللهِ مِنْ قَتْلِ رَجُلٍ مُسْلِمٍ. سنن الترمذي والنسائي وابن ماجه، مشكواة، كتاب القصاص.

[333] On the authority of ʿAbdullāh b. ʿAmr ﵄ that the Prophet ﷺ said, "The perishing of the world is truly lighter before Allah than the murder of a Muslim." Tirmidhī and Nasā'ī (*Mishkāt*, Book of Retaliation, *Ḥadīth* nos. 3462-3). Ibn Mājah narrates the *Ḥadīth* on the authority of al-Barā' b. ʿĀzib.

عَنْ ابْنِ عَبَّاسٍ ﵄، أَنَّ النَّبِيَّ ﷺ قَالَ: أَبْغَضُ النَّاسِ إِلى اللهِ ثَلاثَةٌ: مُلْحِدٌ في الْحَرَمِ، وَمُبْتَغٍ فِي الْإِسْلَامِ سُنَّةَ الْجَاهِلِيَّةِ، وَمُطَّلِبُ دَمِ امْرِئٍ مُسْلِمٍ بِغَيْرِ حَقٍّ لِيُهَرِيقَ دَمَهُ. صحيح البخاري، مشكواة، باب الاعتصام.

[334] On the authority of Ibn ʿAbbās ﵄, who said: The Messenger of Allah ﷺ said, "The most hated of people to Allah are three types: one who spreads heresy in the *Ḥaram* [Sacred Land], one who seeks the way of *Jāhiliyyah* in Islam, and one who pursues a Muslim to shed his blood unjustly." Bukhārī (*Mishkat*, Chapter on Holding Fast, *Ḥadīth* no. 142).

Commentary

Spreading heresy is a major sin everywhere; however, to spread it in the *Ḥaram* (the noble city of Makkah) that is the centre of guidance in Islam is a serious crime for which the punishment is multiplied. Similarly, to call for ways of unbelief and wickedness in Islam is a major crime.

14.30 DECEPTION AND DISHONESTY

عَنْ أَبِي هُرَيْرَةَ ﵁، أَنَّ رَسُولَ اللهِ ﷺ مَرَّ عَلى صُبْرَةِ طَعَامٍ، فَأَدْخَلَ يَدَهُ فِيهَا، فَنَالَتْ أَصَابِعُهُ بَلَلًا، فَقَالَ: مَا هَذَا يَا صَاحِبَ الطَّعَامِ. قَالَ: أَصَابَتْهُ السَّمَاءُ يَا رَسُولَ اللهِ. قَالَ: أَفَلا جَعَلْتَهُ فَوْقَ الطَّعَامِ كَيْ يَرَاهُ النَّاسُ، مَنْ غَشَّ فَلَيْسَ مِنِّي. صحيح مسلم.

[335] On the authority of Abū Hurayrah ﵁, who said: The Messenger of Allah ﷺ passed by a heap of grain [in the market]. He inserted his hand into it and felt some moisture, so he asked, "What is this, O grain-merchant?" The man replied, "Rain affected it, O Messenger of Allah!" He said, "Why did you not

then place the wet grain on top of the heap so that the people could see it? Whoever deceives has nothing to do with me!" Muslim (*Mishkāt*, *Ḥadīth* no. 2860).

14.31 HOARDING

عَنْ مَعْمَرٍ ۞ قَالَ: قَالَ رَسُولُ الله ﷺ: مَنِ احْتَكَرَ فَهُوَ خَاطِئٌ. صحيح مسلم، مشكواة، باب الاحتكار.

[336]   On the authority of Ma'mar ۞, who said: The Messenger of Allah ﷺ said, "Whoever hoards is in error."

In another narration, the Prophet ﷺ said, "Whoever hoards is cursed." Muslim (*Mishkāt*, Chapter on Hoarding, *Ḥadīth* no. 2892).

Commentary

Hoarding refers to withholding a foodstuff from the market with the intention of selling it when its price soars. Such traders are actually exploiting the needs and necessities of people for selfish gains, and this cannot be tolerated by a Muslim society. In the view of some of the people of knowledge amongst the early Muslims, prohibited hoarding is not restricted to foodstuffs, but applies to all items of public necessity such that their absence in the market for a while would lead to public unease, e.g. fuel, medicines, sugar, etc.

14.32 EXPLOITING LEGAL TRICKS

عَنْ جَابِرِ بْنِ عَبْدِ الله ۞، أَنَّهُ سَمِعَ رَسُولَ الله ﷺ يَقُولُ عَامَ الْفَتْحِ وَهُوَ بِمَكَّةَ: إِنَّ اللهَ وَرَسُولَهُ حَرَّمَ بَيْعَ الْخَمْرِ وَالْمَيْتَةِ وَالْخِنْزِيرِ وَالْأَصْنَامِ. فَقِيلَ: يَا رَسُولَ الله أَرَأَيْتَ شُحُومَ الْمَيْتَةِ، فَإِنَّهَا يُطْلَى بِهَا السُّفُنُ وَيُدْهَنُ بِهَا الْجُلُودُ وَيَسْتَصْبِحُ بِهَا النَّاسُ؟ فَقَالَ: لَا هُوَ حَرَامٌ، ثُمَّ قَالَ رَسُولُ الله ﷺ عِنْدَ ذَلِكَ: قَاتَلَ اللهُ الْيَهُودَ إِنَّ اللهَ لَمَّا حَرَّمَ شُحُومَهَا جَمَلُوهُ، ثُمَّ بَاعُوهُ، فَأَكَلُوا ثَمَنَهُ. صحيح البخاري ومسلم.

[337]   On the authority of Jābir b. 'Abdullāh ۞ that he heard the Messenger of Allah ﷺ saying in Makkah in the year of its

conquest, "Truly, Allah and His Messenger have prohibited the sale of wine, carrion, pigs and idols." He was asked, "O Messenger of Allah! What about the fat of carrion? Boats are coated with it, leather is softened with it and people burn it in their lamps." He replied, "No. It is prohibited." He then said, "May Allah destroy the Jews! Truly, when Allah forbade them [from eating] the fat of carrion, they would melt it, sell it and devour its profit."[59] Bukhārī and Muslim (*Mishkāt*, *Ḥadīth* no. 2766).

Commentary

To legalise something unlawful through a legal trick is such a dangerous affliction that dishonesty and deception spreads throughout society because of it. Further, the original purpose of the *Sharīʿah* becomes slowly lost from view.

14.33 IRRESPONSIBLE ACTIONS

عَنْ عَمْرِو بْنِ شُعَيْبٍ، عَنْ أَبِيهِ، عَنْ جَدِّهِ ﷺ، قَالَ: قَالَ رَسُولُ اللهِ ﷺ: مَنْ تَطَبَّبَ وَلَمْ يُعْلَمْ مِنْهُ طِبٌّ فَهُوَ ضَامِنٌ. النسائي وأبي داود وابن ماجه، مشكواة، باب الديات.

[338] On the authority of ʿAmr b. Shuʿayb from his father from his grandfather ◈ that the Messenger of Allah ﷺ said, "Whoever becomes a doctor without being qualified in medicine will be responsible [for a patient's death or worsening in condition]." Abū Dāwūd and Nasāʾī (*Mishkāt*, Chapter on Blood-Money, *Ḥadīth* no. 3504).

Commentary

To practise medicine without licence from a reputable body or institution is such a major crime that it can be tried by an Islamic government and the offender can be given an extremely severe punishment.

---

59. This curse applies only to those Jews, and by extension anyone else, including Muslims, who exploit legal devices to oppose the spirit of the Law whilst maintaining its letter. – Trans. Note

14.34 SELFISHNESS

عَنْ أَبِي هُرَيْرَةَ ﷺ، أَنَّ رَسُولَ اللهِ ﷺ قَالَ: لا يَخْطُبْ أَحَدُكُمْ عَلى خِطْبَةِ أَخِيهِ حَتَّى يَنْكِحَ أَوْ يَتْرُكَ. متفق عليه، مشكواة، باب اعلان النكاح والخطبة.

[339] On the authority of Abū Hurayrah ﷺ, who said: The Messenger of Allah ﷺ said, "A man should not propose over the marriage proposal of his [Muslim] brother: he should wait until the latter marries or calls the engagement off." Bukhārī and Muslim (*Mishkāt*, Chapter: Announcing Marriage and Engagement, *Ḥadīth* no. 3144).

Commentary

If a man has initiated a marriage proposal somewhere, it is not permissible for another Muslim to propose on his own or another's behalf to the same woman before a definite decision has been reached regarding the first proposal. Behaviour contrary to this is a sign of extreme selfishness and ignobility in Islamic law, which has set similar limits in other mutual dealings such as buying and selling.

14.35 MISERLINESS

عَنْ أَبِي هُرَيْرَةَ ﷺ، أَنَّ رَسُولَ اللهِ ﷺ قَالَ: مَطْلُ الْغَنِيِّ ظُلْمٌ، فَإِذَا أُتْبِعَ أَحَدُكُمْ عَلى مَلِيٍّ فَلْيَتْبَعْ. صحيح البخاري، مشكواة، باب الافلاس والانظار.

[340] On the authority of Abū Hurayrah ﷺ that the Messenger of Allah ﷺ said, "A rich man's delaying payment [of a debt or due] is injustice. If one of you is appointed to pursue a wealthy person [for payment of a debt or due], he should pursue him." Bukhārī and Muslim (*Mishkāt*, Chapter on Bankruptcy and Deferral, *Ḥadīth* no. 2907).

Commentary

This means that such a person should accept the responsibility and use his influence and contacts to obtain the right of his Muslim brother from the wealthy person. If anyone's rights are suppressed, it is the duty of the influential members of society to defend those rights using their power, rather than remaining as passive onlookers.

14.36 INGRATITUDE

عَنِ أَسْمَاءَ بِنْتَ يَزِيدَ الأَنْصَارِيَّة ﵂: مَرَّ بِيَ النَّبِيِّ ﷺ وأنا في جوار أتْرَاب لي، فَسَلَّمَ عَلَيْنَا، وَقَالَ: إِيَّاكُنَّ وَكُفْرَ الْمُنْعِمِينَ. قَالَ: لَعَلَّ إِحْدَاكُنَّ أَنْ تَطُول أَيْمَتُهَا مِنْ أَبَوَيْهَا، ثُمَّ يَرْزُقَهَا اللهُ زَوْجًا، وَيَرْزُقَهَا مِنْهُ وَلَدًا، فَتَغْضَبَ الْغَضْبَةَ، فَتَكْفُرَ، فَتَقُولُ: مَا رَأَيْتُ مِنكَ خَيْرًا قَطُّ. الأدب المفرد، باب التسليم على النساء.

[341] On the authority of Asmā' bint Yazīd the Anṣārī ﵂, who said: The Prophet ﷺ passed by me whilst I was in the company of friends of the neighbourhood. He greeted us with peace and said, "Beware of ingratitude to those who show kindness. One of you may remain with her parents, unmarried for a long time, but then Allah grants her a husband and bestows children with him upon her. She then becomes angry with her husband over a matter and shows ingratitude [for the long companionship, despite all its blessings], saying, 'I never saw any kindness from you'." Bukhārī's *Al-Adab al-Mufrad*, Chapter on Greeting Women, *Ḥadīth* no. 1047).

Commentary

A couple of matters are learnt from this *Ḥadīth*:

1. If there is a group of women and there is no danger of impropriety, a male non-relative may greet them.
2. A specific quality and natural disposition of the woman has been explained in this *Ḥadīth*. It is that if she is ever annoyed with her husband, she momentarily forgets all his kindnesses. The household atmosphere can only really be happy if the husband's kindnesses and good qualities are appreciated, rather than only his weaknesses and faults being remembered. This same teaching is given to husbands in another *Ḥadīth*, "No male believer [i.e. a husband] should ever hate a female believer [i.e. his wife]: if he dislikes one of her qualities, he will be pleased with another."

14.37 CONTRIVED AND FALSE APPEARANCES

عَنْ أَسْمَاءَ رضي الله عنها، أَنَّ امْرَأَةً قَالَتْ: يَا رَسُولَ اللهِ ﷺ إِنَّ لِي ضَرَّةً، فَهَلْ عَلَيَّ جُنَاحٌ إِنْ تَشَبَّعْتُ مِنْ زَوْجِي غَيْرَ الَّذِي يُعْطِينِي؟ فَقَالَ رَسُولُ اللهِ ﷺ: الْمُتَشَبِّعُ بِمَا لَمْ يُعْطَ كَلَابِسِ ثَوْبَيْ زُورٍ. صحيح البخاري ومسلم، مشكواة، باب عشرة النساء.

[342] On the authority of Asmā' رضي الله عنها that a woman asked, "O Messenger of Allah ﷺ! I have a co-wife. Is there any harm if I display my own possessions [garments etc.] to her in such a way as to make out that my husband has given them to me?" He replied, "One who makes a false display of prosperity is like someone who wears two garments of falsehood." Bukhārī and Muslim (*Mishkāt*, Chapter: Treatment of Women, *Ḥadīth* no. 3247).

Commentary

A person should only make a display in attire and appearance according to his or her means. To exaggerate one's own status and position for pomp and pride or in order to annoy others is a form of lying.

14.38 HAVING AN INFERIORITY COMPLEX AND IMITATING OTHERS

عَنْ ابْنِ عُمَرَ رضي الله عنه قَالَ: قَالَ رَسُولُ اللهِ ﷺ: مَنْ تَشَبَّهَ بِقَوْمٍ فَهُوَ مِنْهُمْ. سنن أبي داود وأحمد، مشكواة، باب اللباس.

[343] On the authority of Ibn 'Umar رضي الله عنه, who said: The Messenger of Allah ﷺ said, "Whoever imitates a people is of them." Aḥmad and Abū Dāwūd (*Mishkāt*, Book of Dress, *Ḥadīth* no. 4347).

Commentary

There are two forms of prohibited imitation of non-Muslims:

1. A Muslim disfigures his appearance and way of living in such a way that there remains nothing to distinguish him from non-Muslims.

2. A Muslim individual or society adopts a symbol or characteristic of a non-Muslim nation.

Other than that, it does not contradict this *Ḥadīth* to adopt a beneficial aspect of the customs and culture of non-Muslim nations. For example, the Prophet ﷺ wore a tight-sleeved Roman cloak. Further, upon the advice of Umm Ḥabībah, he had curved sticks used for women's funeral biers, an Abyssinian practice. Also, upon the advice of Salmān al-Fārisī, he had a trench dug around Madīnah during the Battle of al-Aḥzāb, a Persian tactic.

14.39 IDOLATRY AND PERSONALITY-WORSHIP

عَنْ أَبِي الْهَيَّاجِ الْأَسَدِيِّ رضي الله عنه قَالَ: قَالَ لِي عَلِيُّ بْنُ أَبِي طَالِبٍ رضي الله عنه: أَلا أَبْعَثُكَ عَلى مَا بَعَثَنِي عَلَيْهِ رَسُولُ اللهِ ﷺ، أَنْ لا تَدَعَ تِمْثَالًا إِلا طَمَسْتَهُ، وَلا قَبْرًا مُشْرِفًا إِلا سَوَّيْتَهُ. صحيح مسلم، مشكواة، باب دفن الميت.

[344] On the authority of Abū'l-Hayyāj al-Asadī رضي الله عنه, who said: 'Alī b. Abī Ṭālib said to me, "Should I not despatch you upon the same mission with which the Messenger of Allah ﷺ despatched me? It is that you must neither leave any image without obliterating it nor any raised grave without levelling it." Muslim (*Mishkāt*, Chapter: Burying the Deceased, *Ḥadīth* no. 1696).

Commentary

Two major causes of idolatry and personality-worship have been explained in this *Ḥadīth*.

14.40 ROYAL POMP

عَنْ قُدَامَةَ رضي الله عنه قَالَ: رَأَيْتُ النَّبِيَّ ﷺ يَرْمِي جَمْرَةَ الْعَقَبَةِ يَوْمَ النَّحْرِ عَلى نَاقَةٍ لَهُ صَهْبَاءَ لَيْسَ ضَرْبٌ وَلا طَرْدٌ وَلَيْسَ قِيلَ إِلَيْكَ إِلَيْكَ. رواهُ الشافعي والنسائي وابن ماجه وأحمد والدرامي، مشكواة، باب رمي الجمار.

[345] On the authority of Qudāmah ﵁, who said: I saw the Prophet ﷺ stoning [the Devil] on the Day of Sacrifice, riding a reddish-brown she-camel. There was no beating or pushing [of the crowd], no scolding [of anyone] and no shouting, "Make way!"[60] Shāfi'ī, Tirmidhī, Nasā'ī, Ibn Mājah and Dārimī (*Mishkāt*, Chapter: Stoning the Devils, *Ḥadīth* no. 2623).

Commentary

The life of the Prophet ﷺ was totally free of the pomp, show and displays of protocol that usually accompany royal processions.

14.41 *JĀHILĪ* ROYAL SPECIAL TREATMENT

وَعَنْ أَبِي مَسْعُودٍ الأَنْصَارِيِّ ﵁ قَالَ: نَهَى رَسُولُ اللهِ ﷺ أَنْ يَقُومَ الإِمَامُ فَوْقَ شَيْءٍ وَالنَّاسُ خَلْفَهُ، يَعْنِيَ أَسْفَلَ مِنْهُ. رواه الدارقطني في المجتبى، مشكواة، باب المشي بالجنازة.

[346] On the authority of Abū Mas'ūd al-Anṣārī ﵁, who said: The Messenger of Allah ﷺ forbade that the *imām* should stand on a high place [or object], the people praying behind him being lower than him. Abū Dāwūd and Darāquṭnī (*Mishkāt*, Chapter on Walking with the Funeral, *Ḥadīth* no. 1692).

14.42 ELITISM

عَنْ عَبْدِ اللهِ ابْنِ مَسْعُودٍ ﵁، عَنِ النَّبِيِّ ﷺ قَالَ: بَيْنَ يَدَيْ السَّاعَةِ تَسْلِيمُ الْخَاصَّةِ وَفُشُوُ التِّجَارَةِ حَتَّى تُعِينَ الْمَرْأَةُ زَوْجَهَا عَلَى التِّجَارَةِ وَقَطْعُ الْأَرْحَامِ وَشَهَادَةُ الزُّورِ وَكِتْمَانُ شَهَادَةِ الْحَقِّ وَظُهُورُ الْقَلَمِ. مسند أحمد، الأدب المفرد، باب من كره تسليم الخاصة.

[347] On the authority of 'Abdullāh [b. Mas'ūd] ﵁ that the Prophet ﷺ said, "Before the Hour there will be: (1) greeting only

60. The same Companion has narrated an identical description of the Prophet's riding a camel between Mounts Ṣafā and Marwah as part of pilgrimage rites without any special privileges (*Mishkāt*, *Ḥadīth* no. 2583). – Trans. Note

of the elite; (2) the spread of trade, until the woman assists her husband in trade;[61] (3) the severing of family relations; (4) the prevalence of false witness and the concealment of true witness; (5) the spread of knowledge[62] and writing." Aḥmad and Bukhārī's *Al-Adab al-Mufrad*, Chapter on Whoever Disliked to Greet the Elite Only, *Ḥadīth* no. 1049.

Commentary

The first sign mentioned means that only people of status will be greeted and talked to, not the common masses. The second sign means that greed for wealth will increase to such an extent that instead of fulfilling her household duties (such as bringing up children, etc.), women will be forced to help their husbands in business matters. The fourth sign means that wickedness and corruption will be so dominant that noble and good people will find safety in silence, thus protecting themselves from the evil of the selfish and wicked. The fifth sign is critical of the spread of knowledge: there will be much hue and cry about knowledge, but the standards of nobility, politeness and character will decline on a daily basis.

14.43 PARTISANSHIP FOR ONE'S GROUP, TRIBE OR NATION

عَنْ عَائِشَةَ ﵂ قَالَتْ: قَالَ رَسُولُ اللهِ ﷺ: إِنَّ أَعْظَمَ النَّاسِ جُرْمًا: إِنْسَانٌ شَاعِرٌ يَهْجُو الْقَبِيلَةَ مِنْ أَسْرِهَا، وَرَجُلٌ انْتَفَى مِنْ أَبِيهِ. الأدب المفرد، باب ما يكره من الشعر.

[348] On the authority of 'Ā'ishah ﵂ that the Prophet ﷺ said, "Truly, the greatest criminals amongst mankind are [two types

61. This *Ḥadīth* speaks of a situation where women are forced to help earn a living against their wishes. Women who choose to participate in economic life are, of course, free to do so. The Prophet's first and most beloved wife, Khadījah, was an extremely successful businesswoman. – Trans. Note

62. Two versions of this narration variously mention *al-qalam* (the pen, i.e. writing) and *al-'ilm* (knowledge), hence the translation given. – Trans. Note

of people]: a poet who satirises and criticises a tribe in its totality, and a man who disowns [his lineage to] his father." Bukhārī's *Al-Adab al-Mufrad*, Chapter on What is Disliked in Poetry, *Ḥadīth* no. 874.

Commentary

This means that the poet totally ignores the good qualities of a tribe or group of people when criticising them based upon partisanship towards his own tribe or group. Justice dictates that if anyone is being criticised for their faults or weaknesses, their positive qualities should also be kept in mind.

14.44 CLASS DISTINCTION

عَنْ أَبِي هُرَيْرَةَ ﷺ قَالَ: قَالَ رَسُولَ اللهِ ﷺ: شَرُّ الطَّعَامِ طَعَامُ الْوَلِيمَةِ يُدْعَى لَهَا الْأَغْنِيَاءُ وَيُتْرَكُ الْفُقَرَاءُ، وَمَنْ تَرَكَ الدَّعْوَةَ فَقَدْ عَصى اللهَ وَرَسُولَهُ. متفق عليه.

[349] On the authority of Abū Hurayrah ﷺ, who said: The Messenger of Allah ﷺ said, "The worst food is that of a feast to which the rich are invited but the poor are excluded. Whoever declines an invitation [without an excuse] has disobeyed Allah and His Messenger." Bukhārī and Muslim (*Mishkat*, *Ḥadīth* no. 3218).

14.45 BLOCKING THE HIDDEN AVENUES TO OBSCENITY

عَنْ ابْنِ عَبَّاسٍ ﷺ، أَنَّهُ سَمِعَ النَّبِيَّ ﷺ يَقُولُ: لا يَخْلُوَنَّ رَجُلٌ بِامْرَأَةٍ، وَلا تُسَافِرَنَّ امْرَأَةٌ إِلا وَمَعَهَا مَحْرَمٌ. فَقَامَ رَجُلٌ، فَقَالَ: يَا رَسُولَ اللهِ اكْتُتِبْتُ فِي غَزْوَةِ كَذَا وَكَذَا، وَخَرَجَتْ امْرَأَتِي حَاجَّةً. قَالَ: اذْهَبْ فَحُجَّ مَعَ امْرَأَتِكَ. صحيح البخاري ومسلم، مشكواة، كتاب المناسك.

[350] On the authority of Ibn ʿAbbās ﷺ, that he heard the Prophet ﷺ saying, "A man must not seclude himself with a [non-*maḥram*] woman. A woman must not travel unless she is accompanied by a *maḥram* [close male relative]." A man asked,

"O Messenger of Allah! My name has been written down to participate in such-and-such a military expedition, and my wife has left for the Pilgrimage." He replied, "Go and perform the Pilgrimage with your wife." Bukhārī and Muslim (*Mishkāt*, Book of *Ḥajj* Rituals, *Ḥadīth* no. 2513).

Commentary

From this *Ḥadīth*, it can be understood that Islam leaves no stone unturned in closing the doors to immorality and obscenity and in protecting the honour of women, even disregarding an act of worship as important as *Jihād* in this regard.

عَنْ أُمَيْمَةَ بِنْتَ رُقَيْقَةَ ﵂ تَقُولُ: بَايَعْتُ رَسُولَ اللهِ ﷺ فِي نِسْوَةٍ، فَقَالَ لَنَا: فِيمَا اسْتَطَعْتُنَّ وَأَطَقْتُنَّ. قُلْتُ: اللهُ وَرَسُولُهُ أَرْحَمُ بِنَا مِنَّا بِأَنْفُسِنَا، قُلْتُ: يَا رَسُولَ اللهِ بَايِعْنَا، تَعْنِي صَافِحْنَا، فَقَالَ رَسُولُ اللهِ ﷺ: إِنَّمَا قَوْلِي لِمِائَةِ امْرَأَةٍ كَقَوْلِي لِامْرَأَةٍ وَاحِدَةٍ. سنن الترمذي والنسائي وأحمد ومالك، مشكواة، باب الصلح.

[351] On the authority of Umaymah bint Ruqayqah ﵂, who said: I gave the pledge of allegiance to the Prophet ﷺ, amongst a group of women. He said, "I am taking your pledge regarding those matters that you are capable of and can manage." I said, "Allah and His Messenger are more merciful to us than us ourselves." I then said, "O Messenger of Allah! Take our pledge", meaning, shake our hands in accepting allegiance. He replied, "My verbal acceptance of a hundred women is like my verbal acceptance of one woman." Mālik, Tirmidhī, Nasā'ī and Ibn Mājah (*Mishkāt*, Chapter on Reconciliation, *Ḥadīth* no. 4048).

Commentary

A Prophet is a father to his nation; in fact, he is even greater than that. Despite that, the Prophet ﷺ refrained from shaking women's hands at the time of their pledging allegiance. Had he not done so, there would have been a wrongful exploitation of religious authority, justifying a storm of indecency and shamelessness in the name of the *Sunnah* until the Day of Judgment.

عَنْ أُمِّ سَلَمَةَ رَضِيَ اللهُ عَنْهَا، أَنَّهَا كَانَتْ عِنْدَ رَسُولِ اللهِ ﷺ وَمَيْمُونَةَ، قَالَتْ: فَبَيْنَا نَحْنُ عِنْدَهُ أَقْبَلَ ابْنُ أُمِّ مَكْتُومٍ، فَدَخَلَ عَلَيْهِ، وَذَلِكَ بَعْدَ مَا أُمِرْنَا بِالْحِجَابِ، فَقَالَ رَسُولُ اللهِ ﷺ: احْتَجِبَا مِنْهُ. فَقُلْتُ: يَا رَسُولَ اللهِ أَلَيْسَ هُوَ أَعْمَى لا يُبْصِرُنَا وَلا يَعْرِفُنَا؟ فَقَالَ رَسُولُ اللهِ ﷺ: أَفَعَمْيَاوَانِ أَنْتُمَا؟ أَلَسْتُمَا تُبْصِرَانِهِ؟ سنن الترمذي وأبي داود وأحمد، مشكواة، باب النظر إلى المخطوبة.

[352] On the authority of Umm Salamah ﵂ that she and Maymūnah were with the Messenger of Allah ﷺ when Ibn Umm Maktūm entered his chamber, and this was after veiling had been commanded. The Messenger of Allah ﷺ directed the two of them, "Veil yourselves from him." I asked, "O Messenger of Allah! Is he not blind, and cannot see us or recognise us?" The Messenger of Allah ﷺ replied, "But are you blind? Do you not see him?" Aḥmad, Abū Dāwūd and Tirmidhī (*Mishkāt*, Chapter on Looking at the One to Whom a Marriage Proposal is Made, *Ḥadīth* no. 3116).

Commentary

Ibn Umm Maktūm was an eminent Companion and, furthermore, he was blind. Despite this, pure women such as the Mothers of the Believers were ordered to veil themselves from him.

عَنْ عُمَرَ رَضِيَ اللهُ عَنْهُ، عَنِ النَّبِيِّ ﷺ، قَالَ: لا يَخْلُوَنَّ رَجُلٌ بِامْرَأَةٍ إِلا كَانَ ثَالِثَهُمَا الشَّيْطَانُ. رواه الترمذي.

[353] On the authority of ʿUmar ﵁, that the Prophet ﷺ said, "A man must not seclude himself with a [non-*maḥram*] woman, otherwise the third of them will be Satan." Tirmidhī (*Mishkāt*, *Ḥadīth* no. 3116).

Commentary

This means that wherever a man and woman are alone, Satan is there to exploit his opportunity. There is the continuous danger that the two of them will be afflicted by temptation.

عَنْ أَبِي سَعِيدٍ الْخُدْرِيِّ ﵁ يَقُولُ: قَالَ رَسُولُ الله ﷺ: إِنَّ مِنْ أَشَرِّ النَّاسِ عِنْدَ اللهِ مَنْزِلَةً يَوْمَ الْقِيَامَةِ، الرَّجُلُ يُفْضِي إِلى امْرَأَتِهِ وَتُفْضِي إِلَيْهِ، ثُمَّ يَنْشُرُ سِرَّهَا. صحيح مسلم، مشكواة، باب المباشرة.

[354] On the authority of Abū Saʿīd al-Khudrī ﵁, who said: The Messenger of Allah ﷺ said, "Truly, amongst the people worst in station with Allah on the Day of Judgment will be the man who has intimate relations with his wife and then spreads her secrets [amongst the people]." Muslim (*Mishkāt*, Chapter on Sexual Intercourse, *Ḥadīth* no. 3190).

عَنْ جَرِيرِ بْنِ عَبْدِ اللهِ ﵁ قَالَ: سَأَلْتُ رَسُولَ اللهِ ﷺ عَنْ نَظَرِ الْفُجَاءَةِ، فَأَمَرَنِي أَنْ أَصْرِفَ بَصَرِي. صحيح مسلم، مشكواة، باب النظر إلى المخطوبة.

[355] On the authority of Jarīr b. ʿAbdullāh ﵁ who said: I asked the Messenger of Allah ﷺ about the unintentional glance. He ordered me to avert my gaze. Muslim (*Mishkāt*, Chapter on Looking at the One to Whom a Marriage Proposal is Made, *Ḥadīth* no. 3104).

Commentary

In Islam, unlawful sexual intercourse (*zinā*) has been declared an extremely dangerous moral disease. Therefore, all roads and doors to it have been closed.

عَنْ أَبِي هُرَيْرَةَ ﵁ قَالَ: قَالَ رَسُولُ اللهِ ﷺ: طِيبُ الرِّجَالِ مَا ظَهَرَ رِيحُهُ وَخَفِيَ لَوْنُهُ، وَطِيبُ النِّسَاءِ مَا ظَهَرَ لَوْنُهُ وَخَفِيَ رِيحُهُ. سنن الترمذي والنسائي، مشكواة.

[356] On the authority of Abū Hurayrah ﵁ who said: The Messenger of Allah ﷺ said, "A man's perfume is that which has a strong scent but light colour. A woman's perfume is that which has a strong colour but light scent." Tirmidhī and Nasā'ī (*Mishkāt*, *Ḥadīth* no. 4443).

Commentary

Islam strives to keep a righteous society free from shamelessness and indecency and whatever provokes these. This is why women are forbidden from wearing perfume that can arouse lustful passions. Contrarily, men are allowed to wear strong perfume since there is not the risk of temptations that are created by women acting similarly. Men have been forbidden from wearing strongly-coloured perfume. This is because it is appropriate for their nature, duties and obligations that their dress and appearance should be as simple as possible. On the other hand, women are allowed to wear colourful scent. Clearly, it is in the nature of women to love adornment and beautification, and this natural instinct has been considered in Islam. However, restrictions have also been placed on the expression of this natural tendency so that Islamic society is protected from indecency and moral chaos.

14.46 SPREADING INDECENCY

عَنْ عَلِيِّ بْنِ أَبِيْ طَالِبٍ ﷺ قَالَ: القَائِلُ الفَاحِشَةَ، وَالَّذِي يُشِيعُ بِهَا فِي الإِثْمِ سَوَاءٌ. الأدب المفرد، باب إثم من سمع فاحشة فافشاها.

[357] On the authority of ʿAlī b. Abī Ṭālib ﷺ who said, "The one who utters an obscenity and the one who spreads it [in society] are equal in sin." Bukhārī's *Al-Adab al-Mufrad*, Chapter on The Sin of One who Hears an Obscenity and then Spreads It, *Ḥadīth* no. 324.

14.47 A CORRUPTING ENVIRONMENT

عَنْ أَبِي هُرَيْرَةَ ﷺ قَالَ: قَالَ رَسُولُ اللهِ ﷺ: مَا مِنْ مَوْلُودٍ إِلا يُولَدُ عَلَى الْفِطْرَةِ، فَأَبَوَاهُ يُهَوِّدَانِهِ ، وَيُنَصِّرَانِهِ، أَوْ يُمَجِّسَانِهِ، كَمَا تُنْتِجُ الْبَهِيمَةُ بَهِيمَةً جَمْعَاءَ، هَلْ تُحِسُّونَ فِيهَا مِنْ جَدْعَاءَ؟ ثُمَّ يَقُولُ أَبُو هُرَيْرَةَ رَضِيَ اللهُ عَنْهُ: فِطْرَةَ اللهِ الَّتِي فَطَرَ النَّاسَ عَلَيْهَا لا تَبْدِيلَ لِخَلْقِ اللهِ ذَلِكَ الدِّينُ الْقَيِّمُ. صحيح البخاري ومسلم، مشكواة، باب الإيمان بالقدر.

[358] On the authority of Abū Hurayrah ﷺ who said: The Messenger of Allah ﷺ said, "Every newborn child is born upon

the natural state [*fiṭrah*]. His parents then turn him into a Jew, Christian or Magian. This is just as animals produce sound and healthy young: do you see any born with ears cut?" Abū Hurayrah then recited, "*The true nature on which Allah has created human beings. The mould fashioned by Allah cannot be altered. That is the true Straight Faith* [*Sūrah al-Rūm*, 30: 30]." Bukhārī and Muslim (*Mishkāt*, Chapter on Faith in Predestination, *Ḥadīth* no. 90).

Commentary

This means that Allah has created every human being upon the natural state (*fiṭrah*, i.e. Islam). Subsequently, a person may lose his way because of the wrong upbringing given by his parents and the harmful effects of his environment.

14.48 GREED FOR POWER

عَنْ أَبِي هُرَيْرَةَ ﷺ، عَنْ النَّبِيِّ ﷺ قَالَ: إِنَّكُمْ سَتَحْرِصُونَ عَلى الْإِمَارَةِ، وَسَتَكُونُ نَدَامَةً يَوْمَ الْقِيَامَةِ، فَنِعْمَ الْمُرْضِعَةُ وَبِئْسَتْ الْفَاطِمَةُ. صحيح البخاري، مشكواة، كتاب الإمارة.

[359] On the authority of Abū Hurayrah ﷺ that the Prophet ﷺ said, "You will certainly crave after leadership, and it will be a source of regret on the Day of Judgment. How excellent is the suckler and how bad the weaner!" Bukhārī (*Mishkāt*, Book of Leadership, *Ḥadīth* no. 3681).

Commentary

Here, government and leadership have been compared to the suckler and weaner. A person thoroughly enjoys a position of authority but when this position is taken away from him by death or dismissal, the memory of those delights and joys continually haunts him in the form of regret and sorrow.

14.49 INTERCEDING ON BEHALF OF A CRIMINAL

عَنْ عَائِشَةَ ﵂، أَنَّ قُرَيْشًاقَدْ أَهَمَّهُمْ شَأْنُ الْمَرْأَةِ الْمَخْزُومِيَّةِ، الَّتِي سَرَقَتْ. فَقَالُوا: وَمَنْ يُكَلِّمُ فِيهَا رَسُولَ اللهِ ﷺ، فَقَالُوا: وَمَنْ يَجْتَرِئُ عَلَيْهِ إِلا أُسَامَةُ بْنُ زَيْدٍ حِبُّ رَسُولِ اللهِ ﷺ، فَكَلَّمَهُ أُسَامَةُ، فتلوَّنَ وَجْهُ رَسُولُ اللهِ ﷺ وَقَالَ: أَتَشْفَعُ فِي حَدٍّ مِنْ حُدُودِ اللهِ، ثُمَّ قَامَ، واخْتَطَبَ، ثُمَّ قَالَ: إِنَّما أَهْلَكَ الَّذِينَ قَبْلَكُمْ، أَنَّهُمْ كَانُوا إِذَا سَرَقَ فِيهِمْ الشَّرِيفُ تَرَكُوهُ، وَإِذَا سَرَقَ فِيهِمْ الضَّعِيفُ أَقَامُوا عَلَيْهِ الْحَدَّ، وَايْمُ اللهِ لَوْ أَنَّ فَاطِمَةَ بِنْتَ مُحَمَّدٍ سَرَقَتْ لَقَطَعْتُ يَدَهَا. متفق عليه، مشكواة، باب الشفاعة في الحدود.

[360] On the authority of 'Ā'ishah ﵂ that the Quraysh were concerned about the case of the Makhzūmī woman who had committed theft. They wondered as to who would speak to the Messenger of Allah ﷺ regarding her, and decided that no one would dare do so except Usāmah b. Zayd, the beloved of the Messenger of Allah ﷺ. Usāmah spoke to him about it, upon which the colour of the face of the Messenger of Allah ﷺ changed. He said, "Are you interceding regarding one of the limits [*ḥudūd*] laid down by Allah?" He then stood and addressed the people, saying, "The only thing that destroyed the people before you was that when one of their nobles committed theft, they would spare him but when one of the weak committed theft, they would punish him. By Allah! If Fāṭimah, daughter of Muḥammad, were to steal, I would cut off her hand." Bukhārī and Muslim (*Mishkāt*, Chapter on Intercession Regarding *Ḥudūd*, *Ḥadīth* no. 3610).

14.50 BREAKING COVENANTS

عَنْ صَفْوَانَ بْنَ سُلَيْمٍ ﵁، أَخْبَرَهُ عَنْ عِدَّةٍ مِنْ أَبْنَاءِ أَصْحَابِ رَسُولِ اللهِ ﷺ، عَنْ آبَائِهِمْ، عَنْ رَسُولِ اللهِ ﷺ قَالَ: أَلا مَنْ ظَلَمَ مُعَاهِدًا، أَوْ انْتَقَصَهُ، أَوْ كَلَّفَهُ فَوْقَ طَاقَتِهِ، أَوْ أَخَذَ مِنْهُ شَيْئًا بِغَيْرِ طِيبِ نَفْسٍ، فَأَنَا حَجِيجُهُ يَوْمَ الْقِيَامَةِ. سنن أبى داود، مشكواة، باب الصلح.

[361] On the authority of Ṣafwān b. Sulaym ﵁ from a number of sons of the Companions of the Messenger of Allah ﷺ from their fathers from the Messenger of Allah ﷺ, who said, "Lo!

Whoever oppresses one [individual or people] protected by [our] covenant, withholds part of his due, imposes an unbearable task upon him or takes anything from him without his consent, I will contend with him on the Day of Judgment [on behalf of the oppressed party]." Abū Dāwūd (*Mishkāt*, Chapter on Reconciliation, *Ḥadīth* no. 4047).

14.51 DANGEROUS SOCIAL ILLS

عن عَبْدِ الله بْنِ عَبَّاس ﵄، أَنَّهُ قَالَ: مَا ظَهَرَ الْغُلُولُ فِي قَوْمٍ قَطُّ إلا أُلْقِيَ فِي قُلُوبِهِمْ الرُّعْبُ، وَلا فَشَا الزِّنَا فِي قَوْمٍ قَطُّ إلا كَثُرَ فِيهِمْ الْمَوْتُ، وَلا نَقَصَ قَوْمٌ الْمِكْيَالَ وَالْمِيزَانَ إلَّا قُطِعَ عَنْهُمْ الرِّزْقُ، وَلا حَكَمَ قَوْمٌ بِغَيْرِ الْحَقِّ إلا فَشَا فِيهِمِ الدَّمُ، وَلا خَتَرَ قَوْمٌ بِالْعَهْدِ إلَّا سَلَّطَ الله عَلَيْهِمْ الْعَدُوَّ. رواه مالك، مشكواة، باب تغير الناس.

[362] On the authority of ʿAbdullāh b. ʿAbbās ﵄, who said, "Whenever treachery becomes widespread amongst a people, Allah places fear [of their enemy] in their hearts. Whenever unlawful sexual intercourse becomes widespread amongst a people, death becomes common amongst them. Whenever a people cheat in weights and measures, sustenance is cut off from them. Whenever people judge unjustly, bloodshed becomes rife amongst them. Whenever a people break covenants, their enemy is made dominant over them." Mālik (*Mishkāt*, Chapter: Changes in the Condition of the People, *Ḥadīth* no. 5370).

14.52 GREED FOR THE WORLD

عَنْ ثَوْبَانَ ﵁ قَالَ: قَالَ رَسُولُ الله ﷺ: يُوشِكُ الْأُمَمُ أَنْ تَدَاعَى عَلَيْكُمْ كَمَا تَدَاعَى الْأَكَلَةُ إِلَى قَصْعَتِهَا. فَقَالَ قَائِلٌ: وَمِنْ قِلَّةٍ نَحْنُ يَوْمَئِذٍ. قَالَ: بَلْ أَنْتُمْ يَوْمَئِذٍ كَثِيرٌ وَلَكِنَّكُمْ غُثَاءٌ كَغُثَاءِ السَّيْلِ، وَلَيَنْزَعَنَّ الله مِنْ صُدُورِ عَدُوِّكُمْ الْمَهَابَةَ مِنْكُمْ، وَلَيَقْذِفَنَّ الله فِي قُلُوبِكُمْ الْوَهْنَ. فَقَالَ قَائِلٌ: يَا رَسُولَ الله وَمَا الْوَهْنُ؟ قَالَ حُبُّ الدُّنْيَا وَكَرَاهِيَةُ الْمَوْتِ. سنن أبى داود.

[363] On the authority of Thawbān ﵁, who said: The Messenger of Allah ﷺ said, "Very soon, nations will invite each other to

gather around you [to devour you] as diners invite each other to a feast." Someone asked, "Will it be due to our lack of numbers at that time?" He replied, "Rather, you will be great in number, but you will be like the froth on the surface of the floodwater. Allah will have snatched away from the hearts of your enemies their awe of you, and He will have cast weakness into your hearts." Someone asked, "O Messenger of Allah! What is that weakness?" He replied, "Love of the world and hatred of death."
Abū Dāwūd (*Mishkāt*, Chapter on Changes in the Condition of the People, *Ḥadīth* no. 5369).

Commentary

Islam does not forbid the heart's inclination towards worldly blessings, as long as this is within limits. However, if this love for worldly matters increases to the extent that cowardice and a lack of spiritual motivation take root, then a person is neither regarded with dignity in this world nor blessed with happiness in the Hereafter.

15

A Sound Social System

15.1 SOCIAL ORDER

عَنْ أَبِي سَعِيدٍ الْخُدْرِيِّ ﷺ، أَنَّ رَسُولَ الله ﷺ قَالَ: إِذَا كَانَ ثَلَاثَةٌ فِي سَفَرٍ فَلْيُؤَمِّرُوا أَحَدَهُمْ. رواه أبي داود، مشكواة، باب آدب السفر.

[364] On the authority of Abū Sa'īd al-Khudrī ﷺ that the Messenger of Allah ﷺ said, "When there are three people travelling, they should appoint one as *amīr* [leader, chief]." Abū Dāwūd (*Mishkāt*, Chapter: Etiquette of Travelling, *Ḥadīth* no. 3911).

Commentary

In explanation of this *Ḥadīth*, Imām Ibn Taymiyyah has written that since the establishment of an organised order has been emphasised in a temporary situation such as that of a journey, it follows by implication that the formation of an organised order and leadership is obligatory in settled life. This is supported by another *Ḥadīth* where the Prophet ﷺ said, "If there are three people in even a wilderness, one of them should be appointed as *amīr*."

15.2 HOLDING TO THE CONGREGATION

عَنْ أَبِي الدَّرْدَاءِ ﷺ قَالَ: سَمِعْتُ رَسُولَ الله ﷺ يَقُولُ: مَا مِنْ ثَلَاثَةٍ فِي قَرْيَةٍ وَلا بَدْوٍ لَا تُقَامُ فِيهِمُ الصَّلَاةُ إِلا قَدِ اسْتَحْوَذَ عَلَيْهِمُ الشَّيْطَانُ، فَعَلَيْكُمْ بِالْجَمَاعَةِ، فَإِنَّمَا يَأْكُلُ الذِّئْبُ الْقَاصِيَةَ. رواه داود، مشكواة، باب الجماعة.

[365] On the authority of Abū'l-Dardā' ﷺ who said: I heard the Messenger of Allah ﷺ saying, "If there are three people in a village or wilderness amongst whom the [congregational] prayer is not established, Satan will have dominance over them. Therefore, stay with the congregation, for the wolf only eats the stray sheep!" Aḥmad, Abū Dāwūd and Nasā'ī (*Mishkāt*, Chapter on the Congregation, *Ḥadīth* no. 1067).

Commentary

The forces of falsehood, evil and wickedness are united and well-organised. In order to break their influence, it is necessary that the people of truth and piety also become organised and united. This is why congregational life has been emphasised repeatedly in the Qur'ān and the *Sunnah*.

15.3 THE IMPORTANCE OF A SOCIAL ORDER

عَنْ أَبِي هُرَيْرَةَ رضي الله عنه قَالَ: قَالَ رَسُولُ اللهِ ﷺ: الْجِهَادُ وَاجِبٌ عَلَيْكُمْ مَعَ كُلِّ أَمِيرٍ بَرًّا كَانَ أَوْ فَاجِرًا وَإِنْ عمل الْكَبَائِرَ، وَالصَّلَاةُ وَاجِبَةٌ عَلَيْكُمْ خَلْفَ كُلِّ مُسْلِمٍ بَرًّا كَانَ أَوْ فَاجِرًا وَإِنْ عَمِلَ الْكَبَائِرَ، وَالصَّلَاةُ وَاجِبَةٌ عَلى كُلِّ مُسْلِمٍ بَرًّا كَانَ أَوْ فَاجِرًا وَإِنْ عَمِلَ الْكَبَائِرَ. سنن أبي داود، مشكواة، باب الإمامة.

[366] On the authority of Abū Hurayrah ﷺ who said: The Messenger of Allah ﷺ said, "*Jihād* is a duty upon you behind every leader, whether he is righteous or wicked, even if he commits major sins. Prayer is a duty upon you behind every leader, whether he is righteous or wicked, even if he commits major sins. The funeral prayer is a duty over every [deceased] Muslim, whether he is righteous or wicked, even if he commits major sins. Abū Dāwūd (*Mishkāt*, Chapter on Imamate, *Ḥadīth* no. 1125).

Commentary

A number of matters are learnt from this *Ḥadīth*:

1. Whatever may be the character and behaviour of the leader of the Muslims, he must nevertheless be obeyed in matters of righteousness.

2. Whether an *imām* is righteous or impious and wicked, prayer is valid behind him. This applies when the *imām* or *amīr* has been appointed beforehand or has seized control through influence and force. In normal circumstances, when the Muslims have the opportunity to appoint their own *amīr* or *imām*, they should choose the best person with regards to character and piety, as in the *Ḥadīth*, "Make the best of you your leaders."
3. No matter how wicked a Muslim's actions may be, his funeral prayer must not be abandoned. However, if a person deservedly has a bad reputation or has done something that impinges upon the rights of others, people of knowledge and piety may avoid praying over his funeral in order to alert and remind the masses. Thus, it is transmitted in the *Ḥadīth* that the Prophet ﷺ did not pray over the funeral of the person who committed suicide. Similarly, he ﷺ did not pray over the funeral of the one who died while indebted, but said to the people, "Pray over your companion." It should remain clear that such a policy of boycott and breaking of relations can only work in a society that has truly been established upon Islamic principles.

15.4 ABIDING BY RULES

عَنْ بَشِيرِ ابْنِ الْخَصَاصِيَّةِ ﷺ قَالَ: إِنَّ أَهْلَ الصَّدَقَةِ يَعْتَدُونَ عَلَيْنَا، أَفَنَكْتُمُ مِنْ أَمْوَالِنَا بِقَدْرِ مَا يَعْتَدُونَ عَلَيْنَا؟ فَقَالَ: لَا. سنن أبي داود، مشكواة، كتاب الزكاة.

[367] On the authority of Bashīr b. al-Khaṣāṣiyyah ﷺ who said: We asked the Prophet ﷺ, "The *zakāt*-collectors transgress upon us. Should we therefore conceal part of our wealth commensurate with their transgression?" He replied, "No." Abū Dāwūd (*Mishkāt*, Book of *Zakāt*, *Ḥadīth* no. 1784).

Commentary

The importance of obedience to authority and abiding by rules in Islam can be judged from this *Ḥadīth*. Even if the representatives of an Islamic government commit injustice when collecting *zakāt* and charity, one cannot take wrongful steps in return.

15.5 THE LIMITS OF OBEDIENCE TO AUTHORITY

عَنْ ابْنِ عُمَرَ ؓ، عَنْ النَّبِيِّ ﷺ أَنَّهُ قَالَ: عَلَى الْمَرْءِ الْمُسْلِمِ السَّمْعُ وَالطَّاعَةُ فِيما أَحَبَّ وَكَرِهَ، إلا أَنْ يُؤْمَرَ بِمَعْصِيَةٍ، فَإِنْ أُمِرَ بِمَعْصِيَةٍ، فَلا سَمْعَ وَلَا طَاعَةَ. متفق عليه.

[368] On the authority of Ibn ʿUmar ؓ who said: The Messenger of Allah ﷺ said, "Hearing and obeying [authority] are a duty upon the Muslim, whether he likes [the orders] or not, as long as he is not ordered to disobey Allah: if he is ordered to disobey Allah, then there is [to be] neither hearing nor obeying." Bukhārī and Muslim (*Mishkāt*, Book of Leadership, *Ḥadīth* no. 3664).

15.6 NO AGREEMENT OR DECLARATION IS ALLOWED THAT CONTRAVENES DIVINE LIMITS

عَنْ عَمْرِو بْنِ عَوْفٍ الْمُزَنِيِّ ؓ، أَنَّ رَسُولَ الله ﷺ قَالَ: الصُّلْحُ جَائِزٌ بَيْنَ الْمُسْلِمِينَ إِلَّا صُلْحًا حَرَّمَ حَلَالًا، أَوْ أَحَلَّ حَرَامًا، وَالْمُسْلِمُونَ عَلَى شُرُوطِهِمْ إلا شَرْطًا حَرَّمَ حَلَالًا، أَوْ أَحَلَّ حَرَامًا. سنن الترمذي وأبي داود وابن ماجه وأحمد.

[369] On the authority of ʿAmr b. ʿAwf al-Muzanī ؓ that the Prophet ﷺ said, "Reconciliation is allowed amongst Muslims, except a reconciliation that prohibits the permitted or permits the prohibited. The Muslims must abide by their commitments [i.e. those to which they agree], except for agreements that prohibit the permitted or permit the prohibited." Tirmidhī and Ibn Mājah (*Mishkāt*, Chapter on Bankruptcy, *Ḥadīth* no. 2923).

Commentary

All financial and political dealings, social relationships, international agreements and formulations of national law must be agreed in the light of this *Ḥadīth*. It is not necessary for every particular issue that specific evidence be found in the Qur'ān and *Sunnah* for these types of dealings. Rather, it is enough to ascertain that we are not taking any steps that go against an unequivocal revealed text. On the other hand, for ritual worship, it is necessary to prove every detail from the Qur'ān and *Sunnah*, otherwise we run the risk of innovation finding a foothold in our worship.

15.7 RESPONSIBILITIES OF THE *AMĪR* (LEADER)

عَنْ مَعْقِل بْنِ يَسَار ﷺ قَالَ: سَمِعْتُ رَسُولَ الله ﷺ يَقُولُ: أَيُّما وَالٍ وَلِيَ مِنْ أَمْرِ الْمُسْلِمِيْنَ شَيْئَاً، فَلَمْ يَنْصُح لَهُمْ وَلَمْ يَجْهَدْ لَهُمْ كَنُصْحِهِ وَجُهْدِهِ لِنَفْسِهِ كَبَّهُ اللهُ عَلى وَجْهِهِ فِي النَّارِ. المعجم الصغير للطبراني.

[370] On the authority of Ma'qil b. Yasār ﷺ who said: I heard the Messenger of Allah ﷺ saying, "Anyone who takes responsibility for a matter concerning the Muslims and shows neither dedication nor efforts for them as he would be dedicated and strive for his own affairs, Allah will cast him upon his face into the Fire." Ṭabarānī's *Al-Mu'jam al-Ṣaghīr*.

عَنْ عَائِشَةَ ﷺ قَالَتْ: قَالَ رَسُولُ اللهِ ﷺ اللَّهُمَّ مَنْ وَلِيَ مِنْ أَمْرِ أُمَّتِي شَيْئًا، فَشَقَّ عَلَيْهِمْ، فَاشْقُقْ عَلَيْهِ، وَمَنْ وَلِيَ مِنْ أَمْرِ أُمَّتِي شَيْئًا، فَرَفَقَ بِهِمْ، فَارْفُقْ بِهِ. صحيح مسلم، مشكواة، كتاب الامارة.

[371] On the authority of 'Ā'ishah ﷺ who said: The Messenger of Allah ﷺ said, "O Allah! Whoever is given authority over any matter of my nation and is severe upon them, be Thou severe upon him! Whoever is given authority over any matter of my nation and is gentle with them, be Thou gentle with him!" Muslim (*Mishkāt*, Book of Leadership, *Ḥadīth* no. 3689).

عَنْ ابْنِ عَبَّاس ﷺ قَالَ: قَالَ رسولُ الله ﷺ: ما مِنْ أَحَدٍ مِن أُمَّتي وُلِّيَ مِنْ أَمْرِ الْمُسْلِمِينَ شَيْئَاً لَمْ يَحْفَظْهُمْ بِما يَحْفَظُ بِهِ نفسَهُ وَأَهْلَهُ إلا لَمْ يَجِدْ رَائِحَةَ الْجَنَّةِ. المعجم الصغير للطبراني.

[372] On the authority of Ibn 'Abbās ﷺ who said: The Messenger of Allah ﷺ said, "Any one of my nation who takes responsibility for a matter concerning the Muslims and does

not safeguard it as he would safeguard his own self and family, he will not smell the fragrance of the Garden." Ṭabarānī's *Al-Muʿjam al-Ṣaghīr*. A similar *Ḥadīth* is transmitted by Bukhārī.

وَعَنْ أَنَسِ بْنِ مَالِكٍ ﷺ قَالَ: قَالَ رَسُولُ الله ﷺ: مَنْ وُلِّيَ مِنْ أَمْرِ المُسْلِمِينَ شَيْئاً فَغَشَّهُمْ فَهُوَ فِي النَّارِ. المعجم الصغير للطبراني.

[373]   On the authority of Anas b. Mālik ﷺ, who said: The Messenger of Allah ﷺ said, "Whoever takes responsibility for a matter concerning the Muslims and then betrays them, he will be in the Fire." Ṭabarānī's *Al-Muʿjam al-Ṣaghīr*.

15.8 THE OBLIGATIONS OF ISLAMIC GOVERNANCE

عَنْ أَبِي هُرَيْرَةَ ﷺ، أَنَّ رَسُولَ الله ﷺ كَانَ يُؤْتَى بِالرَّجُلِ المُتَوَفَّى عَلَيْهِ الدَّيْنُ، فَيَسْأَلُ هَلْ تَرَكَ لِدَيْنِهِ مِنْ قَضَاءٍ، فَإِنْ حُدِّثَ أَنَّهُ تَرَكَ وَفَاءً، صَلَّى عَلَيْهِ، وَإِلَّا قَالَ: صَلُّوا عَلَى صَاحِبِكُمْ، فَلَمَّا فَتَحَ الله عَلَيْهِ الفُتُوحَ، قَالَ: أَنَا أَوْلَى بِالمُؤْمِنِينَ مِنْ أَنْفُسِهِمْ، فَمَنْ تُوُفِّيَ وَعَلَيْهِ دَيْنٌ فَعَلَيَّ قَضَاؤُهُ وَمَنْ تَرَكَ مَالًا فَهُوَ لِوَرَثَتِهِ. متفق عليه، مشكوة، باب الافلاس.

[374]   On the authority of Abū Hurayrah ﷺ who said: People who had died in debt used to be brought to the Messenger of Allah ﷺ. He would ask whether or not the man had left enough wealth to pay the debt. If he was told that the man had left enough surplus wealth, he would pray over his funeral, otherwise he would say to the Muslims, "Pray over your companion." When Allah opened up the conquests to him, he stood and addressed the people saying, "I have more right to the believers than their own selves. Therefore, any believer who dies in debt, its settlement is my responsibility. Whoever leaves surplus wealth, it is for his inheritors." Bukhārī and Muslim (*Mishkāt*, Chapter on Bankruptcy, *Ḥadīth* no. 2913).

Commentary

It is known from this *Ḥadīth* that an Islamic government is responsible for all the basic necessities of people who are unable to support themselves. The basic necessities are: (1) food, (2) clothing, (3) accommodation, (4) healthcare and (5) education. If the citizens of any state are deprived of these basic necessities, the government cannot be regarded as Islamic in the true sense. 'Umar b. al-Khaṭṭāb did not enforce the corporal punishment of amputating the hand of the thief during a period of famine. The reason for this is obvious: if a government cannot provide food for its subjects, how can it punish the thief who is likely to have stolen due to dire circumstances?

15.9 THE QUALITIES OF IMAMATE AND LEADERSHIP

عَنْ أَبِي مَسْعُودٍ الْأَنْصَارِيِّ ﷺ قَالَ: قَالَ رَسُولُ الله ﷺ: يَؤُمُّ الْقَوْمَ أَقْرَؤُهُمْ لِكِتَابِ الله، فَإِنْ كَانُوا فِي الْقِرَاءَةِ سَوَاءً، فَأَعْلَمُهُمْ بِالسُّنَّةِ، فَإِنْ كَانُوا فِي السُّنَّةِ سَوَاءً، فَأَقْدَمُهُمْ هِجْرَةً، فَإِنْ كَانُوا فِي الْهِجْرَةِ سَوَاءً، فَأَقْدَمُهُمْ سِنًّا، وَلَا يَؤُمَّنَّ الرَّجُلُ الرَّجُلَ فِي سُلْطَانِهِ، وَلَا يَقْعُدْ فِي بَيْتِهِ عَلَى تَكْرِمَتِهِ إِلَا بِإِذْنِهِ. صحيح مسلم والترمذي والنسائي وأبى داود، مشكواة، باب الامامة.

[375]   On the authority of Abū Mas'ūd al-Anṣārī ☙ who said: The Messenger of Allah ☙ said, "A people should be led [in prayer] by the most well-versed of them in the Book of Allah. If they are equal in recitation, they should be led by the one most knowledgeable about the *Sunnah*. If they are equal in knowledge of the *Sunnah*, they should be led by the earliest one to migrate. If they are equal in the matter of [sacred] migration, they should be led by the eldest. A man must neither lead another man [in prayer] in the latter's place of authority nor sit in his house upon his seat without his permission." Muslim (*Mishkāt*, Chapter on Imamate, Ḥadīth no. 1117).

Commentary

I.   As politics is also subservient to religion in Islam, the qualities that are considered for seniority in the mosque should also be considered at the time of selecting the president or prime minister of a country. Here, four such qualities have been explained:

a. Precedence in knowledge of the Qur'ān.
b. Precedence in familiarity with the *Sunnah*.
c. Precedence in *hijrah* (sacred migration) or other important service to the religion.
d. Seniority in terms of age.

2. If the influence and acceptance of a person learned in the religion is widespread in a particular location, it could be divisive for the Muslims' social life for another person to usurp the position of imamate and leadership there, unless the former gives his own consent. Similarly, no-one should sit on another's special seat or chair without the latter's permission, for this can also open the door to bad feelings and misunderstandings.

عَنْ ابْنِ عَبَّاسٍ ﵄، عَنْ رَسُولِ اللهِ ﷺ، قَالَ: ثَلَاثَةٌ لا تَرْتَفِعُ صَلَاتُهُمْ فَوْقَ رُءُوسِهِمْ شِبْرًا: رَجُلٌ أَمَّ قَوْمًا وَهُمْ لَهُ كَارِهُونَ، وَامْرَأَةٌ بَاتَتْ وَزَوْجُهَا عَلَيْهَا سَاخِطٌ، وَأَخَوَانِ مُتَصَارِمَانِ. سنن ابن ماجه، مشكواة، باب الإمامة.

[376] On the authority of Ibn 'Abbās ﵄ who said: The Messenger of Allah ﷺ said, "There are three whose prayers are not raised above their heads even a handspan [i.e. their prayers are not accepted]: a person who leads, in prayer, people who dislike him; a woman who spends a night while her husband is angry at her; two [Muslim] brothers who cut off relations with each other." Ibn Mājah (*Mishkāt*, Chapter on Imamate, *Ḥadīth* no. 1128).

Commentary

A leading quality of the *amīr* or *imām* is that there is affection and acceptance amongst the public for him, based on his life and character. Whenever he feels that the majority of the people are unhappy with him, he should voluntarily resign from this responsibility.

15.10 SEEKING POSITION

عَنْ عَبْدِ الرَّحْمَنِ بْنِ سَمُرَةَ ﷺ قَالَ: قَالَ لِي رَسُولُ اللهِ ﷺ: لَا تَسْأَلِ الْإِمَارَةَ، فَإِنَّكَ إِنْ أُعْطِيتَهَا مِنْ غَيْرِ مَسْأَلَةٍ أُعِنْتَ عَلَيْهَا، وَإِنْ أُعْطِيتَهَا عَنْ مَسْأَلَةٍ وُكِلْتَ إِلَيْهَا. صحيح البخاري ومسلم، مشكواة، كتاب الإمارة.

[377]   On the authority of ʿAbd al-Raḥmān b. Samurah ☙ who said: The Messenger of Allah ﷺ said to me, "Do not seek a position of authority, for if you are given it after seeking it you will be entrusted [and abandoned] to it, but if you are given it without seeking it you will be helped in it [by Allah]." Bukhārī and Muslim (*Mishkāt*, Book of Leadership, *Ḥadīth* no. 3680).

Commentary

The responsibilities of leadership and government are so numerous that a pious person of understanding could never put himself forward to shoulder this burden. If a person nevertheless runs after such positions, one of two things must be true about him: either he is naïve, unaware of the sensitive nature and responsibilities of such positions, or he is hungry for authority and afflicted by greed for power. Either of these cases is enough to make the person unfit to wield authority.

عَنْ أَنَسِ بْنِ مَالِكٍ ☙ قَالَ: قَالَ رَسُولُ اللهِ ﷺ: مَنْ سَأَلَ الْقَضَاءَ وُكِلَ إِلَى نَفْسِهِ، وَمَنْ أُجْبِرَ عَلَيْهِ يُنْزِلُ اللهُ عَلَيْهِ مَلَكًا فَيُسَدِّدُهُ. سنن الترمذي وابن ماجة، مشكواة، باب العمل في القضاء.

[378]   On the authority of Anas b. Mālik ☙, who said: The Messenger of Allah ﷺ said, "Whoever seeks to be a judge, he is entrusted [and abandoned] to himself. Whoever is forced into [accepting] such a position, Allah sends down an angel to keep him on the right path." Tirmidhī and Ibn Mājah (*Mishkāt*, Chapter on Judgment, *Ḥadīth* no. 3734).

15.11 THE LIMITS OF SEEKING POSITIONS

عَنْ أَبِي هُرَيْرَةَ ﷺ، عَنِ النَّبِيِّ ﷺ، قَالَ: مَنْ طَلَبَ قَضَاءَ الْمُسْلِمِينَ حَتَّى يَنَالَهُ، ثُمَّ غَلَبَ عَدْلُهُ جَوْرَهُ فَلَهُ الْجَنَّةُ، وَمَنْ غَلَبَ جَوْرُهُ عَدْلَهُ فَلَهُ النَّارُ. سنن أبي داود، مشكواة، باب العمل في القضاء.

[379] On the authority of Abū Hurayrah ﷺ, who said: The Messenger of Allah ﷺ said, "Whoever seeks to be a judge amongst Muslims and attains such a position: if his justice dominates his injustice, for him is the Garden; if his injustice dominates his justice, for him is the Fire." Abū Dāwūd (*Mishkāt*, Chapter on Judgment, *Ḥadīth* no. 3736).

Commentary

Usually, the *Sharī'ah* necessitates that a Muslim should not run after positions of responsibility, otherwise his personal piety will be adversely affected. However, if a person puts himself forward for such positions without coveting them greedily, anticipating that he can really establish some truth and justice and combat the forces of evil and corruption, then this case is an exception to the rule. Further, this is true only when no other person of reliable character and integrity exists in society.

This clarification is necessary to reconcile the *Aḥādīth* opposed to, and in favour of, seeking positions of responsibility. However, the most cautious approach is to save oneself from being immersed in such a trial, as in the other *Ḥadīth*, "Whoever is appointed as a judge has been slaughtered without a knife."

15.12 REFORM OF THE GOVERNMENT DEPENDS ON REFORM OF THE PUBLIC

وَعَنْ يَحْيَى بْنِ هَاشِمٍ، عَنْ يُونُسَ بْنِ أَبِي إِسْحَاقَ، عَنْ أَبِيهِ ﷺ قَالَ: قَالَ رَسُوْلُ اللهِ ﷺ: كَمَا تَكُوْنُوْنَ كَذَلِكَ يُؤَمَّرُ عَلَيْكُمْ. رواه البيهقي، مشكواة، باب كتاب الإمارة.

[380] On the authority of Yaḥyā b. Hāshim from Yūnus b. Abī Isḥāq from his father ﷺ, who said: The Messenger of Allah ﷺ

said, "As you will be, thus will be the leaders appointed over you." Bayhaqī (*Mishkāt*, Chapter on Leadership, *Ḥadīth* no. 3717).

Commentary

Usually, the ruling class is the cream of the society. However, if the public is corrupt, how can its elite be of righteous character, especially in our democratic age when the public are free to choose their representatives and rulers? Another possible meaning of this *Ḥadīth* is that if the people of a land are fond of evil deeds, Allah will punish them by imposing evil-doing governors upon them.

15.13 THE IMPORTANCE OF A SYSTEM OF CONSULTATION

عَنْ أَبِي هُرَيْرَةَ ﷺ قَالَ: قَالَ رَسُولُ اللهِ ﷺ: إِذَا كَانَ أُمَرَاؤُكُمْ خِيَارَكُمْ، وَأَغْنِيَاؤُكُمْ سُمَحَاءَكُمْ، وَأُمُورُكُمْ شُورَى بَيْنَكُمْ، فَظَهْرُ الأَرْضِ خَيْرٌ لَكُمْ مِنْ بَطْنِهَا. وَإِذَا كَانَ أُمَرَاؤُكُمْ شِرَارَكُمْ، وَأَغْنِيَاؤُكُمْ بُخَلَاءَكُمْ، وَأُمُورُكُمْ إِلَى نِسَائِكُمْ، فَبَطْنُ الأَرْضِ خَيْرٌ لَكُمْ مِنْ ظَهْرِهَا. سنن الترمذي، مشكواة، باب تغير الناس.

[381] On the authority of Abū Hurayrah ﷺ, who said: The Messenger of Allah ﷺ said, "When your leaders are the best of you, your rich are the most generous of you and your [social] matters are decided by consultation amongst yourselves, then the surface of the earth [i.e. life] is better for you than its interior [i.e. death]. When your leaders are the worst of you, your rich are the most miserly of you and your matters are left [entirely] to your women, the interior of the earth is better for you than its surface [i.e. such a Muslim people who bring humiliation and disgrace upon themselves are also a shame upon Islam]." Tirmidhī (*Mishkāt*, Chapter: The Changing Condition of the People, *Ḥadīth* no. 5368).

Commentary

In this *Ḥadīth*, three matters have been declared as the fountainhead of happiness for a Muslim society in both this world and the Hereafter. If all three of these qualities exist in a society, it will achieve success and felicity:

1. God-fearing leadership and government.
2. Generous wealthy classes who have concern for the poor.
3. The spirit of mutual consultation prevails in all social transactions.

In contrast, if the leadership is corrupt in nature, the wealthy are miserly and greedy and the inclination towards lusts and luxuries is excessive, then such a society will disintegrate sooner rather than later. This *Ḥadīth* also clarifies that the best forms of government are found in societies based on mutual consultation and trust.

15.14 RESPONSIBILITIES OF THE JUDICIARY

عَنْ بُرَيْدَةَ ﷺ، عَنْ النَّبِيِّ ﷺ قَالَ: الْقُضَاةُ ثَلَاثَةٌ: وَاحِدٌ فِي الْجَنَّةِ وَاثْنَانِ فِي النَّارِ، فَأَمَّا الَّذِي فِي الْجَنَّةِ فَرَجُلٌ عَرَفَ الْحَقَّ فَقَضَى بِهِ، وَرَجُلٌ عَرَفَ الْحَقَّ فَجَارَ فِي الْحُكْمِ فَهُوَ فِي النَّارِ، وَرَجُلٌ قَضَى لِلنَّاسِ عَلَى جَهْلٍ فَهُوَ فِي النَّارِ. سنن أبى داود، مشكواة، باب العمل في القضاء.

[382] On the authority of Buraydah ﷺ, that the Prophet ﷺ said, "There are three types of judges: one will be in the Garden whilst the other two will be in the Fire. The one who will be in the Garden is the person who recognised the truth and judged by it. The two who will be in the Fire are the one who recognised the truth but judged unjustly and the one who judged amongst people based on ignorance." Abū Dāwūd and Ibn Mājah (*Mishkāt*, Chapter on Judgment, *Ḥadīth* no. 3735).

Commentary

For someone to be a judge in an Islamic government, they must fulfil two fundamental conditions:

1. Detailed familiarity with the Law;
2. Concern with fairness and justice in every matter.

If either quality is missing in a person, they are unfit to be a judge in an Islamic court.

عَنْ أَبِي هُرَيْرَةَ ﵁، عَنِ النَّبِيِّ ﷺ قَالَ: مَنْ جُعِلَ قَاضِيًا بَيْنَ النَّاسِ فَقَدْ ذُبِحَ بِغَيْرِ سِكِّينٍ.

سنن أبي داود وابن ماجه.

[383] On the authority of Abū Hurayrah ﵁, that the Prophet ﷺ said, "Whoever is made to judge amongst people, he has been slaughtered without a knife." Abū Dāwūd and Ibn Mājah (*Mishkāt*, Chapter on Judgment, *Ḥadīth* no. 3733).

Commentary

This means that the position of being a judge is an extremely critical responsibility. If the judge behaves unjustly, he will be held accountable by Allah. If he behaves justly, he becomes the target of enmity from influential criminals.

15.15 EQUALITY IN ENFORCING LAWS

عَنْ عُبَادَةَ بْنِ الصَّامِتِ ﵁ قَالَ: قَالَ رَسُولُ اللهِ ﷺ: أَقِيمُوا حُدُودَ اللهِ فِي الْقَرِيبِ وَالْبَعِيدِ، وَلَا تَأْخُذْكُمْ فِي اللهِ لَوْمَةُ لَائِمٍ. سنن ابن ماجه، مشكواة، كتاب الحدود.

[384] On the authority of ʿUbādah b. al-Ṣāmit ﵁, who said: The Messenger of Allah ﷺ said, "Establish the limits of Allah upon those near and far [equally], and let not the blame of the critics affect you in the matters of Allah." Ibn Mājah (*Mishkāt*, Book of Limits, *Ḥadīth* no. 3587).

15.16 LEGAL EQUALITY

عن أُمِّ سَلَمَةَ ﵂، أَنَّ النَّبِيَّ ﷺ، كَانَ فِي بَيْتِهَا، فَدَعَا وَصِيفَةً لَهُ - أَوْ لَهَا - فَأَبْطَأَتْ، فاسْتَبَانَ الغَضَبُ فِي وَجْهِهِ، فقامَتْ أُمُّ سَلَمَةَ إلى الحِجاب، فوَجَدَتْ الوَصِيفَةَ تَلْعَبُ، وَمَعَهُ سِوَاكٌ، فَقَالَ: لَوْلا خَشْيَةُ القَوَدِ يَوْمَ القِيَامَةِ، لَأَوْجَعْتُكِ بِهَذَا السِّوَاكِ. الأدب المفرد، باب قصاص العبد.

[385]   On the authority of Umm Salamah 🙏 that the Prophet 🙏 was in her house when he called a slave-girl belonging to him or her. The girl did not respond and anger became apparent in his face. Umm Salamah went to the curtain and found that the girl was busy playing. The Prophet 🙏 had a tooth-stick in his hand and he said, "Were it not for the fear of retaliation on the Day of Judgment, I would have punished you with this tooth-stick." Bukhārī's *Al-Adab al-Mufrad*, Chapter on Retaliation against Slaves, *Ḥadīth* no. 184.

Commentary

1.   In this *Ḥadīth*, there is mention of justice in the Hereafter. From this, it can be inferred that since there is the possibility of retaliation in the Hereafter for even slight injury or insult, it follows that such justice can also be enforced in the courts of this world.

2.   A lofty ideal for the treatment of slaves and servants is given in this *Ḥadīth*.

15.17 THE LIMITS OF LEGAL PARDON

عَنْ عَائِشَةَ 🙏 قَالَتْ: قَالَ رَسُولُ الله ﷺ: أَقِيلُوا ذَوِي الْهَيْئَاتِ عَثَرَاتِهِمْ إِلا الْحُدُودَ. سنن أبى داود وأحمد، مشكواة، كتاب الحدود.

[386]   On the authority of 'Ā'ishah 🙏 who said: The Messenger of Allah 🙏 said, "Pardon the slips of the respected, except where the limits [laws] of Allah are involved." Abū Dāwūd (*Mishkāt*, Book of Limits, *Ḥadīth* no. 3569).

Commentary

"Respected" here refers to that respect and dignity which is earned in a Muslim society through knowledge, piety and service of religion. If such a person slips up, it is appropriate to overlook this.

In support of this *Ḥadīth*, the incident of Ḥāṭib b. Abī Balta'ah can be presented. This Companion tried to convey a secret plan of the Messenger of Allah ﷺ to the polytheists of Makkah for his own purely-worldly interests. This open crime of his was pardoned because he had risked his life against the enemy in the critical Battle of Badr. However, the caliph does not have the right to suspend Divinely-sanctioned punishments for even the most spiritual or valiant person.

15.18 PRINCIPLES AND ETIQUETTE OF JUDGMENT

عَنْ عَبْدِ اللهِ بْنِ الزُّبَيْرِ رضي الله عنه قَالَ: قَضى رَسُولُ اللهِ ﷺ أَنَّ الْخَصْمَيْنِ يَقْعُدَانِ بَيْنَ يَدَيْ الْحَكَمِ. سنن أبى داود وأحمد، مشكواة، باب الاقضيه.

[387] On the authority of ʿAbdullāh b. Zubayr رضي الله عنه, who said, "The Messenger of Allah ﷺ decreed that the two disputants must sit [i.e. be present] before the judge." Aḥmad and Abū Dāwūd (*Mishkāt*, Book of Judgments, *Ḥadīth* no. 3786).

Commentary

Both parties must appear in court. It should not be the case that one party is exempted from appearance in court on the basis of wealth, position, power or influence.

عَنْ ابْنِ عَبَّاسٍ رضي الله عنهما، أَنَّ النَّبِيَّ ﷺ قَالَ: لَوْ يُعْطَى النَّاسُ بِدَعْوَاهُمْ، لَادَّعَى نَاسٌ دِمَاءَ رِجَالٍ وَأَمْوَالَهُمْ، وَلَكِنَّ الْيَمِينَ عَلَى الْمُدَّعَى عَلَيْهِ. صحيح مسلم، مشكواة، باب الاقضيه.

[388] On the authority of Ibn ʿAbbās رضي الله عنهما that the Prophet ﷺ said, "Were people to be given [judgments] in accordance with their claims, some people would claim everyone's blood and wealth [and no-one's life or wealth would be safe]. Hence, the right of taking an oath [to deny the claim] belongs to the defendant." Muslim (*Mishkāt*, Book of Judgments, *Ḥadīth* no. 3758).

Commentary

In another *Ḥadīth*, it is said that the claimant must produce a witness or evidence in support of his claim. If he cannot do so, then in the light of this *Ḥadīth*, the defendant is absolved of the accusation by taking the required oath.

عَنْ عَائِشَةَ ﵂ قَالَتْ: قَالَ رَسُولُ اللهِ ﷺ: ادْرَءُوا الْحُدُودَ عَنْ الْمُسْلِمِينَ مَا اسْتَطَعْتُمْ، فَإِنْ كَانَ لَهُ مَخْرَجٌ فَخَلُّوا سَبِيلَهُ، فَإِنَّ الْإِمَامَ أَنْ يُخْطِئَ فِي الْعَفْوِ خَيْرٌ مِنْ أَنْ يُخْطِئَ فِي الْعُقُوبَةِ.

سنن الترمذي، مشكواة، كتاب الحدود.

[389] On the authority of 'Ā'ishah ﵂, who said: The Messenger of Allah ﷺ said, "Avoid enforcing the limits [criminal punishments] upon the Muslims as much as you can. If there is any doubt, let the accused go free, for the ruler's mistake in pardoning is better than his mistake in punishing." Tirmidhī (*Mishkāt*, Book of Limits, *Ḥadīth* no. 3570).

Commentary

It is clear from this *Ḥadīth* that even after a court trial, if there is any doubt about the proof of guilt, the accused should not be punished. Furthermore, it goes without saying that to imprison or punish someone without trial is totally opposed to Islamic justice.

15.19 ETIQUETTE OF WAR

عَنْ أَنَسِ بْنِ مَالِكٍ ﵁، أَنَّ رَسُولَ اللهِ ﷺ قَالَ: انْطَلِقُوا بِاسْمِ اللهِ وَبِاللهِ وَعَلَى مِلَّةِ رَسُولِ اللهِ، وَلَا تَقْتُلُوا شَيْخًا فَانِيًا، وَلَا طِفْلًا صَغِيرًا، وَلَا امْرَأَةً، وَلَا تَغُلُّوا، وَضُمُّوا غَنَائِمَكُمْ، وَأَصْلِحُوا وَأَحْسِنُوا، إِنَّ اللهَ يُحِبُّ الْمُحْسِنِينَ. سنن أبى داود، مشكواة، باب القتال في الجهاد.

[390] On the authority of Anas b. Mālik ﵁, that the Messenger of Allah ﷺ said, "Go forth [in *Jihād* against the enemy] with the Name of Allah, by [the capability and support of] Allah and [remain steadfast] upon the Way of the Messenger of Allah. Do not kill the frail, old man, the small child or the woman. Do not steal from the war-booty. Gather your gains and behave with

righteousness and excellence, for truly, Allah loves those who show excellence." Abū Dāwūd (*Mishkāt*, Chapter on Fighting during *Jihād*, *Ḥadīth* no. 3956).

Commentary

Islam has explained the fundamental etiquette of war, that one should only fight enemy combatants. One must not target innocent children, women or decrepit, elderly people.

15.20 INTERNATIONAL RELATIONS

عَنْ سُلَيْم بْنِ عَامِرٍ ﷺ، رَجُلٌ مِنْ حِمْيَرَ، قَالَ: كَانَ بَيْنَ مُعَاوِيَةَ وَبَيْنَ الرُّومِ عَهْدٌ وَكَانَ يَسِيرُ نَحْوَ بِلَادِهِمْ حَتَّى إِذَا انْقَضى الْعَهْدُ أَغَارَ عَلَيْهِمْ، فَجَاءَ رَجُلٌ عَلى فَرَسٍ أَوْ بِرْذَوْنٍ، وَهُوَ يَقُولُ: اللهُ أَكْبَرُ، اللهُ أَكْبَرُ، وَفَاءٌ لا غَدَرَ. فَنَظَرُوا، فَإِذَا عَمْرُو بْنُ عَبَسَةَ، فَأَرْسَلَ إِلَيْهِ مُعَاوِيَةُ فَسَأَلَهُ، فَقَالَ: سَمِعْتُ رَسُولَ اللهِ ﷺ يَقُولُ: مَنْ كَانَ بَيْنَهُ وَبَيْنَ قَوْمٍ عَهْدٌ فَلَا يَحُلَّنَّ عَهْداً وَلَا يَشُدَّنَّهُ حَتَّى يَنْقَضِيَ أَمَدُهَا أَوْ يَنْبِذَ إِلَيْهِمْ عَلى سَوَاءٍ، فَرَجَعَ مُعَاوِيَةُ بِالنَّاسِ. سنن أبى داود، مشكواة، باب الأمان.

[391] On the authority of Sulaym b. ʿĀmir ﷺ, a man of the Ḥimyar, who said: There was a peace treaty between Muʿāwiyah and the Romans [Byzantines]. Muʿāwiyah had set out (with his army) towards Roman [Byzantine] land so that he could attack them as soon as the treaty expired, when a man rode up on his Arabian or Turkish horse, saying, "Allah is the Greatest! Allah is the Greatest! Fulfilment, not treachery!" The people looked and saw that the man was ʿAmr b. ʿAbasah. Muʿāwiyah sent for him and asked him about his statement. He replied, "I heard the Messenger of Allah, ﷺ, saying, 'Whoever has a treaty with another people should not violate it until its period has been completed, otherwise he should fling it evenly back at them'." Upon hearing this, Muʿāwiyah returned back with his army. Abū Dāwūd and Tirmidhī (*Mishkāt*, Chapter: Peace Treaties, *Ḥadīth* no. 3980).

Commentary

Several matters are learnt from this *Ḥadīth*:

1. If there is a peace treaty with another country, it is not permissible to attack it immediately upon expiry of the treaty without giving it fair time for preparation.
2. If war becomes inevitable during the period of the treaty, it is necessary to inform the adversary of this fact. This same meaning is found in the verse of the Qur'ān, "*And if you fear treachery from any people* [*with whom you have a covenant*], *then publicly throw their covenant at them.*" (*Sūrah al-Anfāl*, 8: 58)
3. The lofty example of the noble Companions in the matter of hearing and obeying is apparent from this *Ḥadīth*. As soon as Mu'āwiyah ﵁ learnt that his actions were contrary to the Prophetic guidance, he ordered his advancing army to return home.
4. Another important lesson from the Companions' lives is that they were not afraid of speaking a word of truth in front of people in power, whether they be the caliph or his governors. This courageous step of 'Amr b. 'Abasah presents a lofty example of upholding the truth for every Muslim.

15.21 RELIGION AND POLITICS

وَعَنْ مُعَاذِ بْنِ جَبَلٍ ﵁ قَالَ: سَمِعْتُ رَسُوْلَ اللهِ ﷺ يَقُوْلُ: خُذُوْا الْعَطَاءَ مَا دَامَ عَطَاءً، فَإِذَا صَارَ رِشْوَةً عَلَى الدِّيْنِ، فَلا تَأْخُذُوهُ، ولَسْتُمْ بِتَارِكِيْهِ، يَمْنَعُكُمْ الفَقْرُ وَالْحَاجَةُ، أَلا إِنَّ رَحَى الإِسْلامِ دَائِرَةٌ، فَدُوْرُوْا مَعَ الكِتَابِ حَيْثُ دَارَ، أَلا إِنَّ الْكِتَابَ وَالسُّلْطَانَ سَيَفْتَرِقَانِ فَلا تُفَارِقُوا الكِتَابَ، أَلا إِنَّهُ سَيَكُونُ عَلَيْكُمْ أُمَرَاءُ يَقْضُونَ لأَنْفُسِهِمْ مَا لا يَقْضُونَ لَكُمْ، فَإِذَا عَصَيْتُمُوْهُمْ قَتَلُوْكُمْ، وَإِنْ أَطَعْتُمُوهُمْ أَضَلُّوْكُمْ. قَالُوْا: يَا رَسُوْلَ اللهِ، كَيْفَ نَصْنَعُ؟ قَالَ :كَمَا صَنَعَ أَصْحَابُ عِيْسَى ابْنِ مَرْيَمَ، نُشِرُوْا بِالْمَنَاشِيْرِ، وَحُمِلُوْا عَلَى الخَشَبِ، مَوْتٌ فِيْ طَاعَةِ اللهِ خَيْرٌ مِنْ حَيَاةٍ فِي مَعْصِيَةِ اللهِ. المعجم الصغير للطبراني.

[392]   On the authority of Muʿādh b. Jabal ⬧, who said: I heard the Messenger of Allah ⬧ saying, "Accept gifts as long as they are gifts. If they become bribes in the matter of religion, do not accept them. However, you will not leave them, for poverty and need will prevent you [from rejecting the bribes]. Beware! The mill of Islam is revolving, so follow the Book wherever it turns. Beware! The Book and authority [government] will soon separate, so do not separate from the Book. Beware! There will be rulers who will decree advantages for themselves but not for you: if you obey them, they will mislead you; if you disobey them, they will kill you." People asked, "O Messenger of Allah! What shall we do?" He replied, "Do as the disciples of Jesus son of Mary did: they were sawed into pieces and nailed to wood. Death in obedience to Allah is better than life in disobedience to Allah." Ṭabarānī's *Al-Muʿjam al-Ṣaghīr*.

Commentary

This means that no matter how great the trial, a believer should remain steadfast upon the truth and should not cease to invite to the truth. A couple of matters have been indicated in this *Ḥadīth*:

I.   The mutual exchanging of gifts, presents, invitations and hospitality is a culture of good actions that have been repeatedly encouraged in the *Aḥādīth*. However, if this habit originates from influential governors, the people of truth may become susceptible to compromise: upon seeing open evils, their tongues may not only refrain from criticism but may even give wrong *fatwas* in support of such things. Hence, we see that after Imām Aḥmad b. Ḥanbal's steadfastness in the face of persecution by the ʿAbbāsid Caliphs Maʾmūn, Muʿtaṣim and Wāthiq Bi'Llāh, he was presented with bags of *dirhams* and *dīnars* by Caliph Mutawakkil. In this situation, he responded spontaneously with the words, "This is more severe upon me than what happened before," i.e. that being tested with royal gifts and presents was harder than enduring flogging. There was now the danger that the foot may slip upon seeing worldly wealth and riches. History tells us that he also remained steadfast during this trial.

2. The benefit and happiness of a Muslim environment and righteous social order lies in politics being subservient to religion. Wherever these two become separated, social life will necessarily become dominated by tyranny and barbarism.

عَـنْ تَمِيم الدَّارِيِّ ﵁، أَنَّ النَّبِيَّ ﷺ قَـالَ: الدِّينُ النَّصِيحَـةُ، ثَلاثاً. قُلْنَا: لِمَنْ. قَالَ: لِلّٰهِ وَلِكِتَابِهِ وَلِرَسُولِهِ وَلِأَئِمَّةِ الْمُسْلِمِينَ وَعَامَّتِهِمْ. صحيح مسلم.

[393] On the authority of Tamīm al-Dārī ﵁ that the Prophet ﷺ said, "Religion is sincerity [*naṣīḥah*]" three times. We asked, "To whom?" He replied, "To Allah, to His Book, to His Messenger, to the leaders of the Muslims and their common folk." Muslim (*Mishkāt*, *Ḥadīth* no. 4966).

Commentary

The original meaning of *nuṣḥ* is to be pure from adulteration or mixing. Pure honey, meaning that which has been purified from beeswax and so on, is called *nāṣiḥ al-ʿaṣl* (cf. *Mufradāt Rāghib*). Similarly, the word is applied to the heart of a person when there is no malice or impurity left in it and the person's outwardness corresponds totally to his inwardness.

The same meaning is found in the Qur'ānic commandment (*Sūrah al-Taḥrīm*, 66: 8) to the believers to turn to Allah with sincere repentance (*tawbah naṣūḥah*), i.e. to a repentance that is free from every type of hypocrisy or stain. In another *āyah*, the believers are addressed thus: "*There is no blame on the weak nor on the sick nor on those who have to join [the struggle in the Way of Allah] if they stay behind provided that they are sincere to Allah and His Messenger. There is no cause for reproach against those who do good. Allah is All-Forgiving, Ever Merciful.*" (*Sūrah al-Tawbah*, 9: 91)

This Qur'ānic verse means that usually, abstaining from *Jihād* is contrary to faith and obedience. However, it will not be blameworthy in the sight of Allah when one has an excuse, on condition that the heart is full of sincerity and loyalty. Thus, Allah does not burden a servant with practical service and exertion when the person has an excuse, but the situation of sincerity and goodness is such that every person is required to possess it and his salvation is impossible without it.

The meaning of "sincerity to Allah" is that a person allows no hypocrisy or betrayal between himself and Allah. The depths of his heart should be full of pure faith and loyalty. Such purity and loyalty dictate that a person must not allow any created being to become a partner or equal with Allah in His Essence and Attributes and with regard to His guidance and the etiquette and rights due towards Him. In this way, a person actually does goodness to himself and enriches his own world and the Hereafter. "*Whoever does good, does so to his own benefit.*" (*Sūrah Fuṣṣilat*, 41: 46)

"Sincerity to His Book" dictates that the purpose of the Qur'ān's revelation be fulfilled. This purpose consists of three matters:

1. Recitation, i.e. that the Majestic Qur'ān should be recited slowly with calmness and correct pronunciation, as is stated in the Qur'ān, "*We have revealed the Qur'ān in parts that you may recite it to people slowly and with deliberation; and [for that reason] We have revealed it gradually [to suit particular occasions].*" (*Sūrah Banī Isrā'īl*, 17: 106)
2. Pondering and contemplating deeply, i.e. that it should not simply be recited without understanding, but its signs and verses should be thought about and contemplated. Thus, Allah says, "*This is the Blessed Book that We have revealed to you, [O Muḥammad], that people with understanding may reflect over its verses.*" (*Sūrah Ṣād*, 38: 29)
3. Ruling by the Qur'ān, i.e. that contemplation should not merely be for the sake of contemplation itself; rather, it should be done so that the injunctions and guidance of the

> Wise Qur'ān be applied upon oneself, one's environment, one's country and, in fact, the whole world. Thus Allah says, "[*O Messenger*], *We have revealed to you this Book with the Truth so that you may judge between people in accordance with what Allah has shown you.*" (*Sūrah al-Nisā'*, 4: 105)

"Sincerity to His Messenger" means that his *Sunnah* should be revived and that sacrifice and effort be made to uphold the way of life, for the establishment of which he and his noble Companions fought with blood and sweat. The way of life proved to have come from him must be given priority to all other human ways. His words and deeds must not be abandoned in favour of the views or actions of any member of his nation.

"Sincerity to the leaders of the Muslims" – by "leaders" (*imāms*) here is not meant the religious representatives in today's mosques. It is the wretched fortune of the Muslim nation that the separation between politics and religion has changed the meaning of imamate. In Islam, politics and worldly dealings are subservient to religion. Hence, those who are *imāms* of mosques in a truly Islamic society will also be the leaders and heads of the country.

Being well-disposed towards the Muslim leaders means that when the latter do righteous works, one should co-operate with them. If they stray towards corruption and evil conduct, they should be criticised without hesitation or fear and their evil disposition should be publicly exposed, as is mentioned in the *Ḥadīth*, "The most excellent *Jihād* is to speak a word of truth before a tyrannical ruler." This was the sincerity displayed by Imām Mālik towards the Caliph Manṣūr, by Imām Aḥmad b. Ḥanbal in the shade of the whips of the Caliphs Ma'mūn, Muʿtaṣim and Wāthiq Bi'Llāh, by Imām Ibn Taymiyyah towards the tyrants of Egypt, and by Mujaddid Alf Thānī (Shaykh Aḥmad Sirhindī) in the royal court of Jahangir.

"Sincerity towards the common-folk of the Muslims" has several aspects:

1. If the Muslim public go astray, they should be called towards the straight path with wisdom and beautiful preaching, and Islamic values should be inculcated in them.
2. If the public are ignorant of Islam, knowledge of the religion should be spread amongst them. Religious schools and centres of higher education should be established. The message of Islam should be made so common that the sound of "Allah says, the Messenger says", should echo from every door and wall in the land.
3. If the public are afflicted by disease, they should be treated. Medication should be provided for them. An effective national healthcare system should be devised so that no sick person is left deprived of treatment.
4. If any Muslim faces problems or oppression, the oppressor must be resisted, individually and collectively, and the oppressed must be supported. Such organised institutions should be created so that no weak or oppressed person should feel helpless and unassisted in a Muslim society.
5. If a Muslim dies, one should participate in his funeral and burial and console his relatives. Similarly, mutual co-operation, concern and sharing of grief should become so common that a powerful example of "*Surely the believers are none but brothers unto one another.*" (*Sūrah al-Ḥujurāt*, 49: 10) is manifested to the whole world.

In reality, this *Ḥadīth* summarises the essence of Islam and extracts its fragrance in very few words.

Our final prayer is that All Praise belongs to Allah, Lord of the Worlds.

16

Translator's Bibliography

Dates, whether Hijrī *or Gregorian, are given as listed in the publications*

ʿAbd al-Ghaffar Ḥasan ʿUmarpūrī, *Intikhāb-e-Ḥadīth*, Islamic Publications Ltd., Lahore, 1995.

Muḥammad b. ʿAbdullāh al-Khaṭīb al-Tabrīzī, *Mishkāt al-Maṣābīḥ*, 3 vols., ed. Muḥammad Nāṣir al-Dīn Albānī, Al-Maktab al-Islāmī, Beirut, 3rd ed., 1405/1985.

Muḥammad b. Ismāʿīl al-Bukhārī, *Ṣaḥīḥ al-Bukhārī*, ed. M. M. M. H. Naṣṣār, Dar al-Kutub al-ʿIlmiyah, Beirut, 2nd ed., 1423/2002.

Muslim b. al-Ḥajjāj / al-Nawawī, *Ṣaḥīḥ Muslim* (with Commentary), Dar Ibn Hazm, Beirut, 1423/2002.

Abū Dāwūd Sulaymān b. al-Ashʿath al-Sijistānī, *Sunan*, ed. Mashhūr Salmān / Albānī, Maktabah al-Maʿārif, Riyadh, 1417.

Abū ʿĪsā Muḥammad b. ʿIsā al-Tirmidhī, *Sunan*, ed. Mashhūr Salmān / Albānī, Maktabah al-Maʿārif, Riyadh, 1417.

Abū ʿAbd al-Raḥman Aḥmad b. Shuʿayb b. ʿAlī al-Nasāʾī, *Sunan*, ed. Mashhūr Salmān / Albānī, Maktabah al-Maʿārif, Riyadh, 1417.

Abū ʿAbdullāh Muḥammad b. Yazīd Ibn Mājah al-Qazwīnī, *Sunan*, ed. Mashhūr Salmān / Albānī, Maktabah al-Maʿārif, Riyadh, 1417.

Muḥammad b. Ismāʿīl al-Bukhārī / Muḥammad Nāṣir al-Dīn Albānī, *Ṣaḥīḥ al-Adab al-Mufrad*, Dār al-Ṣiddīq, Jubayl, 2nd ed., 1415/1994.

Jalāl al-Dīn al-Suyūṭī / Muḥammad Nāṣir al-Dīn Albānī, *Ṣaḥīḥ al-Jāmiʿ al-Ṣaghīr*, 2 vols., Al-Maktab al-Islāmī, Beirut / Damascus, 3rd ed., 1408/1988.